THE ORIGINS AND DEVELOPMENT OF THE ENGLISH LANGUAGE

Third Edition

THE ORIGINS AND DEVELOPMENT OF THE *Third Edition* ENGLISH LANGUAGE

Thomas Pyles LATE OF THE UNIVERSITY OF FLORIDA

John Algeo UNIVERSITY OF GEORGIA

HARCOURT BRACE JOVANOVICH, PUBLISHERS

San Diego   New York   Chicago   Austin
London   Sydney   Toronto

COVER: From British Museum Manuscript Cotton Julius E vii, folio 59.

ISBN: 0–15–567608–3

Library of Congress Catalog Card Number: 81–86501

Printed in the United States of America

Preface

The Third Edition of *The Origins and Development of the English Language* was begun in collaboration with Thomas Pyles, but his death brought to an end a collaboration that was a source of great satisfaction to me. I have, however, tried to complete this revision as I think Thomas Pyles would have wanted it.

The changes in the Third Edition are considerably greater than those in the Second. Some material has been reordered, both within and among chapters. New material has been added as needed for fuller explanation or to bring a discussion up to date. Some old material has been reluctantly omitted to keep the book's length within reasonable bounds and to simplify the presentation for students, who often feel lost among the many factual details that make up the history of English. Parts of many chapters have undergone extensive rewriting, and new subheadings and tabular matter have been added to guide students in their reading. The use of footnotes has been radically abridged; references are generally made within the text by the author's name and the date of publication, with full information given in the Selected Bibliography at the back of the book. The suggested readings at the end of each chapter are also keyed to the bibliography.

An aim of this new edition is to make the text more accessible to students who have had no prior study of linguistics or of languages. As in earlier editions, the treatment is descriptive and traditional. Experience has shown that students find it difficult to learn both linguistic theory and the history of English simultaneously. Therefore, although this edition makes some references to work in current linguistics, it devotes less space to discussion of recent theoretical studies than does the Second Edition. The focus throughout remains on the internal history of English. Theoretical implications and purely external history, which are admirably treated in other books, are purposely kept to a minimum.

I have tried to preserve the emphasis that Thomas Pyles placed on the treatment of writing, on the similarities and differences between British and American English, on early Modern English, and on the vocabulary as both lexis and morphology. A somewhat fuller treatment of syntax has been added. The tone and style of the book, which were characteristic of everything Pyles wrote, have been preserved as much as possible, although changing times and sensibilities inevitably call for some adjustments.

The debts that Thomas Pyles acknowledged in the earlier editions are matters of record that are still owing. In the preparation of the Third Edition I am indebted to the extensive critiques made by Samuel C. Monson, Brigham Young University, and E. J. Murphy, California State University, Hayward. I am grateful also for suggestions, corrections, help, or encouragement from many persons, including Robert K. Barnhart of Clarence L. Barnhart, Inc.; William T. Burke, Winston-Salem State University; Thomas L. Clark and his students at the University of Nevada, Las Vegas, from whose reactions I have benefited at every turn; Virginia P. Clark, University of Vermont; Dušan Gabrovšek, University of Ljubljana; Ruth P. M. Lehmann, University of Texas at Austin; Jean Lorrah, Murray State University; Rupert Palmer, Vanderbilt University; Lee Pederson, Emory University; Ralph L. Ward, Hunter College; and Jacqueline de Weever, Brooklyn College. For their scholarly and personal example, I owe much to Harold B. Allen, Frederic G. Cassidy, Raven I. McDavid, Jr., James B. McMillan, and I. Willis Russell. My colleagues at the University of Georgia have been a continual source of stimulation. I am indebted to Edward A. Stephenson, Jared Klein (who also made a detailed critique of chapter 4), Charles C. Doyle, Jane Appleby, and Betty Jean Irwin for advice and conversation. For expert assistance in preparing the manuscript of this edition, I am grateful to Kathryn N. Howell and Katherine Postero. A special word of appreciation is due to Becky Pyles for her friendship and support. Finally and most important, my wife, Adele Algeo, has helped in every stage of the revision; without her it would not have been. After so much help and good counsel, whatever shortcomings remain are, as Thomas Pyles said about the Second Edition, my own unhappy responsibility.

J.A.

Contents

Contents

6 The Middle English Period (1100-1500)   136

7 The Modern English Period to 1800: Sounds and Spellings   167

THE ORIGINS AND DEVELOPMENT OF THE ENGLISH LANGUAGE

Third Edition

1 Language and Languages

An Introduction

Our language is inextricably bound up with our humanity. To be human is to use language, and to talk is to be a person. As biologist and author Lewis Thomas remarks in *The Lives of a Cell* (1974, p. 89):

> The gift of language is the single human trait that marks us all genetically, setting us apart from the rest of life. Language is, like nest-building or hive-making, the universal and biologically specific activity of human beings. We engage in it communally, compulsively, and automatically. We cannot be human without it; if we were to be separated from it our minds would die, as surely as bees lost from the hive.

The contemporary scientific view of language as essential to our human nature agrees with the view expressed in the Book of Genesis, where the first action we see human beings engaged in is talking. In chapter 2 of that book it is said that God brought all the creatures of the earth before Adam to see

1

what he would call them, and whatever Adam called the creatures, so were they named. Those two statements—that of the modern biologist and that of the ancient prophet—however different they are in style and imagery, are saying the same thing: to be human is to have and use language.

The language that is innate in us is, of course, no particular form of speech and need not, in fact, even be **speech**, that is, sounds produced orally by which language is expressed. When we say "Bread is the staff of life," we do not mean any particular kind of bread—whether whole wheat, rye, pumpernickel, French, matzo, pita, or whatever sort; rather we are talking about the kind of thing bread is, that which all bread has in common. So also, when we say that language is the basis of our humanity, we do not mean any particular kind of language—whether English, Spanish, Chinese, Swahili, Hopi, or Ameslan (the sign language of the deaf). Rather we mean the ability to learn and use such particular language systems, which is shared by all human beings. That ability is **language** in the abstract, as distinct from individual languages like those just named.

Why Study the History of English?

Language is an ability, inherent in us. Languages such as English are particular systems that are developments of that ability. We can know the underlying ability only through studying the actual languages that are its expressions. Thus one of the best reasons for studying languages is to find out about ourselves, about what makes us persons. And the best place to start such study is with our own language, the one that has nurtured our minds and formed our view of the world, although any language can be useful for the purpose. A good approach to studying languages is the historical one. To understand how things are, it is often helpful and sometimes essential to know how they got to be that way. If we are psychologists who want to understand a person's behavior, we must know something about that person's origins and development. The same is true of a language.

There are also other, more concrete reasons for studying about the history of English. One is that many of the irregularities of our language today are the remnants of earlier, quite regular patterns. For example, the highly irregular plurals of nouns like *man–men, mouse–mice, goose–geese,* and *ox–oxen* can be explained historically. So can the spelling of Modern English, which may seem chaotic, or at least unruly, to anyone who has had to struggle with it. The orthographic joke attributed to George Bernard Shaw, that in English *fish* might be spelled *ghoti* (*gh* as in *enough, o* as in *women,* and *ti* as in *nation*), has been repeated often, but the only way to understand the anomalies of our spelling is to study the history of our language. The fact that the present-day pronunciation and meaning of *cupboard* do not much suggest a board for cups is also something we need history to explain. Why do we talk about *withstanding* a thing when we mean that we stand in opposition to it, rather than in company *with* it? If people are *unkempt*, can they also be *kempt*, and what does *kempt* mean? Is something wrong with the position of *secretly* in "She wanted to secretly finish writing her novel"? Is there any connection between *heal, whole, healthy, hale,* and *holy*? Knowing about the history of the language can help us to understand and to answer these and many similar questions. Knowledge of the history of English is no *nostrum* or *panacea* for curing all our linguistic ills (why do we call some medicines by those names?), but it can at least alleviate some of the symptoms.

Another reason for studying the history of English is that even a little knowledge about it can help to clarify the literature written in earlier periods, and some written rather recently. In "The Eve of St. Agnes," John Keats describes the sculptured effigies on the tombs of a chapel on a cold winter evening:

> The sculptur'd dead, on each side, seemed to freeze,
> Emprison'd in black, purgatorial rails.

What image should Keats's description evoke with its reference to *rails*? Many a modern reader, taking a cue from the word *emprison'd*, has thought of the *rails* as railings or bars, perhaps a fence around the statues. But *rails* here is from an Old English word that meant 'garments' and refers to the shrouds or funeral garments in which the stone figures are clothed. Unless we are aware of such older usage, we are likely to be led badly astray in the picture we conjure up for these lines. In the General Prologue to his *Canterbury Tales*, Geoffrey Chaucer, in describing an ideal knight, says: "His hors weren goode." Did the knight have one horse, or more than one? *Hors* seems to be singular, but the verb *weren* looks like a plural. The knight did indeed have several horses; in Chaucer's day *hors* was a word like *deer* or *sheep* that had a plural identical in form with its singular. It is a small point, but unless we know what a text means literally, we cannot appreciate it as literature.

A Definition of Language

For our purposes, a **language** will be defined as a system of conventional vocal signs by means of which human beings communicate. There are six important terms in this definition, each of which is examined in some detail in the remainder of this chapter. The terms are *system*, *signs*, *vocal*, *conventional*, *human*, and *communicate*. On the following pages we examine what these words mean and, often just as important, what they imply about the nature of language.

Perhaps the most important word in our definition is *system*. We speak in patterns. A language is not just a collection of words, such as we find in a dictionary. It is also the rules or patterns that relate the words to one another.

Every language has two levels to its system—a characteristic that is called **duality of patterning**. One of these levels consists of meaningful units—for example, the words and word parts *Adam*, *like*, *-d*, *apple*, and *-s* in the sentence "Adam liked apples." The other level consists of units that have no meaning in themselves, although they serve as components of the meaningful units—for example, the sounds represented by the letters *a*, *d*, and *m* in the word *Adam*.

The distinction between a meaningful word (*Adam*) and its meaningless parts (*a*, *d*, and *m*) is important. Without that distinction, language as we know it would be impossible. If every meaning had to be represented by a unique, unanalyzable sound, only a few such meanings could be expressed. We have only about 35 basic sounds in English; we have hundreds of thousands of words. Duality of patterning lets people build an immensely large number of meaningful words out of only a handful of meaningless sounds. It is perhaps the chief characteristic that distinguishes true human language from the simpler communication systems of all nonhuman animals.

The meaningless components of a language make up its **sound system**, or **phonology**. The meaningful units are part of its **grammatical system**. Both have patterning. Thus, according to the sound system of Modern English, the consonant combination *mb* never occurs at the beginning or at the end of any word. As a matter of fact, it did occur in final position in earlier stages of our language, which is why it was necessary in the preceding statement to specify "Modern English." Despite its complete absence in this position in the sound system of English for at least 600 years, we still insist—such is the conservatism of writing habits—that the *b* be written in *lamb*, *climb*, *tomb*, *dumb*, and a number of other words. But this same combination, which now occurs only medially in English (as in *tremble*), may well occur in final or even in initial position in the sound systems of other languages. Initial *mb* is indeed a part of the systems of certain African languages, as in Efik and Ibibio *mbakara* 'white man,' which in the speech of the Gullahs— black Americans living along the coastal region of Georgia and South Carolina who have preserved a number of words and structural features that their ancestors brought from Africa—has become *buckra*. It is notable that the Gullahs have simplified the initial consonant combination of this African word to conform to the pattern of English speech.

The sounds of a language recur again and again according to a well-defined system, not haphazardly; for without system, communication would be impossible. The same is true of all linguistic features, not sound alone. Thus, according to the grammatical system of English, a very large number of words take a suffix written *-s* to indicate plurality or possession (in which case it is a comparatively recent convention of writing to add an apostrophe). This suffix is variously pronounced. *Duck,* for instance, adds the sound that is usually indicated by *s*; *dog* adds the sound that is usually indicated by *z*; and *horse* adds a syllable consisting of a vowel sound plus the *z* sound.

Words that can be thus modified in form are nouns. They fit into certain definite patterns in English utterances. *Alcoholic,* for instance, fits into the system of English in the same way as *duck, dog,* and *horse*: "Alcoholics need understanding" (compare "Ducks need water"), "An alcoholic's perceptions are faulty" (compare "A dog's perceptions are keen"), and the like. But it may also modify a noun and be modified by an adverb: *an alcoholic drink, a somewhat alcoholic taste,* and the like; and words that operate in this way are called adjectives. *Alcoholic* is thus both adjective and noun, depending on the way it functions in the system of English. Such an utterance as "Alcoholic worries" is ambiguous because our system, like all linguistic systems, is not completely foolproof. It might be either a noun followed by a verb (as in a newspaper headline) or an adjective followed by a noun. To know which interpretation is correct, we need a context in which to place the expression. That is, we need to relate it to a larger system.

GRAMMATICAL SIGNALS

The grammatical system of any language has various techniques for relating words to one another and for signaling the structure of the sentences that words make up. Six kinds of signals are especially important.

1. Words can be put in various categories called **parts of speech**, of which there are four major ones in English: nouns, verbs, adjectives, and adverbs. Some words belong primarily or solely to one part of speech: *child* is a noun, *seek* is a verb, *tall* is an adjective, and *anymore* is an adverb. Other words can function as more than one part of speech; in various meanings, *fast* can be any of the four major parts. English speakers move words about pretty freely from one part of speech to another, as when we call a book that is enjoyable to read "a good read," making a noun out of a verb. Part of knowing English is knowing how words can be shifted about in that way and what the limits are to such shifting.

2. A word's part of speech is sometimes signaled by its form, specifically by the affixes—the beginnings or endings—used with it. The prefix *en-* at the beginning of a word, as in *encipher, enrage, enthrone, entomb, entwine,* and *enwrap,* marks the word as a verb. The suffix *-ist* at the end, as in *dentist, geologist, motorist,* and *violinist,* marks the word as a noun. English also has a small number of **inflectional suffixes** (endings that mark distinctions of number, case, person, tense, mood, and comparison). They include the plural *-s* and the possessive *'s* used with nouns (*girls, girl's*); the third person singular present tense *-s,* the past tense and past participle *-ed,* and the present participle

6   -*ing* used with verbs (*aids, aided, aiding*); and the comparative -*er* and superlative -*est* used with some adjectives and adverbs (*slower, slowest*). **Inflection** (change in the form of a word to mark such distinctions) may also involve internal change, as in the singular and plural noun forms *man* and *men* or the present and past verb forms *sing* and *sang*. A language that depends heavily on the use of inflections, either internal or suffixed, is said to be **synthetic**; English used to be far more synthetic than it now is.

3. When a language uses inflections, they are often interconnected by **concord**, or **agreement**. Thus in "The bird sings" and "The birds sing" there is subject-verb concord (it being merely coincidental that the signal for plural in nouns happens to be identical in form with the signal for singular in third person present tense verbs). Similarly, in *this day* both words are singular, and in *these days* both are plural; some languages, such as Spanish, require that all modifiers agree with the nouns they modify in number, but in English only *this* and *that* change their form to show such agreement. Synthetic languages, such as Latin, usually have a great deal of concord; thus Latin adjectives agree with the nouns they modify in number (*bonus vir* 'good man,' *bonī virī* 'good men'), in gender (*bona femina* 'good woman'), and in case (*bonae feminae* 'good woman's'). English used to have more such concord than it now does.

4. **Word order** is a grammatical signal in all languages, though some languages, like English, depend more heavily on it than do others. "The man finished the job" and "The job finished the man" are sharply different in meaning, as are "He died happily" and "Happily he died."

5. Minor parts of speech, also called **function words** (for example, articles, auxiliaries, conjunctions, prepositions, pronouns, and certain adverbial particles), are a kind of grammatical signal used with word order to serve some of the same functions as inflections. For example, in English the indirect object of a verb can be shown by either word order ("I gave *the dog* a bone") or a function word ("I gave a bone *to the dog*"); in Latin it is shown by inflection (*canis* 'the dog,' *Canī os dedī*, literally 'To-the-dog a-bone I gave'). A language like English whose grammar depends heavily on the use of word order and function words is said to be **analytic**.

6. **Prosodic signals**, such as pitch, stress, and tempo, can indicate grammatical meaning. The difference between the statement "He's here" and the question "He's here?" is the pitch used at the end of the sentence. The chief difference between the verb *conduct* and the noun *conduct* is that the verb has a stronger stress on its second syllable and the noun on its first syllable. The tempo of the last two words makes an important difference of meaning between "He died happily" and "He died, happily."

All languages have these six kinds of grammatical signals available to them, but languages differ greatly in the use they make of the various signals. Even a single language may change its use over time, as English has done.

It is obvious that every language must have its own system, though it may share certain features with other languages. What has been said of the capacity of the typical English noun to add -*s* for pluralizing or indicating possession is, for instance, not at all true of the typical Modern French noun, which has no possessive form and which in isolation remains unchanged in the pronunciation of its plural. The fact that singular *ami* and plural *amis* are written differently is merely a historical feature of the French writing system. The two forms are actually identical in speech except when *amis* is "in liaison," that is, followed by a word beginning with a vowel sound, in which case the normally "silent" -*s* is pronounced. The French noun, then, would require a definition different in some of its details from that of the English noun.

Pidgin English and other languages spoken by technologically primitive peoples are just as systematic as English, or as Classical Latin for that matter (Hall 1955). Since system in languages *is* grammar in its widest sense, it is obviously impossible for there to be a grammarless language. When the eighteenth-century lexicographer Dr. Samuel Johnson remarked that English had no grammar, he was thinking of the complicated system of word endings of Latin as constituting grammar. It would have been remarkable if anyone had thought otherwise in his day. But the fact is that English "The fire cooks the meat," Melanesian Pidgin "Fire i-cookim abus," and Latin "Ignis carnem coquit" all have grammar. The systems are, of course, different, but no one system can be said to be superior to another. In the sentence from Pidgin, for instance, the ending -*im* of the verb indicates that a direct object follows; in "The meat cooks," no such ending would be used: "Abus i-cook." This ending is a systematic grammatical device indicating the same grammatical relationship as the accusative ending -*em* (with which it has no connection) of the Latin noun. In the system of English, the position of *meat* in the sentence indicates the same grammatical relationship. Position is, however, relatively unimportant in Latin: "Carnem ignis coquit" means the same thing as "Ignis carnem coquit," inasmuch as the direct object is clearly labeled by the ending. To reverse the meaning (with nonsensical effect) one would have to change only the *form* of the words, as follows: "Caro ignem coquit." The order of the words makes no difference. In English (as also in Pidgin), the same reversal in meaning is accomplished without change of form, but of word order only: "The meat cooks the fire."

Language Signs

In language, what the system organizes are signs. A **sign** is merely something that stands for something else—for example, a word like *apple*, which stands for the familiar fruit. But linguistic signs are not words alone; they may also be either smaller or larger than whole words. The smallest linguistic sign is the **morpheme**, which is a meaningful form that cannot be divided into smaller meaningful parts. The word *apple* is a single morpheme; the word *applejack* consists of two morphemes (each of which can also function independently as a word); the word *apples* also consists of two morphemes, one of which (-*s*) can occur only as part of a word. Morphemes that can be used alone as words (such as *apple* and *jack*) are called **free morphemes**; those that must be combined with other morphemes to make a word (such as -*s*) are **bound morphemes**. The word *reactivation* has five morphemes in it (one free and four bound), as can be seen by analyzing it step by step:

> *re*-activation
> activate-*ion*
> active-*ate*
> act-*ive*

Thus the morphemes of this word are free *act* and bound *re*-, -*ive*, -*ate*, and -*ion*.

A morpheme may have more than one pronunciation. For example, the noun plural ending spelled -*s* has, as noted above, three variations: an *s*-sound as in *backs*, a *z*-sound as in *bags*, and a vowel plus *z*-sound as in *badges*. Each of these variations is called an **allomorph** of the plural morpheme. Similarly, when the morpheme -*ate* has added to it the morpheme -*ion* (as in *activate-ion*), the *t* of -*ate* combines with the *i* of -*ion* to become a *sh*-sound (so that we might spell the word "activashon"). Such allomorphic variation is typical of the morphemes of English, even though it is often not represented by the spelling.

Morphemes can also be divided into **base morphemes** and **affixes**. An affix is a bound morpheme that is added to a base morpheme. An affix may be either a **prefix**, which comes before its base (such as *re*-), or a **suffix**, which comes after its base (such as -*s*, -*ive*, -*ate*, and -*ion*). Most base morphemes are free (such as *apple* and *act*), but some are bound (such as the *insul*- of *insulate*). A word that has two or more bases (such as *applejack*) is called a **compound**.

In addition to being of word size (free morphemes) or smaller (bound morphemes), linguistic signs may also be larger than words. A combination of words whose meaning cannot be predicted from those of its constituent parts is an **idiom**. One kind of idiom that English has come to use extensively is the combination of a verb with an adverb, a preposition, or both—for instance, *turn on* (a light), *call up* (on the telephone), *put over* (a joke), *ask for* (a job), *come down with* (an illness), and *go back on* (a promise). From the standpoint of meaning, such an expression can be regarded as a single unit: to *go back on* is to 'abandon' a promise. But from the standpoint of grammar, it consists of several independent words.

Some of the richness of the system of language is due to the variety of its signs, which has been only hinted at in this brief discussion.

Language is a system that can be expressed in many ways—by the marks on paper that we call writing, by hand signals and gestures as in sign language, by colored lights or moving flags as in semiphore, and by electronic clicks as in telégraphy. However, the signs of language—its words and morphemes—are basically **oral-aural**, sounds produced by the mouth and received by the ear. If human communication had developed primarily as a system of gestures (like the American Sign Language of the deaf), it would have been quite different from what it is. Because sounds follow one another sequentially in time, language has a one-dimensional quality (like the lines of type we use to represent it in printing); gestures can fill the three dimensions of space as well as the fourth of time. The ears can hear sounds coming from any direction; the eyes can see only those gestures made in front of them. The ears can hear through physical barriers, such as walls, which the eyes cannot see through. Speech has both advantages and disadvantages in comparison with gestures; but on the whole, it is undoubtedly superior, as its evolutionary survival demonstrates.

WRITING AND SPEECH

Because writing has become so important in our culture, we sometimes think of it as more real than speech. A little thought, however, will show why speech is primary and writing secondary to language. Human beings have been writing (as far as we can tell from the surviving evidence) for at least 5000 years; but they have been talking for much longer, doubtless ever since there have been human beings When writing did develop, it was derived from and represented speech, albeit imperfectly, as we shall see in chapter 3. Even today there are spoken languages that have no written form. Furthermore, we all learn to talk well before we learn to write; any human child who is not severely handicapped physically or mentally will learn to talk: a normal human being cannot be prevented from doing so. It is as though we were "programmed" to acquire language in the form of speech. On the other hand, it takes a special effort to learn to write; in the past many intelligent and useful members of society did not acquire the skill, and even today many who speak languages with writing systems never learn to read or write, while some who learn the rudiments of those skills do so only imperfectly.

To affirm the primacy of speech over writing is not, however, to disparage the latter. If speaking makes us human, writing makes us civilized. Writing has some advantages over speech. For example, it is more permanent, thus making possible the records that any civilization must have. Writing is also capable of easily making some distinctions that speech can make only with difficulty. We can, for example, indicate certain types of pauses more clearly by the spaces that we leave between words when we write than we ordinarily are able to do when we speak. *Grade A* may well be heard as *gray day*, but there is no mistaking the one phrase for the other in writing.

Similarly, the comma distinguishes "a pretty, hot day" from "a pretty hot day" more clearly than these are often distinguished in actual speech. But the question mark does not distinguish between "Why did you do it?" (I didn't hear you the first time you told me), with rising pitch at the end, and "Why did you do it?" (You didn't tell me), with falling terminal pitch. Nor can we show in writing the very apparent difference between *sound quality* 'tone' and *sound quality* 'good grade' (as in "The sound quality of the recording was excellent" and "The materials were of sound quality")—a difference that we show very easily in speech by strongly stressing *sound* in the first sentence and the first syllable of *quality* in the second. *Incense* 'enrage' and *incense* 'aromatic substance for burning' are likewise sharply differentiated in speech by the position of the stress, as *sewer* 'conduit' and *sewer* 'one who sews' are differentiated by vowel quality. But in writing we can distinguish these words only in context, as we must do with words both written and pronounced identically, like *bear* 'carry' and *bear* 'animal.' On the other hand, some words pronounced alike are distinguished from each other in writing; *bare* is thus distinguished from the words cited in the preceding sentence, as *weak* is distinguished from *week*. Here the written forms rule out the slight possibility of ambiguity inherent in such phrases as "a bear behind" and "a week back" when these are spoken. Homonyms[1] make up the very stuff and substance of much nursery humor, as in the examples just cited, but William Shakespeare was by no means averse to this sort of thing: puns involving *tale* and *tail*, *whole* and *hole*, *hoar* and *whore*, and a good many other homonyms (some, like *stale* and *steal*, are homonyms no longer) are of rather frequent occurrence in the writings of our greatest poet.

The conventions of writing differ somewhat, but not really very much, from those of ordinary speech. For instance, we ordinarily write *was not, do not, would not*, although we usually say *wasn't, don't, wouldn't*. Furthermore, our choice of words is likely to differ occasionally and to be made with somewhat more care in writing than in ordinary, everyday speech. But these are stylistic matters, as is also the fact that writing tends to be somewhat more conservative than speech.

The effort to represent the sounds of one language by the spellings of another may lead to a confusion of **transliteration**, the interpretation of one writing system by another, with **translation**, the interpretation of one language by another. Greek πυρ can be transliterated *pyr*, as in *pyromaniac*, or trans-

---

[1] Such words as have been discussed here are usually called **homonyms**. The overlapping terms **homograph** 'a word written like another word of different meaning that may or may not be pronounced like it' and **homophone** 'a word pronounced like another word of different meaning that may or may not be written like it' may also be used, depending on one's concern with one or the other, writing or pronunciation.

lated *fire*, as in *firebug*. The name of a great Russian writer whom English-speaking people know as *Chekhov* is written in other spelling systems according to the various ways of transliterating Russian, which uses the Cyrillic rather than the Roman alphabet: the French write *Tchékhov*; the Czechs, *Čechov*; the Germans, *Tschechow*; the Swedes, *Tjechov*; and the Spanish, *Tchejoff*, *Tchekov*, or *Chejov*. The fact that these variant writings give a fairly close approximation of the Russian pronunciation to one familiar with the phonetic and orthographic systems of the languages cited is all that is really important. The writer himself wrote his name *Чехов*, which, despite its strangeness to our eyes, does not indicate that Russian is an uncommonly difficult language or that, in the interests of international "understanding," the Russians ought to adopt our way of writing—or, for that matter, that we ought to adopt theirs. Names, like all other words, were in existence long before anybody ever wrote them, and the way one writes them is purely and simply a matter of tradition. Had the Russians long ago settled on Chinese ideograms as the basis of their writing system, their language would have had precisely the same development that it has had, and the great writer would have had the same name as that under which he is known to us. When the president of Turkey, Mustafa Kemal Pasha (later Kemal Atatürk), in 1928 substituted the Roman alphabet for the Arabic in writing Turkish, the Turkish language changed no more than time changed when he introduced the Gregorian calendar in his country.

GESTURES AND SPEECH

Such specialized gestures as the indifferent shrug of the shoulders, the admonitory shaking of the finger, the lifting up of the hand in greeting and the waving of it in parting, the widening of the eyes in astonishment, the scornful lifting of the brows, the approving nod, and the disapproving sideways shaking of the head—all these need not accompany speech at all; they may of themselves be communicative. Indeed, there is some reason to think that gestures are older than spoken language and are the matrix out of which it developed. When gestures accompany speech, they may be more or less unconscious, like the postures assumed by persons talking together, indicating their sympathy (or lack of it) with each other's ideas. The study of such communicative body movements is known as **kinesics**.

The different tones of voice that we employ optionally in speaking—the drawl, the sneer, the shout, the whimper, the simper, and the like—also play a part in communication (which we recognize when we say, "I didn't mind what he said, I just didn't like his tone of voice"). But they and the gestures that accompany speech are not language, but rather parallel systems of communication called **paralanguage**. Other vocalizations that are communicative, like laughing, crying, groaning, and yelping, usually do not accompany speech as tones of voice do, though they may come before or after it.

Language as Speech

Writing is obviously a convention because we can represent the same language by more than one writing system. Japanese, for example, is written with kanji (ideographs representing whole words), with either of two syllabaries (writing systems that present each syllable with a separate symbol), or with the letters of the Roman alphabet. Similarly, we could by general agreement reform English spelling (soe dhat, for egzammpul, wee spelt it liek dhis). <u>We can change the conventions of our writing system merely by agreeing to do so.</u>

Although it is not so obvious, language itself—that is, speech—is also conventional. No one would deny, of course, that there are features shared by all languages—features that must be regarded as natural, inherent, or universal. Thus the human vocal apparatus (lips, teeth, tongue, and so forth) makes it inevitable that human languages will have only a limited range of sounds. Likewise, since all of us live in the same universe and perceive it through the same senses with more or less the same basic mental equipment, it is hardly surprising that we should find it necessary to talk about more or less the same things in more or less similar ways.

Nevertheless, the systems that operate in the world's many languages are conventional and generally arbitrary; that is to say, there is usually no connection between the sounds we make and the phenomena of life. There are a comparatively small number of **echoic words**, like *bow-wow*, which seems to those of us who speak English as our native language to be a fairly accurate imitation of the sounds made by a dog and therefore not to be wholly arbitrary, but it is highly doubtful that a dog would agree, particularly a French dog, which says *gnaf-gnaf*, or a German one, which says *wau-wau*, or a Japanese one, which says *wung-wung*.[2]

Most people think unquestioningly that their language is the best—and so it is for them, inasmuch as they mastered it well enough for their own purposes so long ago that they cannot remember when. It seems to them more logical, more sensible, more right—in short, more *natural*—than the way foreigners talk. But there is nothing really natural about any language, since all these highly systematized and conventionalized methods of human communication must be acquired. There is, for instance, nothing natural in our use of *is* in such a sentence as "The woman is busy." The utterance can be made just as effectively without the meaningless verb form, which is

---

[2] The reader interested in the sounds made by foreign animals will do well to look into Noel Perrin's instructive and highly amusing "Old Macberlitz Had a Farm" (*New Yorker*, 27 January 1962, pp. 28–29), and the erudite comments by the ambassador from Norway, Paul Koht (in a letter to the editor of the *New Yorker*, 24 February 1962, p. 125), from which he may acquire from a native speaker valuable information about the sounds uttered by Norwegian cows (*mmmøøø*), sheep (*mæ*), pigs (*nøff-nøff*), and other creatures. Norwegian hens very sensibly say *klukk-klukk*, though doubtless with a heavy Norwegian accent.

conventional in standard English, and some languages do get along perfectly well without it. This use of *is* (and other forms of the verb *to be*) was, as a matter of fact, late in developing and has never developed in Russian and some other languages of the Balto-Slavic group.

To the speaker of Russian it is thus more "natural" to say "Zhenshchina zanyata"—literally "Woman busy"—which sounds to our ears so much like baby talk that the unsophisticated speaker of English might well (though quite wrongly) conclude that Russian is a childish tongue. The system of Russian also manages to struggle along without the definite article. As a matter of fact, the speaker of Russian never misses it—nor should we if its use had not become conventional with us.

To a naive English-speaking person, calling the organ of sight *eye* will seem to be perfectly natural and right, and those who call it anything else— like the Germans, who call it *Auge*, the Russians, who call it *glaz*, or the Japanese, who call it *me*—are likely to be regarded as either perverse or simply unfortunate because they do not speak languages in which things are properly designated. The fact is, however, that *eye*, which we pronounce exactly like the nominative form of the first person singular pronoun (a fact that might be cited against it by a foreign speaker), is the name of the organ in question only in our present English linguistic system. It has not always been so. Londoners at the time of the accession of King Edward III in 1327 pronounced the word with two syllables, the vowel of the first syllable being that which we pronounce nowadays in *see* and the second like the *-a* in *Ida*. If we chose to go back to King Alfred's day in the late ninth century, we should find yet another pronunciation and, in addition, a different way of writing the word from which Modern English *eye* has developed. When a Scottish plowboy says "ee" for *eye*,[3] he is not being quaint, whimsical, perverse, or stupid. He is merely using a variant form of the word—a perfectly "legitimate" pronunciation that happens not to occur in standard Modern English. Knowledge of such changes within a single language should be sufficient to dissipate the notion that any one word or any one form of a word is more appropriate except in a purely chronological and social sense than any other word or form.

LANGUAGE CHANGE

Change is the normal state of language. Every language is constantly turning into something different, and when we hear a new word or a new pronunciation of an old word or a novel use of a word, we may be catching the early stages of a change. Change is natural because a language system is

---

[3] As in Robert Burns's "To a Mouse":
Still thou art blest, compared wi' me!
The present only toucheth thee:
But och! I backward cast my e'e,
On prospects drear!

14 culturally transmitted. Like other conventional matters—such as fashions of clothing, cooking, entertainment, means of livelihood, and government—language is undergoing revision constantly; with language such revision is slower than with some other cultural activities, but it is happening nonetheless.

There are three general causes of language change. First, words and sounds may affect neighboring words and sounds. For example, *sandwiches* is often pronounced, not as the spelling suggests, but in ways that might be represented as *sanwiches, sanwiges, samwiges,* or even *sammiges.* Such spellings look illiterate, but they represent perfectly normal, though informal, pronunciations that result from the influence of one sound on another within the word. When nearby elements thus influence one another, the result is called **syntagmatic change**. Second, words and sounds may be affected by others that are not immediately present but with which they are associated. For example, the side of a ship on which it was laden (that is, loaded) was called the *ladeboard*, but its opposite, *starboard*, influenced a change in pronunciation to *larboard*. Then, because *larboard* was likely to be confused with *starboard* through their great similarity of sound, it was generally replaced by *port*. Such change is called **paradigmatic** or **associative change**. Third, a language may change because of the influence of external events. New inventions like holography and new theoretical entities like the gluons and quarks of subatomic physics require new words. In addition, new contacts with persons who use speechways different from our own may affect pronunciation, vocabulary, and even grammar. **Social change** thus modifies speech.

The documented history of the English language begins about A.D. 700, with the oldest written records. We can reconstruct some of the prehistory before that time, to as early as about 4000 B.C., but the farther back in time we go, the less certain we can be about what the language was like. The history of our language is traditionally divided into three periods: Old English, from the earliest records (or the Anglo-Saxon settlement of England, around A.D. 450) to about 1100; Middle English, approximately 1100 to 1500; and Modern English, since about 1500. The lines dividing the three periods are based on significant changes in the language that happened about those times, but there were also major cultural changes around 1100 and 1500 that contribute to our sense of new beginnings. These matters are treated in detail in chapters 5 through 8.

THE NOTION OF LINGUISTIC CORRUPTION

A widely held notion resulting from a misunderstanding of change is that there are ideal forms of languages, thought of as "pure," and that existing languages represent corruptions of these. Thus, the Greek spoken today is supposed to be a degraded form of Classical Greek rather than what it really is, a development of it. Since the Romance languages are developments of

Latin, it would follow from this point of view that they also are corrupt, although this assumption is not usually made. Those who admire or profess to admire Latin literature sometimes suppose that a stage of perfection had been reached in Classical Latin and that every divergent development in Latin was indicative of steady and irreparable deterioration. From this point of view the late development of Latin spoken in the early Middle Ages (sometimes called Vulgar, or popular, Latin) is "bad" Latin, which, strange as it may seem, was ultimately to become "good" Italian, French, Spanish, and so on.

It is obvious that such notions, despite their tenacity, are completely invalid. They are based to some extent on yet another notion—that synthetic languages, which make use of complicated systems of endings for case, tense, mood, gender, and the like, are superior ("more expressive of fine shades of meaning" is a frequent description) to analytical languages, like English and French, which do not. Latin *pater Carolī* 'Charles's father,' for instance, came to be expressed in French, Spanish, and Italian, respectively, by *le père de Charles*, *el padre de Carlos*, and *il padre di Carlo* 'the father of Charles.' The Latin genitive has been completely lost in the languages derived from Latin, its function being performed by a preposition meaning 'of.' (English, which has never lost the genitive inflection, can use either construction.) This loss of the genitive in the Romance languages is doubtless considered degenerative by those who believe in linguistic corruption. Such persons are also likely to regard English, which, though it has retained its genitive, has lost most of its other inflectional devices in the course of its development, as crude and barbarous.

Indo-European, the origin of practically all the languages of Europe as well as some Asiatic ones, was even more complex in its inflections than the classical languages. In addition to the case forms found in most Latin nouns, for instance, the Indo-European noun had also an instrumental, a locative, and a vocative form, the last two of which survive only very rarely in Latin. Now, carrying to its logical conclusion the point of view cited, we would have to regard Greek and Latin as corrupt developments of Indo-European. But such notions of corruption result from ill-founded prejudice only.

Because we hear so much about "pure" English, it is perhaps well that we examine this particular notion. When Captain Frederick Marryat, an English novelist, visited the United States in 1837–38, he thought it "remarkable how very debased the language has become in a short period in America," adding that "if their lower classes are more intelligible than ours, it is equally true that the higher classes do not speak the language so purely or so classically as it is spoken among the well-educated English." Both statements are nonsense. The first is based on the captain's apparent notion that the English language had reached a stage of perfection at the time America was first settled by English-speaking people, after which, presumably because of the innate depravity of those English settlers who brought their language to the

New World, it had taken a steadily downward course, whatever that may mean. One wonders also precisely how Marryat knew what constituted "classical" or "pure" English. It is probable that he was merely attributing certain superior qualities to that type of English that he was accustomed to hear from persons of good social standing in the land of his birth and that he himself spoke. Any divergence was "debased": "My speech is pure; thine, wherein it differs from mine, is corrupt."

THE QUESTION OF USAGE

The concept of an absolute and unwavering, presumably God-given standard of linguistic correctness (sometimes confused with "purity") is so widespread, even among the educated, as to merit some attention here. Those who subscribe to this notion become greatly exercised over such matters as the split infinitive, the "incorrect" position of *only*, and the preposition ending a sentence. All these supposed "errors" have been committed time and again by eminent writers and speakers, so that one wonders how those who condemn them know that they are bad. Robert Lowth, who wrote one of the most influential English grammars of the eighteenth century (*A Short Introduction to English Grammar*, 1762), was praised by one of his admirers for showing "the grammatic inaccuracies that have escaped the pens of our most distinguished writers."

One would suppose that the usage of "our most distinguished writers" would be good usage. But Lowth and his followers knew, or thought they knew, better; and their attitude survives to this day. This is not, of course, to deny that there are standards of usage, but only to suggest that even in the reputedly democratic society in which we live any set of standards that is to have validity must be based on the usage of speakers and writers of generally acknowledged excellence. They would include nowadays almost inevitably persons of education, though it has not always been so; other ages have not placed so high a premium on mere literacy as our own. What we think of as "good" English has grown out of the usage of generations of well-born and well-bred persons, many of whom could neither read nor write. In the late fifteenth century, William Caxton, obviously a highly literate man, used to submit his work to the Duchess of Burgundy (an English lady despite her French title), who "oversawe and corrected" it. We have no information as to the speed and ease with which the Duchess read, but it is highly likely that she was considerably less literate than was Caxton himself. Yet to Caxton the "correctness" of the usage of a lady of the court was unassailable, whereas he would seem to have had little faith in what came naturally to him, a brilliant son of the bourgeoisie. His standard of excellence was the usage of persons of good position—quite a different thing from our own subservience to the mandates of badly informed "authorities" who are guided by their own prejudices rather than by a study of actual usage.

Linguistic commentators with a heavily authoritative air about matters of usage are usually to be distrusted when their pronouncements deny social acceptability to locutions that we have read in reputable books and heard from the lips of reputable speakers. Thus, when the writer of a syndicated newspaper column solemnly informs his linguistically insecure readers that it is incorrect to say "There were 400 people present" because one should never use *people* after a number, but only *persons*, we are quite justified in asking how he knows this. And, inasmuch as there could not possibly be any way of knowing other than by divine inspiration, we are equally justified in assuming that the current preference of a large majority of educated speakers for *people* in such a construction is sufficient to establish it as "correct," that is, in good usage. Likewise, when we come upon lists of words that practically everyone is supposed to mispronounce, we are surely justified in asking ourselves how the compilers of such lists know how the words ought to be pronounced, unless they too are divinely inspired by a linguistic Jehovah who watches over the destiny of the English language.

Language as Human

As noted at the beginning of this chapter, language is a specifically human activity. That statement, however, raises several questions. When and how did human beings acquire language? Is language innate, or is it something we learn? How does human language differ from the communication systems of other creatures? We will look briefly at each of those questions.

THEORIES OF THE ORIGIN OF LANGUAGE

We shall not here speculate overmuch on the ultimate origins of language, since we have no real information on the subject. The earliest languages of which we have any records are already in a high stage of development. The same is true of languages spoken by technologically primitive peoples. The problem of how language began has naturally tantalized philosophical minds, and many theories have been advanced, to which waggish scholars have given such fancifully descriptive names as the pooh-pooh theory, the bow-wow theory, the ding-dong theory, and the yo-he-ho theory. The nicknames indicate how seriously the theories need be taken: they are based, respectively, on the notions that language was in the beginning ejaculatory, echoic (onomatopoeic), characterized by a mystic appropriateness of sound to sense in contrast to being merely imitative, or made up of grunts and groans emitted in the course of group actions and coming in time to be associated with those actions.

According to one theory, the early prelanguage of human beings was a mixture of gestures and sounds in which the gestures carried most of the meaning and the sounds were used chiefly to "punctuate" or amplify the gestures—just the reverse of our use of speech and hand signals. Then, about 50,000 years ago, there were a number of related changes in human physiology and behavior. The human brain, which had been expanding in size, lateralized —that is, each half came to specialize in certain activities, and language ability was localized in the left hemisphere of most persons. As a consequence, "handedness" developed (right-handedness for those with left-hemisphere dominance), and there was greater manual specialization. As people had more things to do with their hands, they could use them less for communication and had to rely more on sounds. Therefore, increasingly complex forms of oral signals developed, and language as we know it evolved. The fact that we human beings alone have vocal language but share with our closest animal kin (the apes) an ability to learn complex gesture systems suggests that manual signs may have preceded language as a form of communication.

We cannot know how language really began; we can be sure only of its immense antiquity. However human beings started to talk, they did so a breathtakingly long time ago, and it was not until much later that they devised a system of making marks in or on wood, stone, and the like to represent what they said. Compared with language, writing is a newfangled invention, although certainly none the less brilliant for being so.

INNATE LANGUAGE ABILITY

The acquisition of language—that is, the mastery of one of the complicated linguistic systems by which human beings, and they alone, communicate—would seem to be an arduous task. But it is a task that normal children all over the world seem not to mind in the least. Even children in daily contact with a language other than their "home" language—the native language of their parents—readily acquire that second language, even to the extent of speaking it with a native accent.

Noam Chomsky (1959, p. 42) has pointed out what should be apparent to all, that "a young child of immigrant parents may learn a second language in the streets, from other children, with amazing rapidity . . . while the subtleties that become second nature to the child may elude his parents despite high motivation and continued practice." After childhood, most minds undergo a kind of "hardening" in this respect, perhaps in the late teens. But children seem to be genetically equipped with some sort of built-in "device" that makes the acquisition of languages possible.

It is not, of course, claimed that children of five or so have acquired all of the words they will need to know as they grow up or all of the grammatical constructions available to them. What is true is that they have rather fully mastered the system by means of which they will speak of many things for the rest of their lives. The immensity of the accomplishment can be appreciated by anyone who has learned a second language as an adult. It is clear that, although every particular language has to be learned, the ability to acquire and use language is a part of our genetic inheritance.

DO BIRDS AND BEASTS REALLY TALK?

Although language is an exclusively human phenomenon, many of the lower animals are physically just about as well equipped as human beings to produce speech sounds, and some—certain birds, for instance—have in fact been taught to do so. What we call our speech organs are actually organs with primary functions quite different from the production of speech sounds, functions such as the ingestion and mastication of food. But no other species makes use of a system of sounds even remotely resembling human language, despite a belief that appeals to the popular imagination, but is as yet unsubstantiated by any truly scientific evidence, that porpoises thus "talk" to one another.

Since the late 1960s, a trio of fetching chimpanzees, Sarah, Lana, and Washoe, have greatly modified our ideas about the linguistic abilities of our closest relatives in the animal kingdom. After several efforts to teach chimps to talk had ended in almost total failure (one animal having learned to say *cup* and *papa* in passable fashion), it was generally concluded that apes lack the cognitive ability to learn language. Some psychologists reasoned, however, that the main problem might be a simple anatomical limitation: human vocal organs are so different from the corresponding ones in apes that the animals cannot produce the sounds of human speech. If they have the mental, but not the physical, ability to talk, then they should be able to learn a language using a medium other than sound.

Sarah was taught to communicate by arranging plastic tokens of arbitrary color and shape into groups. Each of the tokens, which were metal-backed and placed on a magnetized board, represented a word in the system, and groups of tokens corresponded to sentences. Sarah learned over a hundred tokens and could manage sentences of the complexity of "Sarah take banana if-then Mary no give chocolate Sarah" (that is, 'If Sarah takes a banana, Mary won't give Sarah any chocolate').

Lana also used word symbols, but hers were on a typewriter connected to a computer. She communicated with the computer and through it with people, and they communicated with her in a similar way. The typed-out messages appeared on a screen and had to conform exactly to the rules of "word" order of the system Lana had been taught if she was to get what she asked for (food, drink, companionship, and the like).

Washoe, in the most interesting of these efforts to teach animals a language, was schooled in the gesture language used by the deaf, **Ameslan.** Her remarkable success in learning to communicate with this quite natural and adaptable system has resulted in a number of other chimpanzees and even gorillas being taught some of the sign language. The apes learn signs, use them appropriately, combine them meaningfully, and when occasion requires even invent new signs or combinations. For example, one of the chimps, Lucy, made up the terms "candydrink" and "drinkfruit" to converse about watermelons. There is even some evidence of one ape learning signs from another.

Work with Sarah, Lana, and especially Washoe and her compeers has taught us that our simian kin are able to acquire and use languagelike systems to an extent hitherto not believed possible. Their accomplishments suggest that interspecies communication may be feasible and that further research along these lines may produce new ideas about the nature of human language and its evolutionary development. The linguistic accomplishment of these apes is remarkable; nevertheless, it is a far cry from the fullness of a human language. The number of signs or tokens the ape learns, the complexity of the syntax with which they are combined, and the breadth of ideas that they represent are all far more restricted than in any human language. Moreover, human linguistic systems have been fundamentally shaped by the fact that they are expressed in sound. Vocalness of language is no mere incidental characteristic but rather is central to the nature of language. We must still say that only human beings have language in the full sense of that term. However, we can expect to learn a great deal more about the question during the coming years.

There is also ample evidence that in the wild certain animals communicate with others of their kind in an elementary and nonlinguistic fashion. Leaving sexual posturings and similar kinesic phenomena out of the question, it has in fact been established that gibbons do so in a very limited way by a system of differentiated vocal noises—warning calls, calls having to do with the search for food, and the like. This is the nearest we get to human language among the lower animals when they are in a natural state. As Charles Hockett suggests (1973, pp. 381–82), language may well have developed out of blendings of such calls, whereby in the course of heaven only knows how many scores of millennia a closed and nonproductive system of nine or ten calls became an open and productive system making possible the production of an infinite number of different sentences. Or it may be that a sudden mutation endowed the human species with the genetic ability to acquire a language system that bears little similarity to the vocalizations of the apes. However it came about, it would seem that only people have developed such a system; human beings alone can talk about the manifold things that concern them, ranging all the way from food, shelter, and sex—the most drastic concerns of our remotest ancestors—to transubstantiation, relativity, and transformational-generative grammar.

The purpose of language is to communicate, whether with others by talking and writing or with ourselves by thinking. The relationship of language to thought has generated a great deal of speculation. At one extreme are those who believe language is merely a clothing for thought, which is quite independent of the form we use to express it. At the other extreme are those who believe that thought is merely suppressed language and that when we are thinking we are just talking under our breath. The truth is probably somewhere between those two extremes. Some, though not all, of the mental activities we identify as "thought" are linguistic in nature. It is certainly true that until we put our ideas into words they are likely to remain vague, inchoate, and uncertain. We may all from time to time feel like the little girl who, on being told to express her thoughts clearly, replied, "How can I know what I think until I see what I say."

If we think—at least some of the time—in language, then presumably the language we speak must influence the way we think about the world and perhaps even the way we perceive it. The idea that language has that kind of influence and thus importance is called the **Sapir-Whorf hypothesis**, after two American linguists, Edward Sapir and Benjamin Lee Whorf. Efforts have been made to test the hypothesis—for example, by giving to persons who spoke quite different languages a large number of chips, each of a different color. Those tested were told to sort the chips into piles so that each pile contained chips of similar color. Each person was allowed to make any number of piles. As might be predicted, the number of piles tended to correspond with the number of basic color terms in the language spoken by the sorter. In English we have eleven basic color terms (*red, pink, orange, brown, yellow, green, blue, purple, black, gray,* and *white*), so English speakers tend to sort color chips into eleven piles. If a language has only six basic color terms (corresponding, say, to our *red, yellow, green, blue, black,* and *white*), speakers of that language will tend to cancel their perception of all other differences and sort color chips into those six piles. Pink is only a tint or light version of red. Because we have different basic terms for those two colors, however, they seem to us to be quite distinct colors; light blue, green, and yellow, on the other hand, are just insignificant versions of the darker colors because we have no basic terms for them. Thus how we think about and respond to colors is a function of how our language classifies them.

Though a relatively trivial matter, color terms illustrate that the way we respond to the world corresponds to the way our language categorizes it. More complex and important is the question of how many of our assumptions about things are just reflexes of our language. In English, as in many other languages, we often use masculine forms (such as pronouns) when we talk about persons of either sex, as in "Everyone has to do his best." Does such masculine language influence our attitudes toward the equality of the sexes in other regards? In English every regular sentence has to have a subject and a verb; so we say things like "It's raining" and "It's time to go," with the word *it* serving as subject, even though the meaning of that *it* is difficult to specify. Does the linguistic requirement for a subject and verb lead us to expect an actor or agent in every action, even though some things may happen without anyone making them happen? The implications of the Sapir-Whorf hypothesis are far-reaching and of considerable philosophical importance, even though no way of confidently testing those implications seems possible.

An idea about the ability of various languages to communicate that has vitiated much of our thinking about language is the notion that certain languages are more "expressive" than others. Now the fact is that all languages are about equally expressive, if by the term we mean 'efficient for purposes of communication.' It is obvious that members of one linguistic community will not need or want to express all that the members of another community might consider important. In short, Eskimos feel no need to discuss Zen Buddhism, the quantum theory, or urban renewal. But they can talk about what is important to their own culture, and doubtless with greater efficiency in some instances than can the anthropologist who must describe that culture in, say, English—a language that might well impress Eskimos as being quite "primitive" because it has only one widely used word for the frozen vapor that falls in white flakes (*snow*), whereas their language has many words for many different kinds of snow. Furthermore, they can make a good many grammatical distinctions in their language that we are not in the least concerned with making in ours. These distinctions also doubtless seem so essential to them that, if they ever gave the matter a thought, they might well regard English as sadly deficient in its grammar as well as in its word stock.

An important aspect of language systems is that they are "open." That is, a language is not a finite set of messages from which the speaker must choose. Instead, any speaker can use the resources of the language—its vocabulary and grammatical patterns—to make up new messages, sentences that no one has ever said before. Because a language is an **open system**, it can always be used to talk about new things. Bees have a remarkable system of communication, using a sort of "dance" in the air, in which the patterns of a bee's flight tell other members of the hive about food sources. However, all bees can communicate about is a nectar supply—its direction, distance, and abundance. As a consequence, a bee would make a very dull conversationalist, at least in human terms.

Another aspect of the communicative function of language is that it can be displaced. That is, we can talk about things not present—about rain when the weather is dry, about taxes even when they are not being collected, and about a yeti even if no such creature exists. The characteristic of **displacement** means that human beings can abstract, can lie, and can talk about talk itself. It allows us to use language as a vehicle of memory and of imagination. A bee communicates with other bees about a nectar source only when it has just found such a source. Bees do not celebrate the delights of nectar by dancing for sheer pleasure. Human beings use language for many purposes quite unconnected with their immediate environment. Indeed, most language use is probably thus displaced.

One of the most important tenets of the lay person's linguistic creed is that all thoughtful, well-educated individuals, no matter what their special training may have been, are competent to make authoritative pronouncements about the language they speak or, for that matter, about any language with which they have a passing acquaintance. Leonard Bloomfield (1944, p. 49), an authority on American Indian languages, tells of being informed by a physician that Chippewa has only a few hundred words—a patently fantastic statement to make concerning any language. Says Bloomfield, "When I tried to state the diagnostic setting, the physician, our host, briefly and with signs of displeasure repeated his statement, and then turned his back to me." This was a more or less typical (to adopt Bloomfield's term) "tertiary response to language"—a response that seems to be practically inevitable when one has tried to enlighten someone else who has made a statement about language (a "secondary response") that is open to question. As we proceed, we hope it will become increasingly obvious that the study of language, like language itself, has order, discipline, and system, and that consequently the lay person's opinions about language are no more reliable than his or her opinions about medicine, physics, or engineering.

In the remainder of this book, we will be concerned with some of what is known about the origins and the development of the English language. Chapter 2 examines the sound system of present-day English, a necessary preliminary to the later discussion of the many phonological changes that have affected our language during its history. Chapter 3 looks at the development of writing and at the orthographic conventions of present-day English. These preliminary matters out of the way, chapters 4 through 9 trace the history of our language from prehistoric times, through the three periods mentioned above, to the present day. Finally, chapters 10 through 12 examine the vocabulary of Modern English, its sources and its changes.

For Further Reading

Full bibliographical information for the works cited is in the Selected Bibliography, pp. 318–41.

General

Allen, *Linguistics and English Linguistics*, 1977.
Hill, *Linguistics Today*, 1969.
Sampson, *Schools of Linguistics*, 1980.

Hockett, "In Search of Jove's Brow," *American Speech*, 1978.
Hockett, *Man's Place in Nature*, 1973, especially chapters 8, 25, and 27.

Apes and Language

Linden, *Apes, Men and Language*, 1974.
Patterson, "Conversations with a Gorilla," *National Geographic*, 1978.
Premack, A. J., *Why Chimps Can Read*, 1976.
Premack, D., *Intelligence in Ape and Man*, 1976.
Rumbaugh, *Language Learning by a Chimpanzee: The Lana Project*, 1977.
Temerlin, *Lucy: Growing Up Human: A Chimpanzee Daughter in a Psychotherapist's Family*, 1975.

Language and Thought

Hayakawa, *Language in Thought and Action*, 1978.
Sapir, *Culture, Language and Personality: Selected Essays*, 1961.
Whorf, *Language, Thought, and Reality*, 1956.

Nonverbal Communication

Key, *Paralanguage and Kinesics (Nonverbal Communication)*, 1975.

2 The Sounds and Spelling of Current English

The Roman alphabet has always been inadequate for the phonetic representation of the English language, most strikingly so for Modern English. We have, for example, only five vowel symbols, *a*, *e*, *i*, *o*, and *u*; that this number is wholly inadequate is indicated by the fact that the first of these alone may have as many as six different sound values, as in *cat*, *came*, *calm*, *any*, *call*, and *was* (riming with *fuzz*). In our treatment of English sounds we shall use a way of writing in which the same symbols consistently represent the same sounds, rather than using the awkward expedient of riming words or of referring to the initial consonant of, say, *thy* in order to distinguish this sound from the phonetically different though identically written consonant of *thigh*.

We have just mentioned "same sounds," and it thus becomes necessary to point out that what are commonly regarded as the same sounds may vary from language to language. In English, for instance, the vowel sound of *sit* and the vowel sound of *seat* are **distinctive**. Many pairs of words, called **contrastive pairs**, differ solely in the distinctive quality that these sounds have for us: *bit–beat*, *mill–meal*, *fist–feast*, *lick–leak* are a few such pairs. But in

Spanish this difference, so important in English, is of no significance at all; there are no such contrastive pairs, and hence the two vowels in question are felt, not as distinctive sounds, but as one and the same. Native speakers of Spanish, when they learn English, are as likely as not to say "I seat in the sit" for "I sit in the seat"—a mistake that would be impossible, except as a slip of the tongue, for native speakers of English.

The Phoneme

What in any language is regarded as the "same sound" is actually a class of similar sounds that make up what is known as a **phoneme**. A phoneme is thus the smallest *distinctive* unit of speech; it consists of a number of **allophones**, that is, similar sounds that are not distinctive. Thus, speakers of English regard as the "same sound" the sound spelled *t* in *tone* and *stone*, though actually a different sound is symbolized by the letter *t* in each of these words: in *tone* the initial consonant is **aspirated**, that is, followed by a breath puff, which may be clearly felt if one holds one's hand before one's lips when pronouncing the word; in *stone*, this aspiration is lacking. Nevertheless, both sounds belong to, or are allophones of, the English *t* phoneme, which differs according to the phonetic environment in which it occurs. To put it in another way, the allophones occur in what is called **complementary distribution**: that is to say, each occurs in a specific environment—in this instance, the unaspirated *t* occurring only after *s*, a position never occupied by the aspirated sound, so that there is no overlapping of these two allophones. In other positions, such as at the end of a word like *fight*, aspirated and unaspirated *t* are in **free variation**: either may occur, depending on the style of speaking.

To put it in yet another way, in English there are no pairs of words whose members are distinguished solely by the presence or absence of aspiration of a *t* sound; hence, from a phonemic point of view, the two *t* sounds in English are the same because they are **nondistinctive**. They merely occur in different environments, one initially, the other after *s*. But the two sounds are phonemic in other languages: in Chinese, for instance, the difference between aspirated and unaspirated *t* is quite significant, and the aspiration or the lack of it distinguishes between words otherwise identical, just as *t* and *p* in English *tone* and *pone* do. Classical Greek had different symbols for these sounds, Θ and Τ, and carefully differentiated them, whereas the Romans had only the unaspirated sound represented by Greek Τ—that which is preceded in English by *s*. It was not until the classical period that they transliterated Θ by TH and presumably tried to pronounce *theta* in loanwords as an aspirate, that is, as *t* plus *h*.

There are other allophones of the phoneme written *t*. For instance, in some varieties of American English the *t* sound that appears medially in words like *item*, *little*, and *matter* is very like a *d*, and in other varieties it has become completely identical with the sound represented by *d* in that position. In a certain type of New York City speech, it is a **glottal stop**, that is, a "catch" in the throat, as in *battle* and *bottle*. In a word like *outcome*, it may be **unreleased**: we pronounce the first part of the *t* and then go directly to the *k* sound that begins *come*.

It is usual to write phonemes within slanting lines, or **virgules** (also called **slashes**), thus /t/. In this book we shall ordinarily use a **broad phonetic transcription** enclosed in **square brackets**, showing only the gross characteristics of speech and for the most part ignoring allophonic features such as the allophones of /t/ that have just been described. Such allophonic detail can be recorded in a **narrow transcription**, using special symbols such as [tʰ] for the *t* of *tone* and [t̺] for the *t* of *item*. Such detail is necessary, however, only for special purposes. Although broad phonetic transcriptions of speech are not in principle the same as phonemic transcriptions, in actual practice they do not differ much. In other words, nonsignificant features will not as a rule concern us any more than if the transcriptions were labeled as phonemic by putting them within slanting lines. But, since we shall have occasion to use some symbols for sounds that are not really distinctive, we shall, to avoid confusion, hereafter use only square brackets for transcriptions. Dwight Bolinger (1975, pp. 60–66) discusses phonemes and phonemic theory in a clear and concise way.

The Organs of Speech

The diagrammatic cross section of a head reproduced on p. 28 shows the principal organs by which speech is produced. As has been pointed out in chapter 1, none of these originally had any such function; all have been adapted to the articulation of speech sounds. Reference to the diagram will clarify such terms as *labial*, *alveolar*, and *velar* used in describing the place of articulation of English consonants.

The Consonants of English

Consonants are classified according to their **place of articulation** (that is, as labial, alveolar, and so on), their **manner of articulation** (that is, stop, fricative, affricate, and so on), and whether or not **voice** (vibration of the vocal cords) is a component of their articulation. The chart on p. 29 exemplifies such a classification for the consonants of Modern English; illustrative words are supplied only for symbols not occurring in conventional writing.

Referring to the chart, we see that [p], [t], and [k] (as in *pup*, *tat*, and *kick*) are voiceless **stops** (also called **plosives** and **explosives**), so designated because in their production an actual stoppage is made at a given point in the mouth and is then broken down by an explosion of breath with no accompanying vibration of the vocal cords. But, if vibration (as in *bub*, *dad*, and *gig*) is added to the articulations necessary to make these sounds, the

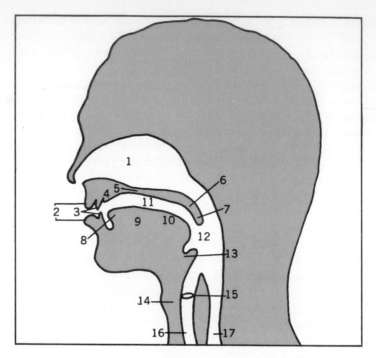

THE ORGANS OF SPEECH

1. Nasal cavity
2. Lips
3. Teeth
4. Alveolar ridge
5. Hard palate
6. Velum
7. Uvula
8. Tip of tongue
9. Front of tongue
10. Back of tongue
11. Oral cavity
12. Pharynx
13. Epiglottis
14. Larynx
15. Vocal cords and glottis
16. Trachea
17. Esophagus

resulting sounds are voiced stops, [b], [d], and [g]. With stoppage at the lips, the result is [p] or [b]; hence these are called, respectively, the voiceless and voiced **bilabial** stops. With stoppage made by the tongue against the gums above the teeth (the alveolar ridge), the result is [t] or [d]; hence these sounds are called, respectively, the voiceless and voiced **alveolar** stops. With stoppage made against the velum, or soft palate, which may be discerned by running the tongue back along the roof of the mouth until it reaches that part which is soft and spongy, the result is [k] or [g]; hence these sounds are called, respectively, the voiceless and voiced **velar** stops. Both [k] and [g] have **palatal** (more forward) varieties, depending on contiguous vowels, as in *kin* contrasted with *calm* and *give* contrasted with *gone*, but these allophonic differences will be ignored where we are dealing with Modern English: one symbol for each is sufficient.

For those sounds called **fricatives** (or **spirants**), a narrow opening is made

The Sounds and Spelling of Current English

PLACE OF ARTICULATION

MANNER OF ARTICULATION		LABIAL		DENTAL			PALATOVELAR		GLOTTAL
		Bilabial	Labiodental	Interdental	Alveolar	Alveolo-palatal	Palatal	Velar	
Stops:	voiceless	p			t			k	
	voiced	b			d			g	
Fricatives:	voiceless		f	θ (*thigh*)	s	š (*shun*)			h
	voiced		v	ð (*thy*)	z	ž (*vision*)			
Affricates:	voiceless					č (*chum*)			
	voiced					ǰ (*gem*)			
Nasals:		m			n			ŋ (*sing*)	
Liquids:	lateral				l				
	retroflex				r				
Semivowels:							y	w	

THE CONSONANTS

The Consonants of English

somewhere in the mouth, so that the air must "rub" (Lat. *fricāre*) its way through instead of breaking down a complete obstruction as with the stops. The fricatives of present-day English include the voiceless and voiced **labiodental** [f] and [v] (as in *fife* and *viva*), **interdental** [θ] and [ð] (as in *thigh* and *thy*), alveolar [s] and [z] (as in *sass* and *zoos*), and **alveolopalatal** [š] and [ž] (as in the middle sounds of *fission* and *vision*). Velar fricatives were current in Old and Middle English, as they still are in German—for example, German *Nacht* 'night.' They had palatal allophones, occurring when the contiguous vowel was front, as in German *nicht* 'not.' The symbols for writing these fricatives are [x] and [ç], but we need not be concerned with them now. The voiceless fricative [h] (as in *hoe*) can probably best be described as a breathing. Although for the sake of convenience it is classified in the chart above as a **glottal** fricative, it has, as Hans Kurath (1964, p. 66) points out, "as many positional allophones as the number of vowels and semivowels that can follow it."

The voiced and voiceless **affricates** begin with articulation as if, respectively, for the stops [d] and [t], followed by, respectively, the fricatives [ž] and [š]. Some analysts in fact write them [dž] and [tš], but it is now more usual to regard them as unitary phonemes and write the first [ǰ] and the second [č]. They are the initial and final sounds of *judge* and *church*, respectively.

Those consonants articulated by obstructing the oral passage and letting the breath and voice flow through the nose are called **nasals**. They include the bilabial [m] (as in *mum*), with lips completely closed; the alveolar [n] (as in *nun*), with stoppage made at the gum line; and the velar [ŋ] (as at the end of *sung*), with stoppage made at the velum. The nasals may by themselves form syllables, as in *open* [-pm] (where the labial [m] is the result of assimilation to the preceding labial [p]), *rotten* [-tn], and *bacon* [-kŋ] (where the velar [ŋ] is the result of assimilation to the preceding velar [k]). Since such words may be, and sometimes are, pronounced with an unstressed vowel sound written [ə] (for which see below), we may write the final syllables as [-pən], [-tən], and [-kən]. But it should be remembered that the intervening [ə] is often, and in some words usually, nonexistent.

The sounds [l] (as in *lull*) and [r] (as in *roar*) are called **liquids** and, like the nasals, may be **syllabic**, as in *ripple* [-pl] and *matter* [-tr]. As with the syllabic nasals, we shall henceforth write such syllabic liquids [-əl] and [-ər]. The similarity in the articulation of [l] and [r] is indicated by their historical alternation, as in *Sarah–Sally*, *Katherine–Kathleen*, and in the related words *stella* (Latin), *astēr* (Greek), and *steorra* (Old English) 'star.' The liquid [l] is called a **lateral** because the breath flows around the sides of the tongue in its production. Its principal allophones are the palatal or **clear *l*** of *lean* as contrasted with the velar or **dark *l*** of *kneel*. Among the allophones of [r] are the fricative sound heard after [t], [d], and [θ], as in *true*, *drew*, and *threw*, and the tongue-flap occurring between vowels in standard British English, as in *America*, *worry*, and *very* (sometimes spelled "veddy" in caricatures of

British speech). The usual description of [r] as **retroflex** ('bent back') refers to the position sometimes assumed by the tongue in its articulation.

Standard British English has no [r] before a consonant sound (as in *farm, far distances*) or in final position in an utterance (as in "The distance is far"); to put it in another way, in this type of speech [r] is pronounced only when a vowel follows in the same word (as in *daring*) or in one immediately following (the **linking r**, as in *there is* and *far away*). This loss of [r], stemming from the folk speech of the eastern counties north of the Thames, occurs also in the speech of eastern New England, New York City, and much of the American coastal South. The speech of the last-named region lacks linking *r* as well. Other varieties of American speech, however, preserve the sound under most conditions, as does the regional speech of the south and the west of England.

Failure to understand that [r] is lacking before a consonant or in final position in standard British English has led to American misunderstanding of such British spellings as *'arf* (for Cockney *half*), *cokernut* (for *coconut*), and *Eeyore*, Christopher Robin's donkey companion. *Eeyore*, which A. A. Milne, creator of Christopher Robin and Winnie-the-Pooh, could just as well have spelled *Eeyaw*, is what Cockney donkeys presumably say instead of *hee-haw*. Similarly, the New England loss of [r] motivates the spelling *marmee* of Louisa May Alcott's *Little Women*, a spelling that represents the same pronunciation most Americans would represent as *mommy*.

An **intrusive r** occurs in the usage of a goodly percentage of the speakers of standard British English, as in *law*[r] *enforcement* and *the idea*[r] *of it*. Analogical with the etymological [r] that is retained before a word beginning with a vowel (linking *r*), this intrusive [r] is also common in eastern New England and New York City, but not in the South, where linking *r* is rare. An intrusive preconsonantal [r] occurs in the speech of some Americans in *wash* and *Washington*.

Because of their vocalic quality, [w] and [y] (as in *woo* and *you*) are called **semivowels**. In their manner of production, they are indeed like vowels (which are described below), the palatal semivowel [y] being like a high front vowel ([i] or [ɪ]) and the velar semivowel [w] being like a high back vowel ([u] or [ʊ]). In historical and comparative studies, the palatal semivowel is often represented by the symbol [j], but we will follow the common American practice of using [y] for this sound.

The Vowels of English

Vowels are the principal sounds of syllables. In the chart that follows, the vowels are shown according to the position of the tongue relative to the roof of the mouth (**high, mid, low**) and to the position of the highest part of the tongue (**front, central, back**). The chart may be taken to represent a cross section of the oral cavity, facing left.

	FRONT	CENTRAL	BACK
HIGH	i (*peat*) ɪ (*pit*)		u (*pooh*) ʊ (*put*)
MID	e (*pate*) ε (*pet*)	ə (*putt, pert, sofa*)	o (*Poe*)
LOW	æ (*pat*)		ɔ (*paw*) ɑ (*pot*)

Some of the tongue positions cited for vowels are only approximate; in particular, there is a range between back and central for some of the nonfront vowels. In considering vowels, it is well to have in mind the words of the great British phonetician Daniel Jones (1967, p. 18):

> It is difficult, though not impossible to describe a vowel-sound in writing in such a manner as to give a reader an idea of what it sounds like. The only way of doing this is to relate the unknown vowels to vowels already known to him. . . . People's vowels vary greatly, and a description based on the vowels presumed to be used in particular words may be correct for one reader, but is sure to be misleading for many others.

For the reader not familiar with phonetic or phonemic transcription, it will be helpful to remember that some of the vowel symbols, specifically [a], [e], and [i], do not represent the various sounds that they usually have in current English spelling but rather approximately those sounds that they represent in languages other than English using the Roman alphabet (for instance, French, Italian, and German). That is to say, in transcribing Modern English words, we use [i] for the sound that is written *i* in other languages but that, except for words recently borrowed by English from these other languages (for example, *police*), is most frequently written *e*, *ee*, *ea*, *ie*, and *ei* in Modern English. We use [e] for that sound usually written *a* (followed by a consonant plus "silent *e*") or *ai* in Modern English (as in *bate*, *bait*). English *o* and *u* frequently correspond to the *o* and *u* of other languages, in which case they are transcribed [o] and [u], as in *roll* [rol] and *rule* [rul]. *A* with its "Italian" value often occurs in the spelling of English words before *r* and *lm* (as in *far* and *calm*); in *father*, *mama*, *papa*, and a few other words like *spa*; and in certain types of American English after *w* (as in *watch*). Its most usual spelling in American English is *o*, as in *pot* and *top*.

Of the vowels listed in the chart, [i], [ɪ], [e], [ε], and [æ], because of the positions assumed by the tongue in their articulation, are classified as front vowels, and [u], [ʊ], [o], [ɔ], and [ɑ] as back vowels. Both series have been given in descending order, that is, in relation to the height of the tongue as indicated by the downward movement of the lower jaw in their articulation: thus [i] is the highest front vowel and [æ] the lowest, as [u] is the highest back vowel and [ɑ] the lowest. All the back vowels save [ɑ] are pronounced with some degree of rounding and protrusion of the lips and hence are called **rounded vowels**. Vowels without lip rounding are called **unrounded** or **spread vowels**.

As regards the position of the body of the tongue, [ə] is central. The symbol, called **schwa**, is here used to represent the stressed central vowel of *putt* and *pert* as well as the unstressed central vowel of *tuba* and *lunar*. Some styles of transcription use [ə] only for the unstressed central vowel of *tuba*, representing the unstressed vowel before *r* (as in *lunar*) by [ɚ], the stressed vowel by [ʌ] when no *r* follows (as in *putt*) and the stressed vowel before *r* (as in *pert*) by [ɝ]. The four sounds are quite distinct from one another and so in a narrow transcription would be written with distinct symbols. However, because they are in complementary distribution, we can use a single symbol for all four sounds in transcribing them broadly. Thus, we will write the words in question as [pət], [pərt], [tubə], and [lunər] (rather than the narrower [pʌt], [pɝt], [tubə], and [lunɚ]).

Not charted is [a], the vowel sound sometimes heard in eastern New England speech in *ask, half, laugh, path*, and in some varieties of Southern speech in *bye, might, tired*, and the like. It is intermediate between [ɑ] and [æ], and is usually the first element of the diphthongs in *right* and *rout*, which we shall write, respectively, as [aɪ] and [aʊ]. We shall have occasion to refer to it later as a phoneme of late Middle English.

Other vowels that are not charted and about which we will have little to say are [ǣ], [ɨ], [ɵ], and [ɒ]. Along the East Coast roughly between New York City and Philadelphia as well as in a number of other metropolitan centers, some speakers use clearly different vowels in *cap* and *cab*, *bat* and *bad*, *lack* and *lag*. In the first word of each of these and many other such pairs, they pronounce the sound represented by [æ]; but in the second word, they use a higher vowel that we may represent as [ǣ]. Some speakers have minimal pairs for these sounds in *have* and *halve* and in *can* 'be able' and *can* 'preserve in tins.' Some Americans pronounce the adverb *just* (as in "They've just left") with a different vowel from that in the adjective ("a just person" with [ə]) or from those in words like *gist* (with [ɪ]) and *jest* (with [ɛ]); this vowel, written [ɨ], may also appear in *children, would*, and various other words. In eastern New England, some speakers, especially of the older generation, use a vowel in *whole* that differs from the one in *hole*. This "New England short *o*" is symbolized by [ɵ] and is found also in *road, stone*, and other words; it is rare and is becoming more so. British English has a lightly rounded vowel symbolized by [ɒ] in *pot, top, rod, con*, and other words in which Americans use the sound [ɑ] for the spelling *o*. Those who do not have these vowel sounds in their pronunciation obviously do not need the symbols to

The Vowels of English

represent their own speech. It is wise, however, to remember that even in English there are sounds one does not use oneself.

Some Americans, especially in western Pennsylvania, in Kansas, and in the Southwest, lack a phonemic contrast between [ɔ] and [ɑ]. For them, *caught* and *cot* are homophones, as are *taught* and *tot*, *dawn* and *don*, *gaud* and *God*, *pawed* and *pod*, *walk* and *wok*, and *maul* and *moll*. They pronounce all such words with either [ɔ] or [ɑ] or with a vowel that is intermediate between those two, namely the [ɒ] mentioned in the preceding paragraph. Other Americans lack a phonemic contrast between two sounds only in a particular environment. For example, in the South, the vowels [ɪ] and [ɛ], although distinguished in most environments (such as *pit* and *pet*), have merged before nasals. Thus *pin* and *pen* are homophones for many Southerners, as are *tin* and *ten*, *Jim* and *gem*, and *ping* and the first syllable of *penguin*. The sound used in the nasal environment is usually [ɪ], though before [ŋ] it may approach [i].

Vowels can be classified not only by their height and their frontness (as in the vowel chart) but also by their tenseness. A **tense vowel** is typically longer in duration than the closest **lax vowel** and also higher and less central (that is, further front if it is a front vowel and further back if a back one). Tense vowels are [i], [e], [u], and [o]; the corresponding lax vowels for the first three are [ɪ], [ɛ], and [ʊ]. The "New England short *o*" is a lax vowel corresponding to tense [o]. For most Americans, the low and the central vowels do not enter into a tense-lax contrast. However, for those who have it, [æ̃] (in *cab*, *halve*, *bag*) is tense, and the corresponding [æ] (in *cap*, *have*, *back*) is lax. Similarly, in standard British English, [ɔ] (in *caught*, *dawn*, *wars*) is tense, and the corresponding [ɒ] (in *cot*, *don*, and *was*) is lax. In earlier times (as we shall see in chapters 5 and 6), English vowels were either long or short; today that difference in duration has generally become a difference in tenseness.

In most types of current English, **vowel length** is hardly ever a distinguishing factor. Most of us distinguish, for example, *bad* from *bat*, *bag* from *back*, and *lab* from *lap* not by the longer vowel in the first of each pair, but by the final consonants. Some speakers, as we have seen, do indeed distinguish *can* 'preserve in tins' from *can* 'be able,' *halve* from *have*, and similarly *balm* from *bomb* and *vary* from *very* by length in the vowel of the first of each pair. In the southeastern American English described by James Sledd (1959, p. 51), *bulb* (with no [l]) is thus distinguished from *bub*, and similarly *burred* (no [r]) from *bud*, *stirred* (no [r]) from *stud*. In *r*-less speech, when [ɑ] occurs before etymological *r*, length may likewise be a distinguishing factor, as in *part* [pɑ̄t] and *pot* [pɑt]. The length mark, or **macron**, can be used to write vowel length when it is necessary to do so. Such distinctions need not concern most of us except for Old, Middle, and early Modern English, when vowel quantity was of considerably more importance.

A **diphthong** is a sequence of two vowels in the same syllable. Many

English vowel sounds tend to have diphthongal pronunciation, most notably [e] and [o], as in *bay* and *toe*, which are usually pronounced in a way that might be written [eɪ] and [oʊ] in narrow transcription. In parts of the United States, most vowels are sometimes diphthongized; thus *bed* may have a centralized **off-glide** (or secondary vowel): [bɛəd]. In keeping with our practice of using broad transcription, however, we will ignore all such diphthongal glides, writing as diphthongs only the [aɪ] and [aʊ] mentioned on p. 33 and the [ɔɪ] in *joy* and *coin*. Words like *few* and *cube* may be pronounced with a semivowel before the vowel, [fyu] and [kyub], or with a diphthong, [fɪu] and [kɪub]. The first pronunciation is more common.

In all three of the diphthongs [aɪ], [aʊ], and [ɔɪ], the tongue moves from the position for the first vowel to that for the second, and the direction of movement is more important than the exact starting and ending points. Consequently, the diphthongs we write [aɪ] and [aʊ] may actually begin with vowels that are more like [ɑ], [æ], or even [ə]. Similarly, [ɔɪ] may begin with [ɒ] or [o] as well as [ɔ]. The ending points are equally variable. The off-glide in [aɪ] and [ɔɪ] may actually be as high as [i] or as low as [ɛ] (and for [aɪ] may disappear altogether, being replaced by a lengthening of the first vowel); and similarly the off-glide in [aʊ] may be as high as [u] or as low as [o]. Thus it is best to understand [aɪ] as a symbol for a diphthong that begins with a relatively low unrounded vowel and moves toward a higher front position, [aʊ] as representing a diphthong that begins the same way but moves toward a higher back rounded position, and [ɔɪ] as representing a diphthong that begins with a relatively low back rounded vowel and moves toward a higher front position. In a narrow transcription, these differences would be represented, for example, in the words *hide* or *white* as [ɑɛ], [a], [əi], or various other possibilities. In a broad transcription, however, we can write [aɪ] and understand that digraph as representing whatever sound we use in words like *hide* and *white*.

VOWELS BEFORE [r]

The sound [r] modifies the quality of a preceding vowel so that the vowel is somewhat different from the same phoneme in other environments. We have already noted that [ə] before [r], as in *curt* or *burst*, is different from [ə] in any other position, as in *cut* or *bust*. Similarly the [o] in *mourn* is not quite the same as that in *moan*, or the [ɑ] in *farther* quite the same as that in *father*. Such allophonic differences can be ignored, however, in a broad transcription such as we are using.

Fewer distinctive vowels occur before [r] than elsewhere. In particular, for many speakers tenseness is not distinctive before [r]. Thus *nearer* and *mirror* may rime, with a vowel in the first syllables that is close to either [i] or [ɪ], the latter being more frequent. Similarly *fairy* and *ferry* may rime, with a first vowel like either [e] or [ɛ], and *tour* may be pronounced with either

[u] or [ʊ]. In all these variations, the lax vowel occurs more frequently. For an increasing number of Americans, *hoarse* and *horse* are homophones. In their traditional pronunciation, *hoarse* has [o] and *horse* [ɔ]; the same difference of vowels was once made by most speakers in *mourning* and *morning*, *borne* and *born*, *four* and *for*, *oar* and *or*, and many other words. Today [o] and [ɔ] are apparently merging before [r]. In some American speech, especially of the lower Mississippi Valley and the West, there is no difference in pronunciation between *form* and *farm*, *or* and *are*, *born* and *barn*, or *lord* and *lard*. Some persons have [ɔ] and others [ɑ] in all such words. There is much variation among speakers from different regions in the vowel allophones used before [r].

When [r] follows a vowel in the same syllable, a schwa glide may intrude, as in *near* [nɪr] or [nɪər]. The schwa glide is especially likely when the sentence stress and consequently a change of pitch fall on the syllable, as in "The time drew néar" with the glide versus "The time dréw near" without it.

UNSTRESSED VOWELS

Although any vowel can be pronounced without stress, three are frequently so used: [i], [ɪ], and [ə]. There is a great deal of variation between [i] and [ɪ] in final position (as in *lucky*, *happy*, *city*, and *seedy*) and before another vowel (as in the second syllables of *various*, *curiosity*, *oriel*, and *carion*). Conservative pronunciation along the Eastern Coast uses [ɪ] in these positions, but the most common pronunciation in the United States has [i].

There is also a great deal of variation between [ə] and [ɪ] before a consonant. In the traditional pronunciation still used in British English, in some regions of the United States, and by linguistically conservative speakers generally, [ɪ] occurs in the final unstressed syllable of words like *bucket* and *college*, and in the initial unstressed syllable of words like *elude* and *illumine*. Increasingly large numbers of Americans, however, use either [ə] or [ɪ] variably in such words, depending in part on the surrounding sounds, though with a strong preference for [ə]. A new rule of pronunciation seems to be emerging that favors unstressed [ɪ] only before velar consonants (as in the first syllable of *ignore* and the final syllable of *comic* or *hoping*) and [ə] elsewhere. Thus, whereas the traditional pronunciation has [ə] in the second syllable of *stomach* and [ɪ] in the first syllable of *mysterious*, many speakers now reverse the vowels in those words, ending *stomach* like *comic* and beginning *mysterious* like *mosquito*. Those who use the traditional pronunciation may regard the new distribution of sounds as substandard; those who use the new distribution will find the traditional distinction bewilderingly arbitrary. Such variation of pronunciation and attitude is to be expected when a change of sound is in progress.

The final and preconsonantal [r] of most Americans is replaced by [ə] in **r-less speech** after [ɪ] as in *ear*, *beard*; after [ɛ] or [æ] as in *their*, *cairn*; after [ɔ] as in *for, form*; after [o] (for those who have this vowel in some words before [r]) as in *four, force*; after [ʊ] as in *tour, bourse* and [yʊ] as in *pure, cured*; after [aɪ] as in *ire, tired*; after [aʊ] as in *our, scoured*; and sometimes after [ɑ] as in *far, farm*.

An intrusive [ə] sometimes occurs between consonants in certain words—for instance, between [l] and [m] in *elm, film*, [n] and [r] in *Henry*, [r] and [m] in *alarum* (an archaic variant of *alarm*), [s] and [m] in *Smyrna* (in the usual local pronunciation of New Smyrna Beach, Florida), [θ] and [r] in *arthritis*, and [θ] and [l] in *athlete*. The name of this phenomenon is **svarabhakti** (from Sanskrit), and such a vowel is called a svarabhakti vowel. If, however, one does not care to use so flamboyant a word, one can always fall back on **epenthesis (epenthetic)** or **anaptyxis (anaptyctic)**. Perhaps it is just as well to say **intrusive schwa**.

Stress

In the occasional transcription of words in the following chapters, **primary stress** will be indicated (as it has already been indicated in a few instances) by an **acute accent** mark (′) over the appropriate vowel symbols; the same mark will be used for conventionally spelled words when stress is involved: thus, [sófə] or *sófa*, [əbáʊt] or *abóut*. For syllables bearing **secondary stress**, a **grave accent** mark (`) will be used: thus, [émənèt] or *émanàte*. What we shall call **unstressed syllables** (which are sometimes said to carry "weak stress") will not be marked in any way.

For our limited purposes in discussing stress on words, the two degrees mentioned above are adequate. In considering the stress in sentences, how-ever, we need to recognize at least one more degree. Thus, in "Hè rán abòut the sófa," *ran* has a stronger stress than either *he* or *about* but a weaker stress than *sofa*. The inherent stress in isolated words is modified when they are combined into a sentence. We shall have no need to consider further these complications.

Kinds of Sound Change

The words of English, as we have already had several occasions to observe, may vary in their pronunciation, in part because sounds do not always change in the same way among different groups. Thus at one time all speakers of English distinguished the members of pairs like *horse–hoarse*, *morning–mourning*, and *for–four*; nowadays most probably do not. Because this change has not proceeded uniformly, the pronunciation of such words is now varied.

Some changes of sound are profound and highly systematic but of un-known cause—for example, the ancient change of consonants that relates

English *brother* and Latin *frater* (the First Sound Shift, pp. 89–94) and the comparatively more recent change of vowels that accounts for the disparity between English *fine* [faɪn] and French *fine* [fin] (the Great Vowel Shift, pp. 172–75). The first of those changes took place perhaps 2000 years ago, and the second about 400 or 500 years ago. Other changes are going on today. In this section we will examine some kinds of sound change that any English speaker can hear.

ASSIMILATION

The most common sound change is **assimilation**, by which one sound becomes more like a neighboring sound. If *pancake* is pronounced carefully, as its parts would be when they are independent words, it is [pæn kek]. However, [n] is an alveolar sound, whereas [k] is a velar; consequently, speakers often anticipate the place of articulation of the [k] and pronounce the word [pæŋkek] with the velar nasal. In addition to such partial assimilation, by which sounds become more alike while remaining distinct, assimilation may be total; that is, the sounds may become completely identical, as when *spaceship* changes in pronunciation from [spes šɪp] to [speš šɪp]. In such cases it is usual for the identical sounds to combine by the omission of one of them, as in [spešɪp]; a much older example is *cupboard*, in which the medial [p b] has become a single [b]. In speech with a moderately fast tempo, assimilation is quite common. Thus, an andante pronunciation of "What is your name?" as [wət ɪz yʊr nem] in allegro tempo might become [wəts yər nem], and in presto tempo [wəčər nem], the latter two suggested by the spellings "What's yer name?" and "Whatcher name?" Such pronunciations, unlike the impressionistic spellings that represent them, are not careless or sloppy (much less substandard) but merely variants we use in speech that is more rapid and less formal than that which requires the unassimilated form. If we never used such assimilated forms in talking, we would sound very stilted indeed.

ELLIPSIS OF UNSTRESSED SOUNDS

The sentence used as an example in the preceding paragraph also exemplifies another kind of sound change: loss of sounds (**ellipsis**) due to lack of stress. The verb *is* usually has no stress and thus is regularly contracted with a preceding word by the ellipsis of its vowel. Vowels may also be lost without the contraction of words. An initial unstressed vowel is lost when *about* is pronounced '*bout* in a process known as **aphesis**. It is a specialized variety of a more general process, **apheresis**, which is the loss of any sounds (not just an unstressed vowel) from the beginning of a word, as in the pronunciation of *almost* in "'Most everybody knows that." Loss of sounds from the end of a word is known as **apocope**, as in the pronunciation of *child* as *chile*.

The most common type of ellipsis in present-day English is **syncope**—loss of a weakly stressed syllable from the middle of a word, as in the usual pronunciation of *family* as *fam'ly*. Indeed many words sound artificial when they are given a full, unsyncopated pronunciation. Like assimilation, syncope is a normal process.

DISSIMILATION

The opposite of assimilation is **dissimilation**, a process by which neighboring sounds become less like one another. In the word *diphthong*, the sequence of two voiceless fricatives [fθ] symbolized by the medial *phth* requires an effort to enunciate. Consequently, many speakers pronounce medial [pθ], replacing fricative [f] with stop [p]—that is, as though the word were spelled *dipthong*. A fair number of them do indeed spell the word in that way.

Another example of dissimilation is the substandard pronunciation of *chimney* as *chimley*, with the second of two nasals changed to an [l]. The ultimate dissimilation is the complete loss of one sound because of its proximity to another similar sound. A frequent example of such ellipsis in present-day English is the omission of one of two [r] sounds from words like *cate(r)pillar*, *Cante(r)bury*, *rese(r)voir*, *terrest(r)ial*, *southe(r)ner*, *barbitu(r)ate*, *gove(r)nor*, and *su(r)prised*.

INTRUSION

The opposite of ellipsis is the **intrusion** of sounds, a process already noted in words like *fil(e)m* and *ath(e)lete* (p. 37). Consonants may also be intrusive; for example, a [p] in *warmth*, so that it sounds as if spelled *warmpth*; a [t] in *sense*, so it is homophonous with *cents*; and a [k] in *length*, so that it sounds as if spelled *lenkth*. These three words end in a nasal [m, n, ŋ] followed by a voiceless fricative [θ, s]; between the nasal and the fricative, many speakers intrude a stop [p, t, k] that is voiceless like the fricative but has the same place of articulation as the nasal (that is, the stop is **homorganic** in place with the nasal and in voicing with the fricative). There is a simple physiological explanation for such intrusion. To move directly from nasal to voiceless fricative, it is necessary simultaneously to release the stoppage and to cease the vibration of vocal cords. If those two vocal activities are not perfectly synchronized, the effect will be to create a new sound between the two original ones; in the examples under discussion, the vocal vibration is ceased an instant before the stoppage is released, and consequently a voiceless stop is created. *Chimney*, cited in the preceding paragraph as an example of dissimilation, has two other substandard variants with intrusion. The two nasals may be separated by an intrusive vowel (as though *chiminey*) or a consonant may intrude between the first nasal and the dissimilated [l] (as though *chimbley*).

Kinds of Sound Change

The order of sounds can be changed in a process called **metathesis**. *Tax* and *task* are variant developments of a single form, with the [ks] represented by *x* metathesized in the second word to [sk]. In present-day English [r] frequently metathesizes with an unstressed vowel; thus the initial [prə] of *produce* may become [pər] and the opposite reordering can be heard in *perform*. The metathesis of a sound and a syllable boundary in the word *another* leads to the reinterpretation of original *an other* as *a nother*, especially in the expression "a whole nother thing."

THE CAUSES OF SOUND CHANGE

The causes of change of sound are often unknown. Some of the major changes that we will take up in more detail in later chapters, such as the First Sound Shift and the Great Vowel Shift, are particularly mysterious. Various causes have been suggested for sound change—for example, that when people speaking different languages come into contact, one group learns the other's language but does so imperfectly, carrying over native habits of pronunciation into the language of the other group. This explanation is known as the **substratum** or **superstratum theory** (depending on whether it is the language of the dominant group or that of the dominated group that is influenced).

A quite different sort of explanation is that languages tend to develop a balanced sound system—that is, to make sounds as different from one another as possible by distributing them evenly in **phonological space**. Thus, it is common for languages to have two front vowels [i, e] and three back ones [u, o, ɑ]; it would be very strange if a language had five front vowels and no back ones at all, because such an unbalanced system would make poor use of its available resources. If, for some reason, a language loses some of its sounds—say, its high vowels—there would be intrasystemic pressure to fill in the gap by changing some of the remaining sounds (for example, by making mid vowels higher in their articulation).

Changes like assimilation, dissimilation, ellipsis, and intrusion are often explained as increasing the **ease of articulation**: some sounds can be pronounced together more smoothly if they are alike, others if they are different. Ellipsis and assimilation both quicken the rate of speech, so the desire or need to talk at "fast" tempo (although more than speed is implied by tempo) would encourage both those processes. Intrusion can also help to make articulation easier. It and metathesis may result from our brains' working faster than our vocal organs; consequently the nerve impulses that direct the movement of those organs sometimes get out of synch, resulting in slips of the tongue.

In addition to such mechanical explanations, some sound changes imply at least partial awareness by the speaker. The remodeling of *chaise longue* as *chaise lounge* because one uses it for lounging is **folk etymology** (pp. 281–84). The sounding of *comptroller* (originally a fancy, and mistaken, spelling for *controller*) with internal [mptr] is a **spelling pronunciation** (pp. 60–62). These are matters that we will consider in more detail later. **Hypercorrection** results from an effort to "improve" one's speech on the basis of too little information. For example, having been told that it is incorrect to "drop your *g*'s" as in *talkin'* and *somethin'*, the earnest but ill-informed self-improver has been known to "correct" *chicken* to *chicking* and *Virgin Islands* to *Virging Islands*. Similarly, one impressed with the elegance of a Bostonian or British pronunciation of *aunt* and *can't* as something like "ahnt" and "cahnt" may be misled into talking about how dogs "pahnt," a pronunciation of *pant* that will amuse any proper Bostonian or Britisher. Speakers have a natural tendency to generalize rules—to apply them in as many circumstances as possible—so in learning a new rule, we must also learn what limitations there are on its application. Another example of such **overgeneralization** is the use of the fricative [ž]. Although it is the most recent and most restricted of the English consonants, it seems to have acquired associations of exotic elegance and is now often used in words where it does not belong historically—for example, *rajah*, *cashmere*, and *kosher*.

As speakers use the language, they often change it, whether mechanically or deliberately. Those changes become for the next generation just a part of the inherited system, available to use or again to change. And so a language varies over the years and centuries and may, like English, eventually become quite a different system from what it was earlier.

Other Kinds of Transcription

The kind of phonetic transcription used in this chapter is not the only one for English, although it or slight variations of it are widely used. Another frequently used style of transcription (Trager and Smith 1951) differs from the present one chiefly in writing the tense vowels as sequences of vowels followed by semivowels functioning as off-glides. Thus, whereas we have represented the vowels of *meet*, *mate*, *moot*, and *mote* as, respectively, [i], [e], [u], and [o] (that is, as unitary segments), this other style of transcription writes the same sounds as binary sequences: /iy/, /ey/, /uw/, and /ow/. It is then free to represent the lax vowels of *mitt*, *met*, and *foot* as /i/, /e/, and /u/ in place of our symbols [ɪ], [ɛ], and [ʊ].

Some analysts, mostly British, follow the example of Daniel Jones (1960, 1967) in writing [i:] for our [i], the colon signifying length, and [i] for our [ɪ]. Similarly, they use [u:] for our [u] and [u] for our [ʊ]. For the mid vowels, they write either [e:] or [eɪ] for our [e], and [o:] or [oʊ] for our [o]; consequently, they also use [e] for our [ɛ].

The fact is that the tense vowels differ from the corresponding lax ones in a number of ways: they are longer, more diphthongal, and of different quality because they are higher and less central. The British style of writing [i:] and [u:] emphasizes the comparative length of those sounds. The binary style of writing /iy/, /ey/, /uw/, and /ow/ emphasizes the diphthongal off-glides. The style of transcription used in this book, namely [i], [e], [u], and [o], emphasizes the difference in quality—that is, of tongue height and frontness. The choice among these or other possible systems of transcription is more a question of convenience in representing the facts than of what the facts are.

It is sometimes convenient to consider sounds, not as whole segments like [b] and [i], but rather as combinations of **distinctive features**. In the latter case [i], for example, might be described as a vowel that is [+ high, − back, + tense]. In treating sounds in this way, phonologists seek to identify the smallest set of features that is adequate to describe any human language. There is so far no agreement about the features that are necessary to describe speech in this way, but one set for English is discussed in John Algeo's *Problems* (1982, exercise 2.26). The traditional articulatory charts for consonants and vowels (as on pp. 29 and 32) imply another set.

Some analysts who use a theory known as **Generative Phonology** seek rules to relate the stressed vowels of word pairs like *define–definitive, seréne–serénity, gráteful–grátitude, cóne–cónic, assúme–assúmption,* and *profóund–profúndity*. To relate the members of these pairs to one another, they postulate highly abstract underlying sounds called **systematic phonemes**; for example, they derive the surface vowels [aʊ] and [ə] in the last pair from an underlying vowel /ū/. Other generative phonologists, however, object that such abstract sounds are psychologically unreal and therefore ought not to be postulated. These analysts, who practice what is called **Natural Generative Phonology**, want to keep underlying forms and all of phonological description as close as possible to actual pronunciation. Because there is such disagreement among the learned about these abstruse matters, we will consider them no further.

For Further Reading

American Pronunciation

Bronstein, *The Pronunciation of American English*, 1960.
Kenyon, *American Pronunciation*, 1950.
Kurath, *A Phonology and Prosody of Modern English*, 1964.
Thomas, *An Introduction to the Phonetics of American English*, 1958.

British Pronunciation

Gimson, *An Introduction to the Pronunciation of English*, 1970.
Jones, *The Pronunciation of English*, 1967.

Pronouncing Dictionaries

Jones and Gimson, *Everyman's English Pronouncing Dictionary*, 1977.
Kenyon and Knott, *A Pronouncing Dictionary of American English*, 1953.
Lewis, *A Concise Pronouncing Dictionary of British and American English*, 1972.

Phonological Theory

Chomsky and Halle, *The Sound Pattern of English*, 1968.
Hooper, *An Introduction to Natural Generative Phonology*, 1976.

For Further Reading

3 Letters and Sounds

A Brief History of Writing

Writing is a product of comparatively recent times. With it, history begins; without it, we must depend on the archaeologist. The entire period during which people have been making conventionalized markings on stone, wood, clay, metal, parchment, paper, or any other surface to symbolize their speech is really no more than a moment in the vast period during which they have been combining vocal noises systematically for the purpose of communicating with each other.

Ideographic and Syllabic Writing

There can be no doubt that writing grew out of drawing, the wordless comic-strip type of drawing done by primitive peoples. The American Indians made many such drawings. It is not surprising that certain conventions should have developed in them, such as horizontal and vertical lines on a chief's gravestone to indicate, respectively, the number of his campaigns and the number of wounds he received in the course of those campaigns (Pedersen 1962, p. 143); the lines rising from an eagle's head were another convention indicating that the figure was the chief of the eagle totem, this in a "letter" from the chief to the president of the United States, represented as a white-faced man in a white house (Sturtevant 1947, p. 20; Gelb 1963, ch. 2). But such drawings, communicative as they may be once one understands their conventions, give no idea of actual words. Any identity of wording in their interpretation would be purely coincidental. No line, no

44

element, even remotely suggests speech sounds or word order, and hence such drawings tell us nothing of the language of those who made them.

When such use of symbols standing for ideas that can be pictured—rather than for the sounds that make up words—reaches a more or less wholly conventional stage and each word is represented by a separate symbol, it becomes **ideographic**, or **logographic**. In Chinese writing, every word originally had a symbol based not on the phonetic structure of the word but on its meaning.

Another method, fundamentally different, probably grew out of ideographic writing: the use of the **phonogram**, which is concerned with sound rather than with meaning. Ultimately, by a sort of punning process, pictures came to be used as in a **rebus**—that is, as if we were to draw a picture of a tie to represent the first syllable of the word *tycoon* and of a coon to represent the second. In such a method we may see the beginnings of a **syllabary**, in which symbols, in time becoming so conventionalized as to be unrecognizable as actual pictures, are used to represent syllables.

From Semitic Writing to Greek Alphabet

Semitic writing, the basis of our own and indeed of all **alphabetic writing**, usually represented consonants only. For that reason it is sometimes called a syllabary, in this case, a system in which each symbol represents a consonant plus an unspecified vowel. It is perhaps simpler to call it an alphabet that wrote consonants but usually not vowels. There were ways of indicating specific vowels, but such devices were used sparingly. Since Semitic had certain consonantal sounds not found in other languages, the symbols for these sounds were readily available for use as vowel symbols by the Greeks when they adopted for their own use the Semitic writing system, which they called Phoenician. (To the Greeks, all eastern non-Greeks were *Phoenices*, just as to the Anglo-Saxons all Scandinavians were *Dene* 'Danes.') The Greeks even used the Semitic names of the symbols, which they adapted to Greek phonetic patterns: thus *aleph* 'ox' and *beth* 'house' became *alpha* and *beta* because words ending in consonants (other than *n*, *r*, and *s*) are not in accord with Greek patterns. The fact that the Greeks used the Semitic names, which had no other meaning for them, is powerful evidence that the Greeks did indeed acquire their writing from the Semites, as they freely acknowledged having done. The order of the letters and their highly similar forms are additional evidence of this fact.

The symbol A indicated in Semitic a glottal consonant that did not exist in Greek. Its Semitic name was *'aleph*, the initial apostrophe here indicating the consonant in question; and, because the name means 'ox,' it has been thought to represent an ox's head, though interpreting many of the Semitic signs as pictorial characters presents as yet insuperable difficulties (Gelb 1963, pp. 140–41). By ignoring the initial Semitic consonant of the letter's name, the Greeks adapted this symbol as a vowel, which they called *alpha*. *Beth* was ultimately somewhat modified in form to B by the Greeks, who wrote it and other reversible letters facing in either direction; in the early days of writing they wrote from right to left, as the Semitic peoples usually did and as Hebrew is still written.[1] From the Greek modifications of the Semitic names of the first two letters, the word *alphabet* is ultimately derived.

The Greek Vowel and Consonant Symbols

The brilliant Greek notion (conceived by the eighth century B.C. or somewhat earlier) of using as vowel symbols those Semitic consonant symbols that did not exist in Greek gave the Greeks an alphabet in the modern sense of the word. Thus Semitic *yod* became *iota* (I) and was used for the Greek vowel *i*; at the time the symbol was taken over, Greek had no need for the corresponding semivowel [y], with which the Semitic word *yod* began. Just as they had changed *aleph* into a vowel symbol by dropping the initial Semitic consonant, so also the Greeks dropped the consonant of Semitic *he* and called it *epsilon* (E), that is, *e psilon* 'e simple, or e without the aspirate.' Semitic *ayin*, symbolizing a syllable beginning with a voiced pharyngeal fricative nonexistent in Greek, became for the Greeks *omicron* (O), that is, *o mikron* 'o little.' Semitic *heth* was at first used as a consonant and called *heta*, but the "rough breathing" sound that it symbolized was lost in several Greek dialects, notably the Ionic of Asia Minor, where the symbol was called *eta* (H) and used for long [e]. The vowel symbol *omega* (Ω), that is, *o mega* 'o big,' was a Greek innovation, as was also *upsilon* (Υ), that is, *u psilon* 'u simple.' *Upsilon* was born of the need for a symbol for a vowel sound corresponding to the Semitic semivowel *waw*. The sound [w], which *waw* represented, was lost in Ionic, as also in other dialects, and *waw*, which came to be called *digamma* because it looked like one gamma on top of another (F), ceased to be used except as a numeral—but not before the Romans had taken it over and assigned a different value to it.

Practically all of the remaining Semitic symbols were used for the Greek consonants, with the Semitic values of their first elements for the most part unchanged. Their graphic forms were also recognizably the same after they had been adopted by the Greeks. *Gimel* became *gamma* (Γ), *daleth* became *delta* (Δ), and so on. The early Greek alphabet ended with *tau* (T). The

[1] Sometimes the early Greeks would change direction in alternate lines, starting, for instance, at the right, then changing direction at the end of the line and going from left to right, and continuing this change of direction throughout. Solon's laws were so written. The Greeks had a word for the fashion—**boustrophedon** 'as the ox turns in plowing,' a wondrous word indeed, which may even be used in English if one is skillful enough to steer conversation in such a way as to make occasion for its use. Those who are fortunate enough to find such occasion stress the first and third syllables (respectively, [bu] or [bau] and [fi]).

consonant symbols *phi* (Φ), *chi* (X), and *psi* (Ψ) were later Greek additions. A good idea of the shapes of the letters and the very slight modifications made by the early Greeks may be obtained from the charts provided by Ignace Gelb (1963, p. 177) and Holger Pedersen (1962, p. 179). Gelb also gives the Latin forms, and Pedersen the highly similar Indian ones, Indian writings from the third century B.C. onward being inscribed in an alphabet adapted from the Semitic.

The Romans Adopt the Greek Alphabet

The Ionic alphabet, adopted at Athens, became the standard for the writing of Greek, but it was the somewhat different Western form of the alphabet that the Romans, perhaps by way of the Etruscans, were to adopt for their own use. The Romans used a curved form of *gamma* (C), the third letter, which at first had for them the same value [g] as for the Greeks but in time came to be used for [k]. Another symbol was thus needed for the [g] sound. This need was remedied in time by a simple modification in the shape of C, resulting in G: thus C and G are both derived from Greek Γ. The C was, however, sometimes used for both [g] and [k], a custom that survived in later times in such abbreviations as *C.* for *Gaius* and *Cn.* for *Gnaeus*.

Rounded forms of *delta* (D), *pi* (P), and *sigma* (S), as well as of *gamma*, were used by the Romans. They were not Roman innovations; all of them occur in Greek also, though the more familiar Greek literary forms are angular (Δ, Π, and Σ). The occurrence of such rounded forms was doubtless due in early times to the use of pen and ink; the angular forms reflect the use of cutting tool on stone.

Epsilon (E) was adopted without change. The sixth position was filled by Ϝ, the Greek *digamma* (earlier *waw*). The Romans gave this symbol the value [f]. Following it came the modified *gamma*, G. H was used as a consonant, as in Semitic and also in Western Greek at the time the Romans adopted it.

The Roman gain in having a symbol for [h] was slight, for the aspirate was almost as unstable a sound in Latin as it is in Cockney English; ultimately, as in Greek, it was lost completely. Among the Romance languages—those derived from Latin, such as Italian, French, Spanish, and Portuguese—there is no need for the symbol, since there is no trace of the sound, though it may be retained in spelling because of conservatism, as in some French and Spanish words—for example, French *heure* and Spanish *hora* 'hour' (but compare Fr. *avoir* with Sp. *haber* 'to have').

Iota (I) was for the Romans both semivowel and vowel, as illustrated, respectively, by the two *i*'s in *iudices* 'judges,' the first syllable of which is like English *you*.[2] The lengthened form of this letter, that is, *j*, did not appear

---

[2] Because of our primary concern with writing in this chapter, editorial macrons (as for the long *u* in this word) will not be used in any cited words.

until medieval times, when the **minuscule** form of writing developed, which used small letters exclusively. (In ancient writing only **majuscules**, that is, capital letters, were used.) The majuscule form of this newly shaped *i*, that is, J, is a product of modern times. *Kappa* (K) was used in only a few words by the Romans, who, as we have seen, used C to represent the same sound. Next came the Western Greek form of *lambda*, L, corresponding to Ionic Λ. M and N, from *mu* and *nu*, require no comment. *Xi* (Ξ), with the value [ks], following Greek *nu*, was not taken over into Latin; thus in the Roman alphabet O immediately followed N. *Pi* (Π) having been adopted in its rounded form P, it was necessary for the Romans to use a tailed form of *rho* (P), as the early Greeks also had sometimes done, and thus create R. The symbol Q (*koppa*) stood for a sound that had dropped out of Greek, though the symbol continued to be used as a numeral in that language. The Romans used it as a variant of C in one position only, preceding V; thus the sequence [kw] was written QV—the *qu* of printed texts. *Sigma* in its rounded form S was adopted unchanged. *Tau* (T) was likewise unchanged. *Upsilon* was adopted in the form V and used for both consonant ([w], later [v]) and vowel ([u], [ʊ]).

The symbol Z (Greek *zeta*), which had occupied seventh place in the early Roman alphabet but had become quite useless in Latin because the sound it represented was not a separate phoneme, was reintroduced and placed at the end of the alphabet in the time of Cicero, when a number of Greek words were coming to be used in Latin. Another form of *upsilon*, Y, was used in such words to indicate the Greek vowel sound, which was like French *u* and German *ü*. *Chi* (X) was used with the Western Greek value [ks], the sound of Ionic X being represented in Classical Latin by CH, just as TH and PH were used to represent Greek *theta* (Θ) and *phi* (Φ) respectively. Actually these were accurate enough representations of the Classical Greek sounds, which most scholars agree were similar to the aspirated initial sounds of English *kin*, *tin*, and *pin*. The Romans in their transcriptions very sensibly symbolized the aspiration, or breath-puff, by H. The sounds symbolized in Latin by C, T, and P apparently lacked such aspiration, as *k*, *t*, and *p* do in English when preceded by *s*—for example, *skin*, *sting*, and *spin*.

Later Developments of the Roman and Greek Alphabets

Even though it lacked a good many symbols for sounds in the modern languages of Europe, the Roman alphabet was taken over by the various European peoples, though not by those Slavic peoples who in the ninth century got their alphabet, called **Cyrillic** from the Greek missionary leader Cyril, directly from the Greek. The Greek missionaries, sent out from Byzantium, added a number of symbols for sounds that were not in Greek—

for example, Ш for [š]. B was used for [v], which was the sound the symbol also stood for in some positions in Greek; a modification, Б, was used for [b]. *Sigma* was written C in later Greek, and C has thus the value [s] in the writing of those Slavic peoples—the Russians, the Bulgarians, and the Serbs—who use this alphabet. Those Slavs whose Christianity stems from Rome—the Poles, the Czechs, the Slovaks, the Croats, and the Slovenians—use the Roman alphabet, adapted by **diacritical markings** (for example, Polish ć and Czech č) and by combinations of letters (for example, Polish *cz*, *sz*) to symbolize sounds for which the Roman alphabet made no provision.

In various ways the Roman alphabet has been eked out by those who have adopted it. Such un-Latin sounds as the *o*-umlaut and the *u*-umlaut of German are written ö and ü. The superposed pair of dots, called an **umlaut** or **dieresis**, is used in many other languages also to indicate vowel quality and in old-fashioned English spellings like *preëminent* to indicate that two adjacent vowel symbols represent separate sounds. Other diacritical marks that have been used to eke out the resources of the Latin alphabet are **accents**—the **acute**, **grave**, and **circumflex** (as, respectively, in French *résumé*, *à la mode*, and *rôle*). The **wedge** is used in Czech and is illustrated by the Czech name for the diacritic, *haček*. The **tilde** is used, for example, in *cañon*, borrowed from Spanish, and in Portuguese to indicate nasalized vowels, as in *São Paulo*. The **cedilla** is familiar in a French loanword like *façade*. Other, less familiar, diacritical markings include the **bar** of Polish ł, the **circle** of Swedish and Norwegian *å*, and the **hook** of Polish ę.

The Use of Digraphs

Digraphs (pairs of letters to represent single sounds), or even longer sequences like the German **trigraph** *sch*, have also been made use of to indicate un-Latin sounds, such as those that we spell *sh*, *ch*, *th*, and *dg*. In *gu*, as in *guest* and *guilt*, the *u* has the sole function of indicating that the *g* stands for the [g] of *go* rather than the [j] that we might expect it to represent before *e* or *i*, as in *gesture* and *gibe*. The *h* of *gh* performs a similar useful function in *Ghent*, but not in *ghost* and *ghastly*. English makes no use of diacritical marks save for the rare dieresis, preferring other devices such as the aforementioned use of digraphs and of entirely different symbols: for example, English writes *man*, *men*; compare the German method of indicating the same vowel change in *Mann*, *Männer*.

Additional Symbols

Other symbols have sometimes been added to the Roman alphabet by those who adopted it. For example, the runic þ (called *thorn*) and ƿ (called *wynn*) were used by the early English, along with their modification of *d* as ð (called *eth*), all now abandoned as far as English writing is concerned. The þ and the ð were also adopted by the Scandinavians, who got the alphabet from the English, and are still used in writing Icelandic.

The **ligature** *œ* (combining *o* and *e*), which indicated a single vowel sound in post–Classical Latin, was used in early Old English for the *o*-umlaut sound (as in German *schön*). When this sound was later unrounded, there was no further need for *œ* in English. It was, however, taken over by the Scandinavians, who have long since given up the symbol, the Danes having devised ø and the Swedes using ö. It has been used in English in a few classical loanwords—for instance, *amœba* and *cœnobite*, more recently written with unligatured *oe* in British English. (American usage has simple *e* in these words.)

For the vowel sound of *cat*, the English used the digraph *ae*, later written prevailingly as a ligature—that is, as *æ*, the symbol used for the same sound in the alphabet of the International Phonetic Association. This digraph they also got from Latin, in which the classical value (as in German *Kaiser*, from *Caesar*) had long before shifted to a vowel sound roughly similar in value to that which the English ascribed to it. The *æ* was called *æsc* 'ash,' the name of the runic symbol that represented the same sound, though it in no way resembled the Latin-English digraph. In Middle English times, beginning around 1100, the symbol went out of use. Today *æ* is used in Danish, Norwegian, and Icelandic. It occurs occasionally, with a quite different value, in loanwords of classical origin, like *encyclopædia* and *anæmia*, spelled *encyclopedia* and *anemia* in current American usage. (British English now usually has unligatured *ae* in such words.)

The Germanic Runes

In the early Middle Ages various script styles—the "national hands"— developed in those lands that had been provinces of the Roman Empire. But Latin writing, as well as the Latin tongue, all but disappeared in the Roman colony of Britannia, which the Romans had perforce practically abandoned even before the arrival of the English. These Germanic invaders of a land whose population was predominantly Celtic had available to them when they wished to write, which was certainly not very often, the twenty-four **runes**, to which they added six. These runes, in the beginning associated with pagan mysteries—the word *rune* means 'secret'—were angular letters intended originally to be cut or scratched in wood and, though perhaps ill adapted to any sustained composition, served well enough for inscriptions, charms, and the like.

The order of the symbols is quite different from that of the Roman alphabet. As modified by the English, the first group of letters consists of characters corresponding to *f*, *u*, *þ*, *o*, *r*, *c*, *g*, and *w*. The English runic "alphabet" is sometimes called **futhorc** from the first six of these. Despite the differences in the order of the letters, their close similarities to both Greek and Latin symbols make it obvious that they are derived from the Roman alphabet, with which the Germanic peoples could easily have acquired familiarity, or from some early Italic alphabet akin to the Roman alphabet.

The Earliest English Writing

Although St. Augustine and his Roman missionaries, who converted the English, must have written the sixth-century Italian script, this hand never established itself in England. The script used in the Old English manuscripts is based on the Irish modification of the Roman alphabet. This so-called **Insular hand** was used for English writings until the Norman Conquest.[3] It is generally accepted that the Irish, whose conversion to Christianity antedated that of the English, taught the English how to write. The Insular hand is still used in the writing of Irish Gaelic.

To read Old English in the Insular hand of the manuscripts requires little adjustment for modern students, once they become accustomed to the aforementioned **æsc**, the peculiar forms of *f*, *g*, and *r*, the **eth**, the runes called **thorn** and **wynn**, and the three forms of *s*, one of which, called **long** *s*, looks very much like an *f* in modern typography except that the horizontal stroke does not go through to the right of the letter. This particular variant of *s* (ſ) was used until the end of the eighteenth century save in final position, printers following what was the general practice of the manuscripts.

Later History of English Writing

When the Normans conquered England in 1066, they introduced a number of Norman-French customs, including their own style of writing. The alphabet itself has remained fairly stable. We have lost a few special letters used in the Insular hand—thorn, eth, and æsc—as well as some special shapes like wynn for *w* and the long *s* described above. We have also distinguished *i* from *j* and *u* from *v*, shapes that were earlier just variants of one another.

When the prolonged and curved *i*—that is, the *j*—came into being, it was used merely as a variant of *i* in final position, especially when preceded by another *i*, as in Latin *filii*. Since English scribes used *y* for *i* in final position (compare *marry* with *marries* and *married*, *holy day* with *holiday*), the use of *j* in English was long more or less confined to the representation of numerals—for instance, *iij* for *three* and *vij* for *seven*. The dot, incidentally, was not

---

[3] The Insular hand is illustrated in *Problems in the Origins and Development of the English Language* (Algeo 1982, exercise 3.12).

originally part of minuscule *i*, but is a development of the faint sloping line that came to be put above this insignificant letter to distinguish it from the strokes of contiguous letters such as *m*, *n*, and *u*, as well as to distinguish double *i* from *u*. It was later extended by analogy to the *j*, where, because of the different shape of the letter, it performed no useful purpose.

The history of the curved and angular forms of *u*—that is, *u* and *v*—was similar to that of *i* and *j*. Although consonantal and vocalic *u* in Latin had come to be sharply differentiated in sound early in the Christian era, when consonantal *u*, hitherto pronounced [w], became [v], the two symbols *u* and *v* continued to be used more or less interchangeably for either vowel or consonant. The later history of these letters will be treated in the chapters on Middle and early Modern English.

CONSONANT DIGRAPHS

After the Norman Conquest, a number of digraphs were introduced, or reintroduced, into English writing. *Th* gradually replaced thorn and eth in a change that made our orthography less efficient rather than more so. The *th* digraph was used to write both the voiceless and the voiced interdental fricatives (as in *thin* and *then*) and to transcribe theta in words ultimately of Greek origin.

Ph, according to Latin custom, was used in a good many English words of Greek origin to indicate the post-Classical value of ϕ in Greek, and, in addition, it replaced *f* in a few words not from Greek—for instance, the proper name *Ralph*, previously and still to a large extent in England pronounced to rime with *safe* or *waif*.[4] (The *l* is also mere window dressing from a historical point of view.) Ordinarily, however, *ph* indicates genuine Greek origin.

Ch was a transliteration of Greek *chi* (X), pronounced [k] in *chorus*, *machination*, and the like, and was sometimes inserted under classical influence in words where it did not belong. *Schism*, though ultimately Greek, was taken from Old French *cisme*, the spelling of which was in the sixteenth century made to conform to the Greek original. The word is, however, still pronounced with initial [s] by those most familiar with it, but pronunciation with [sk] also is frequently heard nowadays.

Gh was used in words like *night* and *though* to write a sound that has been completely lost from standard English. It also came to be used—or rather misused from a purely rational point of view—after 1400 to indicate [g] in some words, the practice surviving in *aghast*, *ghastly*, and *ghost* (earlier *gost*).

[4] As in act 2 of W. S. Gilbert's *H.M.S. Pinafore:*
    In time each little waif
    Forsook his foster-mother,
    The well-born babe was Ralph—
    Your captain was the other!!!

It occurs as well in words of exotic origin as a transliteration of non-Roman symbols indicating non-Roman sounds—for instance, *ghazi* and *ghoul*, and in *Ghent* and *gherkin*, where it performs the genuinely useful purpose of indicating that these words are not to be pronounced like *gent* and *jerkin*.

Sh was introduced as a spelling for the sibilant [š], which Old English scribes wrote as *sc*. The digraph *sc* thus occurs after the Old English period only in borrowed words. In those ultimately Latin or Greek, regardless of their immediate source as far as English is concerned, *sc* may indicate either [s] or [sk], depending on the following sound—for example, [s] in *scene, science, scion*, and [sk] in *scandal, scorpion, scripture, sculpture*. English words of Scandinavian origin use *sc* for [sk] before *a, o, u*, and *r*, as in *scant, scowl, scurf*, and *scrape*, though *sk* may also occur before the cited vowels, as in *skald, skoal*, and *skull*. In *scent* and *scythe* the *c* is a late and an etymologically altogether unjustifiable insertion; in the latter word, as well as in *scissors* (OF *cisoires*), there has been confusion with Latin *scindere* 'to cut' (past participle *scissum*).

For a large part of the English-speaking world the *h* in the graphic sequence *wh*, save for the exceptions noted in the last sentence of this paragraph, has no phonetic significance; it is, however, significant as far as the speech of northern England, Scotland, Ireland, and parts of the United States is concerned. Spoken differentiation of such pairs as *whale–wail, when–wen*, and *which–witch* in American English is doubtless attributable largely to the influence of those Ulster Scots, or Scotch-Irish as they are sometimes called, who began arriving in America in large numbers around the end of the first quarter of the eighteenth century and who settled first the Pennsylvania back country and subsequently a large part of the country away from the Atlantic Coast. In *whole* (OE *hal*) and *whore* (OE *hore*), the *w* indicates what was a dialect pronunciation that seems to have been fairly common in the sixteenth century; the unwritten [w] of *one* and *once* is of the same dialect origin. In *who, whom, whose* there has been loss of earlier [w].

Ck is usual for [k] after short vowels, but the earlier ending *-ick* has been simplified to *-ic* in *critic, music, physic*, and the like. In recent loans, with final stress, the French spelling is used, as in *critique* and *physique*, which are regarded as different words from *critic* and *physic*.

THE VALUES OF VOWEL SYMBOLS

Our knowledge of the scholarly pronunciation of Latin in the early Middle Ages is obviously an important basis for our reconstruction of the pronunciation of English in its earlier periods. The vowel symbols were used in our earliest writing with the values that these symbols had in the Latin alphabet as acquired by the English from the Irish missionaries; for instance, *a, e*, and *i* were approximately as in the later English loanwords *mirage* (never as in *rage*), *café* (never as in *be*), and *machine* (never as in *mine*). *O* and *u*

54 when they symbolize long vowels have had approximately the same values in earlier periods that they now have in *rode* and *rude*, though both letters have symbolized other sounds as well. The other three vowel symbols, however, approximate their Latin values much more closely in other writing systems than they do in Modern English. Because of a radical change in English long vowels that occurred in the course of the fifteenth century (to be discussed in chapter 7), the long sounds indicated by these symbols acquired qualities quite different from their former ones. As a consequence of the retention of earlier spellings for shifted sounds, the vowel symbols *a*, *e*, and *i* have acquired for us values ([e], [i], [aɪ]) quite different from those ([ɑ], [e], [i]) that they have in all other languages using the Greek or Roman alphabets. This fact is undoubtedly one of the reasons why foreigners are so often confused by English spelling.

The Spelling of English Consonant Sounds

The illustrative words supplied below will give some idea of the variety of ways in which our conventional spelling symbolizes the sounds of speech. What we think of as the normal or usual spellings are given first, in the various positions in which they occur (initially, medially, finally). Afterward in parentheses come spellings that are relatively rare, a few of them unique. The words cited to illustrate unusual spellings have been assembled not for the purpose of stocking an Old Curiosity Shop of English orthography or to encourage in any way the popular notion that our spelling is chaotic—which it is not—but to show the diversity of English spelling, a diversity for which, as we shall see in subsequent chapters, there are invariably historical reasons, including the errors of the learned. A few British pronunciations that are, or ought to be, of interest to educated Americans are included; these are labeled BE, for British English. Characteristically American pronunciations are labeled AE, for American English. Because there is variety in how speakers of English pronounce the language, some of the words will not illustrate the intended sounds for all speakers. For example, although *hiccough* usually ends in [p], being merely a respelling of *hiccup*, some speakers now pronounce it with final [f] under the influence of the spelling *-cough*.

THE STOPS

[b] *bib, ruby, rabble, ebb, tribe* (*cupboard, bheesty*)

[p] *pup, stupid, apple, ripe* (*Lapp, grippe, Clapham, hiccough*)

[d] *dud, body, muddle, add, bride, seethed* (*bdellium, dhoti, Gandhi*)

[t] *toot, booty, matter, butt, rate, hopped* (*cigarette*, **Thomas**, **ptomaine**, **receipt**, **debt**, **subtle**, **phth**isic, indict, **victuals**, **veldt**; the sequence [ts] is written *z* in *schizophrenia* and *Mozart*, *zz* in *mezzo*—also pronounced with [dz])

[g] *gag, lager, laggard, egg* (**guess**, **vague**, **ghost**, **aghast**, **Haigh**, **mortgage**, **blackguard**; the sequence [gz] is written *x* in *exalt* and *exist*, and *xh* in *exhaust* and *exhilarate*; the sequence [gž] is written *x* in *luxurious*)

[k] *kit, naked, take, pick, mackerel, car, bacon, music* (**queer**, **piquet**, **queue**, **physique**, **trek**—*k* by itself in final position being rare—**chukker**, **chasm**, **machination**, **school**, **stomach**, **sacque**, **khaki**; the sequence [ks] is written *x* in *fix* and *exit*, *xe* in BE *axe*; the sequence [kš] is written *x* in *luxury*, *xi* in *anxious*, and *cti* in *action*)

THE FRICATIVES

[v] *valve, over* (*Slav*, **Stephen**, sometimes *schwa*)

[f] *fife, if, raffle, off* (**soften**, **rough**, **toughen**, **phantom**, **sphinx**, **elephant**, **Ralph**, **Chekhov**, BE *lieutenant*)

[ð] *then, either, eth, bathe* (*eisteddfod*, *ye*—pseudo archaic spelling for *the*)

[θ] *thin, ether, froth* (**phthalein**, **chthonian**)

[z] *zoos, fizzle, fuzz, ooze, visage, phase* (*fez, possess, Quincy* [Mass.], *clothes,*[5] *xylophone, raspberry, czar*)

[s] *sis, pervasive, vise, passive, mass, cereal, acid, vice* (**sword**, **answer**, **scion**, **descent**, **evanesce**, **schism**, **psychology**, **Tucson**, *façade*, **isthmus**)

[ž] medially: *leisure, azure, delusion, equation*; initially and finally in a few recent borrowings especially from French: *genre* and *rouge* (the sound seems to be gaining ground, perhaps to some extent because of a smattering of school French, though the words in which it is new in English are not all of French provenience—for instance, *adagio, rajah, Taj Mahal,* and *cashmere*)

[š] *shush, marshal* (*chamois, machine, cache, martial, precious, tension, passion, fashion, sure, ocean, luscious, nausea, crescendo, fuchsia*)

[h] *ha, Mohawk* (*who*, school-Spanish *Don Quixote* as "Donkey Hoty," recent *junta*—though the word had since the seventeenth century been regarded as English and therefore pronounced with the beginning consonant and vowel of *junk*—*Mojave, gila*)

[5] As suggested by the rime in Ophelia's song: "Then up he rose, & don'd his clothes" (*Hamlet* 4.5.52). It is still naturally so pronounced by many, who thus distinguish the noun *clothes* from the verb. Speakers on the auditory mass media and other spelling pronouncers say the noun and verb alike with [-ðz].

The Spelling of English Consonant Sounds

[j] *judge, major, gem, regiment,* **George,** *surgeon, region,* **budget** (*exaggerate, raj, educate, grandeur, soldier, spinach, congratulate*—common on the networks, but regarded by many as nonstandard)

[č] **church,** *lecher,* **butcher,** *itch* (*Christian, niche, nature, cello, Czech*)

THE NASALS

[m] **mum,** *clamor, summer, time* (*comb, plumber, solemn, government, paradigm,* BE *programme*)

[n] **nun,** *honor, dine,* **inn,** *dinner* (*know, gnaw, sign, mnemonic, pneumonia*)

[ŋ] *sing,* **wringer,** *finger,* **sink** (*tongue,* **handkerchief,** BE *charabanc,* BE *restaurant, Pago Pago*)

THE LIQUIDS

[l] *lapel, felon, fellow, fell, hole* (*Lloyd, kiln, Miln*[e][6])

[r] *rear, baron, barren, err, bare* (*write,* **rhetoric,** *bizarre,* **hemorrhage,** *catarrh*)

THE SEMIVOWELS

[w] **won,** *which*[7] (*languish,* **question,** *ouija, Oaxaca,* **huarache,** AE *Juan*; in *one,* the initial [w] is not symbolized)

[y] *yet,* **bullion** (*canyon, La Jolla,* BE *capercailzie* 'wood grouse,' BE *bouillon, jaeger, hallelujah,* [ny] *chignon,* [ny] *cañon*)

The Spelling of English Vowel Sounds

As with the consonants, words are supplied below to illustrate the various spellings of each vowel. There is nothing prescriptive implied in the illustrative words, all of which occur in standard English with the vowel sound indicated, though some may have widespread alternative pronunciations. As with the consonant sounds, what may be thought of as ordinary, usual, or common spellings are cited first, and rare or unique spellings are set off by parentheses. It will be convenient to give separate treatment to vowels before [r] and to unstressed [i], [ɪ], and [ə].

[6] The *n* of *kiln* and *Miln(e)* ceased to be pronounced in Middle English times, but pronunciation with *n* is common nowadays because of the spelling.

[7] A fairly large, if decreasing, number of Americans have in *wh*-words not [w] but [hw].

[i] *evil, cede, meter, accretion, eel, lee, eat, sea* (*ceiling, lief, trio, police, people, key, quay, Beauchamp, Aesop, Oedipus, Leigh, camellia,*[8] BE for the Cambridge college *Caius* [kiz])

[ɪ] *it* (*English, sieve, renege, been, symbol, build, busy, women,* old-fashioned *teat*)

[e] *ape, basin, faint, gray* (*great, emir, fey, eh, Baal, rein, reign, maelstrom,* BE *gaol, gauge, weigh,* BE *Ralph,* BE *halfpenny, mesa, fete, chef d'oeuvre, champagne, Montaigne*; alone in final syllables: AE *café, Iowa* locally, *cachet, foyer, melee, Castlereagh*)

[ɛ] *bet, threat* (BE *ate, again, says, many,* BE *Pall Mall, catch* alternating with [æ], *friend, heifer, Reynolds, leopard, eh, phlegm, aesthetic*)

[æ] *at* (*plaid, baa, ma'am, Spokane,* BE *The Mall, salmon, Cædmon,* AE *draught, meringue*)

THE CENTRAL VOWEL

[ə] *but* (*other, blood, does* verb, *young, was* alternating with [ɑ], *pandit, uh, ugh, twopence*)

THE BACK VOWELS

[u] *ooze, too, to, tomb, you, rude, rue, new* (*pooh, shoe, Cowper, boulevard, through, brougham, fruit,* nautical *leeward, Sioux, rheumatic, lieutenant,*[9] *bouillon, rendezvous, ragout,* and alternating with [ʊ] in *room, roof,* and other words written with *oo*)

Spellings other than with *o, oo,* and *ou* usually represent, or have represented, the sequence [yu], occurring after [b] (*bureau, beauty*), [p] (*pew, pure*), [g] (*gules, gewgaw*), [k] (*cue, queue, Kew*), [v] (*view*), [f] (*few, fuel, feud*), and [m] (*music, mew*). After other consonants there is considerable variation between [u] and [yu]—after [n] as in *nuclear, news,* and *neutral*; after [t] as in *tune* and *Teuton*; after [d] as in *dew* and *duty*; after [θ] as in *thew*; after [s] as in *sue* and *sewer*; and after [z] as in *resume*. After [č] and [j], older [yu] is now quite rare. Many older-generation speakers have [yu] after [l] as in *lewd, lute*. Initially and after [h], the [y] is always present in the *o*-less words, as in *use, Europe, ewe, hue, hew,* and *human*. In its spelling the Scottish surname *Home* [hyum] must be regarded as exceptional.

---

[8] This word is exceptional in that the spelling *e* represents [i] rather than the expected [ɛ] before a double consonant symbol.

[9] British English has [lɛfténənt] for the army subaltern, but the naval officer is usually a [lɛténənt].

[ʊ] *good, pull* (*wolf, could, Wodehouse, worsted* 'fabric')

[o] *go, rode, road, toe, tow, owe, oh* (*soul, brooch, folk, beau, chauffeur,* AE *cantaloupe, picot, though, yeoman, cologne, sew, cocoa, Pharaoh,* military *provost*)

[ɔ] *all, law, awe, cause, gone* (*broad, talk, ought, aught, Omaha, Utah, Arkansas, Mackinac,* BE *Marlborough* [mɔ́lb(ə)rə], BE for the Oxford college *Magdalen* [mɔ́dlɪn],[10] *Gloucester, Faulkner, Maugham, Strachan*)

[ɑ] *father, stop*[11] (*solder, ah, calm,*[12] *bureaucracy, baccarat, ennui, aunt,*[13] *kraal*)

Most of the words in which standard British English has [ɑ] in contrast to American English [æ]—for example, *calf, class,* and *path*—are listed in John S. Kenyon's *American Pronunciation* (1950, pp. 179–80).

American English shows considerable variation between [ɑ] and [ɔ]; in certain regions there may be no distinction between *naughty* and *knotty, auto* and *Otto, caller* and *collar*. All may have [ɑ], or all may have [ɔ]. Most types of American speech, however, have [ɔ] in the first of each pair, [ɑ] in the second. Before [g], before [r] followed by a vowel, and after [w], [ɑ] and [ɔ] vary, as Hans Kurath says, "not only regionally, but from word to word" (1964, p. 112). A particular speaker may, for instance, have [ɔ] in *dog, fog,* and *log,* but [ɑ] in *bog, clog,* and *cog*; [ɔ] in *Cloris, florid, oral,* and *sorority,* but [ɑ] in *Doris, Dorothy, Florida,* and *moral*; and a similarly erratic distribution in words like *swamp, swan, wash,* and *watch*. Another speaker might have quite another distribution of the sounds in question.

THE DIPHTHONGS

[aɪ] *ride, hie, my, style, stile, dye* (*buy, I, eye, ay, aye, pi, night, height, isle, aisle, Geiger, Van Eyck, Van Dyck, kaiser, guile, maestro*)

[aʊ] *how, house* (*bough, Macleod, sauerkraut*)

[ɔɪ] *oil, boy* (*buoy* sometimes as [búɪ] in AE, *Reuters* English news agency, *Boulogne, poi*)

---

[10] The name of the Cambridge college is written *Magdalene,* but is pronounced exactly the same.

[11] The [ɑ] in so-called short-*o* words like *clock, collar, got,* and *stop* prevails in American English. It would seem to be gaining ground in standard British English, where the vowel in such words used to be exclusively a slightly rounded one [ɒ].

[12] Because of the spelling, many Americans, mostly younger-generation ones, insert [l] in this word and others spelled *al*—for instance, *alms, balm, palm,* and *psalm.*

[13] Pronunciation of this word with [ɑ], though regarded by many as a mere affectation, is by no means uncommon in American English. It is of course usual in British English.

Letters and Sounds: A Brief History of Writing

[ɪ] or [i] before [r]: *mere, near, peer* (*pier, mirror, weird, lyric*)

[ɛ], [e], or [æ] before [r]: *bare, air, prayer, their* (*aeronaut*)

[ə] before [r]¹⁴: *urge, erg, bird, earn* (*word, journal, masseur, myrrh*¹⁵)

[ʊ] or [u] before [r]: *poor, sure, tour, jury, neural* (*Boer*¹⁶)

[ɔ] or [o] before [r]: *or, oar, ore* (*war, four, door,* AE *reservoir*¹⁷)

[ɑ] before [r]: *art* (*heart, sergeant, soiree* [wɑ] as also in other recent French loans written with *oi*¹⁸)

[aɪ] before [r]: *fire, tyrant* (*choir* [waɪ])

[aʊ] before [r]: *flour, flower* (*dowry, coward, sauerkraut*)

[ɔɪ] before [r] (a rare combination): *coir*

THE UNSTRESSED VOWELS

[i] or [ɪ] unstressed as final sound in a word: *body, honey* (*Macaulay, specie, Burleigh, Ralegh,* BE *Calais* [kǽlɪ], BE *café* [kǽfɪ], *recipe, guinea, coffee,* BE *ballet* [bǽlɪ], *taxi,* BE *Carew, challis, chamois*)

unstressed followed by another vowel: *aerial, area* (*Israel, Ephraim, Nausicaa*)

[ɪ] unstressed followed by a velar consonant: *ignore, topic, running*

[ə] or [ɪ] unstressed in final syllables followed by a consonant other than a velar or [r]: *bias, bucket, college* (*mischief, forfeit, biscuit, minute* noun,

---

¹⁴ In "*r*-less" speech there would of course be no [r]; in such speech the vowel may be transcribed [ɜ].

¹⁵ In words that had earlier [ʊr] followed by a vowel, like *courage, hurry, thorough,* and *worry,* standard British English has a syllabic division different from that of most American English, as in [kə́-rɪj] in contrast to AE [kə́r-ɪj]. The standard British English pronunciation is also current in metropolitan New York and to a lesser extent in other parts of the Atlantic seaboard; the noncoastal American pronunciation is also current in British folk speech (Kurath and McDavid 1961, p. 127).

¹⁶*Poor* and *Boer* are often and *sure* is sometimes pronounced with the vowel [o] or [ɔ].

¹⁷ Many persons in New England and the South, Canada, the English Midland, northern England, and Scotland have [o] before [r] in such words as *four, oar, ore,* and *door.* Such speakers distinguish *oar* and *ore* [or] from *or* [ɔr], *four* and *fore* from *for, hoarse* from *horse, mourn* from *morn, boarder* from *border,* and use [or] in words written *-oor* (though it is of course not implied that the writing has anything to do with the matter), as in *door* and *floor.* The distinction of [or] and [ɔr] is a historical one, but is not maintained in standard British English and in many types of American English, which have the same vowel in all these words; it may be either [ɔr] or, especially among younger-generation Americans, [or].

¹⁸ Some Americans have [ɔ] in all such words.

marriage, portrait, palace, lettuce, tortoise, old-fashioned *Calais* [-ɪs],[19] *dactyl, Tyrwhitt*)

unstressed in initial syllables: *illumine, elude (Aeneas, mysterious*)

[ə] unstressed in final syllables followed by a consonant other than [r]: *bias, melon, bonus, famous (Durham, foreign, Lincoln, Chisholm*)

unstressed standing alone in final syllables: *Cuba (Noah, Goethe, piano, borough, window, bureau, Edinburgh* [-brə],[20] and alternating with [ɪ] or [i] in *Cincinnati, Miami, Missouri*)

unstressed in medial syllables: *malady, remedy, ruminate, melody, syrupy (Aeschylus, Renaissance, limousine*)

unstressed in initial syllables: *alone, molasses, sustain (authority, blancmange*)

unstressed in final syllables ending in [r][21]: *bursar, butter, actor (nadir, femur, glamour, Tourneur*)

unstressed in final syllables with [r] plus another consonant: *coward, shepherd, Cranford, Rayburn (cupboard, Osbourne*)

unstressed in medial syllables with [r] plus another consonant: *gabardine, haberdasher, importunity, bifurcate (avoirdupois*)

unstressed in initial syllables with [r] plus another consonant: *pervade, pursue*

Spelling Pronunciations

Regardless of the method by which they have been taught, or have taught themselves, to read, many literate people attribute sounds to the letters of the alphabet. This is to put the cart before the horse, for, as should be perfectly clear by now, letters do not "have" sounds, but merely symbolize them. Nevertheless, literate people are likely to feel that they do not really know a word until the question "How do you spell it?" has been answered.

Such dependence on spelling is amusingly illustrated in the 1960 motion picture version of H. G. Wells's *The Time Machine*, when the Time Traveler, projected hundreds of thousands of years into the future, asks a beautiful blonde Eloi girl what her name is. Inasmuch as the English language has by

[19] As in the name of the town in Maine. Compare Browning's rime of *malice* with *Calais* in "De Gustibus."

[20] In the last five words cited, [-ə] alternates with a rounded vowel resembling [ʊ], and in *arrow, borough, bureau, narrow, piano, widow, window,* and the like—particularly in younger-generation speech—with [o].

[21] In these words and those cited in the following sections, *r*-less speech has [ə] alone, in contrast to the [ər] of *r*-ish speech.

an unexplained miracle not changed in the least during this vast space of time, the girl understands him perfectly and replies "Weena." "How do you spell it?" immediately asks the Time Traveler. This is too much for Weena, who has no notion of spelling. Wrinkling his brow and taking careful thought, the Traveler proceeds to trace the letters *W, E, E, N, A* in the earth, thus making the name somehow more "real" than it had previously been for him, and presumably for the illiterate girl as well. In justice to H. G. Wells, it should be stated that the incident does not occur in the story as he wrote it.

A knowledge of spelling has been responsible for changing the pronunciation of certain words whose written forms for one reason or another do not indicate pronunciations that had become traditional. For instance, simply because it occurs in writing, the *t* of *often* has come to be pronounced once again, as it was in earlier days and up until well into the seventeenth century.[22] The pronunciation with *t* is sufficiently widespread that it is probably safe to predict that in another generation or so only philologists will get the point of the *orphan–often* dialogue in Gilbert and Sullivan's *The Pirates of Penzance*, culminating in Major-General Stanley's question to the Pirate King, "When you said 'orphan,' did you mean 'orphan'—a person who has lost his parents, or 'often'—frequently?" This will make no sense to those who have restored the *t* in *often*; for such speakers the words are no longer homophones, or even near-homophones as they are in American English with the *r* of *orphan* pronounced. *The Oxford English Dictionary*, whose *O* installments were published in the early years of the present century, records only the pronunciation without *t* but adds the comment that pronouncing the *t* is "now frequent in the south of England, and is often used in singing."

Reanalysis of the compound *forehead*, with restressing of the second element and the *h* pronounced, was also in the beginning due to a mistaken notion of the relationship between writing and speech. This pronunciation is practically universal among younger-generation speakers and is, it must be admitted, perfectly natural with them, since they learned to pronounce the word that way long before they knew how to spell it, the analytical pronunciation having originated, though at first frowned upon, at least a generation ago. Reanalysis of *breakfast* as *break* plus *fast* would be quite parallel to what has happened in the case of *forehead*.

Such is the misunderstanding of writing as it is related to speech that many people suppose that the "best" speech is that which conforms most

---

[22] Otto Jespersen (*A Modern English Grammar on Historical Principles*, 1909–49, 1: 275) is probably overstating somewhat when he says that the *t* seems to have been "always" mute in the eighteenth and nineteenth centuries, for John Walker, though he records only [ɔ́fən], states in the introduction to his *Critical Pronouncing Dictionary* (1791) that in this word "the *t* begins to be pronounced." Though within the memory of living persons such pronunciation has been considered affected—*nouveau riche*, as it were, and hence lacking "status"—it must now be considered both "Queen's English" and "President's English." The fact that the last two kings of England used the form with *t* in public addresses should be sufficient to establish the pronunciation as standard English.

Spelling Pronunciations

closely to the notions that they have acquired about the writing system, though this supposition has not as yet been extended to such words as *through* and *night*. Because of mass education, what is essentially a secondary factor—writing—has begun to affect pronunciation more than it ever did before. This tendency is, as we have seen, quite the reverse of what happened in earlier times, before English spelling became fixed, when writing was made to conform to speech. To put it in different terms: whereas in previous periods the purpose of writing was conceived to be the visual representation of speech, nowadays many conceive speech—ideally, at any rate—as the oral representation of writing.

Words that we have never heard spoken we must necessarily pronounce as their spellings seem to indicate, assuming that there is no dictionary handy. There are no grounds for reproach if a child reads *misled* as if it were the preterit of a hypothetical verb *to misle*. The great scholar W. W. Skeat of Cambridge once declared that "I hold firmly to the belief . . . that no one can tell how to pronounce an English word unless he has at some time or other *heard* it," and refused to hazard an opinion on the pronunciation of a number of very rare words—among them, *aam, abactinal, abrus,* and *acaulose*—going on to say, "It would be extremely dishonest in me to pretend to have any opinion at all as to such words as these."[23] A number of common, everyday words that for one reason or another have become less used than they formerly were have acquired pronunciations based on their written forms—for instance, *clapboard*, pronounced like *clabbered* until fairly recently, but now usually analyzed as *clap* plus *board*; the same sort of analysis might occur also in *cupboard* if houses of the future should be built without cupboards or if builders should think up some fancy name for them, like "food preparation equipment storage areas."[24] A number of generations ago, when people made and sharpened their own tools much more commonly than now, the word *grindstone* rimed with *Winston*.

It is similar with proper names that we have not heard spoken. Our only guide is spelling, and no one, particularly no American, is to be much blamed for pronouncing *Daventry, Shrewsbury,* and *Cirencester* as their spellings seem to indicate they "should" be pronounced; as a matter of fact, many English people treat in exactly the same way these words, whose traditional pronunciations as [déntrɪ], [šrózbərɪ], and [sísɪtə] or [sízɪtər] have become somewhat old-fashioned. A London bus conductor would be baffled at the request to be put down at "Tibbald's" Road; it would be necessary to pronounce *Theobald* as spelled, for the pronunciation indicated by Alexander Pope's spelling "Tibbald" (in reference to the Shakespearean commentator Lewis Theobald) is now quite old-fashioned.

[23] Quoted in *Funk and Wagnalls New Standard Dictionary of the English Language* (1925, p. 2762).

[24] This is not outside the realm of possibility. In luxury advertisements a kitchen is sometimes referred to as a "food preparation area."

Contemporary spelling is the heir of thirteen centuries of English writing in the Latin alphabet. It is hardly surprising, therefore, that our orthography has traces of its earlier history both in its general rules and in its anomalies. Whenever we set pen to paper, we participate in a tradition that started with Anglo-Saxon monks, who had learned it from Irish scribes. The tradition progressed through such influences as the Norman Conquest, the introduction of printing, the urge to reform spelling in various ways (including an impulse to respell words according to their etymological sources), and the recent view that speech should conform to spelling. Nowadays, in fact, we are likely to forget that writing, in the history of humanity or even of a single language like English, is relatively recent. Before writing there were no historical records of language, but languages existed and their histories can be in some measure reconstructed, as we shall see in the next chapter.

For Further Reading

Theory of Writing Systems

Gelb, *A Study of Writing: The Foundations of Grammatology*, 1963.
Haas, *Phono-Graphic Translation*, 1970.

History of Writing

Diringer, *The Alphabet: A Key to the History of Mankind*, 1968.
————, *The Story of the Aleph Beth*, 1960.
Ullman, *Ancient Writing and Its Influence*, 1969.

History of English Spelling

Scragg, *A History of English Spelling*, 1974.
Venezky, "Notes on the History of English Spelling," *Visible Language*, 1976.

Contemporary Spelling

Emery, *Variant Spellings in Modern American Dictionaries*, 1973.
Hanna et al., *Phoneme-Grapheme Correspondences as Cues to Spelling Improvement*, 1966.
Venezky, *The Structure of English Orthography*, 1970.
Wijk, *Rules of Pronunciation for the English Language*, 1966.

Spelling Reform

Dewey, *English Spelling: Roadblock to Reading*, 1971.
Lounsbury, *English Spelling and Spelling Reform*, 1909.
Pitman and St. John, *Alphabets and Reading: The Initial Teaching Alphabet*, 1969.

4 The Backgrounds of English

Even a casual comparison of English with some other languages reveals degrees of similarity among them. Thus English *father* clearly resembles German *Vater* (especially when one is aware that the letter *v* in German represents the same sound as *f*), Dutch *vader*, Icelandic *faðir*, and Norwegian, Danish, and Swedish *fader*. Although there is still a fair resemblance, the English word is not quite so similar to Latin *pater*, Spanish *padre*, Portuguese *pai*, Catalan *pare*, and French *père*. Greek *patēr*, Sanskrit *pitar-*, and Persian *pedar* are all strikingly like the Latin form, and (allowing for the loss of the first consonant) Gaelic *athair* resembles the others as well. It takes no great insight to recognize that those words for 'father' are somehow the "same." When such widespread similarity is reinforced by other parallels among the languages, we are forced to look for some explanation of the resemblances.

The explanation that was first proposed about 200 years ago and is now well supported with evidence from many languages is that there was once a language (now no longer spoken) that developed in different ways in the various parts of the world to which its speakers traveled. We give the name **Proto-Indo-European** (or simply **Indo-European**) to that prehistoric and now dead language because at the beginning of historical times languages that derived from it were spoken from Europe in the west to India in the east. Proto-Indo-European was thus the "ancestor" of most of the languages of Europe and of many of those of south Asia. Its "descendants," which make

up the **Indo-European family**, include all of the languages mentioned in the   65
preceding paragraph, as well as Russian, Polish, Czech, Bulgarian, Albanian,
Armenian, Gypsy, and many others.

Language Typology and Language Families

In talking about a **language family**, we use metaphors like "mother" and
"daughter" languages and speak of degrees of "relationship" just as though
languages had offspring that could be plotted on a genealogical, or family-tree,
chart. The terms are convenient ones; but, in the discussion of so-called
linguistic families that follows, we must bear in mind that a language is not
born, nor does it put out branches like a tree—nor, for that matter, does it
die except when every single one of its speakers dies, as has happened to
Etruscan, Gothic, Cornish, and a good many other languages. We speak of
Latin as a dead language, but in fact it still lives in various developments as
Italian, French, Spanish, and the other Romance languages. In the same
way, Proto-Indo-European continues in the various present-day Indo-
European languages.

Hence the terms *family*, *ancestor*, *parent*, and other genealogical expressions when applied to languages must be regarded as no more than
metaphors. Languages are developments of older languages rather than
descendants in the sense in which people are descendants of their ancestors.
Thus Italian and Spanish are different developments of an earlier, more
unified language, Latin. Latin, in turn, is one of a number of developments
of a still earlier language called Italic. Italic, in its turn, is a development of
Indo-European. Whether or not Indo-European has affinities with other
languages spoken in prehistoric times, and is hence a development of an even
earlier language, no one is prepared to say with certainty; for we are quite
in the dark about how it all began.

Older scholars classified languages as **isolating**, **agglutinative**, **incorporative**,
and **inflective**, these being exemplified, respectively, by Chinese, Turkish,
Eskimo, and Latin. The isolating languages were supposed to represent the
most primitive type: they were languages in which each idea was expressed
by a separate word and in which the words tended to be monosyllabic. But
even the earliest (middle of second millennium B.C.) records of Chinese, an
isolating and monosyllabic language in its modern form, represent not a
primitive but actually a late stage in linguistic development. It obviously
cannot be inferred from such evidence as this that our prehistoric ancestors
prattled in words of one syllable each.

The older scholars also observed, quite correctly, that in certain languages,
such as Turkish and Hungarian, words were made up of parts "stuck together," as it were; hence the term *agglutinative*. In such languages the elements that are put together are usually whole syllables having very definite
meanings. The inflectional suffixes of the Indo-European languages were

supposed likewise once to have been independent words; hence some believed that the inflective languages had grown out of the agglutinative. Little was known of what were called incorporative languages, in which major sentence elements are combined into a single word.

The trouble with such a classification was that, though apparently objective, it was not really so but was instead based on the now discarded theory that early peoples spoke in monosyllables. Furthermore, the difference between agglutinative and inflective was not well defined, and there was considerable overlapping. Nevertheless, the terms are useful and widely used in the description of specific languages or even groups of languages. Modern objective and well-informed **typological classification** has been especially useful in showing language similarities and differences (Greenberg 1960).

From the historical point of view, however, much more satisfactory is the **genetic classification** of languages, made on the basis of such correspondences of sound and structure as indicate relationship through common origin. Perhaps the greatest contribution of nineteenth-century linguistic scholars was the painstaking investigation of those correspondences, many of which had been noted long before.

Such investigation indicated unmistakably that practically all of the languages of Europe (and hence of the Americas and other parts of the world colonized by Europeans) and some of Asia have in common certain characteristics of sound and structure and to some extent a stock of words. Thus it is perfectly obvious that they have all developed out of a single language spoken in prehistoric times that we call Proto-Indo-European.[1] What it was called by those who spoke it we have no way of knowing, nor do we know what they called themselves. We shall here follow the usual practice of referring to them as the Indo-Europeans, but it must always be borne in mind that the term has no racial connotations; it refers only to a group of people who lived in a relatively small area in early times and who spoke a more or less unified language out of which many languages have developed in the course of thousands of years. These languages are spoken today by approximately half of the world's population.

The Non-Indo-European Languages

Before proceeding to a more detailed discussion of the Indo-European group, we may perhaps best delimit it by briefly noting those languages and groups of languages that are *not* Indo-European. Two important groups have names that reflect the biblical attempt to derive all human races from the three sons of Noah: the **Semitic** (from the Latin form of the name of the eldest

[1] The alternative term, *Indo-Germanic*, is not now much used. Another term, *Aryan*, has been used synonymously. Originally this term referred only to the major Asiatic languages of the group. This is still the reference that it has in learned use, where its occurrence is now somewhat rare, *Indo-Iranian* being the preferred term.

son, more correctly called Shem in English) and the **Hamitic**. The term
Japhetic, once used for Indo-European, has long been obsolete. On the basis
of many phonological and morphological features that they share, Semitic
and Hamitic are thought by many scholars to be related through a hypothetical common ancestor, Hamito-Semitic, or **Afroasiatic**, as it is usually
called now; there are also those who believe in an ultimate relationship,
impossible to prove, between Semitic and Indo-European.

The Semitic group includes the following languages in three geographical
subgroups: (Eastern) Akkadian, called Assyrian in the periods of the oldest
texts, and later Babylonian; (Western) Hebrew, Aramaic (the native speech
of Jesus Christ), Phoenician, and Moabitic; (Southern) Arabic and Ethiopic.
Of these, only Arabic is spoken by large numbers of people over a widespread
area. Hebrew has been revived comparatively recently in Israel, to some extent
for nationalistic reasons.[2] Ethiopic survives mainly in Geez, a Christian
liturgical and learned language of Ethiopia, and in Amharic, which is used
in state documents in that country. It is interesting to note that two of the
world's most important religious documents are written in Semitic languages
—the Old Testament in Hebrew (with large portions of the books of Ezra
and Daniel in Aramaic) and the Koran in Arabic.

To the Hamitic group belong Egyptian (called Coptic after the close of
the third century of the Christian era), the Berber dialects of North Africa,
various Cushitic dialects spoken along the upper Nile (named for Cush, a son
of Ham), and Chadic in Chad and Nigeria. Coptic is used in the liturgy of
the Coptic Christian Church in Egypt, much as Geez is used in the Ethiopian
Church and Latin in the Roman Catholic Church, but it is not spoken
elsewhere. Arabic became the national language of Egypt in the course of the
sixteenth century.

Semitic is thus essentially Asiatic, and Hamitic North African. Hamitic
is unrelated to the other languages spoken in central and southern Africa,
the vast region south of the Sahara. Those languages are usually classified
into three main groups: **Nilo-Saharan**, extending to the equator, a large and
highly diversified group of languages whose relationships to one another are
difficult and in some cases impossible to establish; **Niger-Kordofanian**, extending from the equator to the extreme south, a large group of languages
of which the most important belong to the Bantu group, including Swahili;
and the **Khoisan** languages, such as Hottentot and Bushman, spoken by small
groups of people in the extreme southwestern part of Africa. Various of the
Khoisan languages use clicks—the kind of sound used by English speakers
as exclamations and conventionally represented by spellings such as *tsk-tsk*
and *cluck-cluck*, but used as regular speech sounds in Khoisan and transcribed
by slashes or exclamation points, as in the language !O!kung, spoken in
Angola.

[2] Hebrew should not be confused with Yiddish (that is, Jüdisch), a German dialect to
be further defined later. American newspapers printed in Yiddish use Hebrew characters.

The Non-Indo-European Languages

Languages belonging to the **Dravidian** group were once spoken throughout India, where the earlier linguistic situation was radically affected by the Indo-European invasion. They are the aboriginal languages of India but are now spoken mainly in southern India.

The **Sino-Tibetan** group includes the various languages of China, such as Cantonese and Mandarin, as well as Tibetan, Burmese, and others. Japanese is unrelated to Chinese, although it has borrowed the Chinese written characters and many Chinese words. It and Korean are sometimes thought to be members of the Altaic family, mentioned below, but the relationship is not certain. Ainu, the language of the aborigines of Japan, is totally unrelated to any other language of which we have any knowledge; it is now spoken by very few people.

A striking characteristic of the **Malayo-Polynesian** languages is their wide geographical distribution in the islands of the Indian and the Pacific oceans, stretching from Madagascar to Easter Island. The native languages of Australia, spoken by only a few aborigines there nowadays, have no connection at all with Malayo-Polynesian, nor have the more than a hundred languages spoken in New Guinea and neighboring islands.

The American Indian languages constitute a geographic rather than a linguistic grouping, comprising many different language groups and even isolated languages showing very little relationship, if any, to one another. A very important and widespread group of American Indian languages is known as the **Uto-Aztecan**, which includes Nahuatl, the language spoken by the Aztecs, and various closely related dialects. Aleut and Eskimo, which are very similar to each other, are spoken in the Aleutians and all along the extreme northern coast of America and north to Greenland. In the Andes Mountains of South America, **Kechumaran** is a language stock that includes Aymara and Quechua, the speech of the Incan Empire. The isolation of the various groups, small in number to begin with and spread over so large a territory, may account to some extent for the great diversity of American Indian tongues.

Basque, spoken in many dialects by no more than half a million people living in the region of the Pyrenees, has always been something of a popular linguistic mystery. It now seems fairly certain, on the basis of coins and scanty inscriptions of the ancient Iberians, that Basque is related to the almost completely lost language of those people who once inhabited the Iberian peninsula and in Neolithic times were spread over an even larger part of Europe. Efforts to relate it to Etruscan, a language of which we know very little, to the non-Indo-European languages spoken in the Caucasus Mountains (not mentioned elsewhere here), and to the Hamitic languages have not been successful.

An important group of non-Indo-European languages spoken in Europe, as well as in parts of Asia, is the **Ural-Altaic**, which falls into two subgroups: the **Ural**, or **Finno-Ugric**, which includes Finnish, Estonian, Lappish, and

Altaic (though there are those who deny any such connection), which includes several varieties of Turkish, such as Ottoman Turkish (Osmanli) and that spoken in Turkestan and in the Azerbaijan Soviet Socialist Republic, as well as Mongolian and Manchu.

The foregoing is by no means a complete survey of non-Indo-European languages. We have merely mentioned some of the most important groups and individual languages, along with some that are of little significance as far as the numbers or the present importance of their speakers are concerned but that are nevertheless interesting for one reason or another. In their *Classification and Index of the World's Languages*, C. F. and F. M. Voegelin (1977) list about 350 major groups and subgroups of languages and over 4900 languages, of which 188 are Indo-European. One cannot have faith in the accuracy of such counts, for reaching agreement as to what constitutes a language is often impossible.

The line demarcating **dialect** and **language** is difficult to place, and linguists do not always concur on where it should be drawn. The usual distinction is that dialects are mutually comprehensible, whereas languages are not. But chains of dialects create a problem for classification: dialect A may be comprehensible to those who speak dialect B, which is comprehensible to those who speak dialect C, which in turn is comprehensible to speakers of dialect D; yet speakers of dialects A and D may not be able to comprehend each other. That is the situation that Dutch and German speakers face; the two standard languages are very different, but each of the local dialects from Holland to the far side of Germany is readily understandable to the inhabitants of the neighboring areas. In view of the chain of comprehensibility, the Voegelins classify all of those dialects as one language, Netherlandic German, including Dutch, Flemish, and all varieties of German. On the other hand, if we think in terms of standard languages and national boundaries, there are several languages—Dutch, Flemish, German—instead of one. Furthermore, depending largely on one's point of view, Old English, Middle English, and Modern English might be regarded as one, two (on the basis that the transition from Middle English to Modern English is somewhat less well defined than that from Old English to Middle English), or three. And there are yet further difficulties, so that any estimate of the number of languages that are or have been spoken in the world must be grossly imprecise.

The Main Divisions of the Indo-European Group

Of some Indo-European languages—for example, Thracian, Phrygian, Macedonian, and Illyrian—we possess only the scantiest remains. We may be certain that others have disappeared without leaving a trace. Members of the following subgroups survive as living tongues: Indo-Iranian, Balto-Slavic,

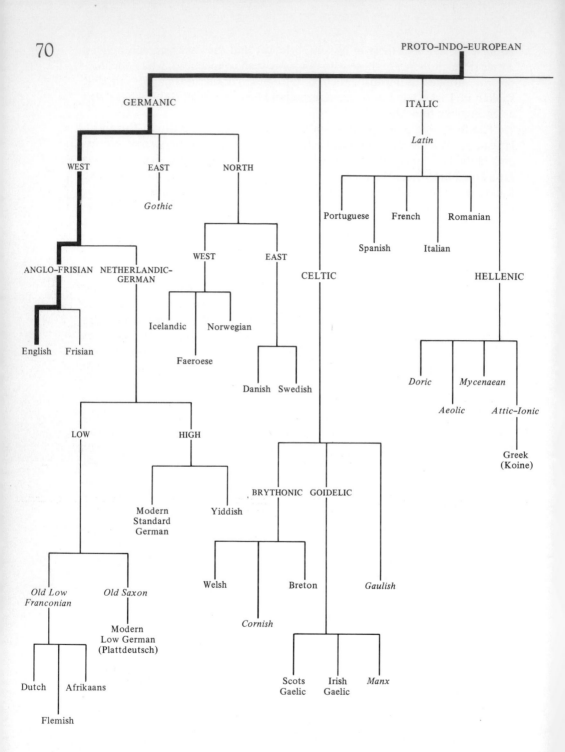

The Backgrounds of English

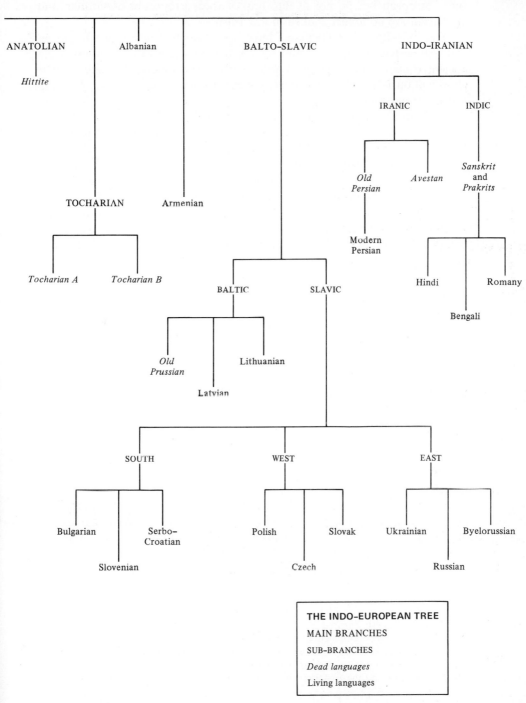

THE INDO-EUROPEAN TREE

MAIN BRANCHES

SUB-BRANCHES

Dead languages

Living languages

The Main Divisions of the Indo-European Group

Hellenic, Italic, Celtic, and Germanic. Albanian and Armenian are also Indo-European but do not fit into any of these subgroups. Anatolian and Tocharian are no longer spoken in any form.

The Indo-European languages have been classified into **satem languages** and **centum languages**, *satem* and *centum* being respectively the Avestan (an ancient Iranian language) and Latin words corresponding to *hundred*. The classification is based on the development, in very ancient times, of Indo-European palatal *k*.

In Indo-European, palatal *k* (as in **kmtóm* 'hundred') was a distinct phoneme from velar *k* (as in the verbal root **kwer-* 'do, make,' which we have in the Sanskrit loanword *karma* and in the name *Sanskrit* itself, which means something like 'well-made'). In the *satem* languages—Indo-Iranian, Balto-Slavic, Armenian, and Albanian—the two *k* sounds remained separate phonemes, and the palatal *k* became a sibilant—for example, Sanskrit (Indic) *śatam*, Lithuanian (Baltic) *šiṁtas*, Old Church Slavic *sŭto*. In the other Indo-European languages, the two *k* sounds became a single phoneme, either remaining a *k* or, in the Germanic group, shifting to *h*, as in Greek (Hellenic) *(he)katon*, Welsh (Celtic) *cant*, and Old English (Germanic) *hund*.[3] In general the *centum* languages tend to be spoken in the West and the *satem* languages in the East, although Tocharian, the easternmost of all Indo-European tongues, belongs to the former group.

THE INDO-IRANIAN LANGUAGES

The **Indo-Iranian** group (*Iranian* is from the same root as the word *Aryan*) is one of the oldest for which we have historical records. The Vedic hymns, written in an early form of Sanskrit, date from about 1000 B.C. but reflect a poetic tradition stretching back to the second millennium B.C. Classical Sanskrit appears about 500 B.C. It is much more systematized than Vedic Sanskrit, for it had been seized upon by early grammarians who formulated rules for its proper use; even so, Classical Sanskrit was probably not systematized until it was ceasing to be widely spoken. The most remarkable of the Indian grammarians was Panini, who, at about the same time (fourth century B.C.) that the Greeks were indulging in fanciful speculations about language and in fantastic etymologizing,[4] wrote a grammar of Sanskrit that to this day holds the admiration of linguistic scholars. But there were yet others whose work, motivated as was Panini's by the importance of preserving unchanged the language of the old sacred literature, puts much of the grammatical writing of the Greeks and Romans to shame.

The written language was fixed by these grammarians, and Sanskrit is

[3] Modern English *hundred* is a compound, first occurring late in the Old English period. The *-red* is a development of what was once an independent word meaning 'number.'
[4] The Romans later did no better, even deriving names of things from what they were *not*. Thus they fancied *bellum* 'war' was so named because it was not *bellus* 'beautiful.' The Middle Ages and the Renaissance failed to improve much on the Romans.

still written by Indian scholars according to their rules. It is in no sense dead as a written language; its status is roughly comparable to that of Latin in medieval and Renaissance Europe.

Indic dialects had developed, as we might expect, long before Sanskrit became a refined and learned language. These are known as Prakrits, and some of them—notably Pali, the religious language of Buddhism—achieved high literary status. From these Prakrits are indirectly derived the various non-Dravidian languages of India, the most widely known of which are Bengali, Hindi, Hindustani (a variety of Hindi, with mixed word stock), and Urdu, derived from Hindustani. Gypsy, or Romany,[5] is also an Indic dialect, with many loanwords from other languages acquired in the course of the Gypsies' wanderings. When they first appeared in Europe in the late Middle Ages, many people supposed them to be Egyptians—whence the name given them in English and some other languages. A long time passed before the study of their language was to indicate unmistakably that they had come originally from northwestern India.

Those Indo-Europeans who settled permanently in the Iranian Plateau developed a sacred language, Avestan, preserved in the religious book the Avesta, after which the language is named. There are no modern descendants of Avestan, which is believed by some to be the language of the Medes, whose name is frequently coupled with that of the Persians, most notably in the phrase "the law of the Medes and Persians, which altereth not" (Daniel 6.8). Avestan was the language of the sage Zarathustra—Zoroaster to the Greeks—many of whose followers fled to India at the time of the Mohammedan conquest of their country in the eighth century. They are the ancestors of the modern Parsees (that is, Persians) of Bombay. Old Persian is a different language from Avestan; it was the language of the district known to the Greeks as Persis, whose inhabitants under the leadership of the great Cyrus in the sixth century B.C. became the predominant tribe.

ARMENIAN AND ALBANIAN

Armenian and Albanian, as we have seen, are independent subgroups. The first has in its word stock so many Persian loanwords that it was once supposed to belong to the Indo-Iranian group; there are also many borrowings from Greek and from Arabic and Syrian.

Albanian also has a mixed vocabulary, with words from Italian, Slavic, Turkish, and Greek. It is possibly related to the ancient language of Illyria in an Illyrian branch of Indo-European. Evidence of the ancient language is so meager, however, and modern Albanian has been so much influenced by neighboring languages that it is difficult to tell much about its affinities.

[5] *Romany* has nothing to do with *Rome*, *Romance*, *Romaic* (Modern Greek), or *Romanian*, but is derived from Gypsy *rom* 'man,' ultimately Sanskrit. Likewise the *rye* of *Romany rye* (that is, 'Gypsy gentlemen') has nothing to do with the cereal crop, but is a Gypsy word akin to Sanskrit *rājan* 'king,' as well as to Latin *rēx* and German *Reich*.

The **Tocharian** languages, of which there are two, called Tocharian A and Tocharian B, are misnamed. When the languages were discovered at the end of the last century in some volumes of Buddhist scriptures and monastic business accounts from central Asia, they were first thought to be forms of Iranian and were named after an extinct Iranian people known to the ancient Greek geographer Strabo as Tocharoi. Later it was discovered that Tocharian is linguistically quite different from Iranian. Nevertheless, the name has stuck; the languages themselves have long been extinct.

ANATOLIAN

Shortly after the discovery of Tocharian, another group of Indo-European languages was identified in Asia Minor. Excavations at the capital city of the Hittites (a people mentioned in the Old Testament and in Egyptian records from the second millennium B.C.) uncovered the royal archives. They contained works in a number of ancient languages, including one otherwise unknown. As the writings in the unknown tongue were deciphered, it became clear that the language, Hittite, was Indo-European, although it had been profoundly influenced by non-Indo-European languages spoken around it. Later scholars identified several different but related languages (Luwian, Palaic, Lydian), and the new branch was named **Anatolian**, after the area where it was spoken. One of the interesting features of Hittite is that it preserves an Indo-European "laryngeal" sound (transliterated *h*) that was lost in all of the other Indo-European languages (for example, in Hittite *pahhur* 'fire' compared with Greek *pûr*, Umbrian *pir*, Czech *pýř*, Tocharian *por*, and Old English *fȳr*).

THE BALTO-SLAVIC LANGUAGES

Although the oldest records of the Baltic and the Slavic languages show them as quite different, most scholars have assumed a common ancestor closer than Indo-European, called **Balto-Slavic**. The chief Baltic language is Lithuanian; the closely related Latvian is spoken in Latvia, to the north of Lithuania and like it now a part of the Soviet Union. Lithuanian is quite conservative phonologically, so that one can find a number of words in it that are very similar in form to cognate words in older Indo-European languages—for example, Lithuanian *Diēvas* and Sanskrit *devás* 'god' or Lithuanian *platùs* and Greek *platús* 'broad.'

Still another Baltic language, Old Prussian, was spoken as late as the seventeenth century in what is now called East Prussia, which was considered outside of Germany until the early years of the nineteenth century. Prussia in time became the predominant state of the new German Empire. The Prussians, like the Lithuanians and the Latvians, were heathens until the end of the

Middle Ages, when they were converted at the point of the sword by the Knights of the Teutonic Order—a military order that was an outcome of the Crusades. The aristocracy of the region (their descendants are the Prussian *Junkers*) came to be made up of members of this order, who, having saved the souls of the heathen Balts, proceeded to take over their lands.

Slavic falls into three main subdivisions: East Slavic includes Great Russian (or just Russian), the common and literary language of Russia; Ukrainian (or Ruthenian), sometimes called Little Russian; and White Russian (or Byelorussian), spoken in the region directly to the north of the Ukraine. West Slavic includes Polish, Czech, the relatively similar Slovak, and Sorbian (or Wendish), a language spoken by a small group of people in East Germany; these languages have lost many of the early forms preserved in East Slavic. The South Slavic languages include Bulgarian, Serbo-Croatian, and Slovenian. The oldest Slavic writing we know is in Old Church Slavic (or Old Church Slavonic), which remained a liturgical language long after it ceased to be generally spoken.

MODERN GREEK AND THE HELLENIC DIALECTS

In ancient times there were many **Hellenic** dialects, among them Mycenaean, Aeolic, Doric, and Attic-Ionic. As in the course of history Athens came to assume tremendous prestige, its dialect, Attic—that of all the giants of the Age of Pericles—became the basis of a standard for the entire Greek world, a **koine** (that is, *koinē* [*dialektos*] 'common [dialect]'), which was ultimately to drive out the other Hellenic dialects. Most of the local dialects spoken in Greece today, as well as the standard language, are thus derived from Attic. With all their glorious ancient literature, the Greeks have not had a modern literary language until comparatively recently. This "purified" literary language makes considerable use of words revived from ancient Greek, as well as a number of ancient inflectional forms; it has become the ordinary language of the upper classes. A more natural development of the Attic koine is spoken by the masses and hence called *demotike*.

THE ITALIC LANGUAGES

In ancient Italia the main Indo-European language was Latin, the speech of Latium, whose chief city was Rome. Oscan and Umbrian have long been thought to be sister languages of Latin within the **Italic** subfamily, but now it appears they may be members of an independent branch of Indo-European whose resemblance to Latin is due to the long period of contact between their speakers. It is well known that languages, even unrelated ones, that are spoken in the same area and share bilingual speakers (in an association called a **Sprachbund**), will influence one another and thus grow more alike.

Whatever its relationship to Osco-Umbrian, Latin early became the most important language of the peninsula. As Rome came to dominate the

Mediterranean world, spreading its influence into Gaul, Spain, and the Illyrian and Danubian countries (and even into Britain, where it failed to displace Celtic), its language became a koine as the dialect of Athens had done.

Spoken Latin, as has been noted, survives in the **Romance** languages. It was quite a different thing from the more or less artificial literary language of Cicero. All the Romance languages—such as Italian, Spanish, Catalan, Galician, Portuguese, French, Provençal, and Romanian—are developments of the **Vulgar Latin** (so called because it was the speech of the *vulgus* 'common people') spoken in various parts of the Roman Empire in the early Middle Ages.

French dialects have included Norman, the source of the Anglo-Norman dialect spoken in England after the Norman Conquest; Picard; and the dialect of Paris and the surrounding regions (the Île-de-France), which for obvious reasons became standard French. In southern Belgium a dialect of French, called Walloon, is spoken. The highly similar varieties of French spoken in Quebec, Nova Scotia, New Brunswick, and Louisiana are developments of the dialects of northern France and are no more to be regarded as "corruptions" of standard (Modern) French than American English is to be regarded as a corruption of the present British standard. The "Cajuns" (that is, Acadians) of Louisiana are descendants of exiles from Nova Scotia, which was earlier a French colony called Acadia.

The speech of the old kingdom of Castile, the largest and most important part of Spain, became standard Spanish. The fact that Spanish America was settled largely by people from Andalusia rather than from Castile accounts for the most important differences in pronunciation between Latin American Spanish and the standard language of Spain.

Because of the cultural preeminence of Tuscany during the Italian Renaissance, the speech of that region—and specifically of the city of Florence—became the standard of Italian speech. Both Dante and Petrarch wrote in this form of Italian. Rhaeto-Romanic comprises a number of dialects spoken in the most easterly Swiss canton called the Grisons (Ger. *Graubünden*) and in the Tyrol.

THE CELTIC LANGUAGES

Celtic shows such striking correspondences with Italic in certain parts of its verbal system and in inflectional endings as to indicate a relationship between them that is rather close, though not so close as that between Indic and Iranian or Baltic and Slavic. Some scholars therefore group them together as developments of a language that they call Italo-Celtic.

The Celts were spread over a huge territory in Europe long before the emergence in history of the Germanic peoples. Before the beginning of the Christian era, Celtic languages were spoken over the greater part of central and western Europe. By the latter part of the third century B.C. Celts had spread even to Asia Minor, in the region called for them Galatia (part of modern Turkey), to whose inhabitants Paul later addressed a famous letter. As the fortunes and the warlike vigor of the Celts declined, their languages were supplanted by those of their conquerors. Thus the Celtic language spoken in Gaul (Gaulish) gave way completely to the Latin spoken by the Roman conquerors, which was to develop into French.

Roman rule did not prevent the British Celts from using their own language, although they borrowed a good many words from Latin. But after the Angles, Saxons, and Jutes arrived—British (Brythonic) Celtic was more severely threatened. It survived, however, and produced a distinguished literature in the later Middle Ages, including the *Mabinogion* and many Arthurian stories. In recent years Welsh (Cymric) has been actively promoted for nationalistic reasons. Breton is the language of the descendants of those Britons who, around the time of the Anglo-Saxon invasion of their island and even somewhat before that time, crossed the Channel and settled in the Gaulish province of Armorica, naming their new home for their old one— Brittany. Breton is thus more closely related to Welsh than to long-extinct Gaulish. There have been no native speakers of Cornish, another Brythonic language, since the early nineteenth century. Efforts have been made to revive it: church services are sometimes conducted in Cornish, and the language is used in antiquarian re-creations of the Celtic Midsummer Eve rituals—but such efforts seem more sentimental than practical.

It is not known whether Pictish, preserved in a few glosses and place-name elements, was a Celtic language. It was spoken by the Picts in the north-western part of Britain, where many Gaelic Celts also settled. These settlers from Ireland, who were called Scots (*Scotti*), named their new home Scotia, or Scotland. The Celtic language that spread from Ireland, called Gaelic or Goidelic, was of a type somewhat different from that of the Britons. It survives in Scots Gaelic, sometimes called Erse, a word that is simply a variant of *Irish*. Gaelic is spoken in the remoter parts of the Scottish high-lands and the Outer Hebrides and in Nova Scotia; in a somewhat different development it survived until recently on the Isle of Man (where it was called Manx).

In Ireland, which was little affected by either the Roman or the later Anglo-Saxon invasions, Irish Gaelic was gradually replaced by English. It has survived in some of the western counties, though most of its speakers are now bilingual. Efforts have been made to revive the language for national-istic reasons in Eire, and it is taught in schools throughout the land; but this resuscitation, less successful than that of Hebrew in modern Israel, cannot be regarded as in any sense a natural development. In striking contrast to their wide distribution in earlier times, today the Celtic languages are re-stricted to a few relatively small areas dotting the Atlantic Ocean on the northwest coast of Europe.

The Main Divisions of the Indo-European Group

The **Germanic** group merits a somewhat fuller treatment than has been given to any of the other groups because English belongs to it. In the course of many centuries certain radical developments occurred in the more or less unified language spoken by those Indo-European peoples living in Denmark and the regions thereabout. The period during which these developments were occurring we may refer to as **Pre-Germanic**. **Proto-Germanic** (or simply **Germanic**) is the usual term for the relatively unified language—distinctive in many of its sounds, its inflections, its accentual system, and its word stock—which resulted from these developments.

Unfortunately for us, those who spoke this particular development of Indo-European did not write. Proto-Germanic is to German, Dutch, the Scandinavian languages, and English as Latin is to Italian, French, and Spanish. But Proto-Germanic, which was probably being spoken shortly before the beginning of the Christian era, must be reconstructed just like Indo-European, whereas Latin is amply recorded.

Spread over a large area as Germanic in time came to be, it was inevitable that more and more marked dialectal differences should have occurred, leading to a division into North Germanic, West Germanic, and East Germanic. The **North Germanic** languages are Danish, Swedish, Norwegian, Icelandic, and Faeroese, the last named highly similar to Icelandic and spoken in the Faeroe Islands, located in the North Atlantic about midway between Iceland and Great Britain. The **West Germanic** languages are High German, Low German (*Plattdeutsch*), Dutch (and the practically identical Flemish), Frisian, and English. Yiddish (Judeo-German) is a development of a number of medieval High German dialects, with many words from Hebrew and Slavic. Before World War II, it was a sort of international language of the Jews, with a literature of high quality. Since that time it has declined greatly in use, with most Jews adopting the language of the country in which they live. The decline of Yiddish has doubtless been accelerated by the revival of Hebrew in Israel. Afrikaans is a development of seventeenth-century Dutch spoken in South Africa.

The only **East Germanic** language of which we have any detailed knowledge is Gothic. The earliest records in any Germanic language, aside from a few proper names recorded by classical authors, a few loanwords in Finnish, and some runic inscriptions found in Scandinavia, are those of Gothic.[6] For almost all our knowledge of Gothic we are indebted to a translation of parts of the New Testament made in the fourth century by Wulfila (*Ulfilas* to the Greeks), bishop of the Visigoths, those Goths who lived north of the Danube.

---

[6] *Gothic* was in the seventeenth and eighteenth centuries extended to mean 'Germanic,' even in the linguistic sense, but this meaning is now obsolete. It also came to mean 'romantically medieval'—a meaning that survives in the name of a fictional genre (*Gothic novel*) and of a style of architecture.

There are also small fragments of two other books of the Bible and of a commentary on the Gospel of John. Late as they are in comparison with the literary records of Sanskrit, Iranian, Greek, and Latin, these remains of Gothic provide us with a clear picture of a Germanic language in an early stage of development and hence are of tremendous importance to the student of Germanic languages. Etymological dictionaries of English cite Gothic cognates of English words (for instance, *light–leihts*, *find–finþan*) when the related Gothic form occurs in the literature cited above. Gothic as a spoken tongue disappeared a long time ago without leaving a trace. No modern Germanic languages are derived from it, nor are there any Gothic loanwords in any of the Germanic languages. Vandalic and Burgundian were apparently also East Germanic in structure, but we know little more of them at first hand than a few proper names.

Cognate Words in the Indo-European Languages

Words of similar structure and of similar or in many instances identical meanings in the various languages of the Indo-European group may be recognized as **cognate**—that is, of common origin (Lat. *co-* and *gnātus* 'born together'), once one knows what to expect in the way of sound shifting. Thus the verb roots meaning 'bear, carry' in Sanskrit (*bhar-*), Greek (*pher-*), Latin (*fer-*), Gothic (*bair-*), and Old English (*ber-*) are of common origin, all being developments of Indo-European **bher-*.[7] Cognate words do not necessarily look much alike: their resemblance may be disguised by sound shifts that have occurred in the various languages of the Indo-European group. (These languages may also be referred to as cognate.) English *work* and Greek *ergon*, for example, are superficially unlike, but they are both developments of Indo-European **wergom* and therefore are cognates. Sometimes, however, there is greater similarity—for example, between Latin *ignis* and Sanskrit *agnis* from Indo-European **egnis* 'fire.'

The most frequently cited cognate words are those that have been preserved in a large number of Indo-European languages; some have in fact been preserved in all. These common related words include the numerals from one to ten; the word meaning the sum of ten tens (*cent-*, *sat-*, *hund-*) in various quite dissimilar-looking but nonetheless quite regular developments;

---

[7] An asterisk before a form indicates that it is a **reconstruction** of what can be assumed to have existed on the basis of comparative study. Since Indo-European was spoken only in prehistoric times, all forms cited as existing in that language are necessarily reconstructions; the same is true of cited forms of any language in a prehistoric stage—for instance, Germanic and very early Old English. The asterisk is also placed before a form assumed to have been current during the historical period though not actually recorded. Square brackets are unnecessary in the discussion of prehistoric sound changes, since it is obvious that the letters under these circumstances are used exclusively as phonetic symbols.

words for certain bodily parts (related, for example, to *heart, lung, head, foot*); words for certain natural phenomena (related, for example, to *air, night, star, snow, sun, moon, wind*); certain plant and animal names (related, for example, to *beech, corn, wolf, bear*); and certain cultural terms (related, for example, to *yoke, mead, weave, sew*). It is interesting to note in passing that cognates of practically all of our taboo words—those monosyllables that pertain to sex and excretion and that seem to cause great pain to many people—are to be found in other Indo-European languages. Historically, if not socially, those ancient words are just as legitimate as any other words.

One needs no special training to perceive the correspondences between the following words:

LATIN	GREEK	WELSH	ENGLISH	ICELANDIC	DUTCH
ūnus	oinē[8]	un	one	einn	een
duo	duo	dau	two	tveir	twee
trēs	treis	tri	three	þrír	drie

Comparison of the forms designating the second digit indicates that non-Germanic *d* (as in the Latin, Greek, and Welsh forms) corresponds to Germanic *t* (English, Icelandic, and Dutch). A similar comparison of the forms for the third digit indicates that non-Germanic *t* corresponds to Germanic θ, the initial sound of *three* and *þrír* in English and Icelandic. Allowing for later changes—as in the case of θ, which became *d* in Dutch, as also in German (*drei* 'three'), and *t* in Danish, Norwegian, and Swedish (*tre*)—these same correspondences are perfectly regular in other cognates in which the consonants in question appear. We may safely assume that the non-Germanic consonants are older than the Germanic ones. Hence we may accept with confidence (assuming a similar comparison of the vowel systems) the reconstructions **oinos, *dwō, *treyes* as accurately representing the Indo-European forms from which the existing forms have developed. The comparative linguists, of course, have used all the Indo-European languages as a basis for their conclusions regarding correspondences, not just a few such as are cited here.

Inflection in the Indo-European Languages

All the Indo-European languages are **inflective**—that is, all are characterized by a grammatical system based on modifications in the form of words, by means of **inflections** (that is, endings and vowel changes),[9] to indicate such

[8] 'One-spot on a die.'

[9] As in Modern English *boy–boys; who–whom–whose; walk–walks–walked–walking; man–man's–men–men's; sing–sings–sang–singing.*

grammatical functions as case, number, tense, person, mood, aspect, and the like. The older inflectional system is very imperfectly represented in most modern languages: English, French, and Spanish, for instance, have lost much of the inflectional complexity that was once characteristic of them; German retains considerably more, with its various forms of the noun and the article and its strong adjective declension. Sanskrit is notable for the remarkably clear picture it gives us of the older Indo-European inflectional system; it retains much that has been lost or changed in the other Indo-European languages, so that its forms show us, even better than Greek or Latin can, what the system of Indo-European must have been.

SOME VERB INFLECTIONS

Once one understands and makes allowances for the regularly occurring sound changes, the relationship of the personal endings of the verb in the various Indo-European languages becomes clear. For example, the present indicative of the Sanskrit verb corresponding to English *to bear* runs as follows:

SANSKRIT

bharā-mi	'I bear'
bhara-si	'thou bearest'
bhara-ti	'he beareth'
bharā-mas	'we bear'
bhara-tha	'you bear'
bhara-nti	'they bear'

The only irregularity here is the occurrence of *-mi* in the first person singular, as against *-ō* in the Greek and Latin forms to be cited immediately below. It was a peculiarity of Sanskrit to extend *-mi*, the regular first person ending of verbs that had no vowel affixed to their roots, to those that did have such a vowel.[10]

Leaving out of consideration for the moment differences in vowels and in initial consonants, compare now the present indicative forms as they have developed from Indo-European into Greek and Latin, with special regard to the personal endings:

[10] This vowel (for example, the *-a* suffixed to the root *bhar-* of the Sanskrit word cited) is called the **thematic vowel**. The root of a word plus such a suffix is called the **stem**. To these stems are added endings. The comparatively few verbs lacking such a vowel in Indo-European are called **athematic**. The *m* in English *am* is a remnant of the Indo-European ending of such athematic verbs.

Inflection in the Indo-European Languages

GREEK	LATIN
pherō[11]	ferō[11]
pherei-s	fer-s[13]
pherei[12]	fer-t
phero-mes (Doric)	feri-mus
phere-te	fer-tis
phero-nti (Doric)	feru-nt

Comparison of the personal endings of the verbs in these and other languages leads to the conclusion that the Indo-European endings were as follows (the Indo-European reconstruction of the entire word is given in parentheses):

-ō, -mi	(*bherō)
-si	(*bheresi)
-ti	(*bhereti)
-mes, -mos	(*bheromes)
-te	(*bherete)
-nti	(*bheronti)

Note now in Gothic and early Old English the Germanic development of these personal endings:

GOTHIC	EARLY OLD ENGLISH
bair-a	ber-u, -o
bairi-s	biri-s
bairi-þ	biri-þ
baira-m	bera-þ[14]
bairi-þ	bera-þ
baira-nd	bera-þ

Germanic þ (that is, [θ]) corresponds as a rule to Proto-Indo-European t (see p. 91). Leaving out of consideration such details as the -nd (instead of

[11] In Indo-European thematic verbs the first person singular present indicative had no ending at all, but only a lengthening of the thematic vowel.

[12] The expected form would be phere-ti. The ending -ti, however, does occur elsewhere in the third person singular—for instance, in Doric didōti 'he gives.'

[13] In this verb the lack of the thematic vowel is exceptional. The expected forms would be feri-s, feri-t, feri-tis in the second and third persons singular and the second person plural, respectively.

[14] From the oldest period of Old English the form of the third person plural was used throughout the plural. This form, beraþ, from earlier *beranþ, shows Anglo-Frisian loss of n before þ.

expected -*nþ*) in the Gothic third person plural form, for which there is a soundly based explanation, it is perfectly clear that the Germanic personal endings correspond to those of the non-Germanic Indo-European languages.

SOME NOUN INFLECTIONS

Indo-European nouns were inflected for eight **cases**: nominative, vocative, accusative, genitive, dative, ablative, locative, and instrumental. The full array of cases is preserved in Sanskrit but not generally in the other descendant

INDO-EUROPEAN NOUN DECLENSION[15]

	INDO-EUROPEAN	SANSKRIT	GREEK	LATIN	OLD IRISH	OLD ENGLISH
Singular						
Nom.	*ekwos	aśvas	hippos	equus	ech	eoh
Voc.	*ekwe	aśva	hippe	eque	eich	
Acc.	*ekwom	aśvam	hippon	equum	ech n-	eoh
Gen.	*ekwosyo	aśvasya	hippou	equī	eich	ēos
Dat.	*ekwōy	aśvāya	hippōi	equō	eoch	ēo
Abl.	*ekwōd	aśvād		equō		
Loc.	*ekwoy	aśve				
Ins.	*ekwō	aśvena				
Plural						
N.–V.	*ekwōs	aśvās	hippoi	equī	eich	ēos
Acc.	*ekwons	aśvān(s)	hippous	equōs	eochu	ēos
Gen.	*ekwōm	aśvānām	hippōn	equōrum	ech n-	ēona
D.–Ab.	*ekwobh(y)os	aśvebhyas	hippois	equīs	echaib	ēom
Loc.	*ekwoysu	aśveṣu				
Ins.	*ekwōys	aśvais				

[15] There are a good many complexities in these forms, some of which are noted here. In Greek, for the genitive singular, the Homeric form *hippoio* is closer to Indo-European in its ending. The Greek, Latin, and Old Irish nominative plurals show developments of the pronominal ending *-oi*, rather than of the nominal ending *-ōs*. Celtic was alone among the Indo-European branches in having different forms for the nominative and vocative plural; the Old Irish vocative plural was *eochu* (like the accusative plural), a development of the original nominative plural *ekwōs*. The Greek and Latin dative-ablative plurals were originally instrumental forms that took over the functions of the other cases; similarly, the Old Irish dative plural was probably a variant instrumental form. The Latin genitive singular -*ī* is not from the corresponding Indo-European ending, but is a special ending found in Italic and Celtic (OIr. *eich* being from the variant *ekwī*). The Old Irish *n*- in the accusative singular and genitive plural is the initial consonant of the following word.

Inflection in the Indo-European Languages

languages, which simplified the noun declension in various ways. The paradigms in the accompanying table show the singular and plural of the word for 'horse' in Proto-Indo-European and five other Indo-European languages. Indo-European also had a dual number for designating two of anything, which is not illustrated.

Word Order in the Indo-European Languages

Early studies of the Indo-European languages focused on cognate words and on inflections. More recently attention has been directed to other matters of the grammar, especially word order in the parent language. Joseph Greenberg, in "Some Universals of Grammar" (1962), has proposed that the orders in which various grammatical elements occur in a sentence are not random, but are interrelated. For example, languages like Modern English that place objects after verbs tend to place modifiers after nouns, to put conjunctions before the second of two words they connect, and to use prepositions:

verb + OBJECT: (The workman) made *a horn.*
noun + MODIFIER: (They marveled at the) size *of the building.*
conjunction + NOUN: (Congress is divided into the Senate) and *the House.*
preposition + OBJECT: (Harold fought) with *him.*

On the other hand, languages like Japanese that place objects before verbs tend to reverse the order of those other elements, placing modifiers before nouns, putting conjunctions after the second of two words they connect, and using postpositions. Most languages can be identified as basically either **VO languages** (like English) or **OV languages** (like Japanese), although it is usual for a language to have some characteristics of both types. English, for example, regularly puts adjectives before the nouns they modify rather than after them, as VO order would imply.

In articles published in *PMLA* (1972) and *Language* (1973), Winfred P. Lehmann has marshaled evidence suggesting that Proto-Indo-European was an OV language, even though the existing Indo-European languages are generally VO in type. Earlier stages of those languages often show OV characteristics that have been lost from the modern tongues or that are less common than formerly. For example, one of the oldest records of a Germanic language is a runic inscription identifying the workman who made a horn about A.D. 400:

ek hlewagastiʀ holtijaʀ   horna tawido
I, Hlewagastiʀ Holtson, [this] horn   made.

The order of words in sentences like this one (subject, object, verb) suggests that Proto-Germanic had more OV characteristics than the languages that evolved from it.

In standard Modern German a possessive modifier, as in *der Garten des Mannes* 'the garden of the man,' normally follows the word it modifies; the other order—*des Mannes Garten* 'the man's garden'—is possible, but it is poetic and old-fashioned. In older periods of the language, however, it was normal. Similarly, in Modern English a possessive modifier can come either before a noun (an OV characteristic), as in *the building's size*, or after it (a VO characteristic), as in *the size of the building*, but there has long been a tendency to favor the second order, which has increased in frequency throughout the recorded history of English under the influence of French, from which the phrasal genitive with *of* (translating Fr. *de*) was perhaps borrowed.

When we want to join two words, we put the conjunction before the second one (a VO characteristic), as in *the Senate and people*, but Latin, preserving an archaic feature of Indo-European, had the option of putting a conjunction after the second noun (an OV characteristic), as in *senatus populusque*, in which *-que* is a conjunction meaning 'and.' Modern English uses prepositions almost exclusively, but Old English often put such words after their objects, using them as postpositions, thus:

> Harold him wið gefeaht
> Harold him with fought.

Evidence of this kind, which can be found in all the older forms of Indo-European and which becomes more frequent the farther back in history one searches, suggests to some linguists that Indo-European once ordered its verbs after their objects. If that is so, by late Indo-European times a change had begun that was to result in a shift of word-order type in many of the descendant languages. This kind of reconstruction depends not only on comparing languages with one another but also on comparing different historical stages of the same language, and it assumes that various kinds of word order are interconnected. For those reasons it is less certain than the reconstruction of inflections and of vocabulary.

Indo-European Culture

On the basis of cognate words, we can infer a good deal about the state of culture attained by the Indo-Europeans before the various migrations began that carried them from their original homeland to many parts of Europe and Asia.[16] Those migrations started probably during the third or

---

[16] See Calvert Watkins, "Indo-European and the Indo-Europeans," particularly the subsection "Lexicon and Culture," in the Appendix to *The American Heritage Dictionary of the English Language* (1976). In an appendix to this Appendix ("Guide to the Appendix"), Watkins lists the Indo-European stems that occur in items listed in the dictionary proper. It all makes for fascinating, and at the same time rewarding, browsing.

fourth millennium B.C. The Indo-Europeans' culture was considerably more advanced than that of some groups of people living today. They had a clear sense of family relationship and hence of the family organization, and they could count. They made use of gold and perhaps silver as well; copper and iron were not to come until later. They drank a honey-based alcoholic beverage whose name has come down to us as *mead*. Words corresponding to *wheel, axle*, and *yoke* make it perfectly clear that they used wheeled vehicles. They were small farmers, not nomads, who worked their fields with plows, and they had domesticated animals and fowl. They had religious feeling, with a conception of multiple gods. This much we can say on the basis of forms that were not actually recorded until long after Indo-European had ceased to be a more or less unified language.

The Indo-European Homeland

Conjectures differ as to the original Indo-European homeland—or at least the earliest for which we have any evidence. Plant and animal names are important clues. The existence of cognates denoting trees that grow in temperate climates (*alder, apple, ash, aspen, beech, birch, elm, hazel, linden, oak, willow, yew*), coupled with the absence of such related words for Mediterranean or Asiatic trees (*olive, cypress, palm*); the similar occurrence of cognates of *wolf, bear, lax*[17] (Old English *leax* 'salmon'), and of a word signifying 'turtle,' but none for creatures indigenous to Asia—all this points to an area between northern Europe and southern Russia as the predispersion home, just as the absence of a common word for *ocean* indicates, though it does not in itself prove, that this homeland was inland.

Paul Thieme, in his cogently reasoned *Die Heimat der indogermanischen Gemeinsprache* (1954) and in "The Indo-European Language" (1958), localizes the Indo-European homeland in the northern part of central Europe, between the Vistula and the Elbe, on the basis of evidence adduced from the prehistoric geographical distribution of the beech, the turtle, and the salmon. Other Indo-Europeanists have argued from similar evidence for southern Russia, the Carpathians, Scandinavia, and southwestern Asia.

Marija Gimbutas, in a number of essays, including "The Beginning of the Bronze Age in Europe and the Indo-Europeans" (1973), would identify the early Indo-Europeans with the "Kurgan" culture of mound builders who lived northwest of the Caucasus and north of the Caspian Sea as early as the fifth millennium B.C. They had domesticated cattle and horses, which they kept for milk and meat as well as for transportation. They combined farming with herding and were a mobile people, using four-wheeled wagons to cart

[17] This word seems to have gone out of general use in English a long time ago. Its Yiddish cognate (written *lox*, in German *Lachs*) has recently entered English as a loanword. There are cognates in Lithuanian, Old Prussian, Russian, Tocharian, and other languages.

their belongings on their treks. They built fortified palaces on hilltops (we have the Indo-European word for such forts in the *polis* of place names like *Indianapolis* and in our word *police*) as well as small villages nearby. Their society was a stratified one, with a warrior nobility and a common laboring class. They worshiped a sky god associated with thunder; the sun, the horse, the boar, and the snake also were important in their religion. They had a highly developed belief in life after death, which led them to the construction of elaborate burial sites, by which their culture can be traced over much of Europe. Early in the fourth millennium B.C., they began expanding into the Balkans and northern Europe, and thereafter into Iran, Anatolia, and southern Europe. We cannot be sure that the Kurgan people were the original Indo-Europeans, but their culture makes the identification a likely one.

The Major Changes from Indo-European to Germanic

One group of Indo-European speakers, the Germanic group, settled in northern Europe near Denmark. Germanic became differentiated from Indo-European principally in the following respects:

1. Germanic has a large number of words that have no known cognates in other Indo-European languages. These could have existed, of course, in Indo-European and have been lost; it is also possible that they were taken from non-Indo-European languages originally spoken in the area occupied by the Germanic peoples. A few words that are apparently distinctively Germanic, given in their Modern English forms, are *broad, drink, drive, fowl, hold, meat, rain,* and *wife.*

2. All Indo-European distinctions of tense and aspect were lost in the verb save for the **present** and the **preterit** (or past) tenses. This simplification of a more complex Indo-European verbal system (though it was not so complex as what developed in Latin, Greek, and Sanskrit) is reflected in all the languages which have developed out of Germanic—in English *bind–bound,* as well as in German *binden–band,* Old Norse *binda–band,* and all the rest. There is in no Germanic language anything comparable to such forms as those of the Latin future, perfect, pluperfect, and future perfect forms (for instance, *laudābō, laudāvī, laudāveram, laudāverō*), which must be rendered in the Germanic languages by verb phrases (for instance, English *I shall praise, I have praised, I had praised, I shall have praised*).

3. Germanic developed a preterit tense form with a **dental suffix**, that is, one containing *d* or *t*. All Germanic languages thus have two types of verbs. Verbs that employ the dental suffix were called **weak** by Jacob Grimm because, being incapable of the type of internal change of *rise–rose* and *sing–sang* (which he called **strong**), they had to make do with suffixes, like *step–stepped* and *talk–talked*. Although Grimm's terminology is not very satisfactory, it has become traditional. An overwhelming majority of our verbs add the dental suffix in the preterit—it is indeed the only living method of inflection for tense in English as in all the other Germanic languages—and this method has thus been thought of as "regular." (For example, new verbs form their preterit so: *elbow–elbowed, televise–televised, rev–revved,* and so forth. Furthermore, as we shall see later, many verbs that were once strong have become weak.) Historically speaking, however, the vowel gradation of the strong verbs is quite regular, and some of the weak verbs are quite irregular. *Bring, think,* and *buy,* for instance, are weak verbs, as the dental suffix of *brought, thought,* and *bought* indicates; the vowel changes do not make them strong verbs. The suffix is the real test. No attempt at explaining the origin of this suffix has been wholly satisfactory. Many have thought that it was originally an independent word meaning, and cognate with, *do.*

4. All the older forms of Germanic had two ways of declining their adjectives. The **weak declension** was used chiefly when preceded by a pronominal adjective, including the demonstrative pronoun that developed into the definite article. The **strong declension** was used otherwise. Thus Old English had *þā geongan ceorlas* 'the young fellows (churls),' with the weak form of *geong,* but *geonge ceorlas* 'young fellows,' with the strong form; the distinction is preserved in present-day German, *die jungen Kerle,* but *junge Kerle.* This particular Germanic characteristic cannot be illustrated in Modern English, inasmuch as in the course of its development English has lost all such declension of the adjective.

5. The "free" accentual system of Indo-European, in which any syllable of a word might be accented, gave way to another type of accentuation in which the first syllable was regularly stressed in all words except verbs like modern *believe* and *forget*—that is, verbs in which the initial syllable was a prefix. None of the Germanic languages has anything comparable to the shifting accentuation of Latin *vírī* 'men,' *virốrum* 'of the men' or of *hábeō* 'I have,' *habḗmus* 'we have.' Compare the paradigms of the Greek and Old English developments of Indo-European **pǝtḗr* 'father':

	GREEK	OLD ENGLISH
Singular nominative	patḗr	fæder
Singular genitive	patrós	fæder(es)
Singular dative	patrí	fæder
Singular accusative	patéra	fæder
Singular vocative	páter	fæder
Plural nominative	patéres	fæderas
Plural genitive	patérōn	fædera
Plural dative	patrási	fæderum
Plural accusative	patéras	fæderas

In these paradigms it will be noted that in the Greek forms the accent may occur on the suffix, the ending, or the root, unlike the Old English forms, which are representative of the Germanic accentual system in having their accent fixed on the first syllable of the root. Germanic accent is predominantly a matter of **stress** (loudness) rather than **pitch** (tone); Indo-European would seem to have had both types of accent at different stages of its development.

6. Indo-European vowels underwent Germanic modification. Indo-European *o*, retained in Latin, became *a* (compare Lat. *octo* 'eight,' Gothic *ahtau*); Indo-European *ā* became *ō* (Lat. *māter* 'mother,' OE *mōdor*); and there were other changes as well, which we shall not go into here.

7. The Indo-European stops *bh, dh, gh, p, t, k, b, d,* and *g*—that is, the *sounds* later symbolized by these letters—all underwent modification in what is called the **First Sound Shift** or **Grimm's Law**. These modifications were gradual, extending over rather long periods of time. The sounds appear in Germanic languages as respectively *b, d, g, f, θ, h, p, t,* and *k*.

Grimm's Law

Because the First Sound Shift, described by Grimm's Law, is such an important difference between Germanic and other Indo-European languages, we may illustrate it more fully by a series of forms consisting of a reconstructed Indo-European root or word (omitting the usual asterisk for convenience), the corresponding word from a non-Germanic language (usually Latin), and the corresponding English word.[18]

1. Indo-European *bh, dh, gh* became, respectively, the Germanic sounds *β, ð, γ,*[19] and later, in initial position at least, *b, d, g*. Stated in phonetic terms, aspirated voiced stops became voiced fricatives and then unaspirated voiced stops. These Indo-European aspirated sounds also underwent changes in most non-Germanic languages. Their developments in Latin, Greek, and Germanic are shown in the following table:

---

[18] Derivatives of many of the Latin and Greek cognates to be cited below occur in English as loanwords, some having entered by way of French. Compare, for instance, such pairs as *fraternity–brotherhood, fragile–breakable, fundament–bottom, horticulture–gardening, paternal–fatherly, pyrotechnics–fireworks, pedal–foot, tenuous–thin, cornet–horn, cordial–hearty, canine–hound, gelid–cold,* and so forth.

[19] The *β* symbolizes a voiced bilabial fricative, the sound symbolized in Spanish by *b* or *v*. The *ð* stands for the initial consonant of *them*. The *γ* indicates a voiced velar fricative (IPA [ɣ]). Authorities identify it with the medial consonant of North German *sagen*; but, unless one has a North German handy, this is of little help. It is made like [g], but with the back of the tongue not quite touching the roof of the mouth. In old English, the voiced velar fricative remained in some positions but became [g] or [y] in others.

Indo-European	bh	dh	gh
Latin[20]	f-	f-	h-
Greek[21]	φ	θ	χ
Germanic	b	d	g

Unless these non-Germanic changes are borne in mind, the examples cited below will not make sense:[22]

INDO-EUROPEAN *bh* (LATIN *f-*, GREEK *ph*)/GERMANIC *b*

---

bhrāter/frāter/brother
bhibhru-/fiber/beaver
bhlē-/flāre/blow
bhreg-/fra(n)go/break
bhudh-/fundus (*for* *fudnus)/bottom
bhāgo-/fāgus/beech
bhəg-/(Gr.) phōgein 'to roast'/bake

INDO-EUROPEAN *dh* (LATIN *f-*, GREEK *th*)/GERMANIC *d*

---

dheigh-/fi(n)gere 'to mold'/dough
dhwer-/foris/door
dhē-/(Gr.) thē- 'to place'/do
dhug(h)ətēr/(Gr.) thugatēr/daughter

INDO-EUROPEAN *gh* (LATIN *h-*, GREEK *ch*)/GERMANIC *g*

---

ghordho-/hortus/OE geard 'yard'
ghosti-/hostis/guest
ghomon-/homo/gome (obsolete)
ghol-/(Gr.) cholē (*whence* cholera)/gall
ghed-/(pre)he(n)dere 'to take'/get
ghaido-/haedus 'kid'/goat

[20] In Latin the sounds developed differently in initial position (shown above) and in medial position in a word. Medially, the sounds became, respectively, *b*, *d* or *b* depending on contiguous sounds, and *g* before or after a consonant.

[21] The Greek sounds were pronounced, respectively, [pʰ], [tʰ], and [kʰ], and are customarily transcribed *ph*, *th*, and *ch*.

[22] Only a single Indo-European root is given for each set, although the following two words may be derived from slightly different forms of that root. Therefore, the correspondence between the two words and the Indo-European root may not be exact in all details other than the initial consonants.

2. Except when preceded by *s*, the Indo-European voiceless stops *p*, *t*, *k* became, respectively, the voiceless fricatives *f*, *θ*, *x*[23] (later *h* in initial position):

INDO-EUROPEAN *p* / GERMANIC *f*

pətēr / pater / father
pisk- / piscis / fish
pel- / pellis / fell 'animal hide'
pūr- / (Gr.) pūr / fire
prtu- / portus / ford
pulo- / pullus / foal
ped- / ped(em) / foot
peku- / pecu 'cattle' / fee (*cf.* Ger. Vieh 'cattle')

INDO-EUROPEAN *t* / GERMANIC *θ*

treyes / trēs / three
ters- / torrēre 'to dry' / thirst
tū / tū / OE þū 'thou'
ten- / tenuis / thin
tum- / tumēre 'to swell' / thumb (*that is,* fat finger)
tonə- / tonāre / thunder

INDO-EUROPEAN *k* / GERMANIC *h*

krn- / cornū / horn
kerd- / cord- / heart
kwod / quod / what (OE hwæt)
ker- / cervus / hart
kmtom / cent- / hund(red)
kel- / cēlāre 'to hide' / hall, hell
kap- / capere 'to take' / heave, have

3. The Indo-European voiced stops *b*, *d*, *g* became, respectively, the voiceless stops *p*, *t*, *k*.

INDO-EUROPEAN *b* / GERMANIC *p*

abel- / (Russ.) jabloko / apple

[23] That is, the velar fricative and doubtless also its palatal allophone. The *x* is thus used here without brackets and similarly throughout this chapter with the value that it has in the alphabet of the International Phonetic Association. (IPA uses [ç] for the more forward variety.) It should not be confused with the letter *x* as used since Old English times to spell [ks].

Grimm's Law

Initial *b* was very infrequent in Indo-European. Greek *kannabis* and Old Norse *hampr* (Eng. *hemp*) have been cited as showing the correspondence of *b* and *p*, as have Latin *turba* 'crowd' and English *thorp* 'town' (as in *Halethorp* and *Winthrop*) and Lithuanian *dubùs* and English *deep*. Other certain examples are hard to come by.

INDO-EUROPEAN *d*/GERMANIC *t*

---

dwō/duo/two
dent-/dentis/tooth
demə-/domāre/tame
drew-/(Gr.) drūs 'oak'/tree
dekm/decem/ten (Gothic taíhun)
ed-/edere/eat

INDO-EUROPEAN *g*/GERMANIC *k*

---

genu-/genu/knee (*loss of* [k-] *is modern*)
agro-/ager 'field'/acre
genə-/genus/kin
gwen-/(Gr.) gunē 'woman'/queen, quean
grəno-/grānum/corn
gnō-/(g)nōscere/know, can

Although we cannot be sure of the chronology of these consonant changes, it is likely that they stretched over centuries—perhaps as much as a millennium. Each set of shifts was completed before the next began; the First Sound Shift was no circular process. It is obvious, for instance, that the shift of Indo-European *b*, *d*, and *g* to Germanic *p*, *t*, and *k* must have occurred after Indo-European *p*, *t*, and *k* had become Germanic *f*, *θ*, and *x*; otherwise, the Germanic *p*, *t*, and *k* from Indo-European *b*, *d*, and *g* would have gone on to become *f*, *θ*, and *x* also, and we should have no native words with *p*, *t*, and *k*.

FIRST SOUND SHIFT (GRIMM'S LAW)

IE bh, dh, gh ⟶ (respectively) **Gmc β, ð, γ** ⟶ **b, d, g**
IE p, t, k ⟶ (respectively) **Gmc f, θ, x** (→ **h** initially)
IE b, d, g ⟶ (respectively) **Gmc p, t, k**

Some words in the Germanic languages appear to have an irregular development of Indo-European *p*, *t*, and *k*. Instead of the expected *f*, *θ*, and *x* (or *h*), we find *β*, *ð*, and *γ* (or their later developments). For example, Indo-European *pətḗr* (represented by Latin *pater* and Greek *patḗr*) would have been expected to appear in Germanic with a medial *θ*. Instead we find Gothic *fadar* (with *d* representing [ð]), Icelandic *faðir*, and Old English *fæder* (in which the *d* is a West Germanic development of earlier [ð]). It appears that Indo-European *t* has become *ð* instead of *θ*.

This seeming anomaly was explained by a Danish scholar named Karl Verner in 1875. Verner noticed that the Proto-Germanic voiceless fricatives (*f*, *θ*, *x*, and *s*) became voiced fricatives (*β*, *ð*, *γ*, and *z*) unless they were prevented by any of three conditions: (1) being the first sound in a word, (2) being next to another voiceless sound, or (3) having the Indo-European stress on the immediately preceding syllable. Thus the *t* of Indo-European *pətḗr* became *θ*, as Grimm's Law predicts it should; but then, because the word is stressed on its second syllable and the *θ* is neither initial nor next to a voiceless sound, that fricative voiced to *ð*.

Verner's Law is that in Proto-Germanic voiceless fricatives became voiced when they were in a voiced environment and the Indo-European stress was not on the immediately preceding syllable. The law was obscured by the fact that, after it had operated, the stress on Germanic words shifted to the first syllable of the root, thus effectively disguising one of its important conditions. The effect of stress on voicing can be observed in some Modern English words of foreign origin, such as *exert* [ɪgzə́rt] and *exist* [ɪgzíst] (compare *exercise* [ɛ́ksərsàɪz] and *exigent* [ɛ́ksɪjənt]). The later history of the voiced fricatives

---

VERNER'S LAW

Later developments in the various Germanic languages that have obscured the workings of the shift are not indicated in the table below.

	GRIMM'S LAW		VERNER'S LAW		STRESS SHIFT	
IE	−p–	⟶ Gmc	−f–	⟶	−β–	⟶	´β–
IE	−t–	⟶ Gmc	−θ–	⟶	−ð–	⟶	´ð– (→ WGmc ´d–)
IE	−k–	⟶ Gmc	−x–	⟶	−γ–	⟶	´γ–
IE	−s–	Gmc	−s–	⟶	−z–	⟶	´z– (→ ´r– except in Gothic)

---

resulting from Verner's Law is the same as that of the voiced fricatives that developed from Indo-European *bh*, *dh*, and *gh*. The *z* that developed from earlier *s* appears as *r* in all recorded Germanic languages except Gothic.[24]

West Germanic Languages

The changes mentioned in the preceding section affected all of the Germanic languages, but among those languages other changes occurred that created three subgroups within the Germanic branch—North, East, and West Germanic. The three subgroups are distinguished from one another by a large number of linguistic features, of which we can mention six as typical:

1. The nominative singular of some nouns ended in -*az* in Proto-Germanic—for example, **wulfaz*. This ending appears as -*r* in North Germanic (Old Icelandic *ulfr*), as -*s* in East Germanic (Gothic *wulfs*), and disappears completely in West Germanic (Old High German *wolf*, Old English *wulf*).

2. In North Germanic the ending for the second person singular in the present tense of verbs came to be used also for the third person:

OLD ICELANDIC	GOTHIC	OLD ENGLISH	
bindr	bindis	bindest	(you bind)
bindr	bindiþ	bindeþ	(he binds)

3. North Germanic developed a definite article that was suffixed to nouns—for example, Old Icelandic *ulfr* 'wolf,' *ulfrinn* 'the wolf.' No such feature appears in East or West Germanic.

4. In East Germanic the *z* that resulted from Verner's Law appears as *s*, but in North and West Germanic as *r*: Gothic *auso*, Old Icelandic *eyra*, Old English *ēare* 'ear.'

5. North and West Germanic had vowel alternations called mutation (to be treated in the next chapter); for example, in Old Icelandic and Old English, the word for 'man' in the accusative singular was *mann*, while the corresponding plural was *menn*. No such alternation exists in Gothic, for which the parallel forms are singular *mannan* and plural *mannans*.

6. In West Germanic, the *ð* that resulted from Verner's Law appears as *d*, but remains a fricative in North and East Germanic: Old English *fæder*, Old Icelandic *faðir*, Gothic *faðar* (though spelled *fadar*).

---

[24] This shift of *z* to *r*, known as **rhotacism** (that is, *r*-ing, from Gr. *rho*, the name of the letter), is by no means peculiar to Germanic: compare Latin *flōs* 'flower,' which has *r* in all forms other than the nominative singular—for instance, the genitive singular *flōris*, from earlier **flōz-*, the original *s* being here voiced because of its position between vowels.

West Germanic itself was divided into smaller subgroups. For example, High German and Low German are distinguished by another change in the stop sounds—the **Second** or **High German Shift**—which occurred comparatively recently as linguistic history goes. It was nearing its completion by the end of the eighth century of our era. This shift began in the southern, mountainous part of Germany and spread northward, stopping short of the low-lying northern section of the country. The *high* in High German (*Hochdeutsch*) and the *low* in Low German (*Plattdeutsch*) refer only to relative distances above sea level. High German became in time standard German, relegating Low German to the status of a peasant patois in Germany.

The Continental home of the English was north of the area in which the High German Shift occurred. But even if this had not been so, the English language would have been unaffected by changes that had not begun to occur at the time of the Anglo-Saxon migrations to Britain, beginning as early as the mid-fifth century. Consequently English has the earlier consonantal characteristics of Germanic, which among the West Germanic languages it shares with Low German, Dutch, Flemish, and Frisian. We may illustrate the High German shift in part by contrasting English and High German forms, as follows:

Proto-Germanic *p* appears in High German as *pf* or, after vowels, as *ff* (*pepper–Pfeffer*).

Proto-Germanic *t* appears as *ts* (spelled *z*) or, after vowels, as *ss* (*tongue–Zunge*; *water–Wasser*).

Proto-Germanic *k* appears after vowels as *ch* (*break–brechen*).

Proto-Germanic *d* appears as *t* (*dance–tanzen*).

The German spoken by more or less simple folk in parts of northern Germany is a development of Old Saxon, and it alone now bears the proper name Low German (*Plattdeutsch*), though as we have seen it is only one type of Low German. Dutch and the practically identical Flemish are the modern forms of Low Franconian, spoken respectively in Holland and, side by side with French, in Belgium. Formerly spoken in a much larger area, including the west coast of Schleswig, Frisian has survived principally in the northern Dutch province of Friesland and in some of the islands off the coast. English and Frisian share certain features not found elsewhere in the Germanic group to such an extent that scholars regard them as a subgroup of West Germanic, developments of a relatively unified prehistoric language called Anglo-Frisian. Old English, Old Frisian, and Old Saxon, sometimes grouped together as Ingvaeonic,[25] share alike the older consonantal characteristics and are

---

[25] From the term used by Tacitus in *Germania* ii (in the form *Ingaevones*) for that group of the Germanic peoples who lived "near to the ocean" (*proximi Oceano*). The name is ultimately Germanic, appearing in Old English as *Ingwine* 'Ing's friends,' Ing having supposedly been a Germanic wonderworker. The *Beowulf* poet somehow connects the term with the Danes. It should be noted that Tacitus' division of the people of Germania into Ingaevones, Herminones, and Istaevones is very ancient and that Tacitus actually knew little about such divisions.

likewise distinguished from Old High German in other rather striking ways. One of these is the loss of nasal consonants before the fricatives *f*, *s*, and *þ*, with lengthening of the preceding vowel: compare (Old) High German *gans* with Old English *gōs* 'goose,' Old High German *fimf* (Modern German *fünf*) with Old English *fíf* 'five,' (Old) High German *mund* (Germanic **munþ-*) with Old English *mūð* 'mouth.' But Old English and Old Frisian are distinguished in equally striking ways from Old Saxon; hence the postulated Anglo-Frisian as the most immediate common source of English and Frisian.[26]

English, then, began its separate existence as a form of Germanic brought by pagan warrior-adventurers from the Continent to the then relatively obscure island that the Romans called Britannia and that had up until a short time before been part of their mighty empire. There, in the next five centuries or so, it was to develop into an independent language quite distinct from any Germanic language spoken on the Continent. Moreover, it had become a language sufficiently rich in its word stock, thanks largely to the impetus given to learning by the introduction of Christianity, that, as Kemp Malone (1948, p. 10) puts it, "by the year 1000, this newcomer could measure swords with Latin in every department of expression, and was incomparably superior to the French speech that came in with William of Normandy."

For Further Reading

History of Linguistics

Jankowsky, *The Neogrammarians: A Re-evaluation of Their Place in the Development of Linguistic Science*, 1972.

Lehmann, *A Reader in Nineteenth-Century Historical Indo-European Linguistics*, 1967.

Pedersen, *The Discovery of Language*, 1962.

Robins, *A Short History of Linguistics*, 1967.

Waterman, *Perspectives in Linguistics*, 1970.

Historical Change in Language

Anderson, *Structural Aspects of Language Change*, 1973.

Anderson and Jones, *Historical Linguistics*, 1974.

Anttila, *An Introduction to Historical and Comparative Linguistics*, 1972.

Bynon, *Historical Linguistics*, 1977.

King, *Historical Linguistics and Generative Grammar*, 1969.

---

[26] It is the belief of some scholars that the Old Saxon that we know mainly from two ninth-century poems (the *Heliand* and the *Genesis*) might have been influenced by Old High German and that in an earlier period Old Saxon might well have exhibited all those features usually regarded as peculiarly Old English and Old Frisian. The attested differences between Old Saxon and Anglo-Frisian are dealt with by Alistair Campbell (1959, pp. 2–3, 50–54, 173–79).

Lehmann, *Historical Linguistics: An Introduction*, 1973.
Palmer, *Descriptive and Comparative Linguistics: A Critical Introduction*, 1972.
Samuels, *Linguistic Evolution, with Special Reference to English*, 1972.
Stockwell and Macaulay, *Linguistic Change and Generative Theory*, 1972.

Indo-European Languages

Birnbaum and Puhvel, *Ancient Indo-European Dialects*, 1966.
Lehmann, "Contemporary Linguistics and Indo-European Studies," *PMLA*, 1972.
Lockwood, *A Panorama of Indo-European Languages*, 1972.
Thieme, "The Indo-European Language," *Scientific American*, 1958.

Indo-European Homeland and Culture

Bender, *The Home of the Indo-Europeans*, 1922.
Cardona, Hoenigswald, and Senn, *Indo-European and Indo-Europeans*, 1970.
Gimbutas, "The Beginning of the Bronze Age in Europe and the Indo-Europeans: 3500–2500 B.C.," *Journal of Indo-European Studies*, 1973.
Mallory, "A History of the Indo-European Problem," *Journal of Indo-European Studies*, 1973.
Puhvel, *Myth and Law among the Indo-Europeans*, 1970.

Germanic Languages

Bennett, *An Introduction to the Gothic Language*, 1980.
Coetsem and Kufner, *Toward a Grammar of Proto-Germanic*, 1972.
Prokosch, *A Comparative Germanic Grammar*, 1939.

5 The Old English Period (449-1100)

The recorded history of the English language begins, not on the Continent, where we know English speakers once lived, but in the British Isles, where they eventually settled. During the period when the language was spoken in Europe, it is known as **pre–Old English**, for it was only after the English separated themselves from their Germanic cousins that we recognize their speech as a distinct language.

The History of the Anglo-Saxons

BRITAIN BEFORE THE ENGLISH

When the English migrated from the Continent to Britain in the mid-fifth century, they found the island already inhabited. A Celtic people had been there for many centuries before Julius Caesar's invasion of the island in 55 B.C. The subsequent occupation, not really begun in earnest until the time of the Emperor Claudius almost a century later (A.D. 43), was to make Britain—that is, Britannia—a part of the Roman Empire for a period somewhat longer than that intervening between the first permanent English settlement in America and our own day. It is therefore not surprising that there are so many Roman remains in modern England, some of them discovered in the very heart of London only in the course of clearing away the rubble of World War II bombings. Despite the long occupation, the British Celts continued to speak their own language, though many of them, particularly those in the towns and cities who wanted to "get on," learned to speak and write the language of their Roman rulers. It was not until Britain became England that the survival of British Celtic was seriously threatened.

After the Roman legionnaires were withdrawn from Britain in the early fifth century (by 410), Picts from the north and Scots from the west savagely attacked the unprotected British Celts, who after generations of foreign domination had neither the heart nor the skill in weapons to put up much resistance. These same Picts and Scots, as well as ferocious Germanic sea raiders whom the Romans called Saxons, had earlier been a very considerable nuisance to the Roman soldiers and their commanders during the latter half of the fourth century.

THE COMING OF THE ENGLISH

According to the Venerable Bede's account in his *Ecclesiastical History of the English Nation*, written in Latin and completed around 730, almost three centuries after the event, the Britons appealed to Rome for help. What relief they got, a single legion, was only temporarily effectual. When Rome could or would help no more, the wretched Britons—still according to Bede—ironically enough called the "Saxons" to their aid "from the parts beyond the sea." As a result of their appeal, shiploads of Germanic warrior-adventurers began to arrive. The date that Bede gives for the first landing—449—cannot be far out of the way, if at all. With it the **Old English** period begins. With it, too, we may in a sense begin thinking of Britain as England—the land of the Angles—for, even though the long ships carried Jutes, Saxons, Frisians, and, doubtless, members of other tribes as well, their descendants a century and a half later were already beginning to think of themselves and their speech as English. (They naturally had no suspicion that it was "Old" English.) The name of a single tribe was thus to be adopted as a national name (prehistoric Old English *Angli*, becoming *Engle*). The term **Anglo-Saxon** is now also sometimes used for either the language of this period or its speakers.

These Germanic sea raiders, ancestors of the English, in short order gave the Pictish and Scottish aggressors what was coming to them. Then, with eyes ever on the main chance, a complete lack of any sense of international morality, and no fear whatever of being prosecuted as war criminals, they very unidealistically proceeded to subjugate and ultimately to dispossess the Britons whom they had come ostensibly to help. Word reached Continental kinsmen and friends of the cowardice of the Britons and the fertility of the island, and in the course of the next hundred years or so more and more of

The History of the Anglo-Saxons

those whom Bede, our primary source for this period, calls Saxons, Angles, and Jutes arrived "from the three most powerful nations of Germania" to seek their fortunes in a new land.

There are only a few events of these exciting times that we can be certain about: the invading newcomers belonged to various Germanic tribes speaking a number of closely related and hence very similar regional types of Germanic; they came from the great North German plain, including the southern part of the Jutland peninsula (modern Schleswig-Holstein); and by the time St. Augustine arrived to convert them to Christianity at the end of the sixth century, they held in their possession practically all of what is now known as England. As for the ill-advised Britons, their plight was hopeless; many fled to Wales and Cornwall, some crossed the Channel to Brittany, others were ultimately assimilated to the English by marriage or otherwise; many, we may be sure, lost their lives in the long-drawn-out fighting.

The Germanic tribes that came first—Bede's *Iutae*, *Iuti*, or "Jutes," led by the synonymously named brothers Hengest[1] and Horsa (both names mean 'horse')—settled principally in the southeastern part of the island, still called by its Celtic name of Kent. Subsequently Continental Saxons were to occupy the rest of the region south of the Thames, and Angles, stemming presumably from the hook-shaped peninsula in Schleswig known as Angeln, settled the large area stretching from the Thames northward to the Scottish highlands, except for the extreme southwestern portion (Wales).

THE ENGLISH IN BRITAIN

The Germanic settlement comprised seven kingdoms, the Anglo-Saxon **Heptarchy**: Kent, Essex, Sussex, Wessex, East Anglia, Mercia, and Northumbria—the last, the land north of the Humber, being an amalgamation of two earlier kingdoms, Bernicia and Deira (see map on next page). Kent early became the chief center of culture and wealth, and by the end of the sixth century its King Ethelbert (Æðelberht) could lay claim to the hegemony over

---

[1] He has been identified with the Hengest who plays a prominent role in the story of the fight at Finn's Borough, recounted in *Beowulf*, lines 1063–1159, and independently in a fragment of another Old English poem. This Hengest of Old English heroic poetry is the retainer of the Danish king Hnæf and, after Hnæf's fall in the treacherous sortie at Finn's Borough, makes peace of a sort with the victorious Finn, king of Frisia, whose subjects also included the Eote (the Old English equivalent of Bede's *Iuti*). The *Beowulf* poet tells us nothing of Hengest's subsequent career but leaves him brooding vengeance for the death of his lord; he is mentioned only as a prominent Danish warrior in the fragment. Vengeance is later executed upon Finn by a Danish fleet, but what part, if any, Hengest took in it we are not told. The identification of this Hengest with the man mentioned by Bede presupposes that somehow after the death of Finn he, presumably a Dane, became king of the Jutes, at the same time acquiring an ancestry befitting an Anglo-Saxon monarch, for Bede tells us that Hengest and Horsa were the great-grandsons of Woden, the chief Germanic god. That the two Hengests were one and the same man seems on the whole unlikely, yet the possibility tantalizes.

all the other kingdoms south of the Humber. Later, in the seventh and eighth centuries, this supremacy was to pass to Northumbria, with its great centers of learning at Lindisfarne, at Wearmouth, and at Jarrow, Bede's own monastery; then to Mercia; and finally to Wessex, with its brilliant line of kings beginning with Egbert (Ecgberht), who overthrew the Mercian king in 825, and culminating in his grandson, the superlatively great Alfred, whose successors after his death in 899 took for themselves the title *Rex Anglorum* 'King of the English.'

The most important event in the history of Anglo-Saxon culture (which in its broadest sense includes the American) occurred in 597, when Gregory I dispatched a band of missionaries to the Angles (*Angli*, as he called them, thereby departing from the usual Continental designation of them as *Saxones*), in accordance with a resolve he had made some years before. The leader of this band was St. Augustine—not to be confused with the African-born bishop of Hippo of the same name who wrote *The City of God* more than a century earlier. The apostle to the English and his fellow bringers of the Word, who landed on the Isle of Thanet in Kent, were received by King Ethelbert

The History of the Anglo-Saxons

courteously, if at the beginning a trifle warily. Already somewhat ripe for conversion through his marriage to a Christian Frankish princess, Ethelbert was himself baptized in a matter of months. Four years later, in 601, Augustine was consecrated first Archbishop of Canterbury, and there was a church in England. Later, Irish missionaries who had come from Iona to found a monastery at Lindisfarne made many converts in Northumbria and Mercia. In the course of the seventh century the new faith spread rapidly (though not without occasional backsliding); and by the end of that century England had become a most important part of Christendom.

THE FIRST VIKING CONQUEST

The Christian descendants of Germanic raiders who had looted, pillaged, and finally taken the land of Britain by force of arms were themselves to undergo harassment from other Germanic invaders, beginning in the later years of the eighth century, when pagan Viking raiders sacked various churches and monasteries, including Lindisfarne and Bede's own beloved Jarrow. During the first half of the following century other more or less disorganized but disastrous raids took place in the south. Then, in 865 a great and expertly organized army landed in East Anglia, led by the unforgettably named Ivar the Boneless and his brother Halfdan, sons of Ragnar Lothbrok (*Loðbrók* 'Shaggy-pants').[2] During the next fifteen years the Vikings gained possession of practically the whole eastern part of England.

In 870 the Vikings attacked Wessex, ruled by Ethelred (Æðelræd) with the able assistance of his brother Alfred, who was to succeed him in the following year. After years of discouragement, very few victories, and many crushing defeats, Alfred in 878 won a signal victory at Edington over Guthrum, the Danish king of East Anglia, who promised not only to depart from Wessex but also to be baptized. Alfred was godfather for him when the sacrament was later administered.

The troubles with the Danes, as the Vikings were called by the English, though there were Norwegians and later Swedes among them, were by no means over. There were further attacks, but these were so successfully repulsed by the English that ultimately, in the tenth century, Alfred's son and grandsons (three of whom became kings) were able to carry out his plans for consolidating England, which by this time had a sizable and peaceful Scandinavian population.

[2] According to the legend, Ivar was born with gristle instead of bone because his father had refused his bewitched bride's plea for a deferment of the consummation of their marriage for three nights. Ragnar is said to have been put to death in a snake pit in York. On this occasion his wife, the lovely Kraka, who felt no resentment toward him, had furnished him with a magical snake-proof coat; but it was of no avail, for his executioners made him remove his outer garment. Ivar Ragnarsson's unique physique seems to have been no handicap to a brilliant if rascally career as warrior.

In the later years of the tenth century, trouble started again with the arrival of a fleet of warriors led by Olaf Tryggvason, later king of Norway, who was in a few years to be joined by Danish King Svein Forkbeard. For more than twenty years there were repeated attacks, most of them crushing defeats for the English, beginning with the glorious if unsuccessful stand made by the men of Essex under the valiant Byrhtnoth in 991, celebrated in the fine Old English poem *The Battle of Maldon*. As a rule, however, the onslaughts of the later Northmen were not met with such vigorous resistance, for these were the bad days of the second Ethelred, known as *Unræd*, that is, 'unadvised,' but frequently misunderstood as 'unready.' After the deaths in 1016 of Ethelred and his son Edmund Ironside, who survived his father by little more than half a year, Cnut, son of Svein Forkbeard, who himself was for a short time recognized as king of England, came to the throne. The line of Alfred was not to be restored until 1042, with the accession of Edward the Confessor, though Cnut in a sense allied himself with that line by marrying Ethelred's widow, Emma of Normandy (the English preferred to call her Ælgifu), who thus became the mother of two English kings by different fathers: by Ethelred, of Edward the Confessor, and by Cnut, of Harthacnut. (She was not the mother of Ethelred's son Edmund Ironside.)

As has been pointed out, those whom the English called Danes (*Dene*) were not all from Denmark. Linguistically, however, this fact is of little significance, for the various Scandinavian tongues were in those days little differentiated from one another. Furthermore, they were sufficiently like Old English as to make communication possible between the English and the Scandinavians. The English were perfectly aware of their racial as well as their linguistic kinship with the Scandinavians, many of whom had become their neighbors: the Old English poem *Beowulf* is exclusively concerned with events of Scandinavian legend and history, and approximately a century and a half after the composition of this great literary masterpiece, Alfred, who certainly had no reason to love the Danes, interpolated in his translation of the history of Orosius the first geographical account of the countries of the North, in the famous story of the voyages of Ohthere and Wulfstan.

THE SCANDINAVIANS BECOME ENGLISH

Despite the enmity and the bloodshed, then, there was a feeling among the English that when all was said and done the Northmen belonged to the same "family" as themselves—a feeling that their ancestors could never have experienced regarding the British Celts. Whereas the earlier raids had been dictated largely by the desire to pillage and to loot—even though a good deal of Scandinavian settlement resulted—the tenth-century and early eleventh-century invaders from the north seem to have been much more interested in colonization than their predecessors had been. This was successfully accomplished in East Anglia (Norfolk and Suffolk), Lincolnshire, Yorkshire, Westmorland, Cumberland, and Northumberland. The Danes settled down peaceably enough in time, living side by side with the English; Scandinavians were good colonizers, willing to assimilate themselves to their new homes. As John Richard Green eloquently sums it up, "England still remained England; the conquerors sank quietly into the mass of those around them; and Woden yielded without a struggle to Christ" (cited by Jespersen 1954, p. 58).

And what of the impact of this assimilation upon the English language, which is our main concern here? Old English and Old Norse (the language of the Scandinavians) had a whole host of frequently used words in common. Otto Jespersen (1954, p. 60) cites, among others, *man, wife, mother, folk, house, thing, winter, summer, will, can, come, hear, see, think, ride, over, under, mine,* and *thine.* In some instances where related words differed noticeably in form, the Scandinavian form has won out—for example, *sister* (ON *systir*; OE *sweostor*). Scandinavian contributions to the English word stock are discussed in more detail in chapter 12.

The Old English Dialects

Four principal dialects were spoken in Anglo-Saxon England: **Kentish**, the speech of the Jutes who settled in Kent; **West Saxon**, spoken in the region south of the Thames exclusive of Kent; **Mercian**, spoken from the Thames to the Humber exclusive of Wales; and **Northumbrian**, whose localization (north of the Humber) is adequately indicated by its name. Mercian and Northumbrian have certain characteristics in common that distinguish them from West Saxon and Kentish, and they are sometimes grouped together as **Anglian**, since those who spoke these north-of-the-Thames dialects were predominantly Angles. Other dialects presumably existed, but we possess no written remains of them. The records of Anglian and Kentish are scant, but much West Saxon writing has come down to us, though probably only a fraction of what once existed. Old English dialect differences were slight as compared with those that were later to develop and nowadays sharply differentiate the speech of a lowland Scottish shepherd from that of his south-of-England counterpart.

Hence, although standard Modern English is in large part a descendant of Mercian speech, the dialect of Old English that will be described in this chapter is West Saxon. During the time of Alfred and for a long time thereafter, Winchester, the capital of Wessex and therefore in a sense of all England, was a center of English culture, thanks to the encouragement given by Alfred himself to learning. Though London was at the same time an important and thriving commercial city, it did not acquire its cultural or even its political importance until later.

It is thus in West Saxon that most of the extant Old English manuscripts—all in fact that may be regarded as literature—are available to us. Fortunately, however, we are at no great disadvantage when we study the West Saxon dialect in relation to Modern English. Because differences in dialect were not great, Old English forms are usually cited from West Saxon rather than Mercian writings. Occasionally a distinctive Mercian form (labeled Anglian if it happens to be identical with the Northumbrian form) is cited as more obviously similar to the standard modern form than is the West Saxon form—for instance, Anglian *ald*, which regularly developed into Modern English *old*. The West Saxon form was *eald*.

The Old English to be described here is of about the year 1000—roughly that of the period during which Ælfric, the most representative writer of the late tenth and early eleventh centuries, was flourishing. This development of English, in which most of the surviving literature is preserved, is sometimes called classical Old English; that of the Age of Alfred, who reigned in the later years of the ninth century, is usually included in what is called early West Saxon, though it is actually rather late in the early period. It is, however, about all that we know of the early West Saxon dialect from manuscript evidence.

The Old English period spans somewhat more than six centuries, the dates ascribed to it being more or less arbitrary. In a period of more than 600 years many changes are bound to occur in sounds, in grammar, and in vocabulary. Some are evident from a comparison of the earliest writings with the later ones. (Written records of English are, incidentally, older than those of any other West Germanic language.) By a comparative study of all the Germanic languages and dialects, linguists are able to reconstruct prehistoric Old English and to infer changes that took place in that stage in the development of our language. With such early changes we shall be concerned here only incidentally.

The Pronunciation and Spelling of Old English

For the pronunciation of the Old English words cited in the following discussion, it must be remembered that our knowledge of the phonology of an older form of any language can be only approximate. The precise quality of any speech sound during the vast era of the past before phonographs and tape recordings can never be determined with absolute certainty. Moreover, in Old English times, as today, there were regional and individual differences, and doubtless social differences as well. A period in which all members of a given linguistic community speak exactly alike, let alone an entire nation, is inconceivable.

The vowel letters in Old English were *a, æ, e, i, o, u,* and *y.* They represented either short or long sounds, vowel length being phonemically distinct. The five vowel letters *a, e, i, o,* and *u* symbolized what are sometimes referred to as "Continental" values—approximately those of Italian, Spanish, German, and to some extent of French as well. In other words, the *a* of the Old English texts indicates a vowel of the quality of [ɑ] short or long; likewise, to long *e, i, o,* and *u* may be assigned the same values that these symbols have when written in square brackets in phonetic transcription. When short, they were approximately [ɛ], [ɪ], [ɔ], and [ʊ] respectively. Short *æ* was as in *mat*; long *æ* was approximately the same sound prolonged, but somewhat tenser. *Y,* used exclusively as a vowel symbol in Old English, indicated a rounded front vowel, long as in German *Bühne,* short as in *fünf.* This sound, which has not survived in Modern English, was made with the tongue position of [i] (long) or [ɪ] (short) but with the lips rounded as for [u] or [ʊ] respectively. The sounds may be represented phonetically as [ü] and [Ü].

In the examples that follow, the Modern English form in parentheses illustrates a typical Modern English development of the Old English sound:[3]

a as in *habban* (have)	*ī* as in *rīdan* (ride)
ā as in *hām* (home)	*o* as in *moððe* (moth)
æ as in *þæt* (that)	*ō* as in *fōda* (food)
ǣ as in *dǣl* (deal)	*u* as in *sundor* (sunder)
e as in *settan* (set)	*ū* as in *mūs* (mouse)
ē as in *fēdan* (feed)	*y* as in *fyllan* (fill)
i as in *sittan* (sit)	*ȳ* as in *mȳs* (mice)

Late West Saxon had two long diphthongs, *ēa* and *ēo,* to the first elements of which may be assigned respectively the values [æ] and [e]. The second elements of both, once differentiated, had been reduced to unstressed [ə], which in the course of the eleventh century was lost; consequently these long diphthongs became monophthongs that continued to be differentiated, at least in the standard pronunciation, until well into the Modern English period but ultimately fell together as [i], as in *beat* from Old English *bēatan, creep* from *crēopan.* According to the traditional view, *ea* and *eo* in such words as *eall* 'all,' *geard* 'yard,' *seah* 'saw' and *eoh* 'horse,' *meolc* 'milk,' and *weorc* 'work' indicated short diphthongs of similar quality to the identically written long ones, approximately [æə] and [ɛə]. In early Old English, there were other diphthongs written *ie* and *io,* but they had disappeared by the time of classical Old English, being replaced usually by *y* and *eo,* respectively.

---

[3] The macron in Old English forms is editorial. Vowel quantity was not customarily indicated in Old English writing, for readers needed no such indication of what they unconsciously did in speaking their native language.

The consonant letters in Old English were *b, c, d, f, g, h, k, l, m, n, p, r, s, t, þ* or *ð, w, x,* and *z.* (The letters *j, q,* and *v* were not used for writing Old English, and *y* was always a vowel.) The symbols *b, d, k* (rarely used), *l, m, n, p, t, w* (which had a much different shape, namely, *ƿ*), and *x* had in all positions the same values that these letters represent in Modern English.

The sound represented by *c* depended on contiguous sounds. Preconsonantal *c* was always [k], as in *cnāwan* 'to know,' *cræt* 'cart,' and *cwellan* 'to kill.' If *c* was next to a back vowel, it indicated the velar stop [k] (*camp* 'battle,' *corn* 'corn,' *cūð* 'known,' *lūcan* 'to lock,' *acan* 'to ache,' *bōc* 'book'). If it was next to a front vowel (or one that had been front in early Old English), the sound indicated was the affricate [č] (*cild* 'child,' *cēosan* 'to choose,' *ic* 'I,' *lǣce* 'physician,' *rīce* 'kingdom,' *mēce* 'sword').

To be sure of the pronunciation of Old English *c,* it is often necessary to know the history of the word in which it appears. In *cēpan* 'to keep,' *cynn* 'race, kin,' and a number of other words, the root vowels were mutated back vowels (Germanic **kōpjan, *kunjō*); hence the palatalization of [k] resulting in Old English [č] did not occur. **Mutation** is a change in a vowel sound brought about by a sound in the following syllable. The mutation of a vowel by a following *i* or *j* (as in the examples) is called *i*-**mutation**. In *bēc* 'books' from prehistoric Old English **bōci* and *sēcan*[4] 'to seek' from prehistoric Old English **sōcjan,* the immediately following *i* and *j* brought about both palatalization of the original [k] (written *c* in Old English reconstructions) and mutation of the original vowel. Thus, they were pronounced [bēč] and [sēčan]. In *swylc* 'such,' *ǣlc* 'each,' and *hwylc* 'which,' an earlier *ī* before the *c* has been lost; but even without this information, we have a guide in the pronunciation of the modern forms cited as definitions. Similarly we may know from modern *keep* and *kin* that the Old English initial sound was [k]. Unfortunately for easy tests, *seek* does not show palatalization (though *beseech* does) and the mutated plural of *book* has not survived.

The digraphs *cg* and *sc* were in post–Old English times replaced by *dg* and *sh,* respectively—spellings that indicate to the modern reader exactly the sounds the older spellings represented, [j] and [š]—for example, *ecg* 'edge,' *scīr* 'shire,' *scacan* 'to shake,' and *fisc* 'fish.'

The pronunciation of *g* (usually written in a form more like *ȝ*) also depended on neighboring sounds. In late Old English the symbol indicated the voiced velar stop [g] before consonants (*gnēað* 'niggardly,' *glæd* 'glad, gracious'), initially before back vowels (*galan* 'to sing,' *gōs* 'goose,' *gūð* 'war'), and initially before front vowels that had resulted from the mutation of back

---

[4] For this word, Old English scribes frequently wrote *secean,* the extra *e* functioning merely as a diacritic to indicate that the preceding *c* symbolized [č] rather than [k]. Compare the Italian use of *i* after *c* preceding *a, o,* or *u* to indicate precisely the same thing, as in *ciao* 'goodbye' and *cioccolata* 'chocolate.'

The Pronunciation and Spelling of Old English

vowels (*gēs* 'geese' from prehistoric Old English **gōsi, gǣst* 'goest' from **gāis*). In the combination *ng* the letter indicated the same sound—that of Modern English *linger* as contrasted with *ringer* (*bringan* 'to bring,' *hring* 'ring').[5]

However, *g* indicated [y] initially before *e, i*, and the *y* that was usual in late West Saxon for earlier *ie* (*gecoren* 'chosen,' *gēar* 'year,' *giftian* 'to give a woman in marriage,' *gydd* 'song'), medially between front vowels (*slǣgen* 'slain,' *twēgen* 'twain'), and after a front vowel at the end of a syllable (*dæg* 'day,' *mægden* 'maiden,' *legde* 'laid,' *stigrāp* 'stirrup,' *manig* 'many').

In practically all other circumstances *g* indicated the voiced velar fricative referred to above (p. 89, n. 19) as the earliest Germanic development of Indo-European *gh*—a sound difficult to describe for English-speaking people nowadays. It is made like [g] except that the back of the tongue does not quite touch the velum (*dragan* 'to draw,' *lagu* 'law,' *hogu* 'care,' *folgian* 'to follow,' *sorgian* 'to sorrow,' *swelgan* 'to swallow'). It later became [w], as in Middle English *drawen, lawe, howe*, and so on.

In Old English, [v], [z], and [ð] were not phonemes; they occurred only medially. There were thus no contrastive pairs like *feel–veal, leaf–leave, thigh–thy, mouth* (n.)–*mouth* (v.), *seal–zeal, face–phase*, and hence there were no distinctive symbols for the voiceless and voiced sounds. The symbols *f, s*, and *þ* (or *ð*, used more or less interchangeably with it) thus indicated both the voiceless fricatives [f], [s], [θ] (as in *fōda* 'food,' *lof* 'praise'; *sunu* 'son,' *mūs* 'mouse'; *þorn* 'thorn,' *pæð* 'path') and, between voiced sounds, the corresponding voiced fricatives [v], [z], [ð] (as in *cnafa* 'boy,' *hæfde* 'had'; *lēosan* 'to lose,' *hūsl* 'Holy Communion'; *brōðor* 'brother,' *fæðm* 'fathom'). Some scribes in late Old English times preferred to write *þ* initially and *ð* elsewhere, but generally the letters were interchangeable. (Note that, although the Old English letter *ð* could represent either the voiceless or voiced fricative, the phonetic symbol [ð] represents the voiced sound only.)

Initially, *r* may have been a trill, but preconsonantally and finally in West Saxon it was probably the so-called retroflex *r* general in American English.

Initial *h* was about as in Modern English, but elsewhere it stood for the velar fricative [x] or the palatal fricative [ç], depending on the neighboring vowel—for example (with [x]), *seah* 'saw,' *þurh* 'through,' *þōhte* 'thought' (verb); (with [ç]), *syhð* 'sees,' *miht* 'might,' *fēhð* 'takes.' Of the sequences *hl* (as in *hlāf* 'loaf'), *hn* (as in *hnitu* 'nit'), *hr* (as in *hræfn* 'raven'), and *hw* (as in *hwæl* 'whale'), only the last survives, now less accurately spelled *wh*. In Old English, both consonants were pronounced in all these combinations.

The letter *z* was rare, and when it was used it had the value [ts], as the variant spellings *miltse* and *milze* 'mercy' indicate.

The doubling of consonant symbols between vowels indicated length;

---

[5] Thus [ŋ] was not an Old English phoneme, but merely an allophone of *n*. There were no contrastive pairs like *sin–sing* and *thin–thing*, nor were there to be any such in English until the Modern English loss of [g] in what had previously been a consonant sequence.

thus the *t*'s of *sittan* indicated the double or long [t] sound in *hot tamale*, in contrast to the single consonant [t] in Modern English *hotter*. Similarly *ll* in *fyllan* indicated the lengthened medial *l* of *full-length*, in contrast to the short *l* of *fully*. The *cc* in *racca* 'part of a ship's rigging' was a long [k], as in *bookkeeper*, in contrast to *beekeeper*, and hence *racca* was distinguished from *raca* 'rake'; and so on.

STRESS

Old English words of more than one syllable, like those in all other Germanic languages, were regularly stressed on their first syllables. Exceptions to this rule are verbs with prefixes, which were generally stressed on the first syllable of their second element: *wiðféohtan* 'to fight against,' *onbíndan* 'to unbind,' *ofdrǽdan* 'to dread.' *Be-*, *for-*, and *ge-* were not stressed, regardless of the part of speech of the word they began: *bebód* 'commandment,' *forsóð* 'forsooth,' *gehǽp* 'convenient.' Compounds had the customary Germanic stress on the first syllable, with a secondary stress on the first syllable of their second element: *lárhùs* 'school,' *híldedèor* 'fierce in battle.'

This heavy stressing of the first syllable of practically all words has had a far-reaching effect on the development of English. Because of it, the vowels of final syllables began to be reduced to a uniform sound as early as the tenth century, as not infrequent interchanges of one letter for another in the texts indicate, though most scribes continued to spell according to tradition. In general the stress system of Old English was simple as compared to that of Modern English, with its many loanwords of non-Germanic origin, like *matérnal*, *philósophy*, *sublíme*, and *tabóo*.

The Vocabulary of Old English

The vocabulary of Old English differed from that of later historical stages of our language in two important respects. First, there were relatively few loanwords, most of the word stock being of native Germanic origin. And second, the gender of nouns was more or less arbitrary rather than determined by the sex or sexlessness of the thing named.

THE GERMANIC WORD STOCK

The word stock of Old English was more thoroughly Germanic than the present-day vocabulary. To be sure, many Old English words of Germanic origin were identical, or at least highly similar, in both form and meaning to the corresponding Modern English words—for example, *god*, *gold*, *hand*, *helm*, *land*, *oft*, *under*, *winter*, and *word*. Others, although their Modern English forms continue to be similar in shape, have changed drastically in meaning. Thus, Old English *brēad* meant 'bit, piece' rather than 'bread'; similarly, *drēam* was 'joy' not 'dream,' *dreorig* 'bloody' not 'dreary,' *hlāf* 'bread' not 'loaf,' *mōd* 'heart, mind, courage' not 'mood,' *scēawian* 'look at' not 'show,' *sellan* 'give' not 'sell,' *tīd* 'time' not 'tide,' *winnan* 'fight' not 'win,' and *wiþ* 'against' not 'with.'

Some Old English words and meanings have survived in Modern English only in disguised form or in set expressions. Thus, Old English *guma* 'man' (cognate with the Latin word from which we have borrowed *human*) survives in the compound *bridegroom*, literally 'bride's man,' where it has been remodeled under the influence of the unrelated word *groom*. Another Old English word for 'man,' *wer*, appears today in *werewolf* 'man-wolf' and in the archaic *wergild* 'man money, the fine to be paid for killing a person.' *Tīd*, mentioned in the preceding paragraph, when used in the proverb "Time and tide wait for no man," preserves an echo of its earlier sense. Doubtless most persons today who use the proverb think of it as describing the inexorable rise and fall of the sea, which mere humans cannot alter; originally, however, *time* and *tide* were just synonyms. *Līc* 'body' continues feebly in compounds like *lich-house* 'mortuary' and *lych-gate* 'roofed gate of a graveyard, where a corpse awaits burial,' and vigorously in the *-ly* endings of adverbs and some adjectives; what was once an independent word has been reduced to a suffix marking parts of speech.

Other Old English words have not survived at all: *blīcan* 'shine, gleam,' *cāf* 'quick, bold,' *duguþ* 'band of noble retainers,' *frætwa* 'ornaments, treasure,' *galdor* 'song, incantation,' *here* 'army, marauders (especially the Danes),' *leax* 'salmon,' *mund* 'palm of the hand, (hence) protection, trust,' *nīþ* 'war, evil, trouble,' *racu* 'account, explanation,' *scēat* 'region, surface of the earth, bosom,' *tela* 'good,' and *ymbe* 'around.' Some of these words continued for a while after the Old English period (for example, *nīþ* lasted through the fifteenth century in forms like *nithe*), but they gradually disappeared and were replaced by other native expressions or, more often, by loanwords. Old English also made extensive use of compounds that we have now replaced by borrowing: *āþwedd* 'oath-promise, vow,' *bōchord* 'book-hoard, library,' *cræftspræc* 'craft-speech, scientific language,' *dēorwurþe* 'dear-worth, precious,' *folcriht* 'folk-right, common law,' *galdorcræft* 'incantation-skill, magic,' *lustbære* 'pleasure-bearing, desirable,' *nīfara* 'new-farer, stranger,' *rīmcræft* 'counting-skill, computation,' *wiþerwinna* 'against-fighter, enemy.'

If Germanic words like these had continued to our own time and if we had not borrowed the very great number of foreign words that we have in fact adopted, English today would be very different.

GENDER IN OLD ENGLISH

Aside from its pronunciation and its word stock, Old English differs markedly from Modern English in having **grammatical gender** in contrast to the Modern English system of gender based on sex or sexlessness. The three genders of Indo-European were preserved in Germanic and survived in English well into the Middle English period; they survive in German and Icelandic to this day. Doubtless the gender of a noun originally had nothing to do with sex, nor does it necessarily have sexual connotations in those languages that have retained grammatical (as opposed to **natural**) gender. Old English *wīf* 'wife, woman' is neuter, as is its German cognate *Weib*; so is *mægden* 'maiden,' like German *Mädchen*. *Bridd* 'young bird' is masculine; *bearn* 'son, bairn' is neuter. *Brēost* 'breast' and *hēafod* 'head' are neuter, but *brū* 'eyebrow,' *wamb* 'belly,' and *eaxl* 'shoulder' are feminine. *Strengðu* 'strength' is feminine, *broc* 'affliction' is neuter, and *drēam* 'joy' is masculine.

Where sex was patently involved, however, this complicated and to us illogical system was beginning to break down even in Old English times. It must have come to be difficult, for instance, to refer to one who was obviously a woman—that is, a *wīf*—with the pronoun *hit* 'it,' or to a *wīfmann*—the compound from which our word *woman* is derived—with *hē* 'he,' the compound being masculine because of its second element. There are in fact a number of instances in Old English of the conflict of grammatical gender with the developing concept of natural gender.

Inflection in Old English

One of the principal grammatical differences between Old English and Modern English is the amount of inflection in the noun, the adjective, and the demonstrative and interrogative pronouns. The personal pronouns, however, have preserved much of their ancient complexity in Modern English.

Old English nouns, pronouns, and adjectives had four **cases**, used according to the word's function in the sentence. The **nominative case** was used for the subject, the complement of linking verbs like *beon* 'be,' and direct address. The **accusative case** was used for the direct object, the object of some prepositions, and certain adverbial functions (like those of the italicized expressions of duration and direction in Modern English "They stayed there *the whole day*, but finally went *home*"). The **genitive case** was used for most of the meanings of Modern English *'s* and *of* phrases, the object of a few prepositions and of some verbs, and certain adverbial functions (like the time expression of Modern English "He works *nights*," in which *nights* was originally a genitive singular). The **dative case** was used for the indirect object and the only object of some verbs, the object of many prepositions, and a variety of other functions that can be grouped together loosely as adverbial (like the time expression of Modern English "I'll see you *some day*").

Adjectives and the demonstrative and interrogative pronouns had a fifth case, the **instrumental**, whose functions were served by the dative case of nouns. A typical example of the instrumental is the italicized phrase in the following sentence: "Worhte Ælfred cyning *lȳtle werede* geweorc" (literally

'Built Alfred King [with a] *little troop* [a] work,' that is, 'King Alfred with a *small troop* built a fortification'). The nominative of the expression for 'small troop' was *lȳtel wered*; the final *-e* marked the adjective as instrumental and the noun as dative, here functioning as an instrumental. The instrumental was used to express the means or manner of an action and was therefore used adverbially: "folc ðe *hlūde* singeþ" ('people that *loud*[*ly*] sing').

Adjectives and adverbs were compared much like Modern English *fast, faster, fastest*. Adjectives were inflected for **definiteness** as well as for gender, number, and case. The **weak declension** of adjectives was used to indicate that the modified noun was definite—that it named an object whose identity was known or expected or had already been mentioned. Generally speaking, the weak form occurred after a demonstrative or a possessive pronoun, as in "se *gōda* dæl" ('that *good* part') or "hire *geonga* sunu" ('her *young* son'). The **strong declension** was used when the modified noun was indefinite because not preceded by a demonstrative or possessive or when the adjective was in the predicate, as in "*gōd* dæl" ('[a] *good* part') or "se dæl wæs *gōd*" ('that part was *good*').

Nouns

Old English will inevitably seem to the modern reader a crabbed and difficult language full of needless complexities. Actually the inflection of the noun was somewhat less complex in Old English than it was in Germanic, Latin, and Greek and, naturally, considerably less so than in Indo-European, with its eight cases (nominative, accusative, genitive, dative, ablative, instrumental, locative, and vocative). No Old English noun had more than six distinct forms; but even this number will seem exorbitant to the speaker of Modern English, who uses only two forms for all but a few nouns: a general form without ending and a form ending in *-s*. The fact that the modern forms ending in *-s* are written differently is quite irrelevant; the apostrophe for the genitive is a fairly recent convention. As far as speech is concerned, *boys, boy's,* and *boys'* are the same.

Old English had a large number of patterns for declining its nouns, each of which is called a **declension**. Only the most common of the declensions or those that have survived somehow in Modern English are illustrated here. The most important of the Old English declensions was that of the **a-stems**, so called because *a* was the sound with which their stems ended in Proto-Germanic. They corresponded to the *o*-stems of Indo-European, as exemplified by nouns of the Greek and Latin second declensions: Greek *philos* 'friend' and Latin *servos* (later *servus*) 'slave,' Indo-European *o* having become Germanic *a* (p. 89). The name for the declension had only historical significance as far as Old English was concerned. For example, Germanic **wulfaz* (nominative singular) and **wulfan* (accusative singular) had an *a* in

	MASCULINE *a*-STEM	NEUTER *a*-STEM	*z*-STEM	*n*-STEM	ROOT-CONSONANT STEM	*ō*-STEM
Singular						
Nom.	hund	dēor	cild	oxa	fōt	lufu
Acc.	hund	dēor	cild	oxan	fōt	lufe
Gen.	hundes	dēores	cildes	oxan	fōtes	lufe
Dat.	hunde	dēore	cilde	oxan	fēt	lufe
Plural						
N.–Ac.	hundas	dēor	cildru	oxan	fēt	lufa
Gen.	hunda	dēora	cildra	oxena	fōta	lufa
Dat.	hundum	dēorum	cildrum	oxum	fōtum	lufum

their endings, but those forms appeared in Old English simply as *wulf* 'wolf,' having lost the *a* of the stem as well as the grammatical endings. The *a*-stems are illustrated in the table of Old English noun declensions by the masculine *hund* 'dog' and the neuter *dēor* 'animal.'

More than half of all commonly used nouns were inflected according to this pattern, which was in time to be extended to practically all nouns. The Modern English possessive singular and general plural forms in -*s* come directly from the Old English genitive singular (-*es*) and the masculine nominative-accusative plural (-*as*) forms—two different forms until very late Old English times, when they fell together because the unstressed vowels had merged, probably as a schwa. In Middle English times both endings were spelled -*es*. Only in Modern English have they again been differentiated in spelling by the use of the apostrophe. Nowadays, new words invariably conform to what survives of the *a*-stem declension—for example, *hobbit's*, *hobbits*, *hobbits'*—so that we may truly say it is the only living declension.

Neuter *a*-stems differed from masculines only in the nominative-accusative plural. If a neuter noun had a **short syllable** for its stem—that is, one containing a short vowel followed by a single consonant—the ending of the nominative-accusative plural was -*u*, as in *lim* 'limb' and *limu* 'limbs.' On the other hand, if the neuter noun had a **long syllable**—that is, one containing a long vowel—or a short vowel followed by two or more consonants, the nominative-accusative plural had no ending, as in *dēor*. Such "endless plurals" survive in Modern English for words like *deer*.

A very few neuter nouns, of which *cild* 'child' is an example, had an *r* in the plural. Such nouns are known as *z*-**stems** in Germanic; the *z*, which

Nouns

became *r* by rhotacism, corresponds to the *s* of Latin neuters like *genus*, which also rhotacized to *r* in oblique forms such as *genera*. The historically expected plural of *child* in Modern English is *childer*, and that form indeed survives in the northern dialects of British English. In standard use, however, *children* acquired a second plural ending from the nouns discussed in the next paragraph.

An important declension in Old English was the **n-stems**. Nouns that follow this pattern were masculine (for example, *oxa* 'ox,' illustrated in the table) or feminine (such as *tunge* 'tongue'); the two genders differed only in the endings for the nominative singular, *-a* versus *-e*. There were also two neuter nouns in the declension, *ēage* 'eye' and *ēare* 'ear'; they had the forms cited here for their nominative and accusative singular cases but were otherwise like *oxa*.

For a time, *-n* rivaled *-s* (from the *a*-stems) as a typical plural ending in English. Plurals like *eyen* 'eyes,' *fon* 'foes,' *housen* 'houses,' *shoen* 'shoes,' and *treen* 'trees' continued well into the Modern English period. The only original *n*-plural to survive as standard today, however, is *oxen*. *Children*, as noted above, has its *-n* by analogy rather than historical development. Similarly *brethren* and the poetic *kine* for 'cows' are post–Old English developments.

The *n* that is so prominent in the endings of this declension was originally a part of the noun stem, not of the inflectional endings. Although by Old English times the *n* had been reinterpreted as part of the inflectional endings, our name for this group of nouns recalls the earlier state of affairs. The *n*-stem pattern is also sometimes called the **weak declension**, in contrast with the **strong declensions**, which have stems that originally ended in a vowel, such as the *a*-stems.

Another declension whose nouns were frequently used in Old English and whose forms have contributed to the irregularities of Modern English consisted of the **root-consonant stems**. In early stages of the language, the case endings of these nouns were attached directly to their roots without an intervening stem-forming suffix (like the *-a*, *-z*, and *-n* of the declensions already discussed). The most striking characteristic of these nouns was the change of root vowel in several of their forms. This declension is exemplified by the masculine noun *fōt* 'foot' in the table. Also belonging to the declension were feminine nouns, which differed only in having a genitive singular without the *-s* ending, often identical with the form of the dative singular. (*Gōs* 'goose' has genitive-dative singular *gēs*.)

It will be noted that the dative singular and the nominative-accusative plural forms were identical for all nouns of the declension. This was so because, although in prehistoric Old English the dative singular and the nominative-accusative plural forms had the same root vowel as all other forms, each had an *i* in the ending, thus: dative singular **fōti*, nominative-accusative plural **fōtiz*. As mentioned earlier, anticipation of the *i*-sound caused

mutation of the root vowel—a kind of assimilation, with the vowel of the root moving in its articulation in the direction of the *i*-sound, but stopping somewhat short of it. English *man–men, foot–feet* show the same development as German *Mann–Männer, Fuss–Füsse,* though German has chosen to indicate the mutated vowel in writing by placing a dieresis over the same symbol used for the unmutated vowel, whereas English uses an altogether different letter. The process, which Jacob Grimm called **umlaut,** occurred in different periods and in varying degrees in the various languages of the Germanic group, in English beginning probably in the sixth century. The fourth-century Gothic recorded by Bishop Wulfila shows no evidence of it.

Vowel mutation was originally a phonetic phenomenon only; but after the endings that caused the change had been lost, the mutated vowels served as markers for the two case forms. Mutation was not in Old English a sign of the plural, for it was found also in the dative singular and not all plural forms had it. Only later did it become a distinctive indication of plurality for those nouns like *feet, geese, teeth, mice, lice,* and *men* which have retained mutated forms into Modern English.[6] Modern English *breeches* is a double plural (OE nominative singular *brōc* 'trouser,' nominative plural *brēc*), as is the already cited *kine* (OE nominative singular *cū* 'cow,' nominative plural *cȳ*).

Somewhat fewer than a third of all commonly used nouns were feminine, most of them **ō-stems** (corresponding to the *ā*-stems, or first declension, of Latin). In the nominative singular, these had -*u* after a short syllable, as in *lufu* 'love' and no ending at all after a long syllable, as in *lār* 'learning' and *wund* 'wound.' The words were otherwise declined alike.

Some very frequently used words (**r-stems**) that denoted family relationships—*fæder* 'father,' *brōðor* 'brother,' *mōdor* 'mother,' *dohtor* 'daughter,' and *sweostor* 'sister'—exhibited a number of peculiarities, as did a variety of other nouns (**u-stems** like *sunu* 'son,' **i-stems** like *wine* 'friend,' and **nd-stems** like *hettend* 'enemy'). Such complications are treated in grammars of Old English and need not be considered here because they have had no important effect on Modern English.

MODERN SURVIVALS OF CASE AND NUMBER

It will be noted that in all declensions the genitive plural form ended in -*a*. This ending survived as [ə] (written -*e*) in Middle English in the "genitive of measure" construction, and its effects continue in Modern English (with loss of [ə]), in such phrases as *sixty-mile drive* and *six foot tall* (rather than *miles* and *feet*). Though *feet* may more often occur in the latter construction, only *foot* is idiomatic in *three-foot board* and *six-foot man. Mile* and *foot* in such

---

[6] Mutation is not limited to the nouns of this declension. Its effects can be seen also in such pairs as *strong–strength, old–elder,* and *doom–deem.* In all these pairs the second word originally had an ending containing an *i*-sound (either a vowel or its consonantal equivalent [y]) that caused the mutation of the root vowel and was thereafter lost.

expressions are historically genitive plurals derived from the Old English forms *mīla* and *fōta*, rather than the irregulars they now appear to be.

The dative plural, which was *-um* for all declensions, survives in the antiquated form *whilom*, from Old English *hwīlum* 'at times,' and in the analogical *seldom* (earlier *seldan*). The dative singular ending *-e*, characteristic of the majority of Old English nouns, survives in the word *alive*, from Old English *on līfe*. The Old English voiced *f* between vowels, later spelled *v*, is preserved in the Modern English form, though the final vowel is no longer pronounced.

There are a very few relics of Old English feminine genitives without *-s* —for instance, *Lady Chapel* and *ladybird*, for *Our Lady's Chapel* and *Our Lady's bird*. The *ō*-stem genitive singular ended in *-e*. This ending was completely lost in pronunciation by the end of the fourteenth century, along with all other final *e*'s of whatever origin.

The forms discussed in these paragraphs are about the only traces left of the Old English declensional forms of the noun other than the genitive singular and the general plural forms in *-s* (along with a few mutated plurals). One of the most significant differences between Old English and Modern English nouns is that Old English had no device for indicating plurality alone—that is, unconnected with the concept of case. It was not until Middle English times that the plural nominative-accusative *-es* (from OE *-as*) drove out the other case forms of the plural (save for the comparatively rare genitive of measure construction discussed above). Even in the root-consonant stems, the mutated forms were, as we have seen, not exclusively plural forms. The *-en* ending (from OE *-an*), surviving in *oxen*, likewise did not indicate plurality alone in earlier periods; in Old English, as a backward glance at the declension of *oxa* will show, the oblique singular forms had *-an* and were thus identical with the nominative-accusative plural form, *oxan*.

Demonstratives

There were two demonstratives in Old English. The more frequently used was that which came to correspond in function to our definite article and may be translated 'the' or 'that, those.' Its forms were as follows:

	MASCULINE	NEUTER	FEMININE	PLURAL
Nom.	sē, se	þæt	sēo	þā
Acc.	þone	þæt	þā	þā
Gen.	þæs	þæs	þǣre	þāra
Dat.	þǣm	þǣm	þǣre	þǣm
Ins.	þȳ, þon, þē	þȳ, þon, þē		

Genders were distinguished only in the singular; in the plural no such distinction existed. The masculine and neuter forms were alike in the genitive, dative, and instrumental. There was no distinct instrumental in the feminine or the plural. Because of the analogy of all the other forms, *sĕ* and *sēo* were in late Old English superseded by the variants *þĕ* and *þeo*.

The definite article *the* of Modern English has developed from the masculine nominative *þe*, remodeled by analogy from *se*. When we use *the* in comparisons, however, as in "The sooner, the better," it is a development of the neuter instrumental form *þē*, the literal sense being something like 'By this [much] sooner, by this [much] better.' The Modern English demonstrative *that* is from the neuter nominative-accusative *þæt*, and its plural *those* has been borrowed from the other demonstrative.

The other, less frequently used Old English demonstrative (usually translated 'this, these') had the nominative singular forms *þēs* (masculine), *þis* (neuter, whence ModE *this*), and *þēos* (feminine). Its nominative-accusative plural, *þās*, developed into *those* and was confused with *tho*, the earlier plural of *that*. Consequently in Middle English a new plural was developed for *this*, namely *these*.

Adjectives

The adjective in Old English, like that in Latin, agreed with the noun it modified in gender, case, and number; but Germanic, as noted in chapter 4, had developed a distinctive adjective declension—the **weak declension**, used after the two demonstratives and after possessive pronouns, which made the following noun definite in its reference. In this declension *-an* predominated as an ending, as shown in the following paradigms for *se dola cyning* 'that foolish king,' *þæt dole bearn* 'that foolish child,' and *sēo dole ides* 'that foolish woman.' Like the demonstratives, the weak adjectives did not vary for gender in the plural.

SINGULAR

Nom.	se dola cyning	þæt dole bearn	sēo dole ides
Acc.	þone dolan cyning	þæt dole bearn	þā dolan idese
Gen.	þæs dolan cyninges	þæs dolan bearnes	þære dolan idese
Dat.	þæm dolan cyninge	þæm dolan bearne	þære dolan idese
Ins.	þȳ dolan cyninge	þȳ dolan bearne	þære dolan idese

PLURAL

Nom., acc.	þā dolan cyningas, bearn, idesa
Gen.	þāra dolra (*or* dolena) cyninga, bearna, idesa
Dat.	þǣm dolum cyningum, bearnum, idesum

The **strong declension** was used when the adjective was not preceded by a demonstrative or a possessive pronoun or when it was predicative. Paradigms for the strong adjective in the phrases *dol cyning* 'a foolish king,' *dol bearn* 'a foolish child,' and *dolu ides* 'a foolish woman' follow. The genders of the plural forms were different only in the nominative-accusative.

SINGULAR

Nom.	dol cyning	dol bearn	dolu ides
Acc.	dolne cyning	dol bearn	dole idese
Gen.	doles cyninges	doles bearnes	dolre idese
Dat.	dolum cyninge	dolum bearne	dolre idese
Ins.	dole cyninge	dole bearne	dolre idese

PLURAL

Nom., acc.	dole cyningas	dolu bearn	dola idesa
Gen.	dolra cyninga, bearna, idesa		
Dat.	dolum cyningum, bearnum, idesum		

The nominative-accusative plural strong forms are exemplified in *dole cyningas* (masculine), *dolu bearn* (neuter), and *dola idesa* (feminine). The genitive and dative plural endings for all genders—respectively, *-ra* and *-um*—were the same as those of the weak declension.

The comparative of adjectives was regularly formed by suffixing *-ra*, as in *heardra* 'harder,' and the superlative by suffixing *-ost*, as in *heardost* 'hardest.' A few adjectives originally used the alternative suffixes **-ira, *-ist* and consequently had mutated vowels. In recorded Old English they took the endings *-ra* and *-est* but retained mutated vowels—for example, *lang* 'long,' *lengra, lengest*, and *eald* 'old,' *yldra, yldest* (Anglian *ald, eldra, eldest*). A very few others had comparative and superlative forms from a different root from that of the positive, among them *gōd* 'good,' *betra* 'better,' *betst* 'best' and *micel* 'great,' *māra* 'more,' *mǣst* 'most.'

Certain superlatives were formed originally with an alternative suffix *-(u)ma*—for example, *forma* (formed from *fore* 'before'). When the ending with *m* ceased to be felt as having superlative force, these words and some others took by analogy the additional ending *-est*. Thus double superlatives (though not recognized as such) like *formest, midmest, ūtemest*, and *innemest* came into being. The ending appeared to be *-mest* (rather than *-est*), which was even in late Old English times misunderstood as 'most'; hence our Modern English forms *foremost, midmost*, and *inmost*, in which the final

syllable is and has long been equated with *most*, though it has no historical
connection with it. Beginning thus as a blunder, this *-most* has subsequently
been affixed to other words—for example, *uppermost*, *furthermost*, and
topmost.

Adverbs

Old English adverbs give no particular trouble. Those formed from
adjectives (the great majority) added the suffix *-e* (historically, the instrumental case ending)—for example, *wrāð* 'angry,' *wrāðe* 'angrily.' This *-e* was
lost along with all other final *e*'s by the end of the fourteenth century, with
the result that many Modern English adjectives and adverbs are identical in
form—for instance, *loud*, *deep*, and *slow*—though Modern English idiom
sometimes requires adverbial forms with *-ly* ("He plunged deep into the
ocean" but "He thought deeply about religious matters"; "Drive slow" but
"He proceeded slowly").

In addition, other case forms of nouns and adjectives might be used
adverbially, notably the genitive and the dative. The adverbial genitive is
used in "He hwearf dæges ond nihtes" (He wandered [by] day and [by]
night), in which *dæges* and *nihtes* are genitive singulars. The construction
survives in "He worked nights" (labeled "dial[ect] and U.S." by the *OED*),
sometimes rendered analytically as "He worked of a night." The usage is,
as the *OED* says, "in later use prob[ably] apprehended as a plural," though
historically, as we have seen, it is not so. The *-s* of *homewards* (OE *hām-
weardes*), *towards* (*tōweardes*), *besides*, *betimes*, *needs* (as in *must needs be*,
sometimes rendered analytically as *must of necessity be*) is from the genitive
singular ending *-es*. The same ending is merely written differently in *once*,
twice, *thrice*, *hence*, and *since*. Examples of the adverbial dative are the singular
elne 'with valor, valiantly,' *wihte* 'at all' and the plural *hwīlum* 'at times,
sometimes,' *þrymmum* 'with forces, mightily.'

Adverbs regularly formed the comparative with *-or* and the superlative
with *-ost* or *-est* (*wrāðor* 'more angrily,' *wrāðost* 'most angrily').

Personal Pronouns

Except for the loss of the **dual number** and the old second person singular
forms, the personal pronouns are almost as complex today as they were in
Old English times. In some respects (particularly the two genitive forms of
Modern English), they are more complex today.

The Old English forms of the pronouns for the first two persons are as
follows:

	SINGULAR	DUAL	PLURAL
Nom.	ic 'I'	wit 'we both'	wē 'we all'
Ac.–D.	mē 'me'	unc 'us both'	ūs 'us all'
Gen.	mīn 'my, mine'	uncer 'our(s) (both)'	ūre 'our(s) (all)'
Nom.	þū 'you (sg.)'	git 'you both'	gē 'you all'
Ac.–D.	þē 'you (sg.)'	inc 'you both'	ēow 'you all'
Gen.	þīn 'your(s) (sg.)'	uncer 'your(s) (both)'	ēower 'your(s) (all)'

The dual forms, which were used to talk about exactly two persons, were disappearing even by late Old English times. The second person singular (*th*-forms) and the second person plural nominative (*ye*) survived well into the Modern English period, especially in religious and poetic language, but they are seldom used today and almost never with traditional correctness. When used as modifiers, the genitives of the first and second persons were declined like the strong adjectives.

Gender appeared only in the third person singular forms, exactly as in Modern English:

	MASCULINE	FEMININE	NEUTER	PLURAL
Nom.	hē 'he'	hēo 'she'	hit 'it'	hī 'they'
Acc.	hine 'him'	hī 'her'	hit 'it'	hī 'them'
Dat.	him 'him'	hire 'her'	him 'it'	him, heom 'them'
Gen.	his 'his'	hire 'her(s)'	his 'its'	hira, heora 'their(s)'

The masculine accusative *hine* has survived only in southwestern dialects of British English as [ən], as in "Didst thee zee un?" that is, "Did you see him?" (*OED*, s.v. *hin, hine*). Modern English *she* has an unclear history, but it is perhaps a development of the demonstrative *sēo* rather than of the personal pronoun *hēo*. A new form was needed because *hēo* became by regular sound change identical in pronunciation with the masculine *hē*—an obviously unsatisfactory state of affairs. The feminine accusative *hī* has not survived.

The neuter *hit* has survived when stressed, notably at the beginning of a sentence, in some types of nonstandard Modern English. The loss of [h-] is due to lack of stress and is paralleled by a similar loss in the other *h-* pronouns when they are unstressed, as for example, "Give her his book," which in the natural speech of people at all cultural levels would show no trace of an [h]; compare also "raise her up" and "razor up," "rub her gloves" and "rubber gloves." In the neuter, however, the older stressed form in standard English has been lost completely, even in writing, whereas in the other *h-* pronouns we have two spoken forms but only one written form, preserving the *h*. *Its* is obviously not a development of the Old English form, but a new analogical form occurring first in Modern English.

Of the third person plural forms only the dative has survived; it is the regular spoken, unstressed, objective form in Modern English, with loss of *h-* as in the other *h-* pronouns—for example, "I told 'em what to do." The Modern English stressed form, *them*, like *they* and *their*, is of Scandinavian origin.

In all of the personal pronouns except *hit*, as also in the interrogative *hwā* 'who' considered in the next section, the accusative form has been displaced by the dative. In the first and second persons, that displacement began very early; for example, *mec*, an earlier accusative for the first person singular, had been lost by the time of classical Old English and its functions assumed by the original dative *mē*. A similar change had taken place in each of the first and second person paradigms and would later do so in the third person (except the neuter).

Interrogative and Relative Pronouns

The interrogative pronoun *hwā* 'who' was declined only in the singular and had only masculine and neuter forms:

	MASCULINE	NEUTER
Nom.	hwā	hwæt
Acc.	hwone	hwæt
Gen.	hwæs	hwæs
Dat.	hwǣm, hwām	hwǣm, hwām
Ins.	hwǣm, hwām	hwȳ

Hwæt is the source of our *what* and *hwām* of *whom*. *Hwone* did not survive beyond the Middle English period, its functions being taken over by the dative *hwām* (or *hwǣm*). *Whose* is from *hwæs* with its vowel influenced by *who* and *whom*. The distinctive neuter instrumental *hwȳ* is the source of our *why*. Other Old English interrogatives included *hwæðer* 'which of two' and *hwilc* 'which of many.' They were both declined like strong adjectives.

Hwā was exclusively interrogative in Old English. The particle *þe* was the usual relative pronoun. Since this word had only a single form, it is a great pity that we ever lost it; it involved no choice such as that which we must make—in writing, at least—between *who* and *whom*, now that these have come to be used as relatives. Sometimes, however, *þe* was preceded by the appropriate form of the demonstrative *sē* to make a compound relative.

Like their Modern English counterparts, Old English verbs were either **weak**, adding a -*d* or -*t* to form their preterits and past participles (as in modern *dive*, *dived*), or **strong**, changing their stressed vowel for the same purpose (as in modern *dive*, *dove*). Old English had several kinds of weak verbs and seven groups of strong verbs distinguished by their patterns of vowel change; and it had a considerably larger number of strong verbs than has Modern English. Old English also had a fair number of irregular verbs in both the weak and strong categories—grammatical irregularity being frequent at all periods in the history of language, rather than a recent "corruption."

The **conjugation** of a typical weak verb, *cēpan* 'to keep,' and of a typical strong verb, *helpan* 'to help,' is as follows:

PRESENT SYSTEM

Indicative

ic	cēpe 'I keep'	helpe 'I help'
þū	cēpest 'you keep'	hilpst 'you help'
hē, hēo, hit	cēpeð 'he, she, it keeps'	hilpð 'he, she, it helps'
wē, gē, hī	cēpað 'we, you, they keep'	helpað 'we, you, they help'

Subjunctive

Singular	cēpe 'I, you, he, she, it keep'	helpe 'I, you, he, she, it help'
Plural	cēpen 'we, you, they keep'	helpen 'we, you, they help'

Imperative

Singular	cēp '(you) keep!'	help '(you) help!'
Plural	cēpað '(you all) keep!'	helpað '(you all) help!'

Infinitive

Simple	cēpan 'to keep'	helpan 'to help'
Inflected	tō cēpenne 'to keep'	tō helpenne 'to help'
Participle	cēpende 'keeping'	helpende 'helping'

PRETERIT SYSTEM

Indicative

ic	cēpte 'I kept'	healp 'I helped'
þū	cēptest 'you kept'	hulpe 'you helped'
hē, hēo, hit	cēpte 'he, she, it kept'	healp 'he, she, it helped'
wē, gē, hī	cēpton 'we, you, they kept'	hulpon 'we, you, they helped'

The Old English Period (449–1100)

Subjunctive		
Singular	cēpte 'I, you, he, she, it kept'	hulpe 'I, you, he, she, it helped'
Plural	cēpten 'we, you, they kept'	hulpen 'we, you, they helped'
PAST PARTICIPLE	gecēped 'kept'	geholpen 'helped'

Weak verbs had three **principal parts** (basic forms on which all of the others are built), and strong verbs had four. The principal parts for these verbs were the infinitives *cēpan* and *helpan* (with the stems *cēp-* and *help-*, on which the whole present system was built), the first and third persons singular of the preterit indicative *cēpte* and *healp* (for weak verbs, the whole preterit system was built on the stem of this part, *cēpt-*), the preterit plural of the strong verbs *hulpon* (with its stem *hulp-*, on which the rest of the preterit system of strong verbs was built), and the past participles *gecēped* and *geholpen*.

Counting identical forms (such as *cēpe*, first person singular present indicative and singular present subjunctive) once only, there were fourteen distinct forms for each of these verbs. The corresponding Modern English verbs have only four distinct forms each. Thus, although the Old English verb was much simpler than those of some other Indo-European languages (such as Latin, which had over a hundred distinct forms for the typical verb), it was considerably more complex than Modern English verbs are.

INDICATIVE FORMS OF VERBS

The **indicative** forms of the verbs, present and preterit, were used for making statements and asking questions; they are the most frequent of the verb forms and the most straightforward and ordinary in their uses. The Old English **preterit** was used for events that happened in the past, and the **present tense** was used for all other times, that is, for present and future events and for habitual actions.

In the present indicative, the *-t* of the second person singular was not a part of the original ending; it came from the frequent use of *þū* as an **enclitic**, that is, an unstressed word following a stressed word (here the verb) and spoken as if it were a part of the stressed word. For example, *cēpes þū* became *cēpesþu*, then assimilated to *cēpestu*, and later lost the unstressed *-u*.

The *-e-* of the endings of the second and third persons singular was usually syncopated in West Saxon, often resulting in various changes in the consonants thereby brought together. For example, with loss of the vowel, *bīdeð* 'waits' became *bītt*. Alternative forms for *cēpest* and *cēpeð* in the paradigm above were *cēpst* and *cēpð*. Strong verbs had mutation of their root vowels—if those vowels were capable of it—in the second and third persons of the present indicative because of the earlier form of their endings, *-ist* and *-iŏ*. Thus we find *hilpst* and *hilpŏ* instead of the unmutated and unsyncopated *helpest* and *helpeŏ*.

Weak and strong verbs had strikingly different personal endings in the preterit singular. The strong second person singular was built on the preterit plural stem (the third principal part), rather than on the preterit singular of the other two persons (the second principal part).

SUBJUNCTIVE AND IMPERATIVE FORMS

The **subjunctive** did not indicate person but only tense and number. The endings were alike for both tenses: singular *-e* and plural *-en*. In strong verbs, the preterit subjunctive of both numbers was built on the preterit plural stem (the third principal part).

The subjunctive was used in main clauses to express wishes and commands: *God ūs helpe* '(May) God help us'; *Ne hēo hundas cēpe* 'She shall not keep dogs.' It was also used in a wide variety of subordinate clauses, including constructions in which we still use it: *swelce hē tam wǣre* 'as if he were tame.' But it was also used in many subordinate clauses where we would no longer employ it: *Ic heom sægde þæt hēo blīŏe wǣre* 'I told them that she was happy.'

The **imperative** singular of *cēpan* and *helpan* was without ending, but for some verbs it ended in *-e* or *-a*. All three types are illustrated in the following passage from *Beowulf*, lines 658–60:

> *Hafa* nū ond *geheald* hūsa sēlest,
> *gemyne* mǣrþo, mægen-ellen *cȳŏ*,
> *waca* wiŏ wrāþum!

> *Have* now and *hold* (of) houses the best,
> *remember* fame, mighty valor *make known*,
> *watch* against (the) hostile (one)!

As in Modern English, imperatives were used for making commands.

NONFINITE FORMS

In addition to their **finite forms** (those having personal endings), Old English verbs had four **nonfinite forms**: two infinitives and two participles. The simple infinitive ended in *-an* for most verbs; for some weak verbs, its ending was *-ian* (*bodian* 'to proclaim,' *nerian* 'to save'), and for some verbs that underwent contraction, the ending was *-n* (*fōn* 'to seize,' *gān* 'to go'). The inflected infinitive was a relic of an earlier time when infinitives were declined like nouns. The two infinitives were often, but not always, interchangeable. The inflected infinitive was especially used when the infinitive had a noun function, like a Modern English gerund: *Is blīðe tō helpenne* 'It is joyful to help'; 'Helping is joyful.'

The participles were used much like those of Modern English, as parts of verb phrases and as modifiers. The usual ending of the present participle was -*ende* (or -*nde* for those verbs in which the -*a*- of the infinitive is missing). The ending of the strong past participle, -*en*, has survived in many strong verbs to the present day: *bitten, eaten, frozen, swollen*. The ending of weak past participles, -*d* or -*t*, was, of course, the source for all regular past participial inflection in Modern English. The prefix *ge*- was fairly general for past participles but occurred sometimes as a prefix in all forms. It survived in the past participle throughout the Middle English period as *y*- (or *i*-) and is familiar to us in Milton's archaic use in "L'Allegro": "In heaven ycleped Euphrosyne . . ." (from OE *geclypod* 'called').

WEAK VERBS

The great majority of Old English verbs formed their preterits and past participles in the characteristically Germanic way, by the addition of a suffix containing *d* or, immediately after voiceless consonants, *t*. There were three classes of weak verbs, with various subclasses. The kinds of weak verbs can be illustrated by citing the principal parts for a few of them:

		INFINITIVE	PRETERIT	PAST PARTICIPLE
Class I		fremman 'to do'	fremede 'did'	gefremed 'done'
		cēpan 'to keep'	cēpte 'kept'	gecēpcd 'kept'
		hīeran 'to hear'	hīerde 'heard'	gehīered 'heard'
		ferian 'to carry'	ferede 'carried'	gefered 'carried'
		bycgan 'to buy'	bohte 'bought'	geboht 'bought'
		þencan 'to think'[7]	þōhte 'thought'	geþōht 'thought'
		þyncan 'to seem'	þūhte 'seemed'	geþūht 'seemed'
Class II		endian 'to end'	endode 'ended'	geendod 'ended'
Class III		habban 'to have'	hæfde 'had'	gehæfd 'had'
		secgan 'to say'	sægde 'said'	gesægd 'said'
		hycgan 'to think'	hogde 'thought'	gehogod 'thought'

Many of the weak verbs were originally causative verbs derived from nouns, adjectives, or other verbs by the addition of a suffix with an *i*-sound that mutated the stem vowel of the word. Thus, *flȳman* 'to cause to flee' is from the noun *flēam* 'flight'; *fyllan* 'to fill, cause to be full' is from the

---

[7]*þencan* 'think' and *þyncan* 'seem' were early confused and ultimately fell together. Archaic *methinks* is thus not to be interpreted as 'I think,' but as '[it] seems to me.'

Verbs

126   adjective *full*; and *settan* 'to set, cause to sit' is from the verb *sæt*, the preterit singular of *sittan*. Other pairs of words of the same sort are, in their Modern English forms, *feed* 'cause to have *food*,' *fell* 'cause to *fall*,' and *lay* 'cause to *lie*.'

STRONG VERBS

Most other Old English verbs—all others, in fact, except for a few very frequently used ones to be discussed later—formed their preterits by a vowel change called **gradation** (Grimm's **ablaut**), perhaps due to Indo-European variations in pitch and stress. Gradation is by no means confined to these strong verbs, but it is best illustrated by them. Gradation should never be confused with mutation (umlaut), which, as we have seen (pp. 107, 115), is the approximation of a vowel in a stressed syllable to another vowel (or semi-vowel) in a following syllable. Although there are roughly similar phenomena in other languages, the type of mutation we have been concerned with is confined to Germanic languages. Gradation, which is much more ancient, is an Indo-European phenomenon common to all the languages derived from Proto-Indo-European. The vowel differences reflected in Modern English *ride–rode–ridden, choose–chose, bind–bound, come–came, eat–ate, shake–shook*, which exemplify gradation, are thus an Indo-European inheritance.

Like the other Germanic languages, Old English had seven classes of strong verbs. The differences among these classes rested on the particular vowel alternations in their principal parts, of which there were four. Like the Modern English preterit of *be*, which distinguishes between the singular *I was* and the plural *we were*, strong verbs had a singular and a plural preterit. Had that number distinction survived into present-day English, we would be saying *I rode* but *we rid*, and *I fand* but *we found*. Sometimes the old singular has survived into current use and sometimes the old plural (and sometimes neither, but a different form altogether). Some examples of the seven strong classes, with their principal parts, follow:

	INFINITIVE	PRETERIT SINGULAR	PRETERIT PLURAL	PAST PARTICIPLE
Class I	drīfan 'drive'	drāf	drifon	gedrifen
	rīdan 'ride'	rād	ridon	geriden
	rīsan 'rise'	rās	rison	gerisen
	wrītan 'write'	wrāt	writon	gewriten
Class II (1)	clēofan 'cleave'	clēaf	clufon	geclofen
	crēopan 'creep'	crēap	crupon	gecropen
(2)	scūfan 'shove'	scēaf	scufon	gescofen
	sprūtan 'sprout'	sprēat	spruton	gesproten

	(3)	frēosan 'freeze'	frēas	fruron	gefroren
		lēosan 'lose'	lēas	luron	geloren
		sēoðan 'seethe'	sēað	sudon	gesoden
Class III	(1)	drincan 'drink'	dranc	druncon	gedruncen
		findan 'find'	fand	fundon	gefunden
		sincan 'sink'	sanc	suncon	gesuncen
		singan 'sing'	sang	sungon	gesungen
		springan 'spring'	sprang	sprungon	gesprungen
		swimman 'swim'	swamm	swummon	geswummen
	(2)	helpan 'help'	healp	hulpon	geholpen
		meltan 'melt'	mealt	multon	gemolten
		swellan 'swell'	sweall	swullon	geswollen
	(3)	ceorfan 'carve'	cearf	curfon	gccorfen
		feohtan 'fight'	feaht	fuhton	gefohten
		steorfan 'die'	stearf	sturfon	gestorfen
		weorpan 'throw'	wearp	wurpon	geworpen
Class IV		beran 'bear'	bær	bǣron	geboren
		stelan 'steal'	stæl	stǣlon	gestolen
		teran 'tear'	tær	tǣron	getoren
Class V	(1)	metan 'mete'	mæt	mǣton	gemeten
		sprecan 'speak'	spræc	sprǣcon	gesprecen
	(2)	gifan 'give'	gcaf	gēafon	gegifen
Class VI	(1)	faran 'fare, go'	fōr	fōron	gefaren
		scacan 'shake'	scōc	scōcon	gescacen
	(2)	standan 'stand'	stōd	stōdon	gestanden
Class VII	(1)	cnāwan 'know'	cnēow	cnēowon	gecnāwen
		feallan 'fall'	fēoll	fēollon	gefeallen
		flōwan 'flow'	flēow	flēowon	geflōwen
	(2)	hātan 'be called'	hēt	hēton	gchāten
		slǣpan 'sleep'	slēp	slēpon	geslǣpen

Class I strong verbs had the root vowels *i, ā, i, i* in their four principal parts.

Most Class II verbs had the vowels *ēo, ēa, u, o*; but a few have *ū* instead in the first principal part. The change from *s* to *r* in the last two principal parts of *lēosan* and *frēosan* and from *ð* to *d* in those of *sēoðan* were the result of Verner's Law. The Indo-European accent was on the ending of these forms rather than on the stem of the word, as in the first two principal parts, thus creating the necessary conditions for the operation of Verner's Law. The consonant alternation is not preserved in Modern English, except for the adjective *sodden*, originally the past participle of *seethe*.

Class III verbs had two consonants after the root vowel. If the first of those consonants was a nasal, the vowel gradation was *i, a, u, u*. If the first

Verbs

of the two consonants was an *l*, the gradation was *e, ea, u, o*. If the first of the consonants was *r* or *h*, the gradation was *eo, ea, u, o*.

Class IV verbs typically had a single *l* or *r* after the root vowel and the gradation *e, æ, ǣ, o*.

Class V verbs had a single consonant (other than *l* or *r*) after the root vowel and the gradation *e, æ, ǣ, e*. The initial *g* (pronounced [y]) of *gifan* affected the following vowel by a process known as palatal diphthongization and produced the gradation *i* (earlier *ie*), *ea, ēa, i* (*ie*).

Class VI verbs had the gradation *a, ō, ō, a*.

Class VII verbs were less regular than the other strong classes. They had the same root vowel in the first and fourth principal parts (although the identity of that vowel was unpredictable), and they had the same vowel in the two principal parts of the preterit—either *ē* or *ēo*.

PRETERIT-PRESENT VERBS

Old English had a few verbs that were originally strong but whose strong preterit came to be used in a present-time sense; consequently, they had to form new weak preterits. They are called **preterit-present verbs** and are the main source for the important group of modal verbs in Modern English. The following are ones that survive as present-day modals:

INFINITIVE	PRESENT	PRETERIT
āgan 'owe'	āh	āhte (*ought*)
cunnan 'know how'	cann (*can*)	cūðe (*could*)
magan 'be able'	mæg (*may*)	meahte (*might*)
*mōtan 'be allowed'	mōt	mōste (*must*)
sculan 'be obliged'	sceal (*shall*)	sceolde (*should*)

Although not a part of this group in Old English, the verb *willan*, preterit *wolde* 'wish, want' (the origin of Modern English *will*, *would*), also became a part of the present-day modal system.

ANOMALOUS VERBS

It is not really surprising that very commonly used verbs should have developed irregularities. *Bēon* 'to be' was in Old English, as its modern descendant still is, to some extent a badly mixed-up verb, with alternative present indicative forms from several different roots, as follows (with appropriate pronouns):

The Old English Period (449–1100)

(ic) eom *or* bēo 'I am'
(þū) eart *or* bist 'you (sg.) are'
(hē, hēo, hit) is *or* bið 'he, she, it is'

(wē, gē, hī) sindon, sind, sint, *or* bēoð 'we, you, they are'

The forms *eom, is,* and *sind(on)* or *sint* were from an Indo-European root *es-, with the forms *esmi, *esti, and *senti, seen in Sanskrit *asmi, asti,* and *santi* and in Latin *sum, est, sunt.* The second person *eart* was from a different Indo-European root, *er- with the original meaning 'arise.' The Modern English plural *are* is from an Anglian form derived from that same root. The forms beginning with *b* were from a third root *bheu-, from which came also Sanskrit *bhavati* 'becomes' and Latin *fui* 'have been.' The preterit forms were from yet another verb, whose infinitive in Old English was *wesan* (a Class V strong verb):

(ic) wæs
(þū) wǣre
(hē, hēo, hit) wæs
(wē, gē, hī) wǣron

The alternation of *s* and *r* in the preterit was the result of Verner's Law. The Old English verb for 'be,' like its Modern English counterpart, combined forms of what were originally four different verbs (seen in the present-day forms *be, am, are, was*). Paradigms which thus combine historically unrelated forms are called **suppletive**.

Another suppletive verb is *gān* 'go,' whose preterit *ēode* was doubtless from the same Indo-European root as the Latin verb *eō* 'go.' Modern English has lost the *ēode* preterit but has found a new suppletive form for *go* in *went,* the irregular preterit of *wend* (compare *send, sent*). Also irregular, although not suppletive, is *dōn* 'do' with the preterit *dyde.*

It is notable that *to be* alone has preserved distinctive singular and plural preterit forms (*was, were*) in standard Modern English. Nonstandard speakers have carried through the tendency that has reduced the preterit forms of all other verbs to a single form, and they get along very nicely with *you was,* *we was,* and *they was,* which are certainly no more inherently "bad" than *you sang, we sang,* and *they sang*—for *sung* in the plural would be the historically "correct" development of Old English *gē, wē, hī sungon.*

Syntax

Old English syntax has an easily recognizable kinship with that of Modern English. There are, of course, differences—and some striking ones—but they do not disguise the close similarity between an Old English sentence and its

Modern English counterpart. Many of those differences have already been treated in this chapter, but they may be summarized as follows:

1. Nouns, adjectives, and most pronouns had fuller inflection for case than their modern developments do; the inflected forms were used to signal a word's function in its sentence.

2. Adjectives agreed in case, number, and gender with the nouns they modified.

3. Adjectives were also inflected for "definiteness" in the so-called strong and weak declensions.

4. Numbers could be used either as we use them, to modify a noun, as in *þrītig scyllingas* 'thirty shillings,' or as nominals, with the accompanying word in the genitive case, as in *þrītig rihtwīsra*, literally 'thirty of righteous men.' Such use of the genitive was regular with the indeclinable noun *fela* 'much, many': *fela goldes* 'much [of] gold' or *fela folca* 'many [of] people.'

5. Old English used the genitive inflection in many circumstances that would call for an *of* phrase in Modern English—for example, *ðæs īglandes micel dæl* 'a great deal of the island,' literally, 'that island's great deal.'

6. Old English had no articles, properly speaking. Where we would use a definite article, the Anglo-Saxons often used one of the demonstratives (such as *se* 'that' or *þes* 'this'); and, where we would use an indefinite article, they sometimes used either the numeral *ān* 'one' or *sum* 'a certain.' But all of those words had stronger meanings than the Modern English definite and indefinite articles; so, frequently Old English had no word at all where we would expect an article.

7. Although Old English could form verb phrases just as we do by combining the verbs for 'have' and 'be' with participles (as in Modern English *has run* and *is running*), it did so less frequently, and the system of such combinations was less fully developed. Combinations using both those auxiliary verbs, such as *has been running*, did not occur in Old English, and one-word forms of the verb (like *runs* and *ran*) were used more often than today. Thus, although Old and Modern English are alike in having just two inflected tenses, the present and the preterit, Old English used those tenses to cover a wider range of meanings than does Modern English, which has frequent recourse to verb phrases. Old English often relied on adverbs to convey nuances of meaning that we would express by verb phrases; for example, Modern English *He had come* corresponds to Old English *Hē ǣer cōm*, literally 'He earlier came.'

8. Old English formed passive verb phrases much as we do, but it often used the simple infinitive in a passive sense as we do not—for example, *Hēo hēht hine lǣran* 'She ordered him to be taught,' in which *lǣran* is the infinitive with a literal meaning of 'to teach.' Another Old English alternative for the Modern passive was the indefinite pronoun *man* 'one,' as in *Hine man hēng* 'Him one hanged,' that is, 'He was hanged.'

9. The subjunctive mood was more common in Old English. It was used, for example, after some verbs that do not require it in Modern English, as in *Sume men cweðaþ ðæt hit sȳ feaxede steorra* 'Some men say that it [a comet] be a long-haired star.' It is also used in constructions where conservative present-day usage has it: *swilce hē wǣre* 'as if he were' or *þeah hē ealne middangeard gestrȳne* 'though he [the] whole world gain.'

10. Old English had a number of **impersonal verbs** that were used without a subject: *Mē lyst rǣdan* '[It] pleases me to read' and *Swā mē þyncþ* 'So [it] seems to me.' The object of the verb (in these examples, *mē*) comes before it and in the second example gave rise to the now archaic expression *methinks* (literally 'to me seems'), which the modern reader is likely to misinterpret as an odd combination of *me* as subject and the present-day verb *think*.

11. The subject of any Old English verb could be omitted if it was implied by the context, especially when the verb followed a clause that expressed the subject: *Hē þē æt sunde oferflāt, hæfde māre mægen* 'He outstripped you at swimming, [he] had more strength.'

12. On the other hand, the subject of an Old English verb might be expressed twice—once as a pronoun at its appropriate place in the structure of the sentence and once as a phrase or clause in anticipation: *And þā þe þær tō lāfe wǣron, hī cōmon tō þæs carcernes dura* 'And those that were there as survivors, they came to that prison's door.' This construction occurs in Modern English but is often considered inelegant; it is frequent in Old English.

13. The Old English negative adverb *ne* came before (rather than after) the verb it modified: *Ic ne dyde* 'I did not.' Consequently it contracted with certain following verbs: *nis* (*ne is* 'is not'), *nille* (*ne wille* 'will not'), *næfð* (*ne hæfð* 'has not'); compare the Modern English contraction of *not* with certain preceding verbs: *isn't, won't, hasn't.*

14. Old English word order was somewhat less fixed than that of Modern English but in general was about the same. Old English declarative sentences tended to fall into the subject-verb-complement order usual in Modern English—for example, *Hē wæs swīðe spēdig man* 'He was a very successful man' and *Eadwine eorl cōm mid landfyrde and drāf hine ūt* 'Earl Edwin came with a land army and drove him out.' Declarative sentences that did not conform to this pattern sometimes occurred when the object of the verb was a pronoun (*Se hālga Andreas him andswarode* 'The holy Andrew him answered') and usually when the sentence began with *þā* 'then, when' or *ne* 'not' (*Þā sealde se cyning him sweord* 'Then gave the king him a sword'; *Ne can ic nōht singan* 'Cannot I nought sing [I cannot sing anything]'); in sentences of the first type the object often preceded the verb, and in those of the second type the verb usually preceded the subject. In dependent clauses the verb usually came last, as always in German (*God geseah þā þæt hit gōd wæs* 'God saw then that it good was'; *Sē micla here, þe wē gefyrn ymbe sprǣcon . . .* 'The great army, which we before about spoke . . .'). In Old

English interrogative sentences followed the same verb-subject-complement pattern as Modern English now follows (*Hæfst þū ǣnigne gefēran?* 'Hast thou any companion?').

15. Although Old English had a variety of ways of subordinating one clause to another, it favored what grammarians call **parataxis**—the juxtaposing of clauses with no formal signal of their relationship other than perhaps a coordinating conjunction. These three clauses describe how Orpheus lost his wife Eurydice in an Old English retelling of the Greek legend (cited by Mitchell 1968, p. 99): *Ða hē forð on ðæt leoht cōm, ðā beseah he hine under bæc wið ðæs wīfes; ðā losode hēo him sōna* 'Then [when] he came forth into that light, then looked he backward toward that woman; then slipped she from him immediately.'

There are a good many other syntactic differences that could be listed; if all of them were, the resulting list would suggest that Old English was far removed in structure from its modern development. But the suggestion would be misleading, for the two stages of the language are much more united by their similarities than divided by their differences.

Old English Illustrated

The first two of the following passages in late West Saxon are from a translation of the Old Testament by Ælfric, the greatest prose writer of the Old English period. The opening verses of chapters 1 and 2 of Genesis are printed here from the edition of the Early English Text Society (O.S. 160), with abbreviations expanded, modern punctuation and capitalization added, some obvious scribal errors corrected, and a few unusual forms regularized. The third passage is the parable of the Prodigal Son (Luke 15), edited by Walter W. Skeat (*The Holy Gospels in Anglo-Saxon, Northumbrian, and Old Mercian Versions*, 1871–87), also slightly regularized.

I. **1.** On   angynne gescēop God heofonan and eorðan.   **2.** Sēo
In [the] beginning created God heavens   and earth.   The

eorðe sōðlīce wæs īdel and ǣmtig, and þēostra   wǣron over ðǣre
earth truly   was void and empty, and darknesses were   over the

nywelnysse brādnysse; and Godes gāst wæs geferod ofer   wæteru.
abyss's   surface;   and God's spirit was brought over [the] water.

3. God cwæð ðā: Gewurðe lēoht, and lēoht wearð geworht. **4.** God
God said then: Be   light, and light was   made.   God

geseah ðā   ðæt hit gōd   wæs, and hē tōdǣlde ðæt lēoht fram ðām
saw   then that it good was, and he divided the light from the

ðēostrum. **5.** And hēt   ðæt lēoht dæg and þā ðēostru niht: ðā
darkness.   And called the light day and the darkness night: then

wæs geworden ǣfen   and morgen ān dæg.
was   evening and morning one day.

II. **1.** Eornostlīce ðā   wǣron fullfremode heofonas and eorðe and
                Indeed   then were completed   heaven   and earth and

eall heora frætewung. **2.** And God ðā   gefyldc on ðone seofoðan dæg
all their ornaments.   And God then finished on the   seventh day

fram eallum ðām weorcum ðe   hē gefremode. **3.** And God geblētsode
from all   the work   that he made.   And God blessed

ðone seofoðan dæg and hine gehālgode, for ðan ðe hē on ðone dæg
the seventh day and it   hallowcd, because   he on that day

geswāc   his weorces, ðe   hē gescēop tō wyrcenne.
ceased from his work,   that he made   to be done.

XV. **11.** Sōðlīce sum man hæfde twēgen suna. **12.** Þā cwæð se gingra
tō his fæder, "Fæder, syle mē mīnne dǣl mīnre æhte þe mē tō gebyreþ."
Þā dǣlde hē him his æhta. **13.** Đā æfter fēawum dagum ealle his þing
gegaderode se gingra sunu and fērde wrǣclīce on feorlen rīce and forspilde
þǣr his æhta, lybbende on his gǣlsan. **14.** Đā hē hȳ hæfde ealle āmyrrede,
þā wearð mycel hunger on þām rīce and hē wearð wǣdla. **15.** Þā fērde hē
and folgode ānum burhsittendum men þæs rīces; ðā sende hē hine tō his
tūne þæt hē hēolde his swīn. **16.** Đā gewilnode hē his wambe gefyllan of
þām bēancoddum þe ðā swȳn ǣton, and him man ne sealde. **17.** Þā beþōhte
hē hine and cwæð, "Ēalā hū fela yrðlinga on mīnes fæder hūse hlāf genōhne
habbað, and ic hēr on hungre forwurðe! . . ." **20.** And hē ārās þā and cōm
tō his fæder. And þā gȳt þā hē wæs feorr his fæder, hē hine geseah and wearð
mid mildheortnesse āstyred and ongēan hine arn and hine beclypte and cyste
hine. **21.** Đā cwæð his sunu, "Fæder, ic syngode on heofon and beforan
ðē. Nū ic ne eom wyrþe þæt ic þīn sunu bēo genemned." **22.** Đā cwæþ se
fæder tō his þēowum, "Bringað hræðe þone sēlestan gegyrelan and scrȳdað
hine, and syllað him hring on his hand and gescȳ tō his fōtum. **23.** And
bringað ān fætt styric and ofslēað, and uton etan and gewistfullian. **24.** For
þām þes mīn sunu wæs dēad, and hē geedcucode; hē forwearð, and hē is
gemēt."

It is frequently supposed that the Old English period was somehow gray, dull, and crude.[8] Nothing could be further from the truth. England after its conversion to Christianity at the end of the sixth century became a veritable beehive of scholarly activity. The famous monasteries at Canterbury, Glastonbury, Wearmouth, Lindisfarne, Jarrow, and York were great centers of learning where men such as Aldhelm, Benedict Biscop, Bede, and Alcuin pursued their studies. The great scholarly movement to which Bede belonged is largely responsible for the preservation of classical culture for us. It was to the famous cathedral school at York founded by one of Bede's pupils that Charles the Great (Charlemagne) turned for leadership in his Carolingian Renaissance, and especially to the illustrious English scholar Alcuin (Ealhwine), born in the year of Bede's death and educated at York. A Devonshire man, Wynfrith, later known as Boniface, led the band of English missionaries who brought the Christian faith and Christian culture to Germany. Earlier in a brilliant career that ended in his martyrdom by a band of heathen fanatics, Boniface had assisted Willibrord, the English-born and English-educated bishop of Utrecht, in his missionary labors in Frisia (Friesland).

The culture of the north of England in the seventh and eighth centuries was to spread over the entire country, despite the decline that it suffered as a result of the hammering onslaughts of the Danes. Luckily, because of the tremendous energy and ability of Alfred the Great, it was not lost; and Alfred's able successors of the royal house of Wessex down to the time of the second Ethelred consolidated the cultural and political contributions made by their most distinguished ancestor.

With English culture more advanced than any other in western Europe, the Norman Conquest amounted to a crushing defeat of a superior culture by an inferior one, as the Normans themselves were in time to have the good sense to realize—for they, like the Scandinavian invaders who had preceded them, were ultimately to become English. As for the English language, which is our main concern here, it was certainly one of the most highly developed vernacular tongues in Europe—for French did not become a literary language until well after the period of the Conquest—with a word stock capable of

---

[8] Those who think so are advised to examine the marvelous Sutton Hoo treasure the next time they visit the British Museum. This collection of finely wrought gold jewelry, weapons and armor, and luxurious household furnishings, dating from the seventh century, was discovered in Suffolk in 1939. It is the subject of chapter 5 of D. Elizabeth Martin-Clarke's *Culture in Early Anglo-Saxon England* (1947), and of Rupert Bruce-Mitford's *Aspects of Anglo-Saxon Archaeology: Sutton Hoo and Other Discoveries* (1974), which contain illustrations. *The Sutton Hoo Ship-Burial*, published by the Trustees of the British Museum (1947), has a full description of the finds, with many illustrations. *Hoo* is a topographical term, from Old English *hōh* 'spur of land.'

will be dealt with in some detail in a later chapter.

For Further Reading

History and Culture

Anglo-Saxon England 1– (1972–).
Blair, *An Introduction to Anglo-Saxon England*, 1977.
Bruce-Mitford, *Aspects of Anglo-Saxon Archaeology: Sutton Hoo and Other Discoveries*, 1974.
Finberg, *The Formation of England, 550–1042*, 1974.
Fisher, *The Anglo-Saxon Age, c. 400–1042*, 1973.
Hodgkin, *A History of the Anglo-Saxons*, 1952.
Humble, *The Fall of Saxon England*, 1975.
Martin-Clarke, *Culture in Early Anglo-Saxon England*, 1947.
Stenton, *Anglo-Saxon England*, 1947.

Introductory Textbooks

Alston, *An Introduction to Old English*, 1961.
Brook, *An Introduction to Old English*, 1962.
Cassidy and Ringler, *Bright's Old English Grammar and Reader*, 1971.
Kispert, *Old English: An Introduction*, 1971.
Marckwardt and Rosier, *Old English Language and Literature*, 1972.
Mitchell, *A Guide to Old English*, 1968.
Moore and Knott, *The Elements of Old English*, 1955.

Grammar

Andrew, *Syntax and Style in Old English*, 1966.
Campbell, *Old English Grammar*, 1959.
Gardner, *An Analysis of Syntactic Patterns of Old English*, 1971.
Quirk and Wrenn, *An Old English Grammar*, 1955.
Shannon, *A Descriptive Syntax of the Parker Manuscript of the Anglo-Saxon Chronicle from 734 to 891*, 1964.
Wardale, *An Old English Grammar*, 1964.
Wright and Wright, *Old English Grammar*, 1925.

Generative Phonology

Lass and Anderson, *Old English Phonology*, 1975.

Lexicon

Barney, *Word-Hoard: An Introduction to Old English Vocabulary*, 1977.
Hall, *A Concise Anglo-Saxon Dictionary*, 1960.
Toller, *An Anglo-Saxon Dictionary Based on the Manuscript Collections of the Late Joseph Bosworth*, 1898.

6 The Middle English Period (1100-1500)

The dates for the beginning and end of the Middle English period are more or less arbitrary. By 1100 certain changes, which had begun long before, were sufficiently well established to justify our use of the adjective *middle* to designate the language in what was actually a period of transition from the English of the early Middle Ages—Old English—to that of the earliest printed books, which, despite certain superficial differences, is essentially the same as our own.

The changes that occurred during this transitional, or "middle," period may be noted in every aspect of the language: in its sounds, in the meanings of its words, and in the nature of its word stock, where many Old English words were replaced by French ones. During the Middle English period there were such extensive changes in pronunciation, particularly of unaccented inflectional endings, that grammar too was profoundly altered. Many of the grammatical distinctions of the Old English period disappeared, thereby producing a language that is structurally far more like the one we speak. As we proceed, we shall examine these developments in some detail.

136

Almost at the end of the Old English period the great catastrophe of the Norman Conquest befell the English people—a catastrophe more far-reaching in its effects on English culture than the earlier harassment by the Scandinavians who had subsequently become one with them.

After the death without issue of Edward the Confessor, the last king in the direct male line of descent from Alfred the Great, Harold, son of the powerful Earl Godwin, was elected to the kingship. Almost immediately his possession of the crown was challenged by William, the seventh duke of Normandy, who was distantly related to Edward the Confessor and who felt that he had a better claim to the throne for a number of tenuous reasons.

The Norman Conquest—fortunately for Anglo-American culture and civilization, the last invasion of England—was, like the earlier harassments, carried out by Northmen, who under the leadership of William the Conqueror defeated the English under the hapless King Harold at the battle of Hastings in 1066. Harold was killed by an arrow that pierced his eye, and the English, deprived of his effective leadership and that of his two brothers, who also fell in the battle, were ignominiously defeated.

William and the Northmen whose *dux* he was came not immediately from Scandinavia but from France, a region whose northern coast their not-very-remote Viking ancestors had invaded and settled as recently as the ninth and tenth centuries, beginning at about the same time that other pagan Vikings were making trouble for Alfred the Great in England. Those Scandinavians who settled in France are commonly designated by an Old French form of *Northmen*, that is, *Normans*, and the section of France that they settled and governed was called Normandy.

The Conqueror was a bastard son of Robert the Devil, who took such pains in the early part of his life to earn his surname among other things, he was accused, doubtless justly, of poisoning the brother whom he succeeded as duke of Normandy—that he became a figure of legend. So great was his capacity for rascality that he was also called Robert the Magnificent. Ironically, he died in the course of a holy pilgrimage to Jerusalem.

Robert's great-great-grandfather was Rollo (*Hrólfr*), a Danish chieftain who was created first duke of Normandy after coming to terms satisfactory to himself with King Charles the Simple of France. In the five generations intervening between Duke Rollo and Duke William, the Normans had become French culturally and linguistically, at least superficially—though we must always remember that in those days the French had no learning, art, or literature comparable to what was flourishing in England, nor had they ever seen anything comparable, as they themselves were willing to admit, to the products of English artisans: carving, jewelry, tapestry, metalwork, and the like. Their **Norman French** dialect developed in England into **Anglo-Norman**, a variety of French that was the object of amusement even among the English in later times.

For a long time after the Norman Conquest, French was the language of the governing classes in England. Nevertheless there was never any period during which the majority of the country's population did not speak English. The loss of Normandy in 1204 by King John, a descendant of the Conqueror, removed an important tie with France, and subsequent events were to loosen those that remained. The Hundred Years' War, beginning in 1337, saw England and France bitter enemies in a long, drawn-out conflict—though it actually fell somewhat short of a hundred years—which gave the death blow to the already moribund use of French in England. Those whose ancestors were Normans eventually came to think of themselves as English.

The Linguistic Influence of the Conquest

The impact of the Norman Conquest on the English language, like that made by the earlier Norse-speaking invaders, was to a large extent confined to the word stock, though Middle English also showed some instances of the influence of French idiom. A huge body of French words were ultimately to become part of the English vocabulary, many of them replacing English words that would have done for us just as well. This older French element (in contrast with newer borrowings like *chef*, *tête-à-tête*, and *café*) will be discussed in a later chapter dealing specifically with loanwords in English. Suffice it to point out here merely that English acquired, as it were, a new look.

Compare the following pairs, in which the first word or phrase is from the Old English translation of the parable of the Prodigal Son (cited on p. 133), and the second is from the Middle English translation (cited on pp. 165–66):

> æhta, catel 'property'
> burhsittende man, citeseyn 'citizen'
> dæl, porcioun 'portion'
> dælde, departide 'divided'
> forwearð, perischid 'perished'
> gælsa, lecherously 'lechery, lecherously'
> genōh, plente 'enough, plenty'
> gewilnode, coueitide 'wanted, coveted'
> gewistfullian, make we feeste 'let us feast'
> mildheortness, mercy 'mercy'
> rīce, cuntre 'country'
> þēow, seruaunt 'servant'
> wræclīce, in pilgrymage 'abroad, traveling'

The Middle English Period (1100–1500)

In each case, the first expression is native English and the second is, or contains, a word borrowed from French. In a few instances, the corresponding Modern English expression is different from either of the older forms: though Middle English *catel* survives as *cattle*, its meaning has become more specific than it was; and so has that of Middle English *pilgrymage*, which now refers to a particular kind of journey. However, most of the French terms have continued unchanged in present-day use. The French tincture of our vocabulary, which began in Middle English times, has been maintained or even intensified in Modern English.

Middle English Spelling

CONSONANTS

Just as French words were borrowed, so too were French spelling conventions. Some of the apparent innovations in Middle English spelling were, in fact, a return to earlier conventions. For example, the digraph *th* had been used in some of the earliest English texts—those written before 900—but was replaced in later Old English writing by þ and ð; during the Middle English period, *th* was gradually reintroduced, and during early Modern English times printers regularized its use. Similarly, *uu*, used for [w] in early manuscripts, was supplanted by the runic wynn, but was brought back to England by Norman scribes in a ligatured form as *w*. The origin of this symbol is accurately indicated by its name, *double-u*.

Other new spellings were true innovations. The Old English symbol ȝ was an Irish form; *g* entered English writing later from the Continent. In late Old English ȝ had three values, as we have seen (pp. 107–08). In Middle English times it acquired a somewhat different form, ȝ (called **yogh**),[1] and was used for two sounds that came to be spelled *y* and *gh* later in the period. Old English, for instance, wrote *ȝeldan* 'to yield,' *cniht* 'knight,' and *þurh* 'through'; early Middle English wrote the same words *ȝelde(n)*, *cniȝt*, and *þurȝ*; later Middle English (as in Chaucer) wrote them *yelde(n)*, *knyght*, and *thurgh*. The characteristic conservatism of Modern English spelling is reflected in our retention of the Middle English *gh* in the last two words (and others like them) even though the velar fricative sound that the spelling represented has long disappeared from all types of English except Scots.

After the Norman Conquest, the French form *g* supplanted Old English ȝ to indicate [g] in English words; and, with the introduction of French words

[1] This symbol, which continued to be written in Scotland long after the English had given it up, has been mistaken for *z*—the symbol that printers, having no ȝ in their fonts, used for it—as in the pronunciation of the names *Kenzie* (compare *Kenny*, with revised spelling to indicate a pronunciation somewhat closer to the historical one) and *Menzies*. For other examples of this erroneous interpretation of ȝ as *z*, see Otto Jespersen (1909–49, 1: 22–23).

into English, the newer symbol was used also with the value that it had in Old French before *e* and *i*—for instance, *gem* and *age*—which is the same value that it has in Modern English. Modern English thus preserves in loanwords what was formerly the French value of *g* when followed by *e* or *i*; in Modern French the older sound has become that of the final consonant of *rouge*, or the medial sound of English *measure*.

The consonant sound [v] did not occur initially in Old English, which used *f* for the [v] that developed internally, as in *drifen* 'driven,' *hæfde* 'had,' and *scofl* 'shovel.' Except for a very few words that have entered standard English from Southern English dialects, in which initial [f] became [v]—for instance, *vixen*, the feminine of *vox* 'fox'—no standard English words of native origin begin with [v]. Practically all our words with initial *v* have been taken from Latin or French. No matter how familiar such words as *vulgar* (Latin), *vocal* (Latin), *very* (French), and *voice* (French) may be to us now, they were once regarded as foreign words—as indeed they are, despite their long naturalization. The introduction of the letter *v* (a variant of *u*) to indicate the prehistoric Old English development of [f] to [v] was an innovation of Anglo-Norman scribes in Middle English times: thus the Middle English form of Old English *drifen* was written *driven* or *driuen*.

When *v*, the angular form of curved *u*, came to be used in Middle English, scribes followed the Continental practice of using either symbol for either consonant or vowel; as a general thing, though, *v* was used initially and *u* elsewhere, regardless of the sound indicated, as in *very*, *vsury* (*usury*), and *euer* (*ever*), except in the neighborhood of *m* and *n*, where for the sake of legibility *v* was frequently used for the vowel in other than initial position.

Ch was used by French scribes, or by English ones under French influence, to indicate the initial sound of *child*, which in Old English had been spelled simply with *c*, as in *cild*. Following a short vowel, the same sound might also be spelled *cch* or *chch*: *catch* appears as *cache*, *cacche*, and *cachche*.

In early Old English times *sc* symbolized [sk], but during the course of the Old English period the graphic sequence came to indicate [š]. The *sh* spelling was an innovation of Anglo-Norman scribes (OE *sceal*—ME and ModE *shall*), who earlier had used *s*, *ss*, and *sch* for the same purpose.

Middle English scribes preferred the writing *wh* for the phonetically more accurate *hw* used in Old English times, as, for example, in Old English *hwæt*—Middle and Modern English *what*.

Under French influence, scribes in Middle English times used *c* before *e* and *i* (*y*) in French loanwords—for example, *citee* 'city' and *grace*—with an earlier French value of this symbol [ts], later becoming [s]. In Old English writing *c* never indicated [s], but only [k] and [č]. Thus, with the introduction of the newer French value, *c* remained an ambiguous symbol, though in a different way: it came to represent [k] before *a*, *o*, and *u* and before consonants, and [s] before *e* and *i* (*y*). *K*, used occasionally in Old English writing, thus came to be increasingly used before *e* and *i* (*y*) in Middle

English times (OE *cyn(n)* 'race'—ME *kin, kyn*) to indicate the stop sound, so that *c* might be reserved for the sibilant, as in *certain* (compare *curtain*, with *c* indicating [k] before *u*).

French scribal practices are responsible for the Middle English spelling *qu*, which French inherited from Latin, replacing Old English *cw*, as in *quellen* 'to kill,' *queen*, and *quethen* 'to say,' which despite their French look are all native English words (in Old English, respectively, *cwellan, cwen*, and *cweðan*).

Also French in origin is the digraph *gg*, supplanting in medial and final positions Old English *cg* (OE *ecg*—ME *egge*), later written *dg(e)*, as in Modern English *edge*.

VOWELS

To indicate vowel length, Middle English writing frequently employed double letters, particularly *ee* and *oo,* the practice becoming general in the East Midland dialect late in the period. These particular doublings have survived into our own day, though, of course, they do not indicate the same sounds as in Middle English. As a matter of fact, both *ee* and *oo* were ambiguous in the Middle English period, as every student of Chaucer must learn. One of the vowel sounds indicated by Middle English *ee* came generally to be written *ea* in the course of the sixteenth century; for the other sound *ee* was retained, alongside *ie* and, less frequently, *ei*—spellings that were also used to some extent in Middle English.

Double *o* came to be commonly used in later Middle English times for the long low-back rounded vowel [ɔ], the vowel that developed out of Old English long *a*. Unfortunately for the beginning student, the same double *o* was used for the continuation of Old English long *o*. As a result of this duplication, *rood* 'rode' (OE *rād*) and *rood* 'rood, cross' (OE *rōd*) were written with identical vowel symbols, though they were no more nearly alike in pronunciation than are their modern forms.

Final unstressed *e* following a single consonant also indicated vowel length in Middle English, as in *fode* 'food' and *fede* 'to feed'; this corresponds to the "silent *e*" of Modern English, as in *case, mete, bite, rote*, and *rule*. Doubled consonants, which indicated consonant length in earlier periods, began in Middle English times to indicate also that a preceding vowel was short. Surviving examples are *dinner* and *bitter*, as contrasted with *diner* and *biter*. In the North of England *i* was frequently used after a vowel to indicate that it was long, a practice responsible for such modern spellings as *raid* (literally a 'riding,' from OE *rād*, noun), *Reid* (a long-voweled variant of *red*, surviving only as a proper name), and Scots *guid* 'good,' as in Robert Burns's "Address to the Unco Guid, or the Rigidly Righteous."

Short *u* was commonly written *o* during the latter part of the Middle English period if *m, n, u (v, w)* were contiguous. The Middle English writings *sone* 'son' and *sonne* 'sun' thus indicate the same vowel sound [ʊ] that these words had in Old English, when they were written respectively *sunu* and *sunne*. *O* for *u* survives in a number of Modern English words besides *son*— for example, *come* (OE *cuman*), *wonder* (OE *wundor*), *monk* (OE *munuc*), *honey* (OE *hunig*), *tongue* (OE *tunge*), and *love* (OE *lufu*), the last of which, if it had not used the *o* spelling, would have been written *luue* (as indeed it was for a time).

The French spelling *ou* came to be used generally in the fourteenth century to represent English long *u*—for example, *hous* (OE *hūs*)—and sometimes represented the short *u* as well. Before a vowel the *u* of the digraph *ou* might well be mistaken as representing [v], for which the same symbol was used. To avoid confusion (as in *douer*, which was a possible writing for both *dower* and *Dover*), *u* was doubled in this position—that is, written *uu*, later *w*. This use of *w*, of course, would have been unnecessary if *u* and *v* had been differentiated as they are now. *W* also came to be used instead of *u* in final position.

Middle English scribes used *y* for the semivowel [y] and also, for the sake of legibility, as a variant of *i* in the vicinity of stroke letters—for example, *myn homcomynge* 'my homecoming.' Late in the Middle English period there was a tendency to write *y* for long *i* generally. *Y* was also regularly used in final position.

Middle English spelling was considerably more relaxed than present-day orthography. The foregoing remarks describe some of the spelling conventions of Middle English scribes, but there were a good many others, and all of them were used with a nonchalance that is hardly imaginable in the era of the printing press. Within a few lines, a scribe might spell both *water* and *watter*, *treese* and *tres* 'trees,' *nakid* and *nakyd*, *eddre* and *edder* 'adder,' *moneth* and *moneþ* 'month,' *clowdes* and *cloudeȝ* 'clouds,' as did the scribe who copied out a manuscript of the Wycliffite Bible (*Ms. Bodley 959*, ed. Conrad Lindberg, 1959). The notion that every word has, or ought to have, just one correct spelling is a relatively recent idea, which was not entertained by our medieval ancestors.

The Rise of a London Standard

Inasmuch as there is writing in all dialects, it is necessary to take some account of the dialectal diversity of Middle English. The Northern dialect corresponds roughly to Old English Northumbrian, its southernmost eastern boundary being also the Humber. Likewise, the Midland dialects, subdivided into East Midland and West Midland, correspond roughly to Old English Mercian. The Southern dialect, spoken south of the Thames, similarly corresponds roughly to West Saxon, with Kentish a subdivision.

It is not surprising that a type of speech—that of London—essentially

East Midlandish in its characteristics, though showing Northern and to a less extent Southern influences, should in time have become a standard for all of England. London had for centuries been a large (by medieval standards), prosperous, and hence important city.

Until the late fifteenth century, however, authors wrote in the dialect of their native regions—the authors of *Sir Gawain and the Green Knight* and of *Piers Plowman* in the West Midland dialect; the authors of *The Owl and the Nightingale*, of the *Ancrene Riwle*, and of the *Ayenbite of Inwit* in the Southern dialect (including Kentish); the author of the *Bruce* in the Northern dialect; and John Gower and Geoffrey Chaucer in the East Midland dialect, specifically the London variety of East Midland. Standard Modern English—American, however indirectly, as well as British—is a development of the speech of London. To this type of speech people of consequence and those who aspired to be people of consequence or to be the ancestors of people of consequence were endeavoring to conform long before the settlement of America by English-speaking people in the early part of the seventeenth

The Rise of a London Standard

century, though many of those who migrated to the New World obviously retained traces of their regional origins in their pronunciation, their vocabulary, and to a lesser degree in their syntax. Rather than speaking local dialects, most used a type of speech that had been influenced in varying degrees by the London standard. In effect, their speech was essentially that of London, with regional shadings.

Thus it comes about that the language of Chaucer and of Gower is so much easier for us to comprehend at first sight than, say, the Northern speech (specifically lowland Scots) of their contemporary John Barbour, author of the *Bruce*. In the following lines from Chaucer's *House of Fame*, for instance, an erudite eagle explains to Chaucer what speech really is:

> Soune ys noght but eyre ybroken
> And every spech that ys yspoken,
> Lowde or pryvee, foule or faire,
> In his substaunce ys but aire;
> For as flaumbe ys but lyghted smoke,
> Ryght soo soune ys aire y-broke.
> But this may be in many wyse,
> Of which I wil the twoo devyse:
> Of soune that cometh of pipe or harpe.
> For whan a pipe is blowen sharpe
> The aire ys twyst with violence
> And rent. Loo, thys ys my sentence.
> Eke, whan men harpe strynges smyte,
> Whether hyt be moche or lyte,
> Loo, with the stroke the ayre to-breketh:
> Thus wost thou wel what thinge is speche.[2]

Now compare Chaucer's English, so like our own, with that of the following excerpt from the *Bruce*:

> Þan wist he weill þai wald him sla,
> And for he wald his lord succour
> He put his lif in aventur
> And stud intill a busk lurkand
> Quhill þat þe hund com at his hand,
> And with ane arrow soyn hym slew
> And throu the wod syne hym withdrew.

---

[2] Except for modernization of the use of *u* and *v*, this passage is in the spelling of Fairfax MS 16 (Bodleian Library) as reproduced by Frederick Furnivall (1878, pt. 2, pp. 201–02).

The Middle English Period (1100–1500)

Then he knew well they wished to slay him,
And because he wished to succor his lord
He put his life in fortune's hands
And stood lurking in a bush
While the hound came to his hand,
And with one arrow immediately slew him
And through the wood afterward withdrew himself.

Distinctively Northern forms in this passage are *slā* (corresponding to East Midland *slee*), *wald* (E. Midl. *wolde*[*n*]), *stud* (E. Midl. *sto*[*o*]*d*); *weill*, in which the *i* indicates length of the preceding *e*; *lurkand* (E. Midl. *lurking*), *quhīll* (E. Midl. *whȳl*), *āne* (E. Midl. *ǭn*[3]), *intill* (E. Midl. *intō*), and *syne* (E. Midl. *sith*). *Soyn* 'soon, immediately' is merely a matter of spelling: the *y*, like the *i* in *weill*, indicates length in the preceding vowel, and not a pronunciation of the vowel different from that indicated by the usual East Midland spelling *sone*. The nominative form of the third person plural pronoun, *þai* 'they,' was adopted in the North from Scandinavian and gradually spread into the other dialects. The **oblique forms** (that is, non-nominative cases) *their* and *them* were not used in London English or in the Midland and South generally at this time, though common enough in the North. Chaucer uses *they* for the nominative, but he retains the native forms *here* (or *hire*) and *hem* as oblique forms. A Northern characteristic not illustrated in the passage cited is the *-es*, *-is*, or *-ys* ending of the third person singular and all plural forms of the present indicative (*he redys* 'he reads,' *thai redys* 'they read'). Also Northern, but not occurring in the passage, is the frequent correspondence of *k* to the *ch* of the other dialects, as in *birk–birch*, *kirk–chirche*, *mikel* 'much'–*michel*, and *ilk* 'each'–*ęch*.

Throughout this chapter, the focus of attention is on the London speech that is the ancestor of standard Modern English. Unless otherwise qualified the term *Middle English* is used here to refer to the language of the East Midland area and specifically to that of London.

Changes in Pronunciation

THE PRINCIPAL CONSONANTAL CHANGES

Throughout the history of English the consonants have remained relatively stable, as compared with the notable vowel changes that have occurred. The Old English consonant sounds written *b*, *c* (in both its values in late Old English, [k] and [č]), *d*, *f* (in both its values [f] and [v]), *ȝ* (in two of its values [g] and [y]), *h* (as [h] and as [x]), *k*, *l*, *m*, *n*, *p*, *r*, *s*, *t*, *þ* (ð), *w*, and *x*

---

[3] The editorial hook under the *ǭ* indicates the "open *o*" sound [ɔ]. Likewise, *ę* indicates "open *ē*," that is, [ɛ]. For the development of these sounds, see pp. 147–48.

(that is, [ks]) remained unchanged in Middle English. Important spelling differences occur, however, most of them due to Anglo-Norman influence. They have been treated earlier in this chapter.

The more important changes in consonant sounds, other than the part played by *g* in the formations of new diphthongs (see p. 149), may be summarized as follows:

1. The Old English sequences *hl*, *hn*, and *hr* (as in *hlēapan* 'to leap,' *hnutu* 'nut,' and *hraðor* 'sooner') were simplified to *l*, *n*, and *r* (as in *lēpen*, *nute*, and *rather*). To some extent *hw*, written *wh* in Middle English, was also frequently so reduced to *w*, at least in the Southern dialect. In the North, however, the *h* in this sequence was not lost. It survives to this day in some types of English, including the speech of much of the United States. The sequence was frequently written *qu* and *quh* in Northern texts.

2. The Old English voiced velar fricative *g* after *l* or *r* became *w*, as in *halwen* 'to hallow' (OE *halgian*) and *morwe(n)* 'morrow' (OE *morgen*).

3. Between a consonant, particularly *s* or *t*, and a back vowel, *w* was lost, as in *sǭ* (OE *swā*) and *tō* 'two' (OE *twā*). Since Old English times it had been lost in various negative contractions regardless of what vowel followed, as in Middle English *nil(le)* from *ne wil(le)*, *nǫt* from *ne wǫt*, *nas* from *ne was*, and *niste* from *ne wiste* (in which the *w* was postconsonantal because of elision of the *e* of *ne*). *Nille* survives in *willy-nilly*. A number of spellings with "silent *w*" continue to occur—for example, *two*, *sword*, and *answer* (early ME *andswarien*).

4. In unstressed syllables, *-ch* was lost in late Middle English, as in *-ly* (OE *-lic*). The form *ī* for the first person nominative singular pronoun represents a restressing of the *i* that alone remained of *ich* (OE *ic*) after this loss.

5. Before a consonant, though an *e* might intervene, *v* was lost in a few words like *hēd* (by way of *hēvd*, *hēved*, from OE *hēafod*), *lǭrd* (*lǭverd*, OE *hlāford*), *hast*, *hath*, and *had* (OE *hæfst*, *hæfð*, and *hæfde*).

6. The Old English prefix *ge-* became *i-* (*y-*) as in *iwis* 'certain' (OE *gewiss*) and *ilimpen* 'to happen' (OE *gelimpan*).

7. In the Southern dialect, including Kentish, initial *f*, *s*, and doubtless *þ* as well, were voiced. This characteristic is reflected in spelling in the use of *v* for *f* and *z* for *s*. It was noted as current in some of the Southern counties of England by Joseph Wright in his *The English Dialect Grammar* (1905) and is reflected in such standard English words of Southern provenience as *vixen* 'she-fox' (OE *fyxe*) and *vat* (OE *fæt*).

8. Final inflectional *n* was gradually lost (Reed 1950), as was also the final *n* of the unstressed possessive pronouns *mīn* and *þīn* and of the indefinite article before a consonant: compare Old English *mīn fæder* 'my father' with Middle English *mȳ fader* (but *mȳn eye* 'my eye'). This loss of *-n* is indirectly responsible for *a newt* (from *an ewte*) and *a nickname* (from *an ekename* 'an also-name'), where the *n* of the indefinite article has attached itself to the following word. In *umpire* (ME *noumpere*), *adder* (ME *nadder*, compare German *Natter* 'snake'), *auger* (ME *nauger*), and *apron* (ME *napron*, compare *napkin, napery*) just the opposite has happened: the *n* of the noun has attached itself to the article.

9. With the introduction of many words from Old French (and much less frequently from Latin) beginning with [v] (for instance, *veal, virtue, visit*), later with [z] (for instance, *zeal, zodiac*), and with the voicing of initial [θ] in words usually unstressed (for instance, *the, this, they*), the voiced fricatives, in Old English allophones of the voiceless ones, achieved phonemic status. With the loss of final *-e* [ə] (below, p. 152), [v], [z], and [ð] came to occur also in final position, as in *give, lose, bathe.*

THE MIDDLE ENGLISH VOWELS

The Old English long vowel sounds *ē, ī, ō,* and *ū* remained unchanged in Middle English although their spelling altered: thus Old English *fēt*—Middle English *fēt, feet* 'feet'; Old English *rīdan*—Middle English *rīden, rȳden* 'to ride'; Old English *fōda*—Middle English *fōde, foode* 'food'; Old English *hūs*—Middle English *hōus* 'house.'

Except for Old English *æ* and *y*, the short vowels of those Old English stressed syllables that remained short were unchanged in most Middle English speech—for example, Old English *wascan* 'to wash'—Middle English *washen, helpan* 'to help'—*helpen, sittan* 'to sit'—*sitten, hoppian* 'to hop'—*hoppen,* and *hungrig* 'hungry'—*hungry* [húŋgrɪ]. The rest of the vowels underwent the following changes:

1. Old English *ȳ* underwent **unrounding** to [ī] in the Northern and the East Midland areas. It remained unchanged, though written *u* or *ui,* in the greater part of the West Midland and all of the Southwest until the later years of the fourteenth century, when it was unrounded and hence fell together with the Northern and East Midland development. In Kent and elsewhere in the Southeast the Old English sound became [ē]. Hence Old English *hȳdan* 'to hide' is reflected in Middle English in such dialectal variants as *hīden, hūden,* and *hēden.*

2. Old English *ā* remained only in the North (*hām* 'home,' *rāp* 'rope,' *stān* 'stone'), becoming [ē], as in *hame, rape,* and *stane,* in Modern Scots; everywhere south of the Humber it became [ɔ̄][4] and was spelled *o* or *oo* exactly like the [ō] that remained from Old English, as in *fo(o)de.* One can tell certainly how to pronounce a Middle English word so spelled by referring to its Old English form; thus, if the *o(o)* corresponds to Old English *ā* (*stǫǫn*—OE *stān*), the Middle English sound is [ɔ̄]; if the Old English word

---

[4] The [ō] of *twō,* cited above in another spelling (that is, without the *w*), as also of *whō* (OE *hwā*), is a special development of early Middle English [ɔ̄].

148   has ō (*mōne*—OE *mōna*, *roote*—OE *rōt*), the Middle English sound is unchanged. But there is an easier way for, say, the beginning student of Middle English literature, who may not be familiar with Old English, and it is fairly certain: if the modern sound is [o], typically spelled *o* with "silent *e*" (as in *roe, rode*) or *oa* (as in *road*), then the Middle English sound is [ɔ̄].[5] If, however, the Modern English sound is [u], [ʊ], or [ə], spelled *oo*, the Middle English sound is [ō], as in, respectively, Modern English *food, foot*, and *flood*,[6] going back to Middle English [fōdə], [fōt], and [flōd].

    3. <u>Old English *ǣ* became Middle English [ɛ̄]</u>. The history of the sound is, however, complicated by diverse developments in earlier times.[7] Moreover, both [ē] and [ɛ̄] were written *e* or *ee* in Middle English.[8] In early Modern English times *ea* was adopted as a spelling for most of those words that in the Middle English dialects spoken north of the Thames had [ɛ̄] from whatever source, whereas those words that had in the same dialects [ē] from whatever source usually continued the Middle English *e(e)* spelling. This difference in spelling is a great blessing to beginning students of Chaucer. By reference to it they may ascertain that *swete breeth* in the fifth line of the General Prologue to the *Canterbury Tales* is to be read [swḗtə brɛ̄θ]. The Modern English spellings *sweet* and *breath* here, as often, provide the clue to the Middle English pronunciation.

    4. Old English short *æ* fell together with short *a* and came to be written like it in Middle English: Old English *glæd*—Middle English *glad*. In Southwest Midland and in Kentish, however, words that in Old English had short

---

    [5] Exceptions are *gold* and *Rome*, which had [ō] in Middle English and [u] in early Modern English. Compare the proper name form *Gould* and early rimes of *Rome* with *doom, room*, and so forth, in the poetry of the early Modern period—for example, that of Pope and Dryden. The earlier pronunciation of *Rome* is indicated by Shakespeare's pun in *Julius Caesar* 1.2.156: "Now is it Rome indeed, and room enough . . ." which he repeats elsewhere. The change back to [rom] and [gold] has occurred in fairly recent times.

    [6] *Brooch* [broč] is an exceptional instance of *oo* as a spelling for [o] from Middle English [ɔ̄]. A spelling pronunciation [bruč] is occasionally heard.

    [7] West Saxon Old English *ǣ* had two quite distinct sources. It might be either a development of West Germanic **ā* (compare the unchanged vowel of Ger. *Schlāf* 'sleep' with the shifted one of WS *slǣp*), corresponding to non–West Saxon (that is, Kentish, Mercian, and Northumbrian) *ē*; or the result of *i*-mutation of prehistoric Old English *ā*, a development of West Germanic **ai*, as in *dǣl* 'part, deal,' from prehistoric Old English **dāli*. But in non–West Saxon dialects the first *ǣ* (from W. Gmc **ā*) was raised to *ē* early in the Old English period. On the other hand, the Old English *ǣ* resulting from *i*-mutation remained in the Anglian dialects as well as in West Saxon. (In Kentish it merged with the *ē* that had developed from West Germanic **ā*.) It corresponds to [ɛ̄] in the Northern and (what is our principal concern) much of the Midland area.

    [8] These spellings were used for the two vowels regardless of their sources, which also include West Germanic *ē* for [ē] and the *e* that was lengthened in open syllables to [ɛ̄] (p. 151) in the early thirteenth century. Thus West Saxon Old English *slǣp* and *dǣl* correspond to Northern and Midland Middle English *sleep* [slēp] and *dẹẹl* [dɛ̄l]; *mētan* 'to meet' and *etan* 'to eat' to *mēten* [mḗtən] and *ẹten* [ɛ́tən].

æ were written with *e* (for instance, *gled*) in early Middle English times—a writing that may have indicated little change from the Old English sound in those areas.

5. In the Northern and East Midland areas Old English *y* was unrounded to *i*, exactly as *ȳ* was unrounded to *ī* in the same areas. In the Southeast it became *e*, but remained as a rounded vowel [ü], written *u*, in the West Midland and the Southwest until late Middle English times, when it was unrounded.

CHANGES IN DIPHTHONGS

The diphthongal system changed radically between Old English and Middle English. The old diphthongs disappeared and a number of new ones developed:

1. The Old English long diphthongs *ēa* and *ēo* underwent **smoothing**, or **monophthongization**, in late Old English times (eleventh century), occurring in the twelfth century as [ɛ] and (in the greater part of England) [ē], respectively, their subsequent Modern English development coinciding with that of [ɛ] and [ē] from other origins. Thus post-eleventh-century Middle English *lẹẹf* 'leaf' [lɛ̄f] develops out of Old English *lēaf* and *seen* 'to see' [sēn] out of Old English *sēon*. The short diphthongs *ea* and *eo* became by the twelfth century, respectively, *a* and *e*, as in Middle English *yaf* 'gave' from Old English *geaf* and *herte* 'heart' from Old English *heorte*.

2. In early Middle English, two new diphthongs ending in the off-glide [ɪ]—[aɪ] and [eɪ]—developed from Old English sources, a development that had in fact begun in late Old English times. One source of this development was the **vocalization** of *g* to *i* after front vowels (OE *sægde* 'said'—ME *saide*, OE *weg* 'way'—ME *wey*). Another source was the development of an *i*-glide between a front vowel and Old English *h*, which represented a voiceless fricative when it did not begin words (late OE *ehta* 'eight'—ME *eighte*). In late Middle English, these two vowels fell together and became a single diphthong, as we know, for example, from the fact that Chaucer rimes words like *day* (which earlier had [aɪ]) and *wey* (which earlier had [eɪ]). When the off-glide followed *i*, it served merely to lengthen that vowel (OE *lige* 'false-hood'—ME *līe*).

3. Four new diphthongs ending in the off-glide [ʊ] or [u]—[aʊ], [ɔʊ], [ɛʊ], and [ɪu]—also developed from Old English sources. The vocalization of *g* (the voiced velar fricative) to *u* after back vowels contributed to the first two of these new diphthongs (OE *sagu* 'saw, saying'—ME *sawe*, OE *boga* 'bow'—ME *bowe*). Another source for the same two diphthongs was the development of a *u*-glide between a back vowel and Old English *h* (OE *āht* 'aught'—ME *aught*, OE *brohte* 'brought'—ME *broughte*). A third source

150 contributed to all four diphthongs: *w* after a vowel became a *u*-glide but continued usually to be written (OE *clawu* 'claw'—ME *clawe*, OE *grōwan* 'to grow'—ME *growen*, OE *lǣwede* 'unlearned'—ME *lewed*, OE *nīwe* 'new'— ME *newe*). **Diphthongization** often involved a new concept of syllable division —for example, Old English *clawu* [klɑ-wʊ] but Middle English *clawe* [klaʊ-ə]. When the off-glide followed *u*, it merely lengthened it (OE *fugol* 'fowl'—ME *fōul*).

4. Two Middle English diphthongs are of French origin, entering our language in the loanwords borrowed from the French-speaking conquerors of England. The diphthong [ɔɪ] is spelled *oi* or *oy*, as in *joie* 'joy,' *cloistre* 'cloister.' The diphthong [ʊɪ] is also written *oi* or *oy*, as in *boilen* 'to boil,' *poisen* 'to poison,' and *joinen* 'to join.' Words containing the second diphthong have [əɪ] in early Modern English, pronunciations that have survived in nonstandard speech and are reflected in the dialect spellings *bile*, *pizen*, and *jine*.

Other diphthongal developments are taken up in specialized grammars of Middle English. It was noted above that as the Old English diphthongs were smoothed into monophthongs, new diphthongs developed in Middle English. These have, in turn, undergone smoothing in Modern English (for instance, *drawen* [dráʊən]—*draw* [drɔ]), new diphthongs have also developed (for instance, *rīden* [rî́dən]—*ride* [raɪd], *hous* [hūs]—*house* [haʊs]), and others are even now in the course of developing. Some inland Southern American speakers lack off-glides in [aɪ] and [aʊ], so that "My wife is in the house" comes out as something very like [ma waf ɪz ɪn ðə has]; the off-glide may also be lost in *oil*, *boil*, and the like. Comparatively new [ʊ] and [ɪ] off-glides occur in words like *boat* and *bait*. As E. E. Wardale aptly puts it (1962, p. 55), "The constant loss of old and formation of new diphthongs illustrate in a striking manner the life and movement inherent in any spoken language."

THE LENGTHENING AND SHORTENING OF VOWELS

In addition to the qualitative vowel changes mentioned above, there were some important quantitative changes, that is, changes in the length of vowels:

1. In late Old English times originally short vowels were lengthened before *mb*, *nd*, *ld*, *rd*, and *rð*. This **lengthening** frequently failed to maintain itself, and by the end of the Middle English period it is to be found only in *i* and *o* before *mb* (*climben* 'to climb,' *cọmb* 'comb'); in *i* and *u* before *nd* (*binden* 'to bind,' *bōunden* 'bound'); and generally before *ld* (*milde* 'mild,' *yēlden* 'to pay, yield,' *ọld* 'old,' *gọld* 'gold'). Reshortening has subsequently occurred, however, in some words—for instance, *wind* (noun), *held*, *send*, *friend*; compare *wind* (verb), *field, fiend*, in which the lengthening survives. If another consonant followed any of the sequences mentioned, lengthening did not occur; this fact explains Modern English *child, children* (OE nominative-accusative plural *cildru*).

2. Considerably later than the lengthenings due to the consonant sequences just discussed, short *a, e,* and *o* were lengthened when they were in **open syllables,** that is, in syllables in which they were final, such as *bā-ken* 'to bake' (OE *bacan*). To put it somewhat differently, these vowels were lengthened when followed by a single consonant plus another vowel. In Old English short vowels frequently occurred in such syllables—for example, *nama* 'name,' *stelan* 'to steal,' *þrote* 'throat,' which became in Middle English, respectively, *nāme, stęlen, thrǫte.* This lengthening is interestingly reflected in *staff* (from ME *staf*, going back to OE *stæf*) and its plural *staves* (from ME *stāves*, going back to OE *stafas*). Short *i* (*y*) and *u* were likewise lengthened in open syllables, beginning in the fourteenth century in the North, but these vowels underwent a qualitative change also: *i* (*y*) became *ē*, and *u* became *ō*— for example, Old English *wicu* 'week,' *yvel* 'evil,' *wudu* 'wood,' which became, respectively, *wēke, ēvel, wōde.* This lengthening in open syllables was a new principle in English. Its results are still apparent, as in *staff* and *staves*, though the distinction between open and closed syllables became largely historical with the loss of final unstressed *e*, as a result of which the vowels of, say, *staves, week,* and *throat* now occur in closed syllables ([stēvz], [wīk], [θrōt]).

3. Conversely, beginning in the Old English period, originally long vowels in syllables followed by consonant sequences were shortened. The consonant sequences that caused **shortening** included lengthened (doubled) consonants but naturally excluded those sequences mentioned above under (1) that lengthened a preceding vowel. For example, there is shortening in *hidde* 'hid' (OE *hȳdde*), *kepte* 'kept' (OE *cēpte*), *fifty* (OE *fīftig*), *fiftēne* (OE *fīftȳne*), *twenty* (OE *twēntig*), and *wisdom.* It made no difference whether the consonant sequence was in the word originally (as in OE *sōfte*—ME *softe*), was the result of adding an inflectional ending (as in *hidde*), or was the result of compounding (as in OE *wīsdōm* [that is, *wīs* plus *dōm*]—ME *wisdom*). The effects of this shortening can be seen in the following Modern English pairs, in which the first member has an originally long vowel and the second has a vowel that was shortened: *hide–hid; keep–kept; five–fifty;* and *wise–wisdom.* There was considerable wavering in vowel length before the sequence *-st*, as indicated by such Modern English forms as *fist–Christ, lost–ghost,* and *breast–least.*

4. Vowels in unstressed syllables were shortened. Lack of stress on the second syllable of *wisdom* accounts for its Middle English shortening from the Old English *dōm.* Similarly, words that were usually without stress within the sentence were subject to vowel shortening—for example, *an* (OE *ān* 'one'), *but* (OE *būtan*), and *not* (OE *nāwiht*).

5. Shortening also occurred regularly before two unstressed syllables, as reflected in *wilderness* (*wild*), *Christendom* (*Christ*), and *holiday* (*holy*).

As far as the structure of English is concerned, the most significant of all developments in the language occurred with the Middle English falling together of *a, o,* and *u* with *e* in unstressed syllables, all ultimately becoming [ə], as in the following:

OLD ENGLISH	MIDDLE ENGLISH
lama 'lame'	lāme
faran 'to fare,' faren (past part.)	fāren
stānes 'stone's,' stānas 'stones'	stǭnes
feallað 'falleth'	falleth
nacod 'naked'	nāked
macodon 'made' (pl.)	mākeden
sicor 'sure'	sēker
lengðo 'length'	lengthe
medu 'liquor'	mẹde

This **leveling**, or **merging**, has already been alluded to (p. 109), for it began well before the end of the Old English period. The *Beowulf* manuscript (*ca.* A.D. 1000), for instance, has occurrences of *-as* for the genitive singular *-es* ending, *-an* for the preterit plural ending *-on* and the dative plural ending *-um* (the *-m* in *-um* had become *-n* late in the Old English period), *-on* for the infinitive ending *-an,* *-o* for the genitive plural ending *-a* and for the neuter nominative plural ending *-u,* among a number of such interchanges pointing to identical vowel quality in such syllables.

THE LOSS OF SCHWA IN FINAL SYLLABLES

The leveled final *e* [ə] was gradually lost in the North in the course of the thirteenth century and in the Midlands and the South somewhat later. Many words, however, continued to be spelled with *-e,* which had earlier been extended by analogy to a number of words in which it was not historical—for example, *brīde,* from Old English *brȳd* 'bride.' This **inorganic -e,** as it is called, should not be confused with **scribal** *e,* which was certainly never pronounced. That inorganic *-e* was pronounced is indicated in a good many lines of verse, such as, for instance, Chaucer's "A bryde shal nat eten in the halle" (*Canterbury Tales,* E 1890).[9]

Nonfinal unstressed *e* (written *i, y,* and *u* in some dialects) was ultimately

---

[9] As additional examples, Samuel Moore (1951, p. 62) cites *weye* (OE *weg*), *pere* (OF *per*), *bare* (OE *bær*), and *harde* (OE *heard*), all of which appear in the *Canterbury Tales* in lines whose scansion, like that of the line quoted above, requires that the *e* be pronounced. For still further examples, see Joseph Wright and Elizabeth Mary Wright (1928, p. 71).

lost in the inflectional ending -es, except after the sibilants [s], [z], [š], [č], and [j]. This loss was a comparatively late development, beginning in the North in the early fourteenth century. It did not occur in the Midlands and the South until somewhat later.

In the West Saxon and Kentish dialects of Old English the *e* of the ending -eð for the third person singular of the present indicative of verbs was usually lost (above, p. 123). It is hence not surprising to find such loss in this ending in the Southern dialect of Middle English and, after long syllables, in the Midland dialects as well, as in *mākth* 'maketh,' *bẹrth* 'beareth,' as also sometimes after short syllables, as in *comth*. Chaucer uses both forms of this ending; sometimes the loss of [ə] is not indicated by the spelling but is dictated by the meter.

The vowel sound was retained in -ed until the fifteenth century. It has not yet disappeared in the forms *aged*, *blessed*, and *learned* when they are used as adjectives. Compare *learnëd woman*, *the blessëd Lord*, *agëd man* with "The woman learned her lesson," "The Lord blessed the multitude," "The man aged rapidly." (In "aged whiskey" the form *aged* is used as a past participle— one could not say "very aged whiskey"—in contrast to the adjectival use in *agëd man*.) There is, of course, no such loss after *t* or *d*.

Changes in Grammar

THE REDUCTION OF INFLECTIONS

As a result of the merging of unstressed vowels into a single sound, the number of forms in English was drastically reduced. Middle English became a language with few inflectional distinctions, whereas Old English, as we have seen, was relatively highly inflected, though less so than Germanic, which was about as fully inflected as Latin. This reduction of inflections was thus responsible for a structural change of the greatest importance.

In the adjective—for instance, the Old English weak forms (those used after the demonstratives)—the endings -a (masculine nominative) and -e (neuter nominative-accusative and feminine nominative) fell together in a single form as -e. Thus an indication of gender distinguishing the masculine form was lost. Middle English *the ọlde man* corresponds to Old English *se ealda man*, the ending of the adjective being identical with that used for *the ọlde tāle* (OE feminine *sēo ealde talu*) and *the ọlde sword* (OE neuter *þæt ealde swurd*). The Old English weak adjective endings -an and -um had already fallen together as -en and, with the loss of final -n (see p. 146), they also came to have only -e. The Old English genitive plural forms of the weak adjective in -ena and -ra, after first becoming -ene and -re, were made to conform to the predominant weak adjective form in -e, though there are a very few late survivals of the Old English genitive plural in -ra as Middle English -er, notably in *aller* (OE *ealra*) and related forms. Thus the five singular and plural forms of the Old English weak adjective declension (*-a, -e, -an, -ena,* and *-um*) are reduced to a single form ending in *-e,* with gender as well as number distinctions completely obliterated. For the strong function the endingless form of the Old English nominative singular was used throughout the singular, with a generalized plural form (identical with the weak adjective declension) in *-e:* thus (strong singular) *grẹẹt lord* 'great lord' but (generalized plural) *grẹẹte lordes* 'great lords.'

To describe the situation more simply, Middle English monosyllabic adjectives ending in consonants had a single inflection, *-e,* used to modify singular nouns in the weak function and all plural nouns. Other adjectives—for example, *free* and *gentil*—were uninflected. This simple grammatical situation can be inferred from many of the manuscripts only with difficulty, however, because scribes frequently wrote final *e*'s where they did not belong.

Changes resulting from this new identity of vowel in unstressed syllables were considerably more far-reaching than what has been shown in the declension of the adjective. For instance, the older endings *-an* (infinitives, most of the oblique, or non-nominative, forms of *n*-stem nouns), *-on* (indicative preterit plurals), and *-en* (subjunctive preterit plurals, past participles of strong verbs) all fell together as *-en.* With the later loss of final inflectional *-n* in some of these forms, only *-e* [-ə] was left, and this was in time also to go. This fact accounts for endingless infinitives, preterit plurals, and some past particples of strong verbs in Modern English, as, for instance:

OLD ENGLISH	MIDDLE ENGLISH	MODERN ENGLISH
findan (inf.)	finden	find
fundon (pret. pl.)	founde(n)	found
funden (past part.)	founde(n)	found

It was similar with the *-as* nominative-accusative plural of the most important declension, which became a pattern for the plural of most nouns, and the genitive singular of the same declension (OE *hundes* 'hound's' and *hundas* 'hounds' merging as ME *houndes*). So too the noun endings *-eð* and *-að* (OE *hæleð* 'fighting man,' *mōnað* 'month') and the homophonous endings in verbs (OE *findeð* 'he, she, it finds,' *findað* 'we, you, they find')—all ended up as Middle English *-eth.*

THE LOSS OF GRAMMATICAL GENDER

One of the important results of the leveling of unstressed vowels was the loss of grammatical gender. We have seen how this occurred with the adjective. We have also seen that grammatical gender, for psychological reasons rather than phonological ones, had begun to break down in Old English times as far as the choice of pronouns was concerned (see p. 111), as when the English translator of Bede's Latin *Ecclesiastical History* refers to Bertha, the wife of King Ethelbert of Kent, as *hēo* 'she' rather than *hit*, though she is in the same sentence designated as *þæt* (neuter demonstrative used as definite article) *wīf* rather than *sēo wīf*, which would still have been impossible.

In Old English, gender was readily distinguishable in most nouns: *a*-stem masculine nominative-accusative plurals, for instance, ended in *-as*, feminines in *-a*, and short-stemmed neuters in *-u*. In Middle English, on the other hand, all but a handful of nouns acquired the same plural ending, *-es* (OE *-as*). This important development, coupled with the invariable *the* that supplanted the Old English masculine *se*, neuter *þæt*, and feminine *sēo* with all their oblique forms (see pp. 116–17), effectively eliminated grammatical gender as a feature of English.

The Inflection of Nouns

It should be obvious that the structure of English was profoundly affected in all departments by the leveling of unstressed vowels. Among the nouns, to cite some further instances, the Old English distinctive feminine nominative singular form in *-u* fell together with the nominative plural form in *-a*, that is, singular *denu* 'valley' and plural *dena* 'valleys' became for a while Middle English *dēne*. It was similar with the neuter nominative-accusative plurals in *-u* and the genitive plurals in *-a*: all came to have the same *-e* ending. What further happened with *dēne* happened to most other nouns that had not formed their nominative-accusative plurals in *-as* in Old English and has been alluded to before: namely, the *-es* that was the Middle English reduced form of this ending was made to serve as a general plural ending for such words (for example, singular nongenitive *dēne*, general plural *dēnes*). In like fashion, the genitive singular ending *-es* was extended to nouns that had belonged to declensions lacking this ending; thus the genitive singular and the general plural forms of most nouns fell together and have remained that way ever since: Old English genitive singular *speres* and nominative plural *speru* became Middle English *spēres*, Modern English *spear's*, *spears*; Old English genitive singular *tale* and nominative plural *tala* became Middle English *tāles*, Modern English *tale's*, *tales*.

A few *s*-less genitives—feminine nouns and the family-relationship nouns ending in *-r*—remained throughout the period (as in Chaucer's "In hope to stonden in his lady grace" and "by my fader kyn") and survived into early Modern English, along with a few nouns from the Old English *n*-stem declension. Sometimes the genitive *-s* was left off a noun that ended in *s* or that was followed by a word beginning with *s*. The same omission, for the same phonological reason, accounts for the occasional modern loss of the genitive *-s* in "Keats' poems, Dickens' novels," when these are not merely matters of writing. Solely a matter of writing is the occasional modern "for pity sake," which indicates the same pronunciation in conversational speech as "for pity's sake."

The few nouns that did not conform to the pattern of forming the plural by suffixing -*es* nevertheless followed the pattern of using the nominative-accusative plural as a general plural form. They include those that lack -*s* plurals today—for example, *oxen, deer,* and *feet.* There were also in Middle English a number of survivals of weak-declension plurals in -*(e)n* that have subsequently disappeared—for example, *eyen* 'eyes' and *foon* 'foes'. The -*(e)n* was even extended to a few nouns that belonged to the *a*-stem strong declension in Old English—for example, *shoon* 'shoes' (OE *scōs*). A few long-syllabled words that had been neuters in Old English occurred with unchanged plural forms, especially animal names like *sheep, deer,* and *hors.* However, the most enduring of these alternative plurals are those with mutation: *men, feet, geese, teeth, lice,* and *mice.*

During the Middle English period, then, practically all nouns were reduced to two forms, just as in Modern English—one without -*s* used as a general nongenitive singular form, and one with -*s* used as a genitive singular and general plural form. The English language thus acquired a device for indicating plurality without consideration of case—namely, the -*s* ending, which had been in Old English only one of three plural endings in the strong masculine declension. It also lost all trace of any case distinctions except for the genitive, identical in form with the plural. English had come to depend on particles—mainly prepositions and conjunctions—and word order to express grammatical relations that had previously been expressed by inflection. No longer could one say, as the Anglo-Saxon homilist Ælfric had done, "Þās gelæhte se dēma," and expect the sentence to be properly understood as 'The judge seized those.' To say this in Middle English, it is necessary that the subject precede the verb: "The dēme ilaughte thǫs."

Pronouns

PERSONAL PRONOUNS

As we have noted, simplification occurred in other categories as well. Only the pronouns retained, and still do retain, a considerable degree of the complexity that characterized them in Old English. These words alone preserved distinctive subject and object case forms, except for the neuter pronouns (*h*)*it, that, this,* and *what,* which even in Old English had not differentiated the nominative and accusative.

The dual number of the personal pronouns virtually disappeared in Middle English. Such a phrase as *git būtū* 'you two both,' occurring in late Old English, indicates that even then the form *git* had lost much of its idea of twoness and needed the reinforcement of *būtū* 'both.' There was a great deal of variety in the remaining Middle English forms, of which those in the following table are some of the more noteworthy.

	SINGULAR	PLURAL
First Person		
Nom.	ich, I, ik	wē
Obj.	mē	us
Gen.	mī; mīn	ōur(e); ōures
Second Person		
Nom.	thōu	yē
Obj.	thee	yōu
Gen.	thī; thīn	yōur(e); yōures
Third Person		
Nom.	hē	hī, they, thai
Obj.	him, hine	hem, heom, them, thaim, theim
Gen.	his	her(e), their(e); heres, theires
Nom.	shē, hō, hyō, hyē, hī, schō, chō, hē	
Obj.	hir(e), her(e), hī	
Gen.	hir(e), her(e); hires	
Nom.	hit, it	
Obj.	hit, it	
Gen.	his	

The dialects of Middle English differed in the forms they used for the pronouns. For example, *ik* was a Northern form corresponding to *ich* or *I* elsewhere. The nominative forms *they, thai* (and other spelling variants such as *thei, thay*), which were derived from Scandinavian, prevailed in the North and Midlands. The corresponding objective and genitive forms *them, thaim, theim,* and *their* were used principally in the North during most of the Middle English period. The native nominative form *hī* remained current in the Southern dialect, and its corresponding objective and genitive forms *hem, heom,* and *here* were used in both the South and Midlands. Thus in Chaucer's usage, the nominative is *they* but the accusative is *hem* and the genitive *here.* Ultimately the Scandinavian forms in *th-* were to prevail; in the generation following Chaucer, they everywhere displaced the native English forms in *h-* except for unstressed *hem,* which we continue to use as *'em.*

The Old English third person masculine accusative *hine* survived into Middle English only in the South; elsewhere *him* took over. The feminine accusative *hī* likewise survived for a while in the same region, but in the later thirteenth century it was supplanted by the *hir(e)* or *her(e)* current elsewhere. The feminine pronoun had a variety of nominative forms, one of them identical with the corresponding masculine form—certainly a well-nigh intolerable state of affairs, forcing the lovesick author of the lyric "Alysoun" to refer to his sweetheart as *he,* the same form she would have used in referring to him (for example, "Bote he me wolle to hire take" means 'Unless she will take me to her'). The predominant form in East Midland speech, and the one that was to survive in standard Modern English, was *she.*

The genitive forms of the personal pronouns came in Middle English to be restricted in the ways they could be used. A construction like Old English *nǣnig hira* 'none of them' could be rendered in Middle English only by *of* plus the objective pronoun, exactly as in Modern English. The variant forms of the genitive first and second persons singular—*mīn, mī; thīn, thī*—preceding a noun were in exactly the same type of distribution as the forms *an* and *a*; that is, the *n* was lost before a consonant (see p. 146). Following a noun, the forms with *-n* were invariable (as in the rare construction *baby mine,* as also when the possessives were used as in Modern English *That book is mine, Mine is that book,* and *that book of mine*). By analogy with this unvarying use of the forms in *-n* as nominals, *hisen, heren, ōuren, yōuren,* and *theiren* arose. From the beginning their status seems to have been much the same as that of their Modern English descendants *hisn, hern, yourn,* and *theirn.* The personal pronouns in *-r* developed new analogical genitive forms in *-es* rather late in Middle English: *hires, ōures, yōures,* and *heres* (Northern *theires*). These *-es* forms were used precisely like Modern English *hers, ours, yours,* and *theirs*—predicatively, as in "The books on the table are hers (ours, yours, theirs)," and nominally, as in "Hers (ours, yours, theirs) are on the table."

DEMONSTRATIVE PRONOUNS

Old English *se, þæt, sēo,* and plural *þā,* with their various oblique forms, were ultimately reduced to *the, that,* and plural *thō*; however, inflected forms derived from the Old English declensions continued to be used in some dialects, though not in East Midland, until the thirteenth century. The *the,* which at first replaced only the masculine nominative *se,* came to be used as an invariable definite article. *That* and *thō* were thus left for the demonstrative function. Another *the,* from the Old English masculine and neuter instrumental *þē,* has had continuous adverbial use in English, as in "The sooner the better" and "He did not feel the worse for the experience."

Thō ultimately gave way to *thōs* (ModE *those*), from Old English *þās,* though the form with *-s* did not begin to become common in the Midlands and the South until the late fifteenth century. Chaucer, for instance, uses only *thō* where we would use *those.* In the North *thās,* the form corresponding to *thōs* elsewhere, began to appear in writing more than a century earlier.

The other Old English demonstrative was *þes, þis, þēos*. By the thirteenth century, when gender distinction and some traces of inflection that had survived up to that time were lost, the singular nominative-accusative neuter *this* was used for all singular functions, and a new plural form, *thise* or *thēse*, the ending *-e* as in the plural of adjectives, appeared. These developments have resulted in Modern English *that–those* and *this–these*.

INTERROGATIVE AND RELATIVE PRONOUNS

The Old English masculine-feminine interrogative pronoun *hwā* became in Middle English *whō*, and the neuter form *hwæt* became *what*. As with the other pronouns, the dative drove out the accusative (OE *hwone*) of the first of these, the dative *whōm* (OE *hwām, hwǣm*) being used in any objective function. *Hwæt* had the same dative form as *hwā* in Old English, but, as with other neuters, it was given up. The genitive of both *hwā* and *hwæt* was *hwæs*; in Middle English this took by analogy the vowel of *whō* and *whōm*: thus *whōs*.

In Middle English *whō* was customarily used only as an interrogative pronoun or an indefinite relative meaning 'whoever,' as in "Who steals my purse steals trash," a usage that occurs first in the thirteenth century. The simple relative use of *who*, as in the title of Rudyard Kipling's story "The Man Who Would Be King," was not really widespread until the sixteenth century, though there are occasional instances of it as early as the late thirteenth century. The oblique forms *whōs* and *whōm*, however, were used as relatives in late Middle English, at about the same time that another interrogative pronoun, *which* (OE *hwylc*), also began to be so used, in reference to either persons or things. Sometimes *which* was followed by *that*, as in Chaucer's "Criseyde, which that felt hire thus i-take," that is, 'Criseyde, who felt herself thus taken.'

The most frequently used relative pronoun in Middle English is indeclinable *that*. It is, of course, still so used, though modern literary style limits it to restrictive clauses: "The man that I saw was Jones," but "This man, who never did anyone any real harm, was nevertheless punished severely." A relative particle *þe* usually regarded as a survival of the Old English indeclinable relative-of-all-work occurs in early Middle English side by side with *that* (or *þat*, as it would have been written early in the period).

Adjectives: Comparative and Superlative Forms

In the general leveling to *e* of unstressed vowels, the Old English comparative ending *-ra* became *-re*, later *-er*, and the superlative suffixes *-ost* and *-est* fell together as *-est*. If the root vowel of an adjective was long, it was shortened before these endings—for example, *swēte, swetter, swettest*—though the analogy of the positive form, as in the example cited, frequently caused the original length to be restored in the comparative and superlative forms; the doublets *latter* and *later* show, respectively, shortness and length of vowel.

As in Old English, *ēvel* (and its Middle English synonym *badde*, of uncertain origin), *gōd, muchel (mikel)*, and *lītel* had comparative and superlative forms unrelated to them etymologically: *werse, werst; bettre* or *better, best; mōre, mōst; lesse* or *lasse, lęste*. Some of the adjectives that in Old English had mutation in their comparative and superlative forms retained the mutated vowel in Middle English—for instance, *long, lengre* or *lenger, lengest; ǭld, eldre* or *elder, eldest*.

The simplification of the Old English adjective declensions has been already discussed in another connection (see above, pp. 153–54).

Verbs

Verbs continued to conform to the Germanic division into strong and weak, as they still do. Although the vowels of endings were leveled, the gradational distinctions expressed in the root vowels of the strong verbs were fully preserved. The tendency to use exclusively one or the other of the preterit vowel grades, however, had begun, though there was little consistency: the vowel of the older plural might be used in the singular, or vice versa. The older distinction (as in *I sang, we sungen*) was more likely to be retained in the Midlands and the South than in the North.

In strong verbs of the first class, the vowel gradation was ī–ǭ–i–i: *rīde(n)* (infinitive)–*rǭd* (preterit singular)–*riden* (preterit plural)–*(i)ride(n)* (past participle), with perfectly regular development from Old English *rīdan–rād–ridon–(ge)riden*. Examples of the other classes follow,[10] which should be compared with the Old English forms (see pp. 126–28):

II. crēpen–crēp–crupen–crōpen[11]
III. fīnden–fǭnd–foūnden–foūnden
helpen–halp–hulpen–holpen
fighten–faught–foughten–foughten

[10] The forms cited are for the most part those that are the regular developments of the Old English forms. All are attested, but many other "irregular" ones are to be encountered in Middle English writings.

[11] For the sake of consistency, infinitives and past participles will be cited with the *-n*, which was ultimately lost in all infinitives, though retained in the past participial forms of some strong verbs. The initial *i* (*y*) of past participles is omitted, though its use in many parts of the country was, as with Old English *ge*, more or less general.

IV. tēren–tar–tēren–tǭren
V. mēten–mat–mēten–mēten[12]
VI. fāren–fōr–fōren–fāren
VII. fallen–fēl–fēlen–fallen
hǭten–hēt–hēten–hǭten

By analogy with the considerably larger group of weak verbs, a good many strong verbs in the course of the Middle English period acquired, side by side with their strong forms, dental-suffix preterits and past participles. These include (to take a single example from each class of strong verbs) glīden 'to glide,' crēpen 'to creep,' helpen 'to help,' shēren 'to shear,' mēten 'to mete,' āken 'to ache,' and wēpen 'to weep.' Ultimately the strong forms were lost altogether in these and other verbs.

THE PERSONAL ENDINGS

When the Old English endings -ust and -uð, which were characteristic of the second and third persons of the present indicative of those weak verbs that had infinitives in -ian not preceded by r (thus lufian, lufast, lufað), fell together with the endings -est and -eð of verbs with infinitives in -an, a historical distinction of form was broken down. When the Old English present indicative plural ending -að likewise became -eth, the distinction between plural and third person singular was also obliterated: Old English bereð and berað both end up as bēreth, a single form that continued to do double duty in the South of England. The Midland dialects, however, substituted the -en of the plural subjunctive for the plural -eth and thereby achieved a formal distinction in number at the expense of one in mood. In the Northumbrian dialect of Old English -as was somewhat more frequent as the present indicative plural ending, at least in the extant texts (Campbell 1959, p. 302). The development of this ending, -es (sometimes spelled -is), is characteristic of the Northern dialect of Middle English: thus wē, yē, thai bēres 'we, you, they bear.' The same ending is a Northern characteristic in the present indicative third person singular and was in Modern English times to drive out the -eth. In Middle English times it had spread from the North into the Midland dialects, which show both -es and -eth in the third person and -es and -e(n) in the plural. Thus with finden 'to find' (strong) and thanken 'to thank' (weak) as models, the indicative forms were as follows in the Midland dialects:

[12] Some verbs belonging originally to the fifth class moved up into the fourth by acquiring participles with ō—for example, brēken (OE brecan), spēken (OE specan), wēven (OE wefan).

PRESENT SINGULAR	PRESENT PLURAL (ALL PERSONS)
1. fīnde, thanke	fīnde(n)(-s), thanke(n)(-s)
2. fīndest, thankest	
3. fīndeth(-es), thanketh(-es)	

PRETERIT SINGULAR	PRETERIT PLURAL (ALL PERSONS)
1. 3. fǫnd, thanked(e)	foūnde(n), thanked(e)(n)
2. foūnde, thankedest	

The verbs *been* 'to be' (OE *bēon*), *doon* 'to do' (OE *dōn*), *willen* 'to want, will' (OE *willan*), and *gǫǫn* 'to go' (OE *gān*) remained highly irregular in Middle English. Typical Midland indicative forms of *been* and *willen* follow:

been: PRESENT SINGULAR	PRESENT PLURAL (ALL PERSONS)
1. am	bee(n), beeth, sinden, ār(e)n[13]
2. art, beest	
3. is, beeth	

PRETERIT SINGULAR	PRETERIT PLURAL (ALL PERSONS)
1. 3. was	wēre(n)
2. wast, wēre	

willen: PRESENT SINGULAR	PRESENT PLURAL (ALL PERSONS)
1. 3. wil(le), wol(le)[14]	wilen, wol(n)
2. wilt, wolt	

PRETERIT SINGULAR	PRETERIT PLURAL (ALL PERSONS)
1. 3. wolde	wolde(n)
2. woldest	

[13] This form is comparatively rare in Middle English save in the North and in the West Midland. Chaucer seldom uses it.

[14] This late Midland form, with the vowel of the preterit, survives in *won't*, that is, *wol not*.

The Middle English Period (1100–1500)

present verbs are still in frequent use: *o(u)ghte* 'owed, was under obligation to,' *can* 'knows how to, is able,' *cōude* (ModE *could*)[15] 'knew how to, was able,' *shal* 'must,' *mōst(e)* (ModE *must*) 'was able to, must,' *may* 'am able to, may,' *mighte* (preterit of the preceding), *dar* (ModE *dare*), and *durst* (preterit of the preceding).

PARTICIPLES

The ending of the present participle varied from dialect to dialect, with *-and(e)* in the North, *-ende*, *-ing(e)* in the Midlands, and *-inde*, *-ing(e)* in the South. The *-ing* ending, which has prevailed in Modern English, is from the old **verbal noun** ending *-ung*, as in Old English *leornung* 'learning' (that is, knowledge), *bodung* 'preaching' (that is, sermon) from *leornian* 'to learn' and *bodian* 'to announce, preach.'

Past participles might or might not have the initial inflection *i-* (*y-*), from Old English *ge-*; the prefix was lost in many parts of England, including the East Midland, but frequently occurred in the speech of London as this is reflected in the writings of Chaucer.

Word Order

Although all possible variations in the order of subject, verb, and complement occur in extant Middle English literature, as in Old English literature, it must be remembered that much of this is verse, in which even today variations (inversions) of what is thought of as "normal" word order may occur. The prose of the Middle English period has much the same word order as Modern English prose. Sometimes a pronoun as object might precede the verb ("Yef þou me zayst, 'How me hit ssel lyerny?' ich hit wyle þe zigge an haste . . . ," that is, word for word, 'If thou [to] me sayest, "How one it shall learn?" I it will [to] thee say in haste . . . ,' or, in Modern English order, 'If thou sayest to me, "How shall one learn it?" I will say it to thee in haste . . .').

In subordinate clauses nouns used as objects might also precede verbs ("And we, þet . . . habbeþ Cristendom underfonge . . . ," that is, 'And we, that have Christian salvation received . . .'). In the frequently occurring impersonal constructions of Middle English, the object regularly preceded the verb: *me mette* '(it) to me dreamed,' that is, 'I dreamed'; *me thoughte* '(it) to me seemed.' *If you please* is very likely a survival of this construction (parallel to French *s'il vous plaît* and German *wenn es Ihnen gefällt*, that is,

[15] The preterit of *can* (infinitive *cunnen*), this word later acquired an unetymological *l* by analogy with *would*.

164 'if it please[s] you'), though the *you* is now taken as nominative. Other than these, there are very few inversions that would be inconceivable in Modern English.

The following passage in the Northern dialect is from *The Form of Living*, by Richard Rolle of Hampole, a gentle mystic and an excellent prose writer, who died in 1349. Strange as parts of it may look to modern eyes, it is possible to put it word for word into Modern English:

Twa lyves þar er þat cristen   men lyfes: ane es called actyve lyfe, for
Two lives there are that Christian men live: one is called active life, for

it es mare bodili warke; another, contemplatyve lyfe, for it es in mare
it is more bodily work; another, contemplative life, for it is in more

swetnes   gastely.   Actife lyfe es mykel owteward and in mare travel,
sweetness spiritually. Active life is much outward   and in more travail,

and in mare peryle for þe temptacions þat er in þe worlde.
and in more peril   for the temptations that are in the world.

Contemplatyfe lyfe es mykel inwarde, and forþi   it es lastandar   and
Contemplative life is much inward,   and therefore it is more lasting and

sykerar,   restfuller,   delitabiler,   luflyer, and mare medeful,
more secure, more restful, more delightful, lovelier, and more full of reward,

for it hase joy in goddes lufe and savowre in þe lyf þat lastes ay   in
for it has joy in God's love and savor   in the life that lasts forever in

þis present tyme if it be right   ledde. And þat felyng of joy in þe lufe
this present time if it be rightly led.   And that feeling of joy in the love

of Jhesu passes   al other merites in erth, for it es swa harde to com
of Jesus surpasses all other merits on earth, for it is so   hard to come

to for þe freelte of oure flesch and þe many temptacions þat we er
to for the frailty of our flesh and the many temptations that we are

umsett   with þat lettes us nyght and day. Al other thynges er   lyght at
set about with that hinder us night and day. All other things   are easy to

com to in regarde þarof,   for þat may na man deserve, bot anely it es
come to in regard   thereof, for that may no man deserve, but only   it is

gifen of goddes godenes til þam þat verrayli gifes þam   to
given of God's goodness to them that verily   give them(selves) to

contemplacion and til quiete for cristes   luf.
contemplation and to quiet   for Christ's love.

The Middle English Period (1100–1500)

The following passages in late Middle English are from a translation of the Bible made by John Wycliffe or one of his followers in the 1380s. The opening verses of chapters 1 and 2 of Genesis are based on the edition by Conrad Lindberg (*Ms. Bodley 959*, Stockholm Studies in English 6, 1959); the parable of the Prodigal Son (Luke 15) is based on the edition by Josiah Forshall and Frederic Madden (*The New Testament in English*, Oxford, 1879). Punctuation has been modernized, and the letters thorn and yogh have been replaced, respectively, by *th* and *y*, *gh*, or *s*.

These versions may be compared with the parallel passages in chapters 5 and 8.

I. **1.** In the first made God of nought heuen and erth. **2.** The erth forsothe was veyn withinne and voyde, and derknesses weren vp on the face of the see. And the spirite of God was yborn vp on the waters. **3.** And God seid, "Be made light," and made is light. **4.** And God sees light that it was good and dyuidide light from derknesses. **5.** And clepide light day and derknesses night, and maad is euen and moru, o day.

II. **1.** Therfor parfit ben heuen and erthe, and alle the anournyng of hem. **2.** And God fullfillide in the seuenth day his werk that he made, and he rystid the seuenth day from all his werk that he hadde fulfyllide. **3.** And he blisside to the seuenthe day, and he halowde it, for in it he hadde seesid fro all his werk that God schapide that he schulde make.

XV. **11.** A man hadde twei sones. **12.** And the yonger of hem seide to the fadir, "Fadir, yiue me the porcioun of catel that fallith to me." And he departide to hem the catel. **13.** And not aftir many daies, whanne alle thingis weren gederid togider, the yonger sone wente forth in pilgrymage in to a fer cuntre; and there he wastide hise goodis in lyuynge lecherously. **14.** And aftir that he hadde endid alle thingis, a strong hungre was maad in that cuntre, and he bigan to haue nede. **15.** And he wente, and drough hym to oon of the citeseyns of that cuntre. And he sente hym in to his toun, to fede swyn. **16.** And he coueitide to fille his wombe of the coddis that the hoggis eeten, and no man yaf hym. **17.** And he turnede ayen to hym silf, and seide, "Hou many hirid men in my fadir hous han plente of looues; and Y perische here thorough hungir. . . ." **20.** And he roos vp, and cam to his fadir. And whanne he was yit afer, his fadir saigh hym, and was stirrid bi mercy. And he ran, and fel on his necke, and kisside hym. **21.** And the sone saide to hym, "Fadir, Y haue synned in to heuene, and bifor thee; and now Y am not worthi to be clepid thi sone." **22.** And the fadir seide to hise seruauntis, "Swithe brynge ye forth the firste stoole, and clothe ye hym, and

166 yiue ye a ryng in his hoond, and schoon on hise feet. **23.** And brynge ye a
fat calf, and sle ye, and ete we, and make we feeste. **24.** For this my sone
was deed, and hath lyued ayen; he perischid, and is foundun."

For Further Reading

Historical Background

Berndt, "The Linguistic Situation in England from the Norman Conquest to the
 Loss of Normandy," *Philologica Pragensia*, 1965.
Dunn and Byrnes, *Middle English Literature*, 1973.
Freeman, *The History of the Norman Conquest of England*, 1974.
Hussey, *Chaucer's World: A Pictorial Companion*, 1967.
Myers, *England in the Late Middle Ages*, 1971.
Stenton, *English Society in the Early Middle Ages (1066–1307)*, 1951.

Handbooks

Jones, *An Introduction to Middle English*, 1972.
Mossé, *A Handbook of Middle English*, 1952.
Wardale, *An Introduction to Middle English*, 1962.

Sounds and Spellings

Fisiak, *A Short Grammar of Middle English; Part One: Graphemics, Phonemics and
 Morphemics*, 1970.
Jordan, *Handbook of Middle English Grammar: Phonology*, 1974.
Kökeritz, *A Guide to Chaucer's Pronunciation*, 1962.
McLaughlin, *A Graphemic-Phonemic Study of a Middle English Manuscript*, 1963.

Grammar

Brunner, *An Outline of Middle English Grammar*, 1963.
Fisiak, *Morphemic Structure of Chaucer's English*, 1965.
MacLeish, *The Middle English Subject-Verb Cluster*, 1969.
Mustanoja, *A Middle English Syntax, Part I: Parts of Speech*, 1960.
Shores, *A Descriptive Syntax of the Peterborough Chronicle from 1122 to 1154*, 1971.
Wright and Wright, *An Elementary Middle English Grammar*, 1928.

Dictionaries

Kurath and Kuhn, *Middle English Dictionary*, 1954–.
Mayhew and Skeat, *A Concise Dictionary of Middle English from A.D. 1150 to 1580*,
 1888.
Stratmann, *A Middle-English Dictionary*, 1891.

Dialects

Kristensson, *A Survey of Middle English Dialects, 1290–1350: The Six Northern
 Counties and Lincolnshire*, 1967.
Moore, Meech, and Whitehall, "Middle English Dialect Characteristics and Dialect
 Boundaries," *Univ. of Michigan Publications in Language and Literature*, 1935.

7 The Modern English Period to 1800

Sounds and Spellings

The fifteenth century, following the death of Chaucer, marks a turning point in the history of English, for during this period the language underwent greater, more important phonological changes than in any other century before or since. Despite these radical changes in pronunciation, the old spelling was maintained and, as it were, stereotyped. William Caxton, who died in 1491, and the printers who followed him based their spelling norm not on the pronunciation current in their day, but on the usage of the medieval manuscripts. Hence, though the quality of every single one of the long vowels had changed, the graphic representation of the newer values remained the same as it had been for the Middle English ones: for instance, though the [ē] of Middle English *feet, see, three,* and so forth had been raised to [ī], all such words went on being written as if no change had taken place.

The influence of printers and that of men of learning—misguided though they frequently were—has been greater than any other on English spelling. Learned men preferred an archaic spelling; and, as we shall see, they further archaized it by respelling words etymologically. Printers were responsible for a further normalization of the older scribal practices. While it is true that early printed works exhibit a good many inconsistencies, they are nevertheless quite orderly as compared with the everyday writing of the time.

A *Specimen of English in 1525*

The following paragraph is the chapter "Rosemary" from Banckes's *Herball*, a hodgepodge of botanical and medical lore and a good deal of sheer superstition thrown together and "impyrnted by me Richard Banckes, dwellynge in London, a lytel fro ẙ Stockes in ẙ Pultry, ẙ .xxv. day of Marche. The yere of our lorde .M.CCCCC. & xxv." The only known original copies of this old black-letter "doctor book" are one in the British Museum and one in the Huntington Library in California. What became of the many other copies of the work, which went through at least fifteen editions, no man can say. It will be noted that *the* is sometimes printed ẙ, sometimes *the*. The spelling ẙ is also used three times for the form of the second person singular objective pronoun, *thee*, for which *the* is the usual spelling. The second person plural nominative form, if it occurred, would have been written *ye*; when the *e* was above the line, the *y* was always a makeshift for *þ*, and never to be interpreted as *y*. A line over a vowel (Banckes and a good many other printers actually used a tilde-like diacritic) indicates omission of a following *n* or *m*, as in *thē* for *them* and *thā* for *than*. This device is very ancient. The virgules, or slanting lines, are the equivalents of our commas, used to indicate brief pauses in reading. As was the custom, *v* is used initially (*venymous, vnder*) and *u* elsewhere (*hurte, euyll*), regardless of whether consonant or vowel was to be indicated. Some of the final *e*'s are used for "justifying" lines of type— that is, making even right-hand margins—a most useful expedient when type had to be set by hand. Long *s*, which must be carefully distinguished from the similar *f*, is used initially and medially.

Roſemary.

This herbe is hote and dry/ take the flowres and put them in a lynen clothe/ & ſo boyle them in fayre clene water to ẙ halfe & coole it & drynke it/ for it is moche worth agaynſt all euylles in the body. Alſo take the flowres & make powder therof and bynde it to the ryght arme in a lynen clothe/ and it ſhall make the lyght and mery. Alſo ete the flowres with hony faſtynge with ſowre breed and there ſhall ryſe in the none euyll ſwellynges. Alſo take the flowres and put them in a cheſt amonge youre clothes or amonge bokes and moughtes [moths] ſhall not hurte them. Alſo boyle the flowres in gotes mylke & than let them ſtande all a nyght vnder the ayer fayre couered/ after that gyue hym to drynke therof that hath the tyſyke [phthisic] and it ſhall delyuer hym. Alſo boyle the leues in whyte wyne & waſſhe thy face therwith/ thy berde & thy browes and there ſhall no cornes growe out/ but thou ſhall haue a fayre face. Alſo put the leues vnder thy beddes heed/ & thou ſhalbe delyuered of all euyll dremes. Alſo breke ẙ leues ſmall to powder & laye them on a Canker & it ſhall flee it. Alſo take the leues & put thē into a veſſcl of wyne and it ſhall preſerue ẙ wyne fro tartneſſe & euyl sauour/ and yf thou ſell that wyne, thou ſhall haue good lucke & ſpede [success] in the ſale. Alſo yf thou be feble with vnkyndly [unnatural] ſwette/ take and boyle the leues in clene water, & whan ẙ water is colde do [put] therto as moche of whyte wyne/ & than make therin ſoppes & ete thou well therof/ & thou ſhal recouer appetyte. Alſo yf thou haue the flux boyle ẙ leues in ſtronge Ayſell [vinegar] & than bynde them in a lynē [c]lothe and bynde it to thy wombe [belly] & anone the flux ſhal withdrawe. Alſo yf thy legges be blowen with thc goute/ boyle the leues in water/ & than take the leues & bynde them in a lynen clothe aboute thy legges/ & it ſhall do ẙ moche good. Alſo take the leues and boyle them in ſtronge Ayſell & bynde them in a clothe to thy ſtomake/ & it ſhall delyuer ẙ of all euylles. Alſo yf thou haue the coughe/ drynke the water of the leues boyled in whyte wyne/ & thou ſhalbe hole. Alſo take the rynde of Roſemary & make powder therof and drynke it for the poſe [cold in the head]/ & thou ſhalbe delyuered therof. Alſo take the tymbre therof & brūne [burn] it to coles & make powder therof & thā put it into a lynen cloth and rubbe thy tethe therwith/ & yf there be ony wormes therin it ſhall ſlee them & kepe thy tethe from all euyls. Alſo make the a box of the wood and smell to it and it shall preſerne[1] thy youthe. Alſo put therof in thy doores or in thy howſe & thou ſhalbe without daunger of Adders and other venymous ſerpentes. Alſo make the a barell therof & drynke thou of the drynke that ſtandeth thcrin & thou nedes to fere no poyſon that ſhall hurte ẙ/ and yf thou ſet it in thy garden kepe it honeſtly [decently] for it is moche profytahle. Alſo yf a mā haue loſt his ſmellynge of the ayre orelles he maye not drawe his brethe/ make a fyre ot the wood & bake his breed therwith & gyue it hym to ete & he ſhalbe hole.

The Orthography of Early Modern English

In a few words other than *the* and *thee*, early Modern English also used *y* (which þ in its later form had come to resemble) as a representation of þ; for example, *y*ᵗ or *ẏ* was used as an abbreviation for *that*. The abbreviation

---

[1] The printer has inadvertently turned the *u* that was in his copy, to make an *n*.

for *the* survives to our own day in such pseudoantique absurdities as "Ye Olde Choppe Suey Shoppe," in which it is usually pronounced as if it were the same word as the old nominative second person plural pronoun *ye*. Needless to say at this point, there is no justification whatever for such a pronunciation. The two words were carefully distinguished and would have been even had they been printed identically. The fact is, however, that they were also carefully distinguished in printing, as in writing, by the superior *e*, either following the *y* or directly over it, for the definite article. Though *y*ᵗ or *ẏ* could hardly be read as any other word, it too was always written with the superior *t*.

The present use of *i* for vowel and *j* for consonant was not established until the seventeenth century. In the King James Bible (1611) and the First Folio (1623) of Shakespeare, for instance, *i* is used for both values; see, for instance, the passage from the First Folio at the end of this chapter, in which Falstaff's first name occurs as *Iack*. For a long time after the distinction in writing was made, however, the feeling persisted that *i* and *j* were one and the same letter: Dr. Johnson's *Dictionary* (1755) puts them together, and this practice continued well into the nineteenth century.

It was similar with the curved and angular forms of *u*—that is, *u* and *v*; they were used more or less indiscriminately for either vowel or consonant. Continental printers in time came to use *v* and *u* for consonant and vowel, respectively, and by the middle of the seventeenth century English printers were generally making the same distinction. As with *i* and *j*, catalogues, indexes, and the like put *u* and *v* together well into the nineteenth century; in dictionaries *vizier* was followed by *ulcer*, *unzoned* by *vocable*, and *iambic* was set between *jamb* and *jangle*. Many editions of old texts, particularly those used in schools, substitute *j* and *v* for *i* and *u* when these indicate consonants, and *u* for initial *v* when this indicates a vowel, representing, for example, *iaspre*, *liue*, and *vnder* as *jaspre* 'jasper,' *live*, and *under*. Except for the two extended passages reproduced in this chapter, those substitutions are made here when older writers are cited, as also in citations of individual words from older periods. The matter is purely graphic; no question of linguistic evidence is involved.

The sound indicated by *h* was lost in late Latin, and hence the symbol has no phonetic significance in those Latin-derived languages that retain it in their spelling. The influence of Classical Latin had caused French scribes to restore the *h* in the spelling of many words—for instance, *habit*, *herbage*, and *homme*—though it was never pronounced. It was also sometimes inserted in English words of French origin where it was not etymological—for instance, *habundance* (mistakenly regarded as coming from *habere* 'to have') and *abhominable* (supposed to be from Lat. *ab* plus *homine*, explained as 'away from man, hence bestial'). When Shakespeare's pedant Holofernes by implication recommended this latter misspelling and consequent mispronunciation with [h] in *Love's Labour's Lost* 5.1.26 ("This is abhominable, which he would call abbominable"),[2] he was in very good company, at least as far as the writing of the word is concerned, for the error had been current since Middle English times. Writers of Medieval Latin and Old French had been similarly misled by a false notion of the etymology of the word.

During the Renaissance *h* was inserted after *t* in a number of foreign words—for instance, *throne,* from Old French *trone.* The French word is from Latin *thronus,* borrowed from Greek, the *th* being the normal Roman transliteration of Greek θ. The English respelling ultimately gave rise to a change in the initial sound, as also in *theater* and *thesis,* which earlier had initial [t]; similarly with the internal consonant sound spelled *th* in *anthem, apothecary, Catherine* (the pet forms *Kate* and *Kit* preserve the older sound), and *Anthony* (compare *Tony*), which to a large extent has retained its historically correct pronunciation in British, but not in American, English. The only American pronunciation of *Anthony* is precisely parallel with the universal English pronunciation of *anthem* and the other words cited. It is sometimes heard even in reference to Mark Antony, where the spelling does not encourage it. The *h* of *author,* from Old French *autor* (modern *auteur*), going back to Latin *auctor,* was first inserted by French scribes, to whom an *h* after *t* indicated no difference in pronunciation. When in the sixteenth century this fancy spelling began to be used in the English loanword, the way was paved for the modern pronunciation, historically a mispronunciation.

Certain Renaissance respellings ultimately effected changes in traditional pronunciations. *Throne* has already been mentioned. Another example is *schedule* (from OF *cedule*), for which Noah Webster recommended the American spelling pronunciation with initial [sk], as if the word were a Greek loan. The present-day British pronunciation of the first syllable as [šɛd] is also erroneously based on the misspelling. The historically correct pronunciation would begin with [s]. *Debt* and *doubt* are likewise fancy **etymological respellings** of *det* (Middle English, from Old French) and *dout* (ME *doute,* also from Old French), the *b* having been inserted because it was perceived that these words were ultimately derivatives of Latin *debitum* and *dubitare,* respectively; similarly with the *c* in *indict* and the *b* in *subtle.* Those learned men responsible for such respellings perhaps thought to effect a change in pronunciation like that which Shakespeare's schoolmaster Holofernes recommended. In the passage referred to above, he speaks of those "rackers of ortagriphie [orthography]" (for to him, as to many after him, spelling set the standard for pronunciation) who say *dout* and *det* when they should say *doubt* and *debt.* "*D, e, b, t,* not *d, e, t,*" he says, unaware that the word was indeed written *d, e, t* before schoolmasters like himself began tinkering with

---

[2] This (with correction of an obvious printer's error) and all other quotations from Shakespeare's plays are from the First Folio (facsimile ed., London, 1910) with the line numbering of the *Globe* edition (1891) as given in Bartlett's *Concordance.* Roman type will be substituted for the italic used for proper names occurring in speeches in the Folio, except for one instance in the passage cited at the end of the chapter.

The Orthography of Early Modern English

spelling. These etymological respellings have not so far affected pronunciation, but others have.

Comptroller is a pseudolearned respelling of *controller*, taken by English from Old French. The fancy spelling is doubtless due to an erroneous association with French *compte* 'count.' The word has fairly recently acquired a new pronunciation based on the misspelling. *Receipt* and *indict*, both taken from Anglo-French, and *victual*, from Old French, have been similarly remodeled to give them a Latin look; their traditional pronunciations have not as yet been affected. *Parliament*, a respelling of the English loanword *parlement* (a derivative of Fr. *parler* 'to speak'), has also fairly recently acquired a pronunciation such as the later spelling seems to indicate.

Another such change of long standing has resulted from the insertion of *l* in *fault* (ME *faute*, from Old French), a spelling suggested by Latin *fallita* and strengthened by the analogy of *false*, which has come to us direct from Latin *falsus*. For a while the word continued to be pronounced without the *l*, riming with *ought* and *thought* in seventeenth-century poetry. In Dr. Johnson's day there was wavering, as Johnson himself testifies in the *Dictionary*, between the older *l*-less and the newer pronunciation with *l*. The eighteenth-century **orthoepists** indicate the same wavering. These were men who conceived of themselves as exercising a directive function; they recommended and condemned, usually on quite irrelevant grounds. Seldom were they content merely to record variant pronunciations. Thomas Sheridan, the distinguished father of a more distinguished son named Richard Brinsley, in his *General Dictionary of the English Language* (1780) decides in favor of the *l*-less pronunciation of *fault*, as does James Elphinston in his *Propriety Ascertained* (1787). Robert Nares in his *Elements of Orthoëpy* (1784) records both pronunciations and makes no attempt to make a choice between them. John Walker in his *Critical Pronouncing Dictionary* (1791) declared that to omit the *l* made a "disgraceful exception," for the word would thus "desert its relation to the Latin *falsitas*." The history of the *l* of *vault* is quite similar.

Although such tinkering with the orthography is one cause of the discrepancy between spelling and pronunciation in Modern English, another and more important one is the change in the pronunciation of the tense vowels that helps to demark Middle from Modern English. This change, the most salient of all phonological developments in the history of English, is called the **Great Vowel Shift**.

The Great Vowel Shift

Comparison of the modern developments in parentheses in the chapter on Old English (p. 106) shows sufficiently clearly what are the modern representatives of the Old English long vowels. As has been pointed out, the latter changed only slightly in Middle English: [ā], in Old English written *a*, as in *stān*, was rounded except in the Northern dialect to [ɔ], in Middle English written *o(o)*, as in *stoon*. But this was really the only particularly noteworthy change in quality. By the early Modern English period, all the long vowels had shifted: Middle English *ē*, as in *sweete* 'sweet,' had already acquired the value [i] that it currently has, and the others were well on their way to acquiring the values that they have in current English.

In phonological terms, Middle English *ē*, *ę̄*, *ō*, and *ǭ* were raised in their articulation. Middle English *ā*, which comes from Old English short *a* in open syllables, was fronted as well. The two highest Middle English front and back vowels—*ī* and *ū*, respectively—became diphthongs. These changes in the quality of the long, or tense, vowels constitute what is known as the Great Vowel Shift, which is summarized in the following table.

LONG VOWELS

LATE MIDDLE ENGLISH	EARLY MODERN ENGLISH	LATER ENGLISH
[ā] as in *name* ⟶	[æ] > [ɛ]³ ⟶	[e]
[ē] as in *feet* ⟶	[i]	
[ɛ] as in *greet* 'great' ⟶	[e]	
[ī] as in *ride* ⟶	[əɪ] ⟶	[aɪ]
[ō] as in *boote* 'boot' ⟶	[u]	
[ɔ] as in *boot* 'boat' ⟶	[o]	
[ū] as in *hous* ⟶	[əʊ] ⟶	[aʊ]

The stages by which the shift occurred and the cause of it are unknown. There are several theories (Wolfe 1972), but the evidence is ambiguous, so we will not go into them here. By some series of intermediate changes, long *ī*, as in Middle English *rīden* 'to ride,' became a diphthong [əɪ]. This pronunciation survives in certain types of speech, particularly before voiceless consonants. It went on in most types of English to become in the course of the seventeenth century [aɪ], though there are variations in pronunciation.

It was similar with Middle English long *u*, as in *hous* 'house': it became [əʊ]. This [əʊ], surviving in eastern Virginia and in some types of Canadian English, became [aʊ] at about the same time as [əɪ] became [aɪ].

Middle English [ō], as in *ro(o)te* 'root,' became [u]. Laxing of this [u] to [ʊ] has occurred in *book*, *foot*, *good*, *look*, *took*, and other words; in *blood*

³ Vowel quantity is distinctive in early Modern English only for [æ] and [ɛ]; up to about the middle of the seventeenth century it distinguished such pairs of words as *fate* [fæt] and *fat* [fæt] and later, when [æ] had shifted to [ɛ], pairs like *mace* [mēs] and *mess* [mɛs]. Consequently, it is only for these two tense vowels that the macron will be used in transcribing early Modern English pronunciation.

The Great Vowel Shift

and *flood* there has been unrounding in addition to laxing, resulting in [ə] in these two words. The chronology of this subsequent laxing and unrounding is difficult to establish, as is the distribution of the various developments. As Helge Kökeritz (1953, p. 236) points out, Shakespeare's riming of words that had Middle English long close *o* gives no clue to his pronunciation, for he rimes *food* with *good* and *flood*, *mood* with *blood*, *reprove* with *love* and *dove*. If these are not merely traditional rimes, we must conclude that the distribution of [u], [ʊ], and [ə] was not in early Modern English the same as it is in current English, and there is indeed ample evidence that colloquial English did vacillate a good deal. This fact is not particularly surprising when we remember that there is at the present time a certain amount of wavering between [u] and [ʊ] in such words as *roof, broom, room*, and a few others. Pronunciation of *root* with the lax vowel is fairly common in some types of American English.

The development of Middle English [ɔ̄] as in *hǫ(ǫ)m* 'home' and *stǫ(ǫ)n* 'stone' presents no special problems. The sound shifted to [o]. In a few words this [o] was laxed in early Modern English—for instance, *hot*, from Middle English *hǫ(ǫ)t*.

Middle English *ā* as in *name* and *ai* as in *nail* had by the early fifteenth century been leveled as [ā], subsequently going through the stages [ǣ], [ɛ̄], [e]. The resultant homophony of *tale* and *tail* provided Shakespeare and his contemporaries with what seems to have been an almost irresistible temptation for the making of off-color puns (for instance, in *The Two Gentlemen of Verona* 2.3.52ff and *Othello* 3.1.6ff). The current pronunciation of such words—that is, with [e]—became normal in standard English probably in the early years of the eighteenth century. All these pronunciations may have existed side by side, just as **retarded** and **advanced pronunciations** may and do exist in current English. (Some speakers today retain characteristics that, if they are noticed at all, are considered old-fashioned by younger-generation speakers, like *forehead* as [fárɪd] or [fórɪd] in contrast to [fórhɛ̀d].)

The development of Middle English [ē] as in *three* and *kēne* 'keen' is quite regular. It became [i], as we have seen.

Middle English [ɛ̄] as in *hɛ̧ɛ̧th* 'heath' had two developments in early Modern English. One is suggested by Falstaff's *reason–raison* pun of 1598, in the passage cited below (pp. 181–82), and many other such puns—for example, *abased–a beast, grace–grease*. (The fullest treatment of Shakespeare's puns—sometimes childish, but frequently richly obscene—is in part 2 of Kökeritz's *Shakespeare's Pronunciation*.) But there is also convincing evidence that the present English vowel in *heath* existed in such words in early Modern English. The coexistence of two pronunciations presupposes that [ē] occurred in late Middle English times as a variant, perhaps dialectal, of [ɛ̄]. Chaucer very occasionally rimes close *ē* words with words that in his type of English ordinarily had open *ɛ̄*, indicating his familiarity with a pre-1400 raising of [ɛ̄] to [ē] in some types of English. The present English vowel in such words as *meat* and *heath* is thus obviously, as H. C. Wyld (1936, p. 211) put it, "merely the result of the abandonment of one type of pronunciation and the adoption of another." Other authorities agree with Wyld's view—for instance, Kökeritz (1953, pp. 194–209) and E. J. Dobson (1968, 2: 606–16).

After about 1600 the polite pronunciation of words that continued Middle English [ɛ̄] had [e], the vowel that survives to this day in *break*, *great*, *steak*, and *yea*. *Drain* (ME *draynen*, *dreynen*, from OE *drēahnian*), which is in standard English pronounced as its current spelling suggests, is yet another example; a variant with [i] occurs in nonstandard usage. Many rimes from the seventeenth and eighteenth centuries testify to this pronunciation in words that today have only [i]—for instance, Jonathan Swift's "You'd swear that so divine a creature / Felt no necessities of nature" ("Strephon and Chloe"), in which the riming words are to be pronounced [krétər] and [nétər], and "You spoke a word began with H, / And I know whom you meant to teach" ("The Journal of a Modern Lady"), in which the riming words are [eč] and [teč]. A few surnames borne by families with long association with Ireland, like *Yeats* (compare *Keats*), *Re(a)gan*, and *Shea*, have also retained the variant pronunciation with [e], which also occurs in *Beatty* in American speech.

But, according to what seems to be the best-informed interpretation of the facts, there was no sound shift in Modern English of this [e] to [i]. Middle and early Modern English [ɛ̄], having reached [e], stopped there, this [e] surviving in the mere handful of words just cited. Pronunciation of these and all other such words with [i] had, however, been current since the beginning of the Modern English period. The [i] pronunciation of words like *heath* was the regular development of the alternative late Middle English pronunciation mentioned above. As Dobson (1968, 2: 611) points out, "Throughout the [early] ModE period there was a struggle going on between two ways of pronouncing 'ME ē̜ words'"; ultimately the earlier less polite [i] pronunciation was to win out, so that only a few words remain as evidence of the sound that prevailed in fashionable circles from about 1600 to the mid-eighteenth century. The process was gradual, involving first one word, then another.

Other Vowels

The short vowels have remained relatively stable throughout the history of English. The most obvious changes affect Middle English short *a*, which shifted by way of [a] to [æ], and Middle English short *u*, which was unrounded and shifted to [ə], though the older value survives in a good many words in which the vowel was preceded by a labial consonant, especially if it was followed by *l*—for instance, *bull*, *full*, *put* (but compare the variant *putt*), *pull*, and *bush*. It is evident that there was an unrounded variant of short *o*, reflected in late-sixteenth- and seventeenth-century spellings. Wyld (1936, pp. 240–41) cites a number of examples of *a* for *o* in spellings, including Queen Elizabeth I's "I pray you stap the mouthes." This unrounding did not affect the language as a whole, but such doublets as *strop–strap* and *god–gad* remain to testify to its having occurred. Today [ɑ] is also found in the most widespread American pronunciation of words that had short [ɔ] in Middle English (*god, stop, clock*, and so forth). Short *e* has not changed, except occasionally before [ŋ], as in *string* and *wing* from Middle English *streng* and *wenge*, and short *i* remains what it has been since Germanic times.

SHORT VOWELS

LATE MIDDLE ENGLISH	EARLY MODERN ENGLISH	LATER ENGLISH

---

[a] as in *that* ⟶ [æ]
[ɛ] as in *bed*
[ɪ] as in *in*
[ɔ] as in *on* ⟶ [ɔ] or [ɑ]
[ʊ] as in *but* ⟶ [ə]

The first element [ʊ] of a Middle English diphthong written *oi* (for *ui*), as in *poison, join*, and *boil*, and occurring almost exclusively in words of French origin, underwent the shift to [ə] along with other short *u*'s. The diphthong thus fell together with the development of Middle English *ī* as [əɪ], both subsequently becoming [aɪ], so that the verb *boil*, from Old French *boillir* (ultimately Lat. *bullīre*) and the etymologically quite distinct noun meaning 'inflamed, infected sore,' which is of native English origin (OE *bȳl*, occurring in Middle English as *bȳle* or *bīle*), have both become current nonstandard [baɪl]. Many rimes in our older poetry testify to this identity in pronunciation of the reflexes of Middle English *ī* and *ui*—for instance, Alexander Pope's couplet "While expletives their feeble aid to join;/ And ten low words oft creep in one dull line." The current standard pronunciation of words spelled with *oi* for etymological *ui* is based on the spelling. The folk, however, preserve the pronunciation with [aɪ] (Kurath and McDavid 1961, pp. 167–68, maps 143–46). The quite different Middle English diphthong spelled *oi* and pronounced [ɔɪ] is also of French origin, the *o* going back to Latin *au*, as in *joie* (ultimately Lat. *gaudia*) and *cloistre* (Lat. *claustrum*).

The similar Middle English diphthongs [ɛʊ] and [ɪu], written *eu, ew, iu, iw*, and *u* (depending to some extent on when they were written), merged into [yu]. As we saw in chapter 2, this [yu] has tended to be reduced to [u] in such words as *duty, Tuesday, lute*, and *news*, in which it follows an alveolar sound. The [y] has been retained initially (*use* as distinct from *ooze*) and after labials and velars: *b* (*beauty* as distinct from *booty*), *p* (*pew* as distinct from *pooh*), *m* (*mute* as distinct from *moot*), *v* (*view* as distinct from the first syllable of *voodoo*), *f* (*feud* as distinct from *food*), *g* (the second syllable of *argue* as distinct from *goo*), *k* (*c*) (*cute* as distinct from *coot*), and *h* (*hew* as distinct from *who*). After [z] this [y] ultimately gave rise to a new single sound [ž] in *azure*, *pleasure*, and the like. Similarly, the earlier medial and initial [sy] in *pressure*, *nation*, *sure*, and the like has become [š], though this was not a new sound, having occurred under other circumstances in Old English.

Other Middle English diphthongs, [aʊ] in *lawe* and [ɔʊ] in *snow*, were monophthongized to [ɔ] and [o], respectively. The early fifteenth-century merger of [æɪ] as in *nail* with [ā] as in *name* has already been mentioned.

DIPHTHONGS

[aʊ] as in *lawe* ⟶	[ɔ]	
[æɪ] > [ā] as in *nail* ⟶	[æ] > [ɛ̄] ⟶	[e]
[ɛʊ] and [ɪu] as in *fewe* and *knew* ⟶	[yu]	
[ɔʊ] as in *snow* ⟶	[o]	
[ɔɪ] as in *joy*		
[ʊɪ] as in *join* ⟶	[əɪ] ⟶	[ɔɪ]

The loss of *e* [-ə] at the end of words is just as widespread a change as the Great Vowel Shift. As we have seen, however, this wholesale **apocopation**, as it is called, had occurred by the end of the fourteenth century and hence can hardly be regarded as a modern change, though it is frequently so regarded, just as the leveling of all final vowels in inflectional syllables, frequently regarded as a Middle English change, actually began long before the date that is traditionally given for the beginning of the Middle English period. From early Modern spellings, as well as from poetic meter, this tendency to lose an unstressed -*e* seems also to have affected *the*, as in *th'earth* and the like.

The Early Modern English Consonants

The consonants of English, like the short vowels, have been rather stable, though certain losses have occurred within the Modern English period. The Old English and Middle English voiceless palatal fricative [ç] occurring next to front vowels and still represented in our spelling by *gh* disappeared entirely, as in *bright*, *sigh*, and *weigh*. The identically written voiceless velar fricative [x] occurring next to back vowels either disappeared, as in *taught*, *bought,* and *bough,* or became the voiceless labiodental fricative [f], as in *cough, laugh,* and *enough.* These changes occurred as early as the fifteenth century in all England south of the Humber, though there is evidence that still in the later part of the sixteenth century old-fashioned speakers and a few pedants retained the sounds or at least thought that they ought to be retained (Kökeritz 1953, p. 306).

In the final sequence *-mb,* the *b* had disappeared in pronunciation before the beginning of the Modern English period, so that the spelling could be added after final *m* where it did not etymologically belong, in *limb.* There was a similar tendency to reduce final *-nd,* as in *lawn,* from Middle English *laund;* confusion seems to have arisen, and a nonetymological *-d* has been added in *sound* and *lend* (ME *soun* and *lene*), though in the latter word the excrescent *d* occurred long before the Modern English period.

The *l* of Middle English preconsonantal *al* was lost after first becoming a vowel: thus Middle English *al* and *au* fell together as *au,* ultimately becoming [ɔ] (as in *talk, walk*) except before *f, v,* and *m,* where it became [æ] in such words as *half, salve,* and *psalm* (the last of which now usually has [ɑ]). The *l* retained in the spelling of the cited words and others[4] has led to spelling pronunciations, particularly when it occurs before *m;* many speakers now pronounce the *l* except before *f,* and seem to more traditional speakers to be making a special effort to do so: a certain football team known as the *Falcons* is everywhere called [fǽlkənz], a pronunciation widely current among the pseudoliterate long before the appearance of the team. The spelling has as yet had little if any effect on the pronunciation of the name of the writer William Faulkner. Perhaps if the name had been written *Falconer,* which amounts to the same thing, the spelling pronunciation might in time have come to prevail. The *l* of *ol* was similarly lost before certain consonants by vocalization, as in *folk, yolk, Holmes,* and the like. As we have seen, the *l* in *fault* and *vault* has been inserted. The older pronunciation of the first of these words is indicated by Swift's "O, let him not debase your thoughts,/Or name him but to tell his faults" ("Directions for Making a Birth-Day Song").

In French loanwords like *host* and *humble* the *h,* because it is in the spelling, has gradually come to be pronounced in all but a few words; it was generally lacking in such words in early Modern English. Renaissance spelling habits are, as we have seen, responsible for the unetymological *h* in *author, throne,* and other words, but early Modern English continued to use the etymologically correct pronunciation of such words with [t], which gradually was to give way to pronunciation based on misspelling.

There was an early loss of [r] before sibilants, not to be confused with the much later loss (not really normal before the nineteenth century) before any consonant or before a pause: older *barse* 'fish' by such loss became *bass,*

---

[4] It has been restored from the Latin etymon in *falcon* (ME *faucon,* from Old French, in which the vocalization to [ʊ] also occurred).

as *arse* became *ass* and *bust, nuss, fust* develop from *burst, nurse, first*; this was not, however, a widespread change. An early loss of [r] before *l* is indicated by such a word as *palsy* (ME *parlesie*, a variant of *paralisie* 'paralysis'). Just as *l* occasionally generates a svarabhakti vowel, *r* has done likewise in the old form *alarum*, a variant of *alarm*.

The final unstressed syllable -*ure* was pronounced [-ər], with preceding *t, d*, and *s* having the values [t], [d], and [s] or intervocalically [z], as in *nature* [-tər], *verdure* [-dər], *censure* [-sər], and *leisure* [-zər], until the nineteenth century. Though Noah Webster's use of such pronunciations was considered rustic and old-fashioned by his more elegant contemporaries, in his *Elementary Spelling Book* of 1843 he gave *gesture* and *jester* as homophones. The older pronunciation is indicated by many rimes: to mine Dean Swift once more, "If this to clouds and stars will venture,/That creeps as far to reach the centre" ("Verses on Two Celebrated Modern Poets"). Webster was also opposed to [-č-] in *fortune, virtue*, and the like, which he seems to have associated with fast living. He preferred [-t-] in such words. But many of the pronunciations that he prescribed were scorned by the proper Bostonians of his day.

The initial consonant sequences *gn* and *kn*, still represented in our spelling of *gnarl, gnat, gnaw, knave, knead, knee*, and a few other words, had lost their first elements by the early seventeenth century. Loss of [k] is evidenced by the Shakespearean puns *knack–neck, knight–night*, and others cited by Kökeritz (1953, p. 305).

Final *ing* when unstressed, as in verb forms like *walking* or *coming* and in pronouns like *nothing* and *something*, had long been practically universally pronounced [-ɪn]. According to Wyld (1936, p. 289), "This habit obtains in practically all Regional dialects of the South and South Midlands, and among large sections of speakers of Received Standard English." The velarization of the *n* to [ŋ] began as a **hypercorrect pronunciation** in the first quarter of the nineteenth century and, still according to Wyld, "has now a vogue among the educated at least as wide as the more conservative one with -*n*." Long before Wyld wrote these words, which would need some revision for British English today, the [-ɪn] pronunciation had come to be considered substandard in many parts of the United States, largely because of the crusade that teachers had conducted against it, though it continues to occur rather widely in unselfconscious speech on all social levels. Many spellings and rimes in our older literature testify to the orthodoxy of what is popularly called "dropping the *g*"—in phonological terms, using the dental [n] instead of the velar [ŋ], for there is of course no [g]. For instance, Swift wrote the couplets "See then what mortals place their bliss in!/Next morn betimes the bride was missing" ("Phyllis") and the delicate "His jordan [chamber pot] stood in manner fitting/Between his legs, to spew or spit in" ("Cassinus and Peter"). **Inverse spellings** such as Shakespeare's *cushings* (*cushions*), *javelings* (*javelins*), and *napking* (*napkin*) tell the same story (cited by Kökeritz 1953, p. 314).

The Early Modern English Consonants

Quantitative changes in the Modern English period include the lengthening of an originally short vowel before voiceless fricatives (of [æ] as in *staff, glass,* and *path,* the resultant [ǣ] in the late eighteenth century coming to be replaced by [ɑ] in standard British English; of [ɔ] as in *soft, lost,* and *cloth*). Short vowels were also lengthened before voiced velar stops, as in *dog* and *sag;* compare *dock* and *sack,* which have voiceless velar stops, before which the lengthening has not occurred. In *dog* versus *dock* the lengthening has resulted in qualitatively distinct vowels in most varieties of American English, [ɔ] versus [ɑ]. In *sag* versus *sack,* there is only phonetic lengthening in most dialects, although some varieties of American English have different phonemes in those words—a tense, higher vowel or a diphthong [æɪ] in *sag.* The earlier laxing of [u] to [ʊ] in *hood, good,* and so forth has already been referred to in connection with the development of Middle English [ō] in the Great Vowel Shift. In *mother, brother, other,* and *smother,* originally long vowels were shortened (with eventual modification to [ə]). *Father* and (in some types of speech) *rather,* with originally short vowels, have undergone lengthening, for what reason we cannot be sure—quite contrary to the shortening that occurred in *lather* and *gather.*

Stress

A good many words in early Modern English were stressed otherwise than they are in current speech. *Character, illustrate, concentrate, contemplate* were all stressed on their second syllables, and most polysyllabic words in *-able* and *-ible* had initial stress, frequently with secondary stress on their penultimate syllables, as in "'Tis sweet and cómmendàble in your Nature Hamlet" (*Hamlet* 1.2.87). *Antique,* like *complete* and other words that now have final stress, had initial stress; it is a doublet of *antic,* with which it was identical in pronunciation. But it is not always possible to come to a firm conclusion on the basis of verse, as the many instances of variant stress in Shakespeare's lines indicate (Kökeritz 1953, pp. 392–98). It is likely that most of these variant stressings occurred in actual speech; it would be surprising if they had not, considering the variations that occur in current English.

Evidence for Early Modern Pronunciation

Our knowledge of early Modern English pronunciation comes from many sources. Fortunately not all gentlefolk knew how to spell in earlier days, which is to say that they did not know what have become in our own day conventional spellings, and were pretty much so even then, thanks to the printers. So they spelled phonetically, according to their lights. What is by modern standards a "misspelling," like *coat* for *court* or *crick* for *creek*, may tell us a good deal about the writer's pronunciation. A good many such writings have come down to us. Wyld in his *History of Modern Colloquial English* has used many memoirs, letters, diaries, and documents from this period as the basis for his conclusions concerning the pronunciation of early Modern English. Kökeritz relies somewhat more than Wyld on the grammars and spelling books that began to appear around the middle of the sixteenth century, which he considers "our most important sources of information" (p. 17) on the pronunciation of the English of Shakespeare's day—works such as John Hart's *An Orthographie* (1569) and *A Methode or Comfortable Beginning for All Unlearned* (1570), William Bullokar's *Booke at Large* (1580) and *Bref Grammar for English* (1586), Richard Mulcaster's *The First Part of the Elementarie* (1582), and, in the following century, Alexander Gill's *Logonomia Anglica* (1619; 2nd ed., 1621) and Charles Butler's *English Grammar* (1633; 2nd ed., 1634), which has a list of homophones in its "Index of Words Like and Unlike." These same works, with others, provide the basis for Dobson's two-volume *English Pronunciation 1500–1700*. There are special studies of these early Modern writers on language by Otto Jespersen (on Hart), Bror Danielsson (Hart and Gill), Helge Kökeritz (Hart), R. E. Zachrisson (Bullokar), along with general studies of early Modern English by Wilhelm Horn (*Historische neuenglische Grammatik*, reissued in 1954 as *Laut und Leben: Englische Lautgeschichte der neueren Zeit* [*1400–1950*]), Eilert Ekwall (*A History of Modern English Sounds and Morphology*, 1975), and Karl Luick (*Historische Grammatik der englischen Sprache*, 1914–40). The first volume of Jespersen's *Modern English Grammar on Historical Principles* (1909–49) deals with early Modern English phonology and orthography. The use of word-play and rime has already been alluded to a number of times. Kökeritz makes extensive and most effective use of these in *Shakespeare's Pronunciation*, a work that has been cited a number of times heretofore. There is no dearth of evidence, though frequently what we have is difficult of interpretation.

A Sample of Early Modern Pronunciation

In the passage from Shakespeare's *1 Henry IV* (2.4.255–66) that follows, the phonetic transcription indicates a somewhat conservative pronunciation that was probably current in the south of England in the late sixteenth and early seventeenth centuries. Vowel length is indicated only in the single word *reason(s)*, in which it was distinctive. Stress is indicated, but no attempt has been made to show fine gradations. The Prince, Poins, and Falstaff, who has just told a whopping lie, are speaking:

Prin. Why, how could'ſt thou know theſe men in Kendall Greene,
[wəɪ hóu kúdst ðəu nó ðiz mén ɪn kéndəl grín

when it was ſo darke, thou could'ſt not ſee thy Hand? Come,
hwɛn ɪt wəz só dǽrk ðəu kúdst nɔt sí ðəɪ hǽnd kʊm

tell vs your reaſon: what ſay'ſt thou to this?
tél əs yər rézən hwæt sést ðəu tə ðís

Poin. Come, your reaſon *Iack*, your reaſon.
kúm yər rézən jǽk yər rézən

Falst. What, vpon compulſion? No: were I at the Strappado, or
hwǽt əpón kəmpúlsyən nó wér əɪ æt ðə stræpǽdo ər

all the Racks in the World, I would not tell you on
ól ðə rǽks ɪn ðə wúrld əɪ wúld nɔt tél yʊ ɔn

compulſion. Giue you a reaſon on compulſion? If Reaſons
kəmpúlsyən gív yʊ ə rézən ɔn kəmpúlsyən ɪf rézənz

were as plentie as Black-berries, I would giue no man a
wɛr əz plénti əz blǽkbèriz əɪ wəd gív nó mæn ə

Reaſon vpon compulſion, I.
rézən əpón kəmpúlsyən óɪ]

In this transcription it is assumed that Falstaff, a gentleman (even if a somewhat decayed one) and an officer as well, would have been highly conservative in pronunciation, thus preferring slightly old-fashioned [sy] in *compulsion* to the newer [š] to be heard in the informal speech of his time (Kökeritz 1953, p. 317). It is also assumed that Falstaff used an unstressed form of *would* [wəd] in his last sentence, in contrast to the strongly stressed form [wuld] of his second sentence, and that, even though the Prince may have had the sequence [hw] in his speech, he would not have pronounced the [h] in his opening interjectional *Why*, thus following the usual practice of those present-day speakers who have [hw] when the word is interrogative, but [w] when it is an interjection or an expletive (Kenyon 1950, p. 159).

It is a great pity that there was no tape recorder at the Globe playhouse.

For Further Reading

General

Bullock-Davies, *English Pronunciation from the Fifteenth to the Eighteenth Century*, 1970.
Dobson, *English Pronunciation 1500–1700,* 1968.
Ekwall, *A History of Modern English Sounds and Morphology*, 1975.
Wyld, *A History of Modern Colloquial English*, 1936.

Wolfe, *Linguistic Change and the Great Vowel Shift in English*, 1972.
Zachrisson, *Pronunciation of English Vowels, 1400–1700*, 1971.

Shakespearean English

Kökeritz, *Shakespeare's Pronunciation*, 1953.
Zachrisson, *The English Pronunciation at Shakespeare's Time as Taught by William Bullokar*, 1970.

8 The Modern English Period to 1800

Forms and Syntax

The early part of the Modern English period saw the establishment of the standard written language that we know today. The standardization of the language was due in the first place to the need of the central government for regular procedures by which to conduct its business, to keep its records, and to communicate with the citizens of the land. Standard languages are usually the byproducts of bureaucracy, developed to meet a specific administrative need, as prosaic as such a source is, rather than spontaneous developments of the folk or the artifice of writers and scholars. John H. Fisher (1977, 1979) argues that standard English was first the language of the Court of Chancery, founded in the fifteenth century to give prompt justice to English citizens and to consolidate the King's influence in the nation. It was then taken up by the early printers, who adapted it for other purposes and spread it wherever their books were read, until finally it fell into the hands of school teachers, dictionary makers, and grammarians.

Inflectional and syntactical developments in this early Modern English are important, if somewhat less spectacular than the phonological ones. They continue the trend established during Middle English times that changed our grammar from a synthetic to an analytic system.

Nouns

As we have seen, by the end of the Middle English period -*es* had been extended to practically all nouns as a genitive singular and caseless plural suffix. As a result, most nouns had only two forms (*sister, sisters*), as they do today in speech. The use of the apostrophe to distinguish the written forms of the genitive singular (*sister's*) and plural (*sisters'*) was not widely adopted until the seventeenth and eighteenth centuries, respectively.

IRREGULAR PLURALS

The handful of mutated-vowel plurals for the most part resisted the analogical principle, so that *feet, geese, teeth, lice, mice, men,* and *women* have survived to the present and show no tendency to give way to -*s* plurals. A few -*n* plurals remained in early Modern English, including *eyen* 'eyes,' *shoon* 'shoes,' *kine* 'cows,' *brethren, children,* and *oxen*. The first two are now obsolete; *kine* continues to eke out a precarious existence as an archaic poetic word; and *brethren* has a very limited currency, confined in serious use mainly to certain religious groups. In *kine, brethren,* and *children,* the *n* had not been present in Old English but was added by analogy with other -*n* plurals. The regularly developed *ky* and *childer,* which go back, respectively, to Old English *cȳ* and *cildru,* are current in dialect speech, or were so until fairly recently, in the north of England and in Scotland. *Brethren* (Old English *brōðor* or *brōðru*) also added an *n* by analogy and introduced a mutated vowel that did not occur in the Old English plural. *Oxen* is thus the only "pure" survival of the Old English weak declension, which formed its nominative-accusative plural with the suffix -*an* (see p. 114).

Uninflected plurals survive from Old and Middle English times to the present in *deer, sheep, swine, folk,* and *kind*. Analogical *folks* occurred very early in the Modern English period. *Kind* has acquired a new -*s* plural because of the feeling that the older construction was a "grammatical error," despite the precedent of its use in "these (those, all) kind of" by Shakespeare, Dryden, Swift, Goldsmith, Austen, and others. Its synonym *sort,* which is not of Old English origin, acquired an uninflected plural as early as the sixteenth century by analogy with *kind,* as in "these (those, all) sort of," but this construction also is frowned upon by most writers of school grammars, despite its use by Swift, Fielding, Austen, Dickens, Trollope, Wells, and others (Jespersen 1909–49, 2: 68). *Horse* retained its historical uninflected plural, as in Chaucer's "His hors were goode" (*Canterbury Tales,* General

Prologue, line 74) and Shakespeare's "Come on, then, horse and chariots let us have" (*Titus Andronicus* 2.2.18), until the seventeenth century, though the analogical plural *horses* had begun to occur as early as the thirteenth. Doubtless by analogy with *deer, sheep,* and the like, the names of other creatures that had -*s* plurals in earlier times came to have uninflected plurals—for example, *fish* and *fowl,* particularly when these are regarded as game. Barnyard creatures take the -*s* (*fowls, ducks, pigs,* and so forth); and Jesus Christ, it will be remembered, distributed to the multitude "a few little *fishes*" (Matthew 15.34). But one shoots (wild) *fowl* and (wild) *duck,* hunts *pig* (that is, wild boars), and catches *fish.* The uninflected plural may be extended to the names of quite un-English beasts, like *buffalo* ("a herd of buffalo") and *antelope. Webster's New World Dictionary of the American Language* in its entry *plural* has a long list of names of creatures, many of them exotic, which may have uninflected plurals.

THE HIS-GENITIVE

A remarkable construction is the use of *his, her,* and *their* as signs of the genitive (***his*-genitive**), as in "Augustus his daughter" (E. K.'s gloss to Spenser's *Shepherds' Calendar,* 1579), "Elizabeth Holland her howse" (State Papers, 1546), and "the House of Lords their proceedings" (Pepys's *Diary,* 1667). This use began in Old English times but had its widest currency in the sixteenth and seventeenth centuries, as in Shakespeare's "And art not thou Poines, his Brother?" (*2 Henry IV* 2.4.308) and in the "Prayer for All Conditions of Men" in the 1662 Book of Common Prayer, "And this we beg for Jesus Christ his sake."

The use of possessive pronouns as genitive markers seems to have had a double origin. On the one hand, it may have arisen from the sort of topic-comment construction that we still have in present-day English: "My brother—his main interest is football." Such a construction would have provided a way in Old English to indicate possession for foreign proper names and for other expressions in which the inflected genitive was awkward. The oldest examples we have are from King Alfred's ninth-century translation of the history of the world by Orosius: "Nilus seo ea hire æwielme is neh þæm clife," that is, 'Nile, the river—her source is near the cliff,' and "Affrica and Asia hiera landgemircu onginnað of Alexandria," that is, 'Africa and Asia—their boundaries start from Alexandria.' An early example with *his* is from Ælfric's translation of the Book of Numbers (made about 1000): "We gesawon Enac his cynryn," that is, 'We saw Anak's kindred.'

On the other hand, many English speakers came to regard the historical genitive ending -*s* as a variant of *his.* In its unstressed pronunciation, *his* was and is still pronounced without an [h], so that "Tom bets his salary" and "Tom Betts's salary" are identical in pronunciation. Once speakers began to think of "Mars's armor" as a variant of "Mars his armor," an association doubtless reinforced by the use of the latter construction from early times as mentioned above, they started to spell the genitive ending -s as *his* (Wyld 1936, pp. 314–15; Jespersen 1909–49, 6: 301–02). That such confusion did occur is shown by the occasional use of *his* with females, as in "Mrs. Sands his maid" (*OED*, 1607), and by the mixture of the two spellings, as in "Job's patience, Moses his meekness, Abraham's faith" (*OED*, 1568). In the latter example, *his* was used when the genitive ending was pronounced as an extra syllable, and *'s* when it was not, the apostrophe also suggesting that the genitive -s was regarded as a contraction of *his*. Other spellings for the genitive ending were *is* and *ys*, as in "Harlesdon ys name" and "her Grace is requeste," that is, 'her Grace's request' (Wyld 1936, p. 315).

His (with its variants *is* and *ys*) was much more common in this construction than *her* or *their*. The *his*-genitive, whichever pronoun is used, was most prevalent with proper names and especially after sibilants, as in *Mars*, *Moses*, *Sands*, and *Grace*, an environment in which the genitive ending is homophonous with the unstressed pronunciation of *his*. Although the earliest examples of the *his*-genitive must have had another origin, those that were so frequent during the early Modern English period were certainly due, at least in part, to a confusion of inflectional -s and *his*. The construction has survived, somewhat marginally, in printed bookplates: "John Smith His Book."

THE GROUP GENITIVE

The **group-genitive** construction, as in "King Priam of Troy's son" and "The Wife of Bath's Tale," is a development of the early Modern English period. Though there were sporadic occurrences in Middle English, the usual older idiom is illustrated by Chaucer's "the kyng Priamus sone of Troye" and "The Wyves Tale of Bathe," or its variant "The Wyf of Bathe Hire Tale" with a *his*-genitive (in this case, *hire* for 'her'). What has happened is that a word group—usually, as in these examples, two nouns connected by a preposition—has come to be regarded as a unit; the sign of the genitive is thus affixed to the last word of what is in fact a phrase. The construction also occurs with a pronoun plus *else*, as in *everybody else's*, and with nouns connected by a coordinating conjunction, as in "Kenyon and Knott's *Pronouncing Dictionary*" and *an hour or two's time*. There are comparatively few literary examples of clauses so treated, but in everyday speech such constructions as *the little boy that lives down the street's dog* and *the woman I live next door to's husband* are frequent. "He is the woman who is the best friend this club has ever had's husband" is an extreme example from Gracie Allen, a radio and television comedian of a generation ago.

As a consequence of the group genitive, the morpheme we spell *'s* is now strikingly different from other inflectional endings, because it is added to phrases rather than to words. In effect it has ceased to be a member of the inflectional system and has instead become a grammatical particle that is always pronounced as part of the preceding word (an **enclitic**), although it often goes syntactically not with that word, but rather with a whole preceding phrase. Of all the Old English inflectional endings, -es (the origin of our 's) has had the most unusual historical development: it has broken off from the nouns to which it was originally added and moved up to the level of phrases, where it functions syntactically like a word on that higher level, although it continues to be pronounced as a mere word ending.

THE UNINFLECTED GENITIVE

In early Modern English an **uninflected genitive** occurred in a number of special circumstances, especially for some nouns that were feminine in Old English and occasionally for nouns ending in [s] or preceding words beginning in [s]—for example, *for conscience sake* and *for God sake*. A few uninflected genitives, though not generally recognized as such, survive to the present day in reference to the Virgin Mary—for example, *Lady Day* (that is, Our Lady's Day 'Feast of the Annunciation'), *Lady Chapel* (Our Lady's Chapel), and *ladybird* (Our Lady's bird). Sometimes an uninflected genitive was used as an alternative to the group genitive, as in "the duke of Somerset dowther [daughter]." The uninflected genitive of present-day black English (for example, "my brother car"), although of different historical origin, has re-created a structure that was once a part of general English usage.

Adjectives and Adverbs

The distinction between strong and weak adjective forms, already greatly simplified by the Middle English loss of the final *n*, completely disappeared with the further loss of [ə] from the end of words. The loss of final [ə] also eliminated the distinction between plural and singular adjectives. Although the letter *e*, which represented the schwa vowel in spelling, continued to be written in many words and was even extended to words that had not had it in Middle English, adjectives no longer had a grammatical category of number or of definiteness. The Modern English adjective thus came to be invariable in form. The only words that still agree in number with the nouns they modify are the demonstratives *this–these* and *that–those*.

Adjectives and adverbs continued to form comparatives with -*er* and superlatives with -*est*, but increasingly they used **analytical comparison** with *mo(e)* (a semantic equivalent of *more*, though not comparative in form), *more*, and *most*, which had occurred as early as Old English times. The present stylistic objection to affixing the endings to polysyllables had somewhat less force in the early Modern English period, when forms like *eminenter*, *impudentest*, and *beautifullest* are not particularly hard to find, nor, for that matter, are monosyllables with *more* and *most*, like *more near*, *more fast*, *most poor*, and *most foul*. As was true in earlier times also, a good many instances of **double comparison** like *more fitter*, *more better*, *more fairer*, *most worst*, *most stillest*, and (probably the best-known example) *most unkindest* occur in early Modern English. The general rule was that comparison could be made with the ending or with the modifying word or, for emphasis, with both.

Many adverbs that now must end in *-ly* did not require the suffix in early Modern English times. The works of Shakespeare furnish many typical examples: *grievous sick*, *indifferent cold*, *wondrous strange*, and *passing* ['surpassingly'] *fair*. Note also the use of *sure* in the following citations, which would nowadays be condemned as "bad English" in the schools: "If she come in, shee'l sure speake to my wife" (*Othello* 5.2.96); "And sure deare friends my thankes are too deare a halfepeny" (*Hamlet* 2.2.282); "Sure the Gods doe this yeere connive at us" (*Winter's Tale* 4.4.692).

Pronouns

Rather important changes are to be noted in the pronouns. Although they are the most highly inflected part of speech in present-day English, thus preserving the earlier synthetic character of our language in a small way, the system of the pronouns has undergone several major and a number of minor alterations.

PERSONAL PRONOUNS

The early Modern English personal pronouns are shown in the table on page 190. *I* came to be capitalized, not through any egotism, but only because lower-case *i* standing alone was likely to be overlooked, since it is the most insignificant of the letters of the alphabet. In the first and second persons singular, the distinction between *my* and *mine* and between *thy* and *thine* was a purely phonological one, as it had been in Middle English since the thirteenth century on; that is, *mine* and *thine* were used before a vowel, *h*, or a pause, and *my* and *thy* before a consonant. This distinction continued to be made until the eighteenth century, when *my* became the only regular first person possessive in attributive use (as in "That is my coat"). Thereafter *mine* was restricted to use as a nominal (as in "That is mine," "Mine is here," and "Put it on mine"), just as the "*s*-forms" *hers*, *ours*, *yours*, *theirs* had been since late Middle English times. Thus the distinction between attributive and nominal possessive forms spread through most of the personal pronoun system; today the only exceptions are *his*, which uses the same form for both functions, and *its*, which has no nominal function. (We do not usually say things like *"That is its" or *"Its is here.")

Nominative		I	thou	he, a	(h)it	she
Objective		me	thee	him	(h)it	her
Possessive	⎧ Attributive					her
		my/mine	thy/thine	his	his, it, its	
	⎩ Nominal					hers

Nominative		we	ye/you	they	
Objective		us	you/ye	them, (h)em	
Possessive	⎧ Attributive	our	your	their	
	⎩ Nominal	ours	yours	theirs	

When the distinction between the forms with and without *n* was phonological, a confusion sometimes arose about which word the *n* belonged with. The Fool's *nuncle* in *King Lear* is due to his misunderstanding of *mine uncle* as *my nuncle*, and it is likely that *Ned*, *Nelly*, and *Noll* (a nickname usually associated with Oliver Goldsmith) have the same origin from *mine Edward*, *mine Eleanor*, *mine Oliver*. The confusion is similar to that which today produces *a* (*whole*) *nother* from *another* (that is, *an other*).

The loss of the second person singular *thou* and its other forms created a gap in the pronoun system that we have not yet repaired. That loss began with a shift in the use of the *thou* and the *ye* forms. As early as the late thirteenth century, the second person plural forms (*ye, you, your*) began to be used with singular meaning in circumstances of politeness or formality. In imitation of the French use of *tu* and *vous*, the English historical plural forms were used in addressing a superior, whether by virtue of social status or age, and in upper-class circles among equals, though highborn lovers might slip into the *th-* forms in situations of intimacy. The distinction is retained in other languages, which may even have a verb meaning 'to use the singular form'—for example, French *tutoyer*, Spanish *tutear*, Italian *tuizzare*, German *dutzen*. Late Middle English had *thoute*, with the same meaning.

In losing this distinction English obviously has lost a useful device. Even when the two forms were available for choosing, however, the English did not always use them as consistently as the French. There is frequently no apparent reason for their interchange, as in the dialogue between two servants in *The Taming of the Shrew* 4.1.101–104:

> *Cur*[*tis*] Doe you heare ho? you must meete my maister to countenance my mistris.
>
> *Gru*[*mio*] Why she hath a face of her owne.

The Modern English Period to 1800: Forms and Syntax

Cur[*tis*] Who knowes not that?
Gru[*mio*] Thou it seemes. . . .

Frequently, however, our older writers use the forms with artistic discrimination, as in *Hamlet* 3.4.9–21:

Qu[*een*] Hamlet, thou hast thy Father much offended.
Ham[*let*] Mother, you have my Father much offended.
Qu[*een*] Come, come, you answer with an idle tongue.

. . .

Qu[*een*] What wilt thou do? thou wilt not murther me?

This passage is cited by Wilhelm Franz (1924, p. 256), who points out that the Queen's *thou* in "What wilt thou do?" is an expression of strong emotion. In addition, it might be pointed out that her first "Hamlet, thou hast thy Father much offended" is tender and affectionate. Hamlet's "Mother, you have . . ." is appropriate from a son to his mother, but there is more than a hint of a rebuff in her choice of the more formal pronoun in "Come, come, you answer. . . ." Elsewhere also Shakespeare chooses the *y*-forms and the *th*-forms with artistic care, though it is sometimes difficult for a present-day reader, unaccustomed to the niceties offered by a choice of forms, to figure him out.

The *th*-forms of the second person singular, which had become quite rare in upper-class speech by the sixteenth century, were completely lost in standard English in the eighteenth, though they have lingered on in the dialects (Evans 1969, 1970). Our familiarity with them is largely due to their occurrence in poetry and in religious language, especially that of the King James Bible. Though less general than they once were, *th*-forms still occur in the usage of older-generation members of the Society of Friends (Quakers) when speaking to one another. In such occurrences *thee* serves for both the subject and the object functions.

The third person singular masculine pronoun has been relatively stable since late Old English times. The unstressed form of *he* was often written *a*, as in "Now might I doe it, but now a is a-praying,/And now Ile doo't, and so a goes to heaven" from the Second Quarto of *Hamlet* 3.3.73–74. (The Folio has *he* in both instances.) In the feminine, *she* and *her(s)* show no change since Middle English times.

In the neuter, however, an important change took place in the later part of the sixteenth century, when the new possessive form *its* arose. The older nominative and objective *hit* had lost its *h-* when unstressed; then the *h*-less form came to be used in stressed as well as unstressed positions—though, as has already been pointed out, *hit*, the form preferred by Queen Elizabeth I, remains in nonstandard speech as a stressed form. The corresponding older possessive *his* remained the usual form in the early years of the seventeenth century, as in Shakespeare's *Troilus and Cressida* 2.2.53–54: "But value dwels not in particular will,/It holds his estimate and dignitie. . . ." The *OED* cites an interesting American example from 1634: "Boston is two miles North-east from Roxberry: His situation is very pleasant."

Perhaps because of its ambiguity, *his* was nevertheless to some extent avoided as a neuter possessive even in Middle English times: an uninflected *it* occurs from the fourteenth to the seventeenth century, and to this day in British dialect usage. The latest citation by the *OED* of its occurrence in standard English is from 1622: "Each part as faire doth show/In it kind, as white in Snow." Other efforts to replace the ambiguous *his* as a possessive for *it* include paraphrases with *thereof*, as in "The earth is the Lord's, and the fullness thereof" (Psalm 24.1), and *of it*, as in "Great was the fall of it" (Matthew 7.27). By analogy with other possessives ending in 's, the present-day form (at first written *it's*, as many unstylish people still write it) began to be used instead of *his*, *it*, or the other options. *Its* is quite rare in Shakespeare and occurs only twice in Milton's *Paradise Lost* (Jespersen 1909–49, 7: 308); but by the end of the seventeenth century *its* had become the usual form, completely displacing *his* and the less frequent *it* as a neuter possessive.

Similar to the use of the second person plural form to refer to a single person is the "regal *we*," except that here a sense of one's own importance rather than that of someone else is implied. It is still useful in proclamations by a sovereign, and in earlier times, if we can judge by the older drama, it was even used in conversation. The usage is very ancient. Queen Victoria is said to have been the last monarch to employ it as a spoken form, as in her famous but doubtless apocryphal reproof to one of her Maids of Honour who had told a mildly improper story: "We are not amused." The "editorial *we*" dates from Old English times. It is sometimes used by one who is a member of a staff of writers assumed to share the same opinions. It may also be used to include one's readers in phrases like "as we have seen."

In the second person plural, which became singular also, as we have just seen, the old distinction between the nominative *ye* and the objective *you* was still maintained in the King James Bible—for example, "The Lord deal kindly with you, as ye have dealt with the dead, and with me. The Lord grant you that ye may find rest" (Ruth 1.8–9). It was, however, generally lost during the sixteenth century, when some writers made the distinction, while others did not (Wyld 1936, p. 330). In time it was the objective form that prevailed to such an extent as to drive *ye* from standard English.

Present-day nonstandard speech distinguishes singular and plural *you* in a number of ways; examples include the analogical *youse* of the "under-privileged" city dweller (also current in Irish English) and the *you-uns* (that is, *you ones*), which probably stems from Scots English. *You-all* (or *y'all*) is in educated colloquial use in the Southern states, and it is the only new second person plural to have acquired respectability in Modern English.

The Modern English Period to 1800: Forms and Syntax

From the later seventeenth century and throughout the eighteenth, many speakers made a distinction between singular *you was* and plural *you were*. James Boswell used singular *you was* throughout his *London Journal* (1762–63) and even reported it as coming from the lips of Dr. Johnson: "Indeed, when you was in the irreligious way, I should not have been pleased with you" (28 July 1763); but in the second edition of his *Life of Johnson*, he changed over to *you were* for both singular and plural. Bishop Robert Lowth, in his very influential *Short Introduction to English Grammar* (1762), had condemned *you was* in no uncertain terms as "an enormous Solecism," but George Campbell testified in his *Philosophy of Rhetoric* (1776) that "it is ten times oftener heard." *You was* at one time was very common in cultivated American usage also: George Philip Krapp (1925, 2: 261) cites its use by John Adams in a letter of condolence to a friend whose house had burned down: "You regret your loss; but why? Was you fond of seeing or thinking that others saw and admired so stately a pile?" The construction became unfashionable in the early nineteenth century, but Noah Webster continued to defend it.

In the third person plural the native *h*-forms had become all but archaic by the end of the fifteenth century, in the course of which the *th*-forms current in present English gradually took over. The only *h*-form to survive is that earlier written *hem*, and it survives only as an unstressed form; when it is written at all nowadays, it is written *'em*. The plural possessives in *h*- (*here, her, hir*) occurred only very rarely after the beginning of the sixteenth century.

RELATIVE AND INTERROGATIVE PRONOUNS

The usual Old English relative particle was *þe*, which, since it had only one form, would have continued to do very well. It is a pity that it was ever lost. Middle English adapted the neuter demonstrative pronoun *that*, without inflection, for the same relative function, later adding the previously interrogative *which*, sometimes preceded by *the*, and likewise uninflected. It was not until the sixteenth century that the originally interrogative *who* (OE *hwā*) came to be commonly used as a simple relative to refer to persons. It had somewhat earlier been put to use as an indefinite relative, that is, as the equivalent of present *who(m)ever*, a use now rare but one that can be seen in Shakespeare's "Who tels me true, though in his Tale lye death,/I heare him as he flatter'd" (*Antony and Cleopatra* 1.2.102–103) and Lord Byron's "Whom the gods love die young" (*Don Juan* 4.12). The King James Bible, which we should expect to be a little behind the times in its grammar, has *which* where we would today use *who*, as in "The kingdom of heaven is likened unto a man which sowed good seed in his field" (Matthew 13.24) and in "Our Father which art in heaven." This translation was the work of almost fifty theological scholars designated by James I, and it was afterward reviewed by the bishops and other eminent scholars. It is not surprising that these men should have been little given to anything that smacked of innovation. Shakespeare, who with all his daring as a coiner and user of words was essentially conservative in his syntax, also uses *which* in the older fashion to refer to persons and things alike, as in "he which hath your Noble Father slaine" (*Hamlet* 4.7.4).

CASE FORMS OF THE PRONOUNS

In the freewheeling usage of earlier days, there was not so much concern as now with what are conceived to be "proper" choices of case forms. English had to wait until the later years of the seventeenth century for the rise of the schoolmaster's attitude toward language that was to become predominant in the eighteenth century and is still so—a relatively new thing. After a coordinating conjunction, for instance, the nominative form tended to occur invariably, as indeed it yet does, whether the pronoun is object of verb or preposition or second element of a compound subject. H. C. Wyld (1936, p. 332) cites "with you and I" from a letter by Sir John Suckling, as well as seventeenth-century occurrences of "between you and I," to which may be added Shakespeare's "all debts are cleerd betweene you and I" •(*Merchant of Venice* 3.2.321). No doubt at the present time the desire to be "correct" causes many speakers who may have been reproved as children for saying "Mary and me went downtown" to use "Mary and I" under all circumstances; but hypercorrectness is hardly a satisfactory explanation for the phenomenon as it occurs in the writings of well-bred people from the sixteenth to the early eighteenth centuries, a period during which people of consequence talked pretty much as they pleased.

School grammar requires the nominative form after *as* and *than* in such sentences as "Is she as tall as me?" (*Antony and Cleopatra* 3.3.14). Boswell, who wrote in a period in which men of strong minds and characters were attempting to "regularize" the English language, shows no particular pattern of consistency in this construction. In the entry in his *London Journal* for 5 June 1763, he writes "I was much stronger than her," but elsewhere uses the nominative form in the same construction. As Esther K. Sheldon (1956, p. 1080) points out, the grammarians of Boswell's day were not in agreement on this particular matter: some demanded the "same case [after *than* and *as*] as before"; others wanted *than* and *as* regarded as prepositions, and would thus require the objective form of the pronoun to be used consistently; still others thought the choice of case form should be determined by expanding the construction, as in "I know him better than she (knows him)"; "I know him better than (I know) her." The last is the rule laid down by present-day prescriptivists.

In early Modern English the nominative and objective forms of the personal pronouns, particularly *I* and *me*, tend to occur more or less indiscriminately after the verb *be*. In *Twelfth Night*, for instance, Sir Andrew

Aguecheek, who, though a fool, is yet a gentleman, uses both forms within a few lines: "That's mee I warrant you. . . . I knew 'twas I" (2.5.87–89). The generally inconsistent state of things before the prescriptive grammarians took over is exemplified by Shakespeare's use of other pronouns as well: "I am not thee" (*Timon of Athens* 4.3.277); "you are not he" (*Love's Labour's Lost* 5.2.550); "And damn'd be him, that first cries hold, enough" (*Macbeth* 5.8.34); "you are she" (*Twelfth Night* 5.1.334). Instances of *her, us,* and *them* in this construction are infrequent in early Modern English writings. "Here's them" occurs in *Pericles* 2.1.67, but the speaker is a fisherman.

Today also the objective form of personal pronouns continues to occur after *be,* though not without bringing down upon the head of the user the thunder of those who regard themselves as guardians of the language. There are nevertheless a great many speakers of standard English who do not care and who say "It's me" when there is occasion to do so, despite the school doctrine that "the verb *to be* can never take an object." There is little point in labeling the construction colloquial or informal as contrasted with a supposedly formal "It is I," inasmuch as the utterance would not be likely to occur alone in any but a conversational environment. Followed by a relative clause, however, "It is I" is usual, as in "It is I who am responsible," though "It is me" occurs as a rule before relative clauses where the pronoun is the object, as in "It is me that he is hunting." What has been said of *me* after forms of *be* applies also to *us, him, her,* and *them.*

The "proper" choice between *who* and *whom,* whether interrogative or relative, frequently involves an intellectual chore that many speakers from about 1500 on have been little concerned with. The interrogative pronoun, coming as it usually does before the verb, tended in early Modern English to be invariably *who,* as it still does in unselfconscious speech. Otto Jespersen cites interrogative *who* as object before the verb from Marlowe, Greene, Ben Jonson, the old *Spectator* of Addison and Steele, Goldsmith, and Sheridan, with later examples from Thackeray, Mrs. Humphry Ward, and Shaw. Alexander Schmidt's *Shakespeare-Lexicon* furnishes fifteen quotations for interrogative *who* in this construction and then adds an *etc.,* though, as Jespersen (1909–49, 7: 242) points out, "Most modern editors and reprinters add the *-m* everywhere in accordance with the rules of 'orthodox' grammar." Compare his earlier and somewhat bitter statement that they show thereby "that they hold in greater awe the schoolmasters of their own childhood than the poet of all the ages" (*Progress in Language,* 1909, p. 216). It is an amusing irony that *whom*-sleuths, imagining that they are great traditionalists, are actually adhering to a fairly recent standard as far as the period from the fifteenth century on is concerned. In view of the facts, such a sentence as "Who are you waiting for?" can hardly be considered untraditional.

Relative *who* as object of verb or preposition is hardly less frequent. For Shakespeare, Schmidt uses the label *etc.* after citing a dozen instances, and Jespersen cites from a few other authors. The *OED,* along with its statement that *whom* is no longer current in natural colloquial speech, cites Edmund Spenser, among others. There are, however, a good many instances of *whom* for the nominative, especially where the relative may be taken as the object of the verb of the principal clause, as in Matthew 16.13: "Whom do men say that I the Son of man am?" Shakespeare's "Whom in constancie you thinke stands so safe" (*Cymbeline* 1.4.138) and "Yong Ferdinand (whom they suppose is droun'd)" (*Tempest* 3.3.92) would be condemned by all prescriptive grammarians nowadays; but in Shakespeare's usage, which may in this respect as in all others be taken as representative of early Modern English, such constructions stand side by side with "I should do Brutus wrong, and Cassius wrong:/who (you all know) are Honourable men" (*Julius Caesar* 3.2.128–29) and others that employ the "approved" form in the same construction. The fact is, however, that this use of *whom* (or "misuse," according to one's point of view and one's teaching) occurs very frequently during the whole Modern English period. Jespersen, whose *Modern English Grammar* is a storehouse of illustrative material upon which apparently few writers of school grammars have drawn, has many examples ranging from Chaucer to the present day (3: 198–99), and Sir Ernest Gowers (1954, p. 228) cites instances from E. M. Forster, Lord David Cecil, *The Times*, and Somerset Maugham, all of which might be presumed to be standard English.

Verbs

CLASSES OF STRONG VERBS

Throughout the history of English, the strong verbs—always a minority—have fought a losing battle, having either joined the ranks of the weak verbs or been lost altogether. In those strong verbs that survive, the Old English four principal parts (infinitive, preterit singular, preterit plural, past participle) have been reduced to three, with the new preterit sometimes derived from the old singular and sometimes from the old plural. Comparatively few verbs that have survived can be said to show a regular development. The orderly arrangement into classes that prevailed in the older periods thus has now no more than historical relevance. Indeed, today the distinction between strong and weak verbs is less important than that between regular verbs, all of which are weak (like *talk, talked, talked*), and irregular verbs, which may be either strong (like *sing, sang, sung*) or weak (like *think, thought, thought*). In what follows, we will trace the history of the seven classes of Old English strong verbs as they have developed in Modern English, recognizing, however, that the classification is now a purely historical matter.

Class I remains rather clearly defined. The regular development of this class, with the Modern English preterit from the old preterit singular, is illustrated by the following:

drive	drove	driven
ride	rode	ridden
rise	rose	risen
smite	smote	smitten
stride	strode	stridden
strive	strove	striven
thrive	throve	thriven
write	wrote	written

Also phonologically regular, but with the Modern English preterit from the old preterit plural (whose vowel was identical with that of the past participle), are the following, of which *chide* and *hide* are originally weak verbs that have become strong by analogy:

bite	bit	bitten
chide	chid	chidden
hide	hid	hidden
slide	slid	slid(den)

The following verbs, on the contrary, have a vowel in the preterit and past participle derived from the old preterit singular:

abide	abode	abode
shine	shone	shone

Dive–dove (*dived*)–*dived* is another weak verb that has acquired a strong preterit. *Strike–struck–struck* has a preterit of uncertain origin; the regularly developed past participle *stricken* is now used only metaphorically.

In early Modern English many of these verbs had alternative forms, some of which survive either in standard use or in the dialects, whereas others are now archaic. There is a Northern form for the preterit of *drive* in "And I delivered you out of the hand of the Egyptians . . . and drave them out from before you" (Judges 6.9). Other now nonstandard forms are represented by "And the people chode [chided] with Moses" (Numbers 20.3) and "I imagined that your father had wrote in such a way" (Boswell, *London Journal*, 30 December 1762). Other verbs of this class have become weak (for example, *glide, gripe, spew,* and *writhe*). Still others have disappeared altogether from the language.

The verbs of Class II have likewise undergone many changes in the course of their development into their present forms. Only a handful survive in modern use, of which the following have taken the vowel of their preterit from the old past participle:

choose	chose	chosen
cleave	clove	cloven
freeze	froze	frozen

Fly–flew–flown has a preterite formed perhaps by analogy with Class VII verbs.

A development of the Old English past participle of *freeze* is used as an archaism in Shelley's "Snow-fed streams now seen athwart frore [frozen] vapours," which the *OED* suggests is a reflection of Milton's "The parching Air Burns frore" (*Paradise Lost* 2.594–95). Other variant forms are in "This word (Rebellion) it had froze them up" (*2 Henry IV* 1.1.199); "O what a time have you chose out brave Caius/To weare a Kerchiefe" (*Julius Caesar* 2.1.314–15); and "Certain men clave to Paul" (Acts 17.34).

The following surviving verbs of Class II are now weak: *bow* 'bend,' *brew*, *chew*, *creep*, *crowd*, *flee*, *lie* 'prevaricate,' *lose*, *reek*, *rue*, *seethe*, *shove*, *sprout*, and *suck*. *Sodden*, the old strong participle of *seethe* (with voicing according to Verner's Law), is still sometimes used as an adjective. *Crope*, a strong preterit of *creep*, occurs in formal English as late as the eighteenth century and in folk speech to the present day.

Practically all verbs of Class III with nasal consonants that have survived from Old English have retained their strong inflection. The following derive their preterit from the old preterit singular:

begin	began	begun
drink	drank	drunk
ring	rang	rung
shrink	shrank	shrunk
sing	sang	sung
sink	sank	sunk
spring	sprang	sprung
stink	stank	stunk
swim	swam	swum

In *run–ran–run* (ME infinitive *rinnen*) the vowel of the participle was in early Modern English extended into the present tense; *run* is otherwise like the preceding verbs. In the following, the modern preterit vowel is from the old preterit plural and past participle:

cling	clung	clung
slink	slunk	slunk
spin	spun	spun
sting	stung	stung
swing	swung	swung
win	won	won
wring	wrung	wrung

The Modern English Period to 1800: Forms and Syntax

A few verbs entering the language after Old English times have conformed to this pattern—for example, *fling*, *sling*, and *string*. By the same sort of analogy the weak verb *bring* has acquired in nonstandard speech the strong preterit and participial form *brung*. Though lacking the nasal, *dig* (not of Old English origin) and *stick*, which at first had weak inflection, have taken on the same pattern.

The consonant cluster *-nd* had early lengthened a preceding vowel, so the principal parts of the following verbs, although quite different in their vowels from those of the preceding group, have the same historical development:

bind	bound	bound
find	found	found
grind	ground	ground
wind	wound	wound

Allowing for the influence of Middle English [ç, x] (spelled *h* or *gh*) on a preceding vowel, *fight–fought–fought* also has a regular development into Modern English. All other surviving verbs of this class have become weak (some having done so in Middle English times); *bark, braid, burn, burst* (also with an invariant preterit and participle), *carve, climb, delve, help, melt, mourn, spurn, starve, swallow, swell, yell, yelp,* and *yield*. The old participial forms *molten* and *swollen* are still used but only as adjectives. *Holp*, an old strong preterit of *help*, was common until the seventeenth century and survives in current nonstandard usage. The old participial form *holpen* is doubtless familiar to many from its use in the King James Bible—for instance, in "He hath holpen his servant Israel" (Luke 1.54).

Most surviving Class IV verbs have borrowed the vowel of the old past participle for their preterit:

break	broke	broken
heave	hove	hove(n)
speak	spoke	spoken
steal	stole	stolen
weave	wove	woven

Verbs with an [r] after the vowel follow the same pattern, although the [r] has affected the quality of the preceding vowel in the infinitive:

bear	bore	borne
shear	shore	shorn
swear	swore	sworn
tear	tore	torn
wear	wore	worn

The last was originally a weak verb; it acquired strong principal parts by analogy with the verbs of Class IV that it rimed with.

Get was a loanword from Scandinavian. It and tread (like speak originally a Class V verb) have shortened vowels in all their principal parts:

get	got	got(ten)
tread	trod	trodden

Come–came–come has regular phonological development from the Middle English verb, whose principal parts were, however, already irregular in form. A variant preterit come was frequent in early Modern English—for example, in Pepys's Diary: "Creed come and dined with me" (15 June 1666), although Pepys also uses came; today the variant occurs mainly in folk speech. Variant preterits for other verbs were also common in early Modern English, as in "When I was a child, I spake as a child" (I Corinthians 13.11); "And when he went forth to land, there met him . . . a certain man, which had devils long time, and ware no clothes" (Luke 8.27); "And when he had taken the five loaves and the two fishes, he looked up to heaven, and blessed, and brake the loaves" (Mark 6.41); "And they brought him unto him; and when he saw him, straightway the spirit tare him" (Mark 9.20).

Verbs of Class V have all diverged in one way or another from what might be considered regular development. Eat–ate–eaten has in its preterit a lengthened form of the vowel of the Middle English preterit singular (which, if it had survived into Modern English, would have been *at). The preterit in British English, although it is spelled like the American form, is pronounced in a way that would be better represented as et; it is derived perhaps by analogy with the preterit read.

Bid and forbid have two preterits in current English. (For)bade, traditionally pronounced [bæd] but now often [bed] from the spelling, was originally a lengthened form of the Middle English preterit singular. The preterit (for)bid has its vowel from the past participle, which, in turn, probably borrowed it from the present stem, by analogy with verbs that have the same vowel in those two forms.

Give–gave–given is a Scandinavian loanword that displaced the native English form. (The latter appears, for example, in Chaucer's use as yeven–yaf–yeven.) Variants are evidenced by Pepys's "This day I sent my cozen Roger a tierce of claret, which I give him" (21 August 1667) and Shakespeare's "When he did frown, O, had she then gave over" (Venus and Adonis, line 571).

Sit had in early Modern English the preterit forms sat, sate, and (occasionally) sit, the participial forms sitten, sit, sat, and sate. Sit and set were confused as early as the fourteenth century, and continue to be. A nonstandard form sot occurs as preterit and participle of both verbs.

The confusion of lie–lay–lain and lay–laid–laid is as old as that of sit and set. The intransitive use of lay, according to the OED, "was not app[arently] regarded as a solecism" in the seventeenth and eighteenth centuries. It has been so used by some very important writers, including Francis Bacon and Lord Byron—for example, in "There let him lay" (*Childe Harold's Pilgrimage* 4.1620). The brothers H. W. and F. G. Fowler (1931, p. 49) cite with apparently delighted disapproval "I suspected him of having laid in wait for the purpose" from the writing of Richard Grant White, the eminent nineteenth-century American purist—for purists love above all to catch other purists in some supposed sin against English grammar. Today the two verbs are so thoroughly confused that their forms are often freely interchanged, as in the following description of a modern dancer, who "lay down again; then raised the upper part of his body once more and stared upstage at the brick wall; then laid down again" (*Illustrated London News*, January 1979, p. 61).

See–saw–seen has normal development of the Middle English forms of the verb. The alternative preterits *see, seed,* and *seen* are found in folk speech.

Other surviving Class V verbs have become weak: *bequeath, fret, knead, mete, reap, scrape, weigh,* and *wreak.*

Some verbs from Class VI (including *take,* a Scandinavian loanword that ultimately ousted its Old English synonym *niman* from the language) show regular development:

forsake	forsook	forsaken
shake	shook	shaken
take	took	taken

Early Modern English frequently uses the preterit form of these verbs as a participle, as in Shakespeare's "Save what is had or must from you be took" (Sonnet 75), "Have from the forests shook three summers' pride" (Sonnet 104), and "Hath she forsooke so many Noble Matches?" (*Othello* 4.2.125). *Stand* (and the compound *understand*) has lost its old participle *standen;* the preterit form *stood* has served as a participle since the sixteenth century, though not exclusively. *Stand* also occurs as a participle, as does a weak form *standed,* as in "a tongue not understanded of the people" in the fourteenth Article of Religion of the Anglican Communion. Two verbs of this class have formed their preterits by analogy with Class VII:

slay	slew	slain
draw	drew	drawn

Other surviving verbs of this class have become weak: *fare, flay, gnaw, (en)grave, heave, lade, laugh, shave, step, wade,* and *wash.* But strong participial forms *laden* and *shaven* survive as adjectives, and *heave* has an alternative strong preterit *hove.*

Several verbs of Class VII show regular development:

blow	blew	blown
grow	grew	grown
know	knew	known
throw	threw	thrown

Another, *crow–crew–crowed*, has a normally developed preterit that is now rare in American use, but it has only a weak participle. Two other verbs also have normal phonological development, although the vowels of their principal parts are different from those above:

fall	fell	fallen
beat	beat	beaten

Hold–held–held has borrowed its Modern English participle from the Middle English preterit. The original participle is preserved in the old-fashioned *beholden*. Modern English *hang–hung–hung* is a mixture of three Middle English verbs: *hōn* (Class VII), *hangen* (weak), and *hengen* (a Scandinavian loan). The alternative weak preterit and participle, *hanged*, is frequent in reference to capital punishment, though it is by no means universally so used.

Let, originally a member of this class, now has unchanged principal parts. Other verbs surviving from the group have become weak; two of them did so as early as Old English times: *dread, flow, fold, hew, leap, mow, read* (OE preterit *rǣdde*), *row, sleep* (OE preterit *slēpte*), *sow, span* 'join,' *walk, wax* 'grow,' and *weep*. Strong participial forms *sown, mown,* and *hewn* survive, mainly as adjectives.

ENDINGS FOR PERSON AND NUMBER

The personal endings of early Modern English verbs were somewhat simplified from those of Middle English, with the loss of *-e* as an ending for the first person singular in the present indicative (making that form identical with the infinitive, which had lost its final *-n* and then its *-e*): *I sit* (*to sit*) from Middle English *ich sitte* (*to sitten*). Otherwise, however, the early Modern English verb preserved a number of personal endings that have since disappeared, and it had, especially early in the period, several variants for some of the persons:

PRESENT		
	I	sit
	thou	sittest, sitst
	he, she	sitteth, sits
	we, you, they	sit

The Modern English Period to 1800: Forms and Syntax

The early Modern English third person varied between -*(e)s* and -*(e)th*. From the beginning of the seventeenth century the -*s* form began to prevail, though for a while the two forms could be used interchangeably, particularly in verse, as in Shakespeare's "Sometime she driveth ore a Souldiers necke, & then dreames he of cutting Forraine throats" (*Romeo and Juliet* 1.4.82–83). But *doth* and *hath* went on until well into the eighteenth century, and the King James Bible uses only -*th* forms. The -*s* forms are usually attributed to Northern dialect influence.

There are occasional third person plural forms ending in -*s*, also of Northern provenience, as in "Where lo, two lamps, burnt out, in darkness lies" (*Venus and Adonis*, line 1128) and elsewhere in Shakespeare and other Elizabethan writers; these should not be regarded "ungrammatical" uses of the singular for the plural form, although H. C. Wyld (1936, p. 340) believes that this plural form in -*s* is due to analogy with the singular rather than to Northern influence, inasmuch as to this day "certain sections of the people inflect all Persons of both Sing. and Pl. with -*s* . . . while others drop the suffix even in the 3rd Sing." The extension of the -*s* to the first and second persons is indeed particularly noticeable in current speech in the usage of naive raconteurs, with their "I says" and "says I," and is the source of the rude expression of disbelief "Sez you!"

The early Modern English preterit ending for the second person singular, -*(e)st*, began to be lost in the sixteenth century. Thus the preterit tense became invariable, as it is today, except for the verb *be*.

The verb *be*, always the most irregular of English verbs, had the following personal inflections in the early Modern period:

PRESENT   I   am
               thou   art
               he, she   is
               we, you, they   are, be

PRETERIT   I, he, she   was
               thou   were, wast, werst, wert
               you (sing.)   were, was
               we, you, they   were

The plural *be* was widely current as late as the seventeenth century; Eilert Ekwall (1975, p. 118) cites "the powers that ·be" as a survival of it. The preterit second person singular was *were* until the sixteenth century, when the forms *wast*, *werst*, and *wert* began to occur, the last remaining current in literature throughout the eighteenth century. Nineteenth-century poets were also very fond of it ("Bird thou never wert"); it gave a certain archaically spiritual tone to their writing that they presumably considered desirable. *Wast* and *wert* are by analogy with present *art*. In *werst*, the *s* of *wast* has apparently been extended. The locution *you was* has been discussed earlier (p. 193).

Of the other highly irregular verbs little need be said. *Could*, the preterit of *can*, acquired its unetymological *l* in the sixteenth century by analogy with *would* and *should*. Early Modern forms that differ from those now current are *durst*, preterit of *dare*, which otherwise had become weak; *mought*, a variant of *might*; and *mowe*, an occasional present plural form of *may*. *Will* has early Modern variants *wull* and *woll*.

CONTRACTED FORMS

Most of our current contracted negative forms in -*n't* first occur in writing in the seventeenth century. It is likely that all were actually used long before ever getting written down, for **contractions** are in their very nature colloquial and thus would have been considered unsuitable for writing, as most people still consider them. *Won't* is from *wol(l)not*. *Don't* presents several problems. One would expect [dunt] for all forms save the third singular, for which [dəzənt] or, with loss of [z], [dənt] would be the expected form. It has been suggested that the [o] of *don't* is analogical with that of *won't* (Jespersen 1909–49, 5: 431). The *OED* derives third person *don't* from *he* (*she*, *it*) *do*, and cites a number of instances of *do* in the third person from the sixteenth and seventeenth centuries, including Pepys's "Sir Arthur Haselrigge do not yet appear in the House" (2 March 1660). The *OEDS* records a use of third person *don't* in 1670, but Karl W. Dykema (1956) found no occurrence of *doesn't* before 1818. Dykema (p. 90) concludes that "such variants as *don't* and *doesn't* in the third person are considered by speakers of standard English as the recent innovation and the original contraction respectively, whereas it is probably more nearly the case that *don't* is the older form!"

An't (early ModE [ænt]) for *am* (*are*, *is*) *not* is apparently of late seventeenth-century origin; the variant *ain't* occurs about a century later. With the eighteenth-century British English shifting of [æ] to [ɑ] as in *ask*, *path*, *dance*, and the like, the pronunciation of this word shifted to [ɑnt]. At the same time, preconsonantal [r] was lost, thus making *an't* and *aren't* homophones. As a result, the two words were confused, even by those, including most Americans, who pronounce *r* before a consonant; and the form *aren't I?* has gained ground among those who regard *ain't* as a linguistic mortal sin. Although *ain't* has fallen victim to a series of schoolteachers' crusades, Henry Alford (1810–71), dean of Canterbury, testified that in his day "It ain't certain" and "I ain't going" were "very frequently used, even by highly educated persons," and Frederick James Furnivall (1825–1910), an early editor of the *OED* and founder of the Chaucer Society and the Early

English Text Society, is said to have used the form *ain't* habitually (Jespersen 1909–49, 5: 434). Despite its current reputation as a shibboleth of uneducated speech, *ain't* is still used by many cultivated speakers in informal circumstances.

Contractions of auxiliary verbs without *not* occur somewhat earlier than forms with *n't*, though they must be about equally old. *It's* as a written form is from the seventeenth century and ultimately drove out *'tis*, in which the pronoun rather than the verb is reduced. There is no current contraction of *it was* to replace older *'twas*, and, in the light of the practical disappearance of the subjunctive, it is not surprising that there is none for *it were*. *It'll* has replaced older *'twill*; *will* similarly is contracted after other pronouns and, in speech, after other words as well. In older times *'ll*, usually written *le* (as in *Ile*, *youle*), occurred only after vowels and was hence not syllabic, as it must be after consonants. *Would* is contracted as early as the late sixteenth century as *'ld*, later becoming *'d*, which came in the eighteenth century to be used for *had* also. The contraction of *have* written *'ve* likewise seems to have occurred first in the eighteenth century. After a consonant this contraction is identical in pronunciation with unstressed *of* (compare "the wood of the tree" and "He would've done it"), hence such uneducated spellings as *would of* and *should of* frequently are written in dialogue as **eye dialect** to indicate that the speaker is unschooled. (The point seems to be "This is the way the speaker would write *have* if he had occasion to do so.") As indicative of pronunciation the spelling is pointless.

EXPANDED VERB FORMS

Progressive verb forms, consisting of a form of *be* plus a present participle ("I am working"), occur occasionally in Old English but are rare before the fifteenth century and remain relatively infrequent until the seventeenth century. The progressive passive, as in "He is being punished," does not occur until the later part of the eighteenth century. Pepys, for instance, writes "to Hales's the painter, thinking to have found Harris sitting there for his picture, which is drawing for me" (26 April 1668), where we would use *is being drawn*.

Verbs of motion and of becoming in early Modern English frequently have a form of *be* instead of *have* in their perfect forms: "is risen," "are entered in the Roman territories," "were safe arrived," "is turned white."

Do is frequently used as a verbal auxiliary in the early Modern period, though it is used somewhat differently from the way it is used today—for example, "I do wonder, his insolence can brooke to be commanded" (*Coriolanus* 1.1.265–66) and "The Serpent that did sting thy Fathers life / Now weares his Crowne" (*Hamlet* 1.5.39–40), where current English would not use it at all. Compare with these instances "A Nun of winters sisterhood kisses not more religiouslie" (*As You Like It* 3.4.17), where we would say *does not kiss*, and "What say the citizens?" (*Richard III* 3.7.1), where we would use *do the citizens say*. In present-day English, when there is no other auxiliary, *do* is obligatory in negative expressions, in questions, and in contradictions for emphasis ("Despite the weather report, it did rain"). In early Modern English, *do* was optional in any sentence that had no other auxiliary. Thus one finds constructions of both types: *Forbid them not* or *Do not forbid them, Comes he?* or *Does he come?* and *He fell* or *He did fall*.

In Old and Middle English times *shall* and *will* were sometimes used to express simple futurity, though as a rule they implied, respectively, obligation and volition. The present prescribed use of these words, the bane of many an American and Northern British schoolchild, stems ultimately from the seventeenth century, the rules having first been codified by John Wallis, an eminent professor of geometry at Oxford who wrote in Latin a grammar of the English language (*Grammatica Linguae Anglicanae*, 1653). The rule, still unrealistically included in some American school books, is that to express a future event without emotional overtones, one should say *I* or *we shall*, but *you, he, she*, or *they will*; conversely, for emphasis, willfulness, or insistence, one should say *I* or *we will*, but *you, he, she*, or *they shall*. This rule, which may fairly describe the variety of English used in southern England (Moody 1974), has never been ubiquitous in the English-speaking world. It has, however, been promoted by the prestige of that form of English in which it is natural and through the influence of Wallis and his successors. Despite a crusade of more than three centuries on behalf of the distinction, the rule for making it is still largely a mystery to most Americans, who get along very well in expressing futurity and willfulness without it.

OTHER VERBAL CONSTRUCTIONS

Impersonal and **reflexive constructions** were fairly frequent in early Modern English, as they had been to a much greater extent in Middle English. Shakespeare used, for instance, the impersonal constructions "it dislikes [displeases] me," "methinks," "it yearns [grieves] me" and the reflexives "I complain me," "how dost thou feel thyself now?" "I doubt me," "I repent me," and "give me leave to retire myself."

Some now intransitive verbs were used transitively, as in "despair [of] thy charm," "give me leave to speak [of] him," and "Smile you [at] my speeches."

Prepositions

With the Middle English loss of all distinctive inflectional endings for the noun save for the *-s* of the genitive and the plural, prepositions acquired a somewhat greater importance than they had had in Old English. Their number consequently increased during the late Middle and early Modern periods.

Changes in the uses of certain prepositions are illustrated by the practice of Shakespeare, who in this respect as in most others is representative of the early Modern period: "And what delight shall she have to looke on [at] the divell?" (*Othello* 2.1.229); "He came of [on] an errand to mee" (*Merry Wives* 1.4.80); "But thou wilt be aveng'd on [for] my misdeeds" (*Richard III* 1.4.70); "'Twas from [against] the Cannon [canon]" (*Coriolanus* 3.1.90); "We are such stuffe/As dreames are made on [of]" (*Tempest* 4.1.156–57); "Then speake the truth by [of] her" (*Two Gentlemen* 2.4.151); ". . . that our armies joyn not in [on] a hot day" (*2 Henry IV* 1.2.234).

Even in Old English times *on* was sometimes reduced in compound words like *abūtan* (now *about*), a variant of *on būtan* 'on the outside of.' The contracted form was usually written *a*—for instance, *aboard, afield, abed, asleep*—and, with verbal nouns in -*ing*—*a-hunting, a-bleeding, a-praying*, and the like. The *a* of "twice a day" and other such expressions has the same origin. *In* was sometimes contracted to *i*', as in Shakespeare's "'i' the head," "'i' God's name," and so forth. This particular contraction was much later fondly affected by Robert Browning, who doubtless thought it singularly archaic—for example, "would not sink i' the scale" and "This rage was right i' the main" ("Rabbi Ben Ezra," lines 42 and 100).

The Study of Language

EARLY DICTIONARIES

The first dictionaries appeared in the period under discussion. If one had to set up a line of development for these, one would start with the Old and Middle English interlinear glosses in Latin and French texts, then proceed through the bilingual vocabularies produced by schoolmasters and designed for those studying foreign languages, specifically Latin, French, Italian, and Spanish. But the first work designed expressly for listing and defining English words for English-speaking people was the schoolmaster Robert Cawdrey's *A Table Alphabeticall* (1604) ("conteyning and teaching the true writing, and understanding of hard usuall English wordes, borrowed from the Hebrew, Greeke, Latine, or French. &c."). Other dictionaries followed in the same tradition of explicating "hard words," among them, that of J[ohn] B[ullokar], Doctor of Physick, *An English Expositour* (1616); Henry Cockeram's *English Dictionarie* (1623); Thomas Blount's *Glossographia* (1656); Edward Phillips's *New World of English Words* (1658); Edward Cocker's *English Dictionary* (1704); and Nathan Bailey's *Universal Etymological English Dictionary* (1721), with a second volume that was really a supplement appearing in 1727. In 1730, Bailey (and others) produced the *Dictionarium Britannicum*, with about 48,000 entries. In 1755 appeared both the Scott-Bailey *New Universal Etymological English Dictionary* and Samuel Johnson's great two-volume

Dictionary, which was based on the *Dictionarium Britannicum*, though containing fewer entries than it. For the history of dictionaries up to Johnson's, the best study is that of DeWitt T. Starnes and Gertrude E. Noyes, *The English Dictionary from Cawdrey to Johnson, 1604–1755* (1946), on which the foregoing summary is based. For Johnson's dictionary, the best study is that of James Sledd and Gwin J. Kolb, *Dr. Johnson's Dictionary: Essays in the Biography of a Book* (1955).

The publication of Johnson's *Dictionary* was certainly the most important linguistic event of the eighteenth century, not to say the entire period under discussion, for it to a large extent "fixed" English spelling and established a standard for the use of words. Johnson did indeed attempt to exercise a directive function. It would have been strange had he not done so at that time. For most people it is apparently not sufficient even today for the lexicographer simply to record and define the words of the language and to indicate the way in which they are pronounced by those who use them; he is also supposed to have some God-given power of determining which are "good" words and which are "bad" ones and to know how they "ought" to be pronounced. But Johnson had the good sense usually to recognize the prior claims of usage over the arbitrary appeals to logic, analogy, Latin grammar, and sheer prejudice so often made by his contemporaries, even if he did at times settle matters by appeals to his own taste, which was fortunately good taste. The son of a bookseller in Lichfield, Johnson had a tremendous admiration for those who were his social betters: he was a Tory by both denomination and conviction. Hence, along with his typical eighteenth-century desire to "fix" the language went a great deal of respect for upper-class usage. He can thus be said truly to have consolidated a standard of usage that was not altogether of his own making. His use of illustrative quotations, literally by the thousands, was an innovation; but his own definitions show the most discriminating judgment. The quirky definitions, like that for oats—"a grain which in England is generally given to horses, but in Scotland supports the people"— are well-known, so well-known that some people must have the utterly false impression that there are very many others not so well-known. It is in a way unfortunate that these have been "played up" for their sheer amusement value as much as they have been, for they are actually few in number.

EIGHTEENTH-CENTURY ATTITUDES TOWARD USAGE

The purist attitude predominant in eighteenth-century England was simply the manifestation of an attitude toward language that has been current, as it continues to be in our own day, in all times and in all places. Doubtless there are and have been purists—persons who believe in some sort of absolute and unwavering standard of what they deem to be "correctness"—in even the most undeveloped societies, for **purism** is a matter of temperament rather than of culture.

Though very dear to American purists—by no means all of them school-teachers—the "rules" supposed to govern English usage originated not in America, but in the mother country. Those who formulated them were about as ill-informed and as inconsistent as their slightly later American counterparts. Present-day notions of "correctness" are to a large extent based on the notion, prominent in the eighteenth century, that language is of divine origin and hence was perfect in its beginnings but is constantly in danger of corruption and decay unless it is diligently kept in line by wise men who are able to get themselves accepted as authorities, such as those who write dictionaries and grammars. Latin was regarded as having retained much of its original "perfection." No one seems to have been very much aware that it was the culmination of a long development and had undergone many changes of the sort that were deplored in English. Hence when English grammars came to be written, they were based on Latin grammar, even down to the terminology.

The most influential of the eighteenth-century advocates of **prescriptive grammar** was Robert Lowth (1710–87), theologian, Hebraist, professor of poetry at Oxford from 1741 to 1753, later bishop of Oxford, then of London, and dean of the Chapel Royal, who four years before his death was offered the archbishopric of Canterbury, which he turned down. In the Preface to his *Short Introduction to English Grammar* (1762), Lowth agreed with Dean Swift's charge, made in 1712 in his *Proposal for Correcting, Improving, and Ascertaining* [that is, fixing, making certain] *the English Tongue*, that "our language is extremely imperfect," "that it offends against every part of grammar," and that most of the "best authors of our age" commit "many gross improprieties, which . . . ought to be discarded." Lowth was able to find many of the most egregious blunders in the works of our most eminent writers; his footnotes are filled with them. It apparently never occurred to any of his contemporaries to doubt that so famous and successful a man had inside information about an ideal state of the English language. Perhaps they thought he got it straight from a linguistic Yahweh.

In any case, Lowth set out in all earnestness in the midst of a busy life to do something constructive about the deplorable English written by the masters of English literature. Like most men of his time, he believed in universal grammar—a concept that has been revived in our own day by the transformational-generative grammarians. Consequently he believed that English was "easily reducible to a System of rules." Among many other things, he gave wide currency, probably because of his high position in the Establishment, to those rules for *shall* and *will* as they had been formulated by John Wallis in his *Grammatica Linguae Anglicanae*.

In actual practice, as we have seen, the "rules," which everybody continues to think are inflexibly right, have been honored more in the breach than in the observance. Most people, only dimly comprehending their complexities, seem to think that they should observe them more conscientiously than they have actually done. But because of the deference that has been paid to these supposedly omniscient lawgivers of the eighteenth century—even though the names of many may have been long forgotten—the most important eighteenth-century development in the English language was its conscious regulation by those who were not really qualified for the job but who managed to acquire authority as linguistic gurus. Sterling A. Leonard, in *The Doctrine of Correctness in English Usage, 1700–1800* (1929), discusses the contributions of Lowth, George Campbell, Joseph Priestley, Lindley Murray, and others.

One of the most influential of the late eighteenth-century grammarians was Lindley Murray, a Philadelphia-born Quaker who returned to England after the American Revolution and wrote an *English Grammar* for use in Quaker girls' schools. He was motivated by a wish to foster the study of the native language, as opposed to Latin, and by his religious piety, which "predisposed him to regard linguistic matters in terms of right and wrong. His highly moralistic outlook perforce carried over into his attitude toward usage" (Read 1939, p. 531).

Although the grammarians who promulgated the rules for language were children of their age, influenced in linguistic matters by their attitudes toward other aspects of life, they must not therefore be thought contemptible. Bishop Lowth was not—and, heaven knows, Dean Swift, one of the glories of English literature, was certainly not. Nor was Joseph Priestley, who, in addition to writing the original and in many respects forward-looking *Rudiments of English Grammar* (1761), was the discoverer of oxygen, a prominent nonconformist preacher, and a voluminous writer on theological, scientific, political, and philosophical subjects. Like George Campbell, who in his *Philosophy of Rhetoric* (1776) went so far as to call language "purely a species of fashion," Priestley recognized the superior force of usage; he also shared Campbell's belief that there was need for some form of control of language other than that furnished by custom. Being children of the Age of Reason, both would have had recourse to the principle of analogy to settle questions of divided usage, though admitting that it was not always possible to do so.

All these men were indeed typical of their time, in most respects a good time; and they were honest men according to their lights, which in other respects were quite bright indeed. We cannot blame them for not having information that was not available in their day. And, despite the tremendous advances of linguistic science in the nineteenth and twentieth centuries, attitudes toward language have actually changed very little since Bishop Lowth and Lindley Murray were laying down the law. Their precepts were largely based on what they supposed to be logic and reason, for they believed that the laws of language were rooted in the natural order, and this was of course "reasonable." To cite an example, they outlawed, as far as the educated are concerned, the emphatic and still very viable double negative construction on the grounds stated by Lowth that "two Negatives in English destroy one another, or are equivalent to an Affirmative"—in English, that is to say, just as in mathematics, though the analogy implicit in the appeal to logic was quite false. Many very reasonable people before them had spoken and written sentences with two or even more negatives: Chaucer has four in "Forwhy to tellen nas [ne was] nat his entente/To nevere no man" (*Troilus and Criseyde* 1.738–39) and four in his description of the Knight in the General Prologue to the *Canterbury Tales*: "He nevere yet no vileynye ne sayde/In al his lyf unto no maner wight" (lines 70–71). It certainly never occurred to him that these would cancel out and thus reverse his meaning.

Modern linguistic studies have made very little headway in convincing those who have not made a special study of language that language is a living thing, our possession and servant rather than an ideal toward which we should all hopelessly aspire. Many schoolroom grammars and handbooks of English usage widely used today perpetuate the tradition of Bishop Lowth's *Short Introduction to English Grammar*. Indeed, the very word *grammar* means to many highly literate people not the study of language, but merely so simple a thing as making the "proper" choice between *shall* and *will*, *between* and *among*, *different from* and *different than*, *who* and *whom* and the avoidance of terminal prepositions, of *ain't*, and of *It's me*. In the following chapter we examine in more detail the later developments of this comparatively recent tradition in England and America.

Early Modern English Illustrated

The following passages are from the King James Bible, published in 1611. They are the opening verses of chapters 1 and 2 of Genesis and the parable of the Prodigal Son (Luke 15). The punctuation and spelling of the original have been retained, except that "long *s*" has been replaced by the form of the letter generally used today.

I.   1. In the beginning God created the Heauen, and the Earth.   2. And the earth was without forme, and voyd, and darkenesse was vpon the face of the deepe: and the Spirit of God mooued vpon the face of the waters.   3. And God said, Let there be light: and there was light.   4. And God saw the light, that it was good: and God diuided the light from the darkenesse.   5. And God called the light, Day, and the darknesse he called Night: and the euening and the morning were the first day.

II.   1. Thus the heauens and the earth were finished, and all the hoste of them.   2. And on the seuenth day God ended his worke, which hee had made: And he rested on the seuenth day from all his worke, which he had made.   3. And God blessed the seuenth day, and sanctified it: because that in it he had rested from all his worke, which God created and made.

XV. **11.** A certaine man had two sonnes: **12.** And the yonger of them said to his father, Father, giue me the portion of goods that falleth to me. And he diuided vnto them his liuing. **13.** And not many dayes after, the yonger sonne gathered al together, and tooke his iourney into a farre countrey, and there wasted his substance with riotous liuing. **14.** And when he had spent all, there arose a mighty famine in that land, and he beganne to be in want. **15.** And he went and ioyned himselfe to a citizen of that countrey, and he sent him into his fields to feed swine. **16.** And he would faine haue filled his belly with the huskes that the swine did eate: and no man gaue vnto him. **17.** And when he came to himselfe, he said, How many hired seruants of my fathers haue bread inough and to spare and I perish with hunger. . . . **20.** And he arose and came to his father. But when he was yet a great way off, his father saw him, and had compassion, and ranne, and fell on his necke, and kissed him. **21.** And the sonne said vnto him, Father, I have sinned against heauen, and in thy sight, and am no more worthy to be called thy sonne. **22.** But the father saide to his seruants, Bring foorth the best robe, and put it on him, and put a ring on his hand, and shooes on his feete. **23.** And bring hither the fatted calfe, and kill it, and let us eate and be merrie. **24.** For this my sonne was dead, and is aliue againe; hee was lost, and is found.

For Further Reading

General

Barber, *Early Modern English*, 1976.
Fisher, "Chancery and the Emergence of Standard Written English in the Fifteenth Century," *Speculum*, 1977.
Fisher, "Chancery Standard and Modern Written English," *Journal of the Society of Archivists*, 1979.

Early Modern English Grammar

Jespersen, *A Modern English Grammar on Historical Principles*, 7 vols, 1909–49.
Michael, *English Grammatical Categories and the Tradition to 1800*, 1970.
Traugott, *A History of English Syntax: A Transformational Approach to the History of English Sentence Structure*, 1972.
Visser, *An Historical Syntax of the English Language*, 1963–73.

Dictionaries and Usage

Leonard, *The Doctrine of Correctness in English Usage, 1700–1800*, 1929.
Read, "The Motivation of Lindley Murray's Grammatical Work," *Journal of English and Germanic Philology*, 1939.
Sledd and Kolb, *Dr. Johnson's Dictionary: Essays in the Biography of a Book*, 1955.
Starnes and Noyes, *The English Dictionary from Cawdrey to Johnson, 1604–1755*, 1946.

9 Recent British and American English

"The American language," despite the distinguished precedent of H. L. Mencken's use of the term,[1] is as much of a misnomer for the English spoken by Americans as would be "the Mexican language" for the Spanish spoken by Mexicans. There is no essential difference between the English of America and that of Great Britain—or that of Canada, Australia, New Zealand, South Africa, India, or various other countries of the world to which the speech of the small northern European tribe of the English has spread. The English language in all of its national varieties throughout the world is remarkably uniform. There are, to be sure, differences between national varieties, just as there are variations within them, but those differences are insignificant in comparison with the similarities. English is unmistakably one language, with two major national dialects: British and American.

Of those two national dialects, British English has long enjoyed greater prestige in Europe and elsewhere around the world. Its prestige is doubtless based partly on its use as the language of the former British Empire and partly on its centuries of cultivated products, including some of the world's greatest works of literature. The prestige of British English is often assessed, however, in terms of its "purity" (a notion that flies in the face of the facts)

---

[1] He was not the first to use it. Noah Webster and others had already done so.

214 or its elegance and style (highly subjective but nonetheless powerful concepts). Even Americans, though they may be slightly put off by "posh accents" at times, are impressed by them and hence likely to suppose that standard British English is somehow "better" English than what they speak. From a purely linguistic point of view, this is nonsense; but it is a safe bet that it will long survive any past or future loss of British influence in world affairs.

Nevertheless, according to three expert British commentators (Halliday, McIntosh, and Strevens 1964, p. 293), "Standard English as used by the English, spoken with the accent of **RP** [that is, **Received Pronunciation**, a usual term for the pronunciation inculcated by the "public" schools of England], remains the automatic and obvious choice for most Europeans and perhaps for the remaining colonies. . . . But even here we must note the increasing acceptance of American varieties of English, at any rate for adult learners." They go on to say in the succeeding paragraph that "American forms of English are now accepted, either side by side with British forms or even in preference to them, in a number of new countries where before 1945 'English' meant 'British English.'"

Conservatism and Innovation in American English

Since language undergoes no changes as a result of crossing an ocean, the first English-speaking colonists in America continued to speak as they had done in England. But the language gradually changed on both sides of the Atlantic, in England at least as much as in America. People isolated from their mother country tend to be conservative, linguistically as well as in other ways, and the English spoken in America at present has retained a good many characteristics of earlier British English that do not survive in contemporary British English, much as Icelandic has retained older characteristics that have been lost in the other Scandinavian languages.

Thus to regard American English as inferior to British English is to impugn earlier standard British English as well, for there was doubtless little difference at the time of the Revolution. There is a strong likelihood, for instance, that George III and Lord Cornwallis pronounced *after*, *ask*, *dance*, *glass*, *path*, and the like exactly the same as did George Washington and John Hancock—that is, as the overwhelming majority of Americans do to this day. It was similar with the treatment of *r*, whose loss before consonants and pauses (as in *bird* [bə̄d] and *burr* [bə̄]) did not occur in the speech of the London area until about the time of the Revolution.

Other supposed characteristics of American English are also to be found in pre-Revolutionary British English, and there is very good reason indeed for the conclusion of the eminent Swedish Anglicist Eilert Ekwall (1946, pp. 32–33) that, from the time of the Revolution on, "American pronunciation has been on the whole independent of British; the result has been that

American pronunciation has not come to share the development undergone later by Standard British." Ekwall's concern is exclusively with pronunciation, but the principle implied holds good also for many lexical items, some morphological characteristics, and probably to some degree for intonation as well.

American retention of *gotten* is an example of conservatism, though it was of course not consciously preserved. This form, the usual past participle of *get* in older British English, survives in present standard British English mainly in the phrase "ill-gotten gains"; but it is very much alive in American English, being the usual past participial form of the verb except in the senses 'to have' and 'to be obliged to' (for instance, "He hasn't got the nerve to do it" and "He's got to do it"). Similarly, American English has kept *fall* for the season and *deck* for a pack of cards (though American English also uses *pack*); and it has retained certain phonological characteristics of earlier British English to be discussed later in some detail.

It works both ways, however; for American English has lost certain features—mostly vocabulary items—that have survived in British English. Examples include *waistcoat* (the name for a garment that Americans usually call a *vest*, a word that in England usually means 'undershirt'); *fortnight*, a useful term completely lost to American English; and a number of topographical terms that Americans had no need for—words like *copse, dell, fen, heath, moor, spinney*, and *wold*. Americans, on the other hand, desperately needed terms to designate topographical features different from any known in the Old World. To remedy the deficiency, they used new compounds of English words like *backwoods, underbrush*, and *watergap*; they adapted English words to new uses, like *creek*, in British English 'a small arm of the sea,' which in American English may mean 'any small stream'; and they adopted foreign words like *canyon* (Sp. *cañón* 'tube'), *mesa* (likewise Spanish), and *prairie* (ultimately derived from Fr. *pré* 'field').

It was similar with the naming of flora and fauna strange to the colonists. When they saw a bird that somewhat resembled the English robin, they simply called it a *robin*, though it was not the same bird at all. When they saw an animal that was totally unlike anything that they had ever seen before, they might call it by its Indian name, if they could find out what that was—for example, *raccoon* and *woodchuck*. So also with the names of plants: *catalpa* and its variant *catawba* are of Muskhogean origin; *Johnny-jump-up* was inspired by a crude kind of fancy; *sweet potato* might have originated just as well in England as in America except for the fact that this particular variety of potato did not exist in England.

On the whole, though, American English is essentially a development of seventeenth-century British English. Except in vocabulary, there are probably few significant characteristics of New World English that are not traceable to the British Isles. There are also some American English characteristics that were doubtless derived from British dialects in the seventeenth century, for there were certainly dialect speakers among the earliest settlers, though they would seem to have had little influence. The majority of those English men and women to settle permanently in the New World were not illiterate bumpkins but ambitious and industrious members of the upper-lower and lower-middle classes, with a sprinkling of the educated—clergymen, lawyers, and even a few younger sons of the aristocracy. It is likely that there was a cultured nucleus in all of the early American communities. Such facts as these explain why American English resembles present standard British English more closely than it resembles any other British type of speech. The differences between the two national varieties are not many or very great.

National Differences in Word Choice

There are many lists of equivalent British and American words (for instance, Mencken 1936, pp. 233–37; 1945, pp. 457–87; Moss 1973; Zviadadze 1973), but they must not be taken too seriously. On the American side of the page will be found many locutions perfectly well understood, many of them in use, in Britain. For instance, *automobile*, represented as the American equivalent of *car* or *motor car*, is practically a formal word in America, the ordinary term being the supposedly British *car*; moreover, the supposedly American word occurs in the names of two English motoring organizations, the Royal Automobile Club and the Automobile Association. And on the British side will be found many locutions perfectly well known and frequently used in America—for instance, *postman* (as in James M. Cain's very American novel *The Postman Always Rings Twice*) and *railway* (as in *Railway Express* and the *Southern Railway*), though it is certain that *mailman* (or *letter carrier*) and *railroad* do occur more frequently in American speech. Similarly, one usually finds *baggage* as the American equivalent of British *luggage*, though *luggage* has come to be very commonly used in American English, perhaps because of its frequent occurrence in "prestige" advertising. Mencken lists *drawers* (men's) as the American equivalent of British *pants*. It is doubtful that this was true even in 1936 (the date of the fourth edition of Mencken's great work), but one can say with confidence that *drawers* has now become archaic for the nether undergarments of either sex. (Imagine asking to buy a pair in either a men's clothing store or a lingerie shop!) The usual American term is *shorts*, which may also designate outer garments; *pants* for the undergarment has become increasingly feminine, though usually in the diminutive form *panties*. British *knickers*, also originally masculine in reference, likewise became feminine, though the term is now quite old-fashioned for ladies' underpants.

There are many other hardy perennials of such lists. *Mad* is supposedly American and *angry* British, though Americans use *angry* in formal contexts, often under the impression that *mad* as a synonym is "incorrect," and though many speakers of British English use *mad* in the sense 'angry' as it was frequently used in older English (for example, in the King James Bible of 1611, Acts 26.11: "being exceedingly mad against them I persecuted them even unto strange cities"[2]). *Mailbox* is supposedly American and *pillar-box* British, though the English use *letter box* for any receptacle for mailing (that is, "posting") letters in, other than the actual low pillar with a slit for putting the letters through. *Package* is supposedly American and *parcel* British, though the supposedly British word is perfectly well known to all Americans, who have for a long time sent packages by parcel post (not "package mail"). *Sick* is supposedly American and *ill* British, though *sick*, reputed to mean only 'nauseated' in England, is frequently used in the older sense, that which is thought of as American: Sir Ralph Richardson writes, "I was often sick as a child, and so often lonely, and I remember when I was in hospital a kindly visitor giving me a book" (*Books of the Month*, November–December 1952, p. 15), in which only the phrase "in hospital" instead of American "in the hospital" indicates the writer's Britishness, except possibly for "visitor" where many Americans, under the impression that the subject of a gerund must be possessive, would have written "visitor's." *Stairway* is supposedly American and *staircase* British, though Mary Roberts Rinehart's best seller from the early years of the present century was entitled *The Circular Staircase*, though *stairs* is the usual term in both countries, and though *stairway* is recorded in British dictionaries with no notation that it is confined to American usage. Finally, *window shade* is supposedly American and *blind* British, though *blind(s)* is the usual term throughout a thickly populated section of the eastern United States. There are many other equally weak examples; the ones presented here have been chosen almost at random.

There are also many genuine instances of differences in word choice, though most of them would not cause any serious confusion on either side. Americans do not usually say *coach* for *bus* (interurban), *compère* for *M.C.* (or *emcee*, less frequently *master of ceremonies*) in a theatrical or television setting, *first floor* (or *storey* [*sic*]) for *second floor* (or *story*),[3] *lorry* for *truck*, *mental* for *insane*, *petrol* for *gas(oline)*, *pram* (or the full form *perambulator*, either) for *baby carriage*, *treacle* for *molasses*, nor do they call an *intermission* (between divisions of an entertainment) an *interval*, an *orchestra seat* a *seat in the stalls*, a *trillion* a *billion*,[4] or a *raise* (in salary) a *rise*. But most sophisticated Americans are quite aware of the British equivalents. Valid differences

---

[2] The *New English Bible: New Testament* has "My fury rose to such a pitch that I extended my persecution to foreign cities," which does not improve what did not need improvement in the first place.

[3] In England, as on the Continent, the *first floor* is immediately above the *ground floor* (also used in American English, but as a synonym of American *first floor*).

[4] In British English a billion is a million millions, whereas in American English it is what the British call a *milliard*—a mere thousand millions.

National Differences in Word Choice

in the use of words other than those that have been mentioned exist, but, as far as everyday speech is concerned, they are not really very numerous or very significant. Randolph Quirk, an English observer of American speech, put the matter well in the *New York Times Weekly Review*, International Edition (2 December 1956, p. 7):

> The long and imposing lists of so-called distinctively British and American words and usages are 75 per cent misleading; it turns out either that both the words so neatly separated are used in one or the other country, or that both are found in both countries but are used in slightly different contexts or in different proportions.

American Infiltration of the British Word Stock

Because in the course of recent history Americans have acquired greater commercial, technical, and perhaps even political prestige than any other English-speaking group, it is perhaps not unnatural that the British and others should take a somewhat high-handed attitude toward American speech. The fact is that the British have done so at least since 1735, when one Francis Moore, describing for his countrymen the then infant city of Savannah, said, "It stands upon the flat of a Hill; the Bank of the River (which they in barbarous English call a *bluff*) is steep" (Mencken 1936, p. 3). Mencken treats the subject of British attitudes toward American speech fully and with characteristic zest in the first chapter of *The American Language* (1936, pp. 1–48) and also in the first supplement to that wonderful work (1945, pp. 1–100).

But the truth is that, as far as vocabulary is concerned—and most people, when they think of language, think of it in terms of vocabulary items—British English has been rather constantly infiltrated by American usage. The transfer began quite a while ago, long before talking films, radio, and television were ever thought of, although they have certainly hastened the process. Sir William Craigie, the eminent editor of *A Dictionary of American English on Historical Principles* (1938–44), pointed out that although "for some two centuries . . . the passage of new words or senses across the Atlantic was regularly westwards . . . with the nineteenth century . . . the contrary current begins to set in, bearing with it many a piece of drift-wood to the shores of Britain, there to be picked up and incorporated in the structure of the language." He cited such **Americanisms** in British English as *backwoods*, *beeline*, *belittle*, *blizzard*, *bunkum*, *caucus*, *cloudburst*, *prairie*, *swamp*, and a good many others that have long been completely acclimatized (Craigie 1927, p. 208).

In recent years many other Americanisms have been introduced into British usage: *cafeteria*, *cocktail*, *egghead*, *electrocute* (both in reference to the distinctively American mode of capital punishment and in the extended sense 'to kill accidentally by electric shock'), *fan* 'sports devotee,' *filling station,* *highbrow,* and *lowbrow.* American *radio* has superseded British *wireless,* and *TV* has about crowded out the somewhat nurseryish *telly.* The ubiquitous *OK* seems to occur more frequently nowadays in England than in the land of its birth and may be found in quite formal situations, such as on legal documents to indicate the correctness of details therein. These and other Americanisms have slithered into British English in the most unobtrusive way, so that their American origin is hardly regarded at all save by a few crusted older-generation speakers: since they are used by the English, they are "English," and that is all there is to it. Woe be to the American who tries to convince a run-of-the-mill Englishman to the contrary!

Brian Foster, an Englishman who is anything but run-of-the-mill, has written knowingly (1956, p. 329) of the "enormous impact of American idiom on the standard British usage," though "by a strange paradox few people, even among specialists, are conscious of the extent of this influence, and some . . . virtually deny its existence." Foster cites as firmly established in standard British English *ballyhoo, to build up* (by advertising), *disk jockey* (the more usual British spelling is *disc*), *double talk, to get* (something) *across,* *natural* 'something very suitable,' *of all time* (as in "the greatest film of all time"), *to put* (something) *over, show business, star* 'popular performer' (also a verb), and *stooge*—all originally from the usage of the world of entertainment, enormously important in modern America, and all, with the possible exception of *of all time,* more or less nonliterary.

The following Americanisms appear in the formal utterances of VIPs, as well as in the writings of some quite respectable authors on both sides of the Atlantic:[5] *alibi* 'excuse,' *allergy* 'aversion' (and *allergic* 'averse'), *angle* 'viewpoint,' *blurb* ("now used quite solemnly as an indispensable item in the jargon of literary critics and the reading public" [Foster 1968, p. 37]), *breakdown* 'analysis,' *crash* 'collide,' *know-how, maybe, quit* (previously regarded as archaic except in a few stock phrases), *sales resistance, to go back on,* *to slip up, to stand up to, way of life. Fortnight* 'two consecutive weeks,' a stock **Briticism** to most Americans who know the word at all (as all those who read books do), "seems to appear rarely in the speech of the younger generation," who increasingly are using American *two weeks.*

As has been pointed out, words and usages are frequently borrowed from American English quite unconsciously. Even when they are consciously borrowed, the fact that they are of transatlantic origin is soon forgotten. H. W. Horwill testifies that a good many Americanisms he wrote down during a residence in the United States between 1900 and 1905 would not have been recognized by him as of American origin when he wrote *A Dictionary of Modern American Usage* in 1935 if he had trusted to his memory alone, for

[5] The words to be cited, except for *blurb,* are obviously not of American origin; it is the meanings and in some instances the combinations that have developed in the United States.

"usages that to-day are peculiar to America are to-morrow adopted by English writers and speakers, frequently without the least suspicion of their transatlantic origin" (1944, p. viii). He cites *cut* in the sense 'reduction' as an Americanism that became widely used in England during the financial crisis of 1931. By 1935 there was no consciousness of its American provenience; it was thoroughly naturalized, though for a time it was written within quotation marks.

The convenient use of noun as verb in *to contact*, meaning 'to see, call, meet, or in any other way to get in touch with,' seems to have originated in America, though it might just as well have done so in England, since there is nothing un-English about such a conversion: scores of other nouns have undergone the same functional shift. This particular conversion had occurred earlier in British English, but the new verb was confined to technical writing: the *OED* cites "The spark and the gunpowder contacted" from 1834 but calls such use rare. We may thus regard the occurrence in 1929 as to all intents and purposes a new American creation. The verb began to catch on in England around the mid-1940s, though many persons there as well as in the United States objected to it vociferously. No one gets much disturbed over it nowadays. Crane Brinton, in a review of H. C. Allen's *Great Britain and the United States* (New York *Herald-Tribune Book Review*, 1 May 1955, p. 3), cites "Lord North despatched an emissary to contact Benjamin Franklin," written "apparently without a qualm" by the author, an Oxford don. The reviewer concludes that this one word *contact* "carries high symbolic importance. . . . Mr. Mencken was wrong—there will be no American language, for the simple reason that, apart from deviations in ephemeral slang and regional dialects . . . the Queen's English and the President's English grow together."

Actually, though, they were never so far apart as it has been pleasing to American patriotism (which has sometimes manifested itself unpleasingly in a prideful "mucker pose") and British insularity (which has sometimes equally unpleasingly manifested itself in an overweening assumption of superiority) to pretend. "How quaint of the British to call a muffler a silencer!" "How boorish of the Americans to call an egg-whisk an egg beater!" The most striking of such presumably amusing differences, however, are not very important, for they almost inevitably occur on a rather superficial level—in the specialized vocabularies of travel, sports, schools, government, and various trades.

Syntactical and Morphological Differences

Syntactical and morphological differences are quite as trivial as those in word choice. With regard to collective nouns, for instance, the British are much more likely than Americans to use a plural verb form, like "the public

are. . . ." Plural verbs are frequent with the names of sports teams, which,
because they lack the plural -*s*, would require singular verbs in American
usage: "England Await Chance to Mop Up" (a headline, the reference
being to England's cricket team, engaged in a test match with Australia);
"Wimbledon Are Fancied for Double" (also a headline); and "Middlesex
were in a strong position when they continued their innings at Gloucester."
This usage is not confined to sports pages: witness "The village are livid";
"The U.S. Government are believed to favour . . ."; "Eton College break
up for the summer holidays to-day"; "The Savoy [Hotel] have their own water
supply"; "The Government regard . . ."; and "Scotland Yard are. . . ."

The following locutions, all from recent British writings, would have been
phrased as indicated within square brackets by American writers; yet as they
stand they would not puzzle an American reader in the least:

> Thus Mgr. [Monsignor] Knox is faced by a word, which, if translated
> by its English equivalent, will give a meaning possibly very different
> to [from, than] its sense. (Letter to the editor of the *Spectator* by
> Quentin de la Bedoyere)
> When he found his body on Hampstead Heath, the only handkerchief
> was a clean one which had certainly not got [certainly did not have]
> any eucalyptus on it. (Michael Underwood)
> She'd got [she had] plenty of reason . . . for supposing that she would
> count in her father's will. (Ronald Knox)
> He hadn't got [didn't have] any relatives . . . except a sister . . . in
> Canada or somewhere. (Macdonald Hastings)
> You don't think . . . that he did confide in any person?—Unlikely.
> I think he would have done [would have] if Galbraith alone had
> been involved. (Edmund Crispin [Bruce Montgomery])
> I'll tell it you [to you]. (Philip MacDonald)
> Are you quite sure you could not give it me [give it to me, give me it]
> yourself? (Josephine Bell)
> In the morning I was woken up [awakened] at eight by a housemaid.
> (Nancy Mitford)

Although most of the constructions cited are not to be heard in American
English, their bracketed equivalents are common as British variants.

There are certain differences other than *different to* in the choice of
prepositions: for instance, the English householder lives *in* a street, the
American *on* it; the English traveler gets *in* or *out of* a train, the American
on or *off* it; still other variations are equally inconsequential. A recent
proliferation of redundant prepositions and adverbs in English may well have
received its impetus from American usage, but the tendency is by no means
new or native to America. Still, it does seem frequently to have gone haywire
in American English, where it is not enough merely to visit someone—one

must visit *with* them; or to refer to something, when one can refer *back* to it; or to head, say, a committee, when one can head it *up*; or even to continue, when it sounds so much more impressive to continue *on*. Nowadays we plan *on* doing something or other rather than merely plan doing it; we cancel *out*, when just canceling would be sufficient; and we face *up to* something when it might have been in earlier times considered sufficient merely to face it.

National Differences in Idiom

In general it may be said that, perhaps because America lacks a **caste dialect** comparable to the RP of British English, American attitudes toward language lay somewhat greater stress on a more easily acquired "correctness" based on such matters as the supposed "proper" position of *only*, which the British tend to put where it comes more or less naturally to all of us, before the verb, as in A. S. C. Ross's "U and Non-U: An Essay in Sociologica! Linguistics": "At all events I have only come across one case of it" (Mitford 1956, p. 33, n. 2). Ross was Professor of English Language in the University of Birmingham (England). It must not be supposed, however, that *only*-snoopers, to use Sir Ernest Gowers's apt term for those who engage in "the sport of pillorying [what they conceive to be] misplaced *onlys*" (1954, p. 185), are all American. Gowers was writing primarily for British readers. But the British are far more tolerant toward the "illogical" but idiomatic preverbal position of the adverb. Even the frequently crotchety H. W. Fowler was of the very sensible opinion that "when perspicuity is not in danger it is needless to submit to an inconvenient restriction" as to the position of *only* (*Modern English Usage*, 1st ed., 1926, p. 406). It is yet likely that educated American speakers—more particularly writers, and even more particularly teachers and editors—concern themselves more with the matter than do their British counterparts.

Likewise it becomes a matter of tremendous importance—practically a moral obligation—invariably to use *whom* where what is thought of as good grammar seems to call for it; to eschew *can* in asking or giving permission and *like* as a conjunction; to choose forms of personal pronouns strictly in accordance with what is conceived to be their proper case; to refer to *everybody, everyone, nobody, no one, somebody,* and *someone* with a personal pronoun singular in form (that is, *he, she,* or any of their oblique forms); and, not to make too long a story of it, to observe the whole set of fairly simple rules and regulations designed for the timorous—prescriptions and proscriptions that those who are secure have never given much thought to.

Counterexamples to these supposed rules of usage are easy enough to come by. "Who are you with?" (that is, 'What newspaper do you work for?'), asked Queen Elizabeth II of various newspapermen at a reception given for her by the press in Washington (28 October 1957, p. 53); though *who* for *whom* would not pass muster among many grammarians, it is nonetheless literally the Queen's English. In *The Cambridge Murders*, a 1945 novel by Dilwyn Rees (a pseudonym of Glyn E. Daniel, Fellow and Steward of St. John's College, Cambridge), a titled academic writes to a young acquaintance, "Babs dear, can I see you for a few moments, please?" (p. 67). There is no indication that Babs responded, "You *can*, but you *may* not," as American children are taught to say. *Like* has been used as a conjunction—as in Clive Barnes's "These Russians dance like the Italians sing and the Spaniards fight bulls" (*Spectator*, 1 July 1960, p. 21)—in self-assured, cultivated English since the early sixteenth century but has been banned in more recent times, for purely arbitary reasons as far as one can determine. The choice of case for pronouns is governed by principles quite different from those found in the run of grammar books; Winston Churchill quoted King George VI as observing that "it would not be right for either you or I to be where we planned to be on D-Day" (*Life*, 29 October 1951, p. 83), and Somerset Maugham was primly *sic*'ed by an American reviewer for writing "a good deal older than me" (*New York Herald Tribune Book Review*, 5 April 1953, p. 5). The use of *they*, *them*, and *their* with a singular antecedent has long been standard in English. George McKnight (1928, pp. 528–29) has specimens of this "solecism" from Jane Austen, Thomas De Quincey, Lord Dunsany, Cardinal Newman, Samuel Butler, and others. The *OED* cites Lord Chesterfield, who may be taken as a model of elegant eighteenth-century usage, as having written, "If a person is born of a gloomy temper . . . they cannot help it." Recently the National Council of Teachers of English has endorsed such use of the pronouns as a way of avoiding sexism in language; it is certainly less self-conscious and more traditional than the legalistic *he or she* or the variety of concocted pronouns that have been proposed in recent years (Baron 1981).

The paucity of American printed examples of proscribed locutions (other than those that occasionally occur in small-town newspapers) may be due to some extent to the greater care given to such details by American editors, which has given rise to a functional variety of our language known as **edited English**—a type of speech that does not necessarily reflect in all details the actual usage of professional writers. Even so, it is likely that most American writers themselves, because of the widespread American concept of a mechanical sort of correctness supposed to be characteristic of cultivated usage, would more or less habitually employ the forms of speech prescribed as standard for American usage, which are certainly not those that have been cited above from English printed works.

British and American Purism

It is not to be inferred that the British citations necessarily illustrate constructions that occur most of the time in British English. It can only be said that, despite the feelings of horror they evince from some educated speakers of American English, they *do* actually occur within the framework of standard British English—and, for that matter, within standard American English as well. Americans are, on the whole, more likely to have linguistic split personalities than are the British. We talk and write one way but are often convinced that there is some other way that is "right," or at least "better." For example, the members of a much touted usage panel responded to a question about whether they made a distinction in use between *farther* and *further* with such comments as these (Morris and Morris 1975, p. 237): "Yes, but I slip. I still like the difference between the two." "No. But I know there is a difference between the two and strive to do so." "Yes. Or at least I try to, but don't always manage." "When I remember to." The members of this panel were all accomplished writers and speakers of English, most of them men or women of letters; yet, faced with a choice between options, both in standard use, many of the panel members were unwilling to accept their own usage but felt called upon to confess the need for improvement and resolved to mend their linguistic manners. The way Americans talk and the way they think they ought to talk are often thus at variance. (Thomas Creswell [1975] has made a revealing study of how usage questions are handled by lexicographers and usage pundits, and Algeo [1977] has surveyed the grammatical **shibboleths** most often treated in usage books.)

There are plenty of purists in England, where the "rules" originated, just as there are in America. There are plenty everywhere else, for that matter, for the purist attitude toward language is above all a question of temperament. By no means are all of them teachers, either. Moreover, the English variety are about as ill-informed and as inconsistent as their American counterparts.

It is in fact likely that everyone between the cockney and the peer pays lip service to the mossy precepts of the eighteenth-century prescriptive grammarians who formulated most of the "rules" that constitute "grammar" in the lay mind. But in actual practice, few English purists have been accorded the deference enjoyed by the American variety. Standard British English is still essentially the speech of those who are expected to speak standard British English, not a set of precepts in a usage book, even one by such a respected purist as H. W. Fowler.

With the new distinction acquired by a good many graduates from the "red-brick universities" north of the Thames, like the unbrushed young D. H. Lawrence of a generation or so ago, British attitudes toward usage may change. Many of these new educated persons have an emotional bias against the Southern, that is, standard British, pronunciation, which is somewhat like the ambivalent attitude of many Americans toward it. But success and prosperity go a long way in tempering bias, and it may well be that they will want their sons and daughters to acquire the speech as well as the social deportment of the Establishment that they now affect to despise. For there is no snob like a self-made man or woman—a statement that is not in the least irrelevant when we are considering linguistic usages. It will be most interesting to observe developments in standard British English a generation or two hence.

Katharine Whitehorn (1962), an English journalist who is quite familiar with America, has put the matter very well: "In America, where it is grammar, not accent, that places you, anyone can learn the grammar; maybe Bostonians don't accept it, but Bostonians only impress other Bostonians." The "American way" in language has been to make gentility accessible to all not by laying the stress on anything so subtle, let alone aristocratic, as "accent," but by basing "good usage" wholly on certain morphological and syntactical shibboleths—the avoidance of *ain't*, *he don't*, *it's me*, terminal prepositions, split infinitives, dangling participles, and the like. These are rather easy for all to learn, even though not all bother to do so. Those who do not conform to the supposedly inflexible rules are thought to speak "bad English," even though they may be persons of considerable consequence in the national life; it is as simple as all that.

National Differences in Pronunciation

In the pronunciation of individual words, much the same situation holds true as for word choices: the differences are really inconsequential. The most widely current pronunciation of a given word in American English may occur in standard British English as a less frequently used variant; for instance, for *either* and *neither* an overwhelming majority of Americans have [i] in the stressed syllable, though some—largely from the Atlantic coastal cities—have [aɪ], and others all over the country have doubtless affected this pronunciation because they suppose it to have social prestige. In any case, the [aɪ] pronunciation cannot be said to be exclusively British; and it may come as a surprise to some Americans to learn that the [i] pronunciation occurs in standard British English, probably much more frequently than the [aɪ] pronunciation occurs in American English. Pronunciation with [i] is in fact listed first in the *OED*, which notes, however, that the pronunciation [aɪðə] "is in London somewhat more prevalent in educated speech" than [iðə]. All dictionaries of British English, in fact, list the supposedly "American" pronunciation as a variant.

The prevalent standard British English pronunciation of each of the following words differs from the usual or only pronunciation in American English: *ate* [ɛt], *been* [bin], *evolution* [ivəlušən], *fragile* [fræǰaɪl], *medicine* [mɛdsɪn], *nephew* [nɛvyu], *process* [prosɛs], *trait* [tre], *tryst* [traɪst], *valet* [vælɪt], *zenith* [zɛnɪθ]. But it is a fact that the prevalent American pronunciation of each (allowing for an interchange of [ɔ] and [ɑ] in *process*) occurs also in standard British English, as in *ate* [et], *been* [bɪn], *evolution* [ɛvəlušən], *fragile* [fræǰɪl], *medicine* [mɛdɪsɪn], *nephew* [nɛfyu], *process* [prosɛs], *trait* [tret], *tryst* [trɪst], *valet* [væle], and *zenith* [zinɪθ]. The pronunciation [ɛt] for *ate* occurs in American speech but is regarded as substandard. For *nephew*, [nɛvyu] is current in America, according to Hans Kurath and Raven I. McDavid, Jr. (1961, p. 176), "both in folk speech and in cultivated speech, in Eastern New England, in Chesapeake Bay, and especially in South Carolina, rarely elsewhere."

The prevalent American pronunciations of the following words do not occur in standard British English: *figure* [fɪgyər], *leisure* [ližər], *quinine* [kwaɪnaɪn], *squirrel* [skwərəl] (also *stirrup* and *syrup* with the same stressed vowel), *tomato* [təmeto], and *vase* [ves]. But the prevalent British pronunciations of all of them are current, though indeed not widespread, in American English—that is, [fɪgə(r)], [lɛžə(r)], [kwɪnin], [skwɪrəl], [təmato], [vɑz], though the first of these, for *figure*, is regarded as substandard. (The British have [-y-] in *figuration, figurative*, and *figurine*.)

The British pronunciation of *lieutenant* as [lɛftɛnənt] when it refers to the army subaltern is now never heard in American English, though it was usual until [lutɛnənt] was recommended for Americans by Noah Webster in his *American Dictionary of the English Language* (1828). Webster also recommended *schedule* with [sk-]. It is likely, however, that the historical pronunciation with [s-] was that most widely used in both England and America in 1828. The current British pronunciation is with [š-].

Other pronunciations that are nationally distinctive include (with the American pronunciation given first) [šəgrín]/[šǽgrɪn] for *chagrin*, [klərk]/[klɑk] for *clerk*, [kɔ́rəlɛ̀rɪ]/[kərɔ́lərɪ] for *corollary*, [daɪnəstɪ]/[dɪnəstɪ] for *dynasty*, [frəntír]/[frɔ́ntyə] for *frontier*, [lǽbrətɔ̀ri]/[ləbɔ́rət(ə)rɪ] or [lǽbrət(ə)rɪ] for *laboratory*, [mísələni]/[mɪsélənɪ] for *miscellany*, and [prɪmír]/[prémyə] for *premier*. American *carburetor* [kɑrbəretər] and British *carburettor* [kəbyʊrɛtə] are, in addition to being pronounced differently, variant written forms, as are the words *alúminum* (again, old Noah Webster's choice) and *àlumínium*.

A few more items might be added to those cited above, but actually not very many. As for more sweeping differences, what strikes most American ears most strongly is the modern standard British shift of an older [æ], which survives in American English except before *r* (as in *far*), *lm* (as in *calm*), and in *father*, to [ɑ] in a number of very frequently used words. Up to the very end of the eighteenth century, [ɑ] in such words was considered vulgar. This shift cannot, however, be regarded as exclusively British, inasmuch as its effect is evident in the speech of eastern New England and to some extent in the tidewater South. Present American usage in regard to such words is by no means consistent: a Bostonian may, for instance, have [ɑ] in *half* (and then perhaps only some of the time), but not in *can't*, or vice versa. An intermediate [a] is sometimes heard in America as a variant of this [ɑ]. According to John S. Kenyon (1950, p. 183), "The pronunciation of '*ask*' words with [a] or [ɑ] has been a favorite field for schoolmastering and elocutionary

Recent British and American English

quackery." (Bracketed symbols replace his boldface ones.) One cannot but   227
agree when one hears American actresses and actors pronounce [a] in words
like *hat, happy, dishpan hands,* and others that were not affected by the
aforementioned shift.

The use of [ɑ] in what Kenyon calls the **ask words**, supposed by some
naive American speakers to have higher social standing than [æ], is fraught
with danger. With speakers of standard British English, who use it naturally,
in the sense that they acquired it when as children they were learning to talk,
it never occurs in a great many words in which it might be expected if one
were going only by analogy. Thus, *bass, crass, lass,* and *mass* have [æ], in
contrast to the [ɑ] of *class, glass, grass,* and *pass.* But *classic, classical,
classicism, classify, passage, passenger,* and *passive* all have [æ]. *Gastric* has
[æ], but *plaster* has [ɑ]; *ample* has [æ], but *example* and *sample* have [ɑ];
fancy and *romance* have [æ], but *chance, dance,* and *glance* have [ɑ]; *cant*
'hypocritical talk' has [æ], but *can't* 'cannot' has [ɑ]; *mascot, massacre,* and
pastel have [æ], but *basket, master,* and *nasty* have [ɑ], and *bastard, mas-
querade,* and *mastiff* may have either [æ] or [ɑ]. It is obvious that few status
seekers could master such complexities, even if there were any real point in
so doing. There is none, actually, for no one worth fooling would be fooled
by such a shallow display of linguistic virtuosity.

Somewhat less noticeable, perhaps because it is more widespread in
American English than the use of [ɑ] or [a] in the *ask* words, is the standard
British English loss of [r] except when a vowel follows it. The American treatment of this sound is, however, somewhat less consistent and hence more
complicated to describe than the British. In parts of the deep South, it may
be lost even before a vowel, as in *Carolina* and *far away.* But in one way or
another, [r] is lost in eastern New England, in New York City, and in most
of the coastal South. Away from the Atlantic Coast, it is retained in all
positions.

There are other less striking phonological differences, like the British
slightly rounded "short *o*" in contrast to the unrounded [ɑ] in *collar, got,
stop,* and the like used in most dialects of American English. In western
Pennsylvania and eastern New England, a vowel like the British one can be
heard in these words.

Though there are signs of its return, British English long ago lost its
secondary stress on the penultimate syllables of polysyllables in *-ary, -ery,*
and *-ory* (for example, *military, millinery, obligatory*). This subordinate stress
is regularly retained in American English. Many Americans, it is true, are
fond of [díkšən(ə)ri] as a pronunciation of *dictionary*—presumably it gives a
certain social "tone" to the word—but few if any who use this pronunciation
pronounce other such words in any save the usual American and older
British fashion, that is, as *mónastèry, sécretàry, térritòry,* and the like. The
secondary stress is often lacking in *library* (sometimes reduced to disyllabic
[láɪbri]), but it regularly occurs in other such words. A restoration of the

secondary stress in British English, at least in some words, is more likely due to spelling consciousness than to any transatlantic influence. Some well-educated younger-generation British speakers have it in *sécretàry* and in *extraórdinàry*.

Intonational characteristics—risings and fallings in pitch—plus to an unrealized extent timbre of voice distinguish British English from American English far more than pronunciations of individual words. Voice quality in this connection has not been much investigated, and most statements about it are impressionistic; but there can be little doubt of its significance. Even if he were to learn British intonation, the American (say, a Bostonian) whose treatment of *r* and of the vowel of *ask*, *path*, and the like agreed with that of standard British English would never in the world pass among the British for an Englishman. He would still be spotted as a "Yank" by practically any-one in the British Isles. Precision in the description of nationally characteristic voice qualities must, however, be left for future investigators.

In regard to intonation, the differences are most noticeable in questions and requests. Contrast the intonational patterns of the following sentences, very roughly indicated as they are, as they would customarily be spoken in British and American English:

BE: Where are you going to be?

AE: Where are you going to be?

BE: Are you sure?

AE: Are you sure?

BE: Let me know where you're going to be.

AE: Let me know where you're going to be.

BE: Don't tell me that you're sure.

AE: Don't tell me that you're sure.

It is usually difficult or impossible to tell whether a singer is English or American, for the intonational patterns in singing are those of the composer.

It is most unlikely that tempo plays any part in the identification of a British or an American accent. To Americans unaccustomed to hearing it, British speech frequently seems to be running on at a great rate. But this impression of speed is doubtless also experienced by those English people who have not come into contact with American television shows, movies, and tourists, if there be any such remaining, in regard to American English.

Some people speak slowly, some rapidly, regardless of nationality; moreover, the same individuals are likely to speak more rapidly when they know what they are talking about than when they must "make conversation."

The type of American speech that one now hears most frequently on national television, especially in commercials, is highly standardized and essentially synthetic. This speech evinces few if any regional or individual characteristics discernible to untrained ears. The extent of the influence and prestige of those who speak the commercials may be gauged by the astronomical sums spent on such advertising. Who can say that their standardized form of speech, based to a large extent on writing, may not in time become the basis for, or for that matter may itself become, a nationwide caste dialect?

British and American Spelling

Finally, there is the matter of spelling, which looms larger in the consciousness of those who are concerned with national differences than it deserves to. Somewhat exotic to American eyes, though by no means unfamiliar to those of the educated, are *cheque* (for drawing money from a bank), *cyder*, *cypher*, *gaol*, *kerb* (of a street), *pyjamas*, *syren*, and *tyre* (around a wheel). But *check*, *cider*, *cipher*, *jail*, *curb*, *pajamas*, *siren*, and *tire* are also current in England in varying degrees.

Noah Webster, whom many regard as a sort of linguistic guru, was responsible for excising the *u* from a group of words spelled in his day prevailingly in *-our*: *armour*, *behaviour*, *colour*, *favour*, *flavour*, *harbour*, *labour*, *neighbour*, and the like. The resultant American *-or* spellings are today far more obnoxious to the English than the alternative forms with *-our* are to Americans, who, in addition to reading a great many books printed in England, are quite accustomed to seeing *glamour* and *saviour* in books printed in their own country. All such words were current in earlier British English without the *u*, though most Britishers today are probably unaware of the fact; Webster was making no radical change in English spelling habits. Furthermore, the English had themselves struck the *u* from a great many words earlier spelled *-our*, alternating with *-or*: *author*, *doctor*, *emperor*, *error*, *governor*, *horror*, *mirror*, and *senator*, among others.

Webster is also responsible for the American practice of using *-er* instead of the British *-re* in a number of words—for instance, *calibre*, *centre*, *litre*, *manoeuvre*, *metre* (of poetry or of the unit of length in the metric system), *sepulchre*, and *theatre*. The last of these spellings has nowadays probably a wider currency in American English than has *theater*; it is regarded by many of its users as an elegant (because British) spelling and by others as an affectation. Except for *litre*, which did not come into English until the nineteenth century, all these words occur in earlier British English with *-er*.

The fact that *c* before *e* indicates [s] must have irritated Webster. At one time he wanted to have *acre* spelled *aker*, but he was still left with *lucre* and *mediocre*, in the case of which he seems to have given up fighting the good fight. There was also *ogre*, about which little could be done; **oger* would have suggested [ojər].

The American use of *-se* in *defense, offense,* and *pretense,* in which the English usually have *-ce,* is also attributable to the precept and practice of Webster, though he did not recommend *fense* for *fence,* which is simply an aphetic form of *defense* (or *defence*). Spellings with *-se* have occurred in earlier British English for all these words, including *fence. Suspense* is now usually so spelled in British English.

Webster proposed dropping final *k* in such words as *almanack, musick, physick, publick,* and *traffick,* bringing about a change that has occurred in British English as well, though not because old Noah recommended it. His proposed *burdoc, cassoc,* and *hassoc* now regularly end in *k,* whereas *havock,* in which he neglected to drop the *k,* is everywhere spelled without it.

Though he was not the first to recommend doing so, Webster is doubtless to be credited with the American spelling practice of not doubling final *l* when adding a suffix except in words stressed on their final syllables—for example, *grável, groveled, groveler, groveling,* but *propél, propelled, propeller, propelling, propellant.* Modern British spelling usually doubles *l* before a suffix regardless of the position of the stress, as in *grovelled, groveller,* and so forth.

The British use of *ae* and *oe* (or *æ* and *œ*) looks strange to Americans in *anaemic, gynaecology, haemorrhage, paediatrician,* and in *diarrhoeia, homoeopathy, manoeuvre,* and *oesophagus,* but not in *aesthetic, archaeology,* and *encyclopaedia,* which are fairly common in American usage. Some words earlier written with one or the other of these digraphs long ago underwent simplification—for example, *phaenomenon, oeconomy,* and *poenology.* Others are in the process of simplification: *hemorrhage, hemorrhoids,* and *medieval* are frequent British variants of the forms with *ae,* but *haematic, haemoglobin, haemophilia,* and *haemostatic* seem not to have lost the *a* as yet.

Most British writers use *-ise* for the verbal suffix written *-ize* in America in such words as *baptize, organize,* and *sympathize.* However, the *Times* of London, the *OED,* H. C. Wyld's *Universal Dictionary* (1932), the various editions of Daniel Jones's *English Pronouncing Dictionary,* and a number of other publications of considerable intellectual prestige prefer the spelling with *z,* which, in the words of the *OED,* is "at once etymological and phonetic." (The suffix is ultimately from Greek *-izein.*) The *ct* of *connection* and *inflection* is due to the influence of *connect* and *inflect.* The etymologically sounder spellings *connexion* and *inflexion,* reflecting their sources in Latin *connexiōn(em)* and *inflexiōn(em),* are used by most writers, or at any rate by most printers, in England.

Spelling reform has been a recurring preoccupation of would-be language engineers on both sides of the Atlantic. Webster, who loved tinkering with all aspects of language, had contemplated far flashier spelling reforms than those he succeeded in getting adopted. For instance, he advocated lopping off the final *e* of *-ine*, *-ite*, and *-ive* in final syllables (thus *medicin*, *definit*, *fugitiv*), using *oo* for *ou* in *group* and *soup*, writing *tung* for *tongue*, and deleting the *a* in *bread*, *feather*, and the like; but in time he abandoned these unsuccessful, albeit sensible, spellings. The financier Andrew Carnegie and President Theodore Roosevelt both supported a reformed spelling in the early years of this century, including such simplifications as *catalog* for *catalogue*, *claspt* for *clasped*, *gage* for *gauge*, *program* for *programme*, and *thoro* for *thorough* (Vivian 1979). Some of the spellings they advocated have been generally adopted, some are still used as variants, but many are rarely used now.

Variation Within American English

Despite the comparative uniformity of English throughout the world, there clearly are variations within the language, even within a single national variety, such as American English. The kind of English we use depends on both us and the circumstances in which we use it. The variations that depend on us have to do with where we learned our English (**regional** or **geographical dialects**), what cultural groups we belong to (**ethnic** or **social dialects**), and a host of other factors such as our sex, age, and education. The variations that depend on the circumstances of use have to do with whether we are talking or writing, how formal the situation is, the subject of the discourse, the effect we want to achieve, and so on. Differences in language that depend on who we are constitute **dialect**. Differences that depend on where, why, or how we are using language are matters of **style**.

Each of us speaks a variety of dialects; for example, a Minnesota, Swedish-American, female, younger-generation, college-educated person talks differently from a Tennessee, Appalachian, male, older-generation, grade-school-educated person—each of those factors (place, ethnic group, sex, age, education) defining a dialect. We can change our dialects during the course of our lives (an Ohioan who moves to Alabama may start saying *y'all* and dropping *r*'s), but once we have reached maturity, our dialects tend to be fairly well set and not to vary a great deal, unless we are very impressionable or there are very strong influences that lead us to change. Each of us also uses a variety of styles, and we change them often, shifting from one to another as the situation warrants, and often learning new ones. The more varied our experiences have been, the more various the styles that we command are likely to be. But almost everyone uses more than one style of language, even in daily activities like talking with young children, answering the telephone when a friend calls, meeting a new colleague, and saying good night to one's family. The language differences in such circumstances may not be obvious to us, because we are used to them and tend to overlook the familiar, but a close study will show them to be considerable.

One style of language—in fact, the style that has been almost the exclusive concern of this book—is **standard English**. A standard language is one that is used widely, in many places and for many purposes; it is also one that enjoys high prestige, one that people regard as "good" language, to be imitated and taught to others. Standard English is the written form of our language used in books and periodicals; it is also known as **edited English**. It is, to be sure, not a homogeneous thing: there is plenty of what Gerard Manley Hopkins called "pied beauty" in it, more in fact than many persons realize. It is partly because of its variety that it is useful. Standard English is standard, not because it is intrinsically better than other varieties—clearer or more logical or prettier—but only because English speakers have agreed to use it in so many places for so many purposes that they have therefore made a useful tool of it and have come to regard it as a good thing.

REGIONAL DIALECTS

In contrast to standard English are all the regional and ethnic dialects of the United States and of other English-speaking countries. In America, there are three or four main regional dialects in the eastern part of the country: **Northern** (from northern New Jersey and Pennsylvania to New England), **North Midland** (from northern Delaware, Maryland, and West Virginia through southern New Jersey and Pennsylvania), **South Midland**, also called **Inland Southern** (the Appalachian region from southern West Virginia to northern Georgia), and **Southern**, or **Coastal Southern** (from southern Delaware and Maryland down to Florida, along the Atlantic seaboard).

The farther west one goes, the more difficult it is to recognize clearly defined dialect boundaries. The fading out of sharp dialect lines in the western United States is what might be expected from the history of the country. The earliest English-speaking settlements were along the eastern seaboard; because that area has been longest populated, it has had the most opportunity to develop distinct regional forms of speech. The western settlements are generally more recent and were usually made by persons of diverse origins. Thus the older eastern dialect differences were not kept intact by the western pioneers, and new ones have not had the opportunity to develop. Because of the increased mobility of the population and the greater opportunities for hearing and talking with persons from many areas, distinct new western dialects may be slow in coming into existence.

The scholarly study of American geographical dialects began in 1889 with the foundation of the American Dialect Society. The chief purpose of the society was the production of an American dialect dictionary. To that end, the society published the periodical *Dialect Notes* from 1890 to 1939, containing principally word lists from various parts of the country. After the hiatus of World War II, the society brought out a series known simply as *Publication of the American Dialect Society* (or *PADS* for short), which is now a monograph series. In 1925 there was published the first issue of *American Speech*, a magazine founded by the journalist-critic H. L. Mencken (who was also responsible for some of the liveliest writing ever published on American English in his monumental three-volume study, *The American Language*, abridged and updated by Raven I. McDavid in 1963) and by three academics: Kemp Malone, Louise Pound, and Arthur G. Kennedy. In 1970 *American Speech* became the journal of the American Dialect Society and is now published for the society by the University of Alabama Press. During the 1960s and 1970s, work on the society's dictionary was revived by Frederic G. Cassidy; and the *Dictionary of American Regional English* (*DARE*), as it is now known, is currently being edited at Wisconsin for publication by the Belknap Press of Harvard. When it is completed, it will be a thorough and authoritative source for information about all varieties of nonstandard English in America.

Another project to assess the regional forms of American English is the Linguistic Atlas of the United States and Canada, which was originally intended to cover all of English-speaking North America but which has been divided into a series of regional projects, of which two are complete: *Linguistic Atlas of New England*, edited by Hans Kurath and others (1939–43), and *The Linguistic Atlas of the Upper Midwest*, edited by Harold B. Allen (1973–76). Other regional atlases in various stages of publication or editing include the *Linguistic Atlas of the Middle and South Atlantic States* (1980–) and the *Linguistic Atlas of the North Central States*, both under the direction of Raven I. McDavid, Jr., and the *Linguistic Atlas of the Gulf States*, edited by Lee Pederson at Emory University and scheduled for publication by the University of Georgia Press. There are also many published monographs based on the unpublished Linguistic Atlas materials (notably Atwood 1953, Kurath 1949, and Kurath and McDavid 1961).

ETHNIC AND SOCIAL DIALECTS

The concentrated study of ethnic and social dialects is more recent than that of regional ones but is now being vigorously pursued in the United States. As Walt Wolfram and Ralph W. Fasold observe (1974, p. 31), "It was probably Labov's work in the middle 1960s that provided the major impetus for much of the current sociolinguistic inquiry into social dialects." William Labov's first major work was *The Social Stratification of English in New York City* (1966). Among the American ethnic groups that have been most intensively studied (although not all by the same methods or with the same thoroughness) are blacks, Appalachians, Jews, Chicanos, Puerto Ricans, and the Pennsylvania Dutch; almost every distinct ethnic group in the United

States has had some attention to its speechways, and some a great deal of attention. There is, however, a pressing need for a coherent and comprehensive linguistic study of the ethnic minorities in the United States.

Linguistic diversity in the classroom is one of the major problems of public education in the later years of the twentieth century; and an increasing sense of ethnic pride, with a concomitant reluctance to abandon ethnic patterns of behavior, including ways of talking and writing, may prove to be a challenge to the traditional concept of the "melting pot" of American culture. On the one hand are those who view ethnic and linguistic diversity as a defense against the cultural imperialism of Anglo-American society, represented by standard English. On the other hand are those who foresee the cultural balkanization of America if large-sized ethnic groups remain unassimilated and who fear the loss of historical continuity with the Anglo-American heritage that standard English represents. The widespread concern about the present state of the language perhaps results from a conservative reaction to the threat of increased or sustained ethnic diversity in the nation.

The language of black Americans, one of the most prominent ethnic minorities in the United States, has been studied especially from the standpoint of its relationship to the language of whites. Two questions are involved (Fasold 1981): (1) How different are the speechways of present-day blacks and whites? (2) What was the origin of **black English**, that is, the typical language of blacks, especially as it differs from that of their white neighbors?

The extent of the present-day linguistic differences between blacks and whites has often been exaggerated. There are differences in word choice through which black vocabulary exerts a steady and enriching influence on the language of whites; for example, *nitty-gritty* is a black contribution of relatively recent years, *jazz* is an older one, and *yam* a much older one. There are differences of pronunciation; for example, the typical black pronunciation of *aunt* as [ɑnt] is unusual for most whites in the United States (although it is the standard British way of saying the word), and blacks are more likely than whites to drop the [t] from words like *rest* and *soft*. There are differences in grammar; for example, blacks are more likely than whites to use **consuetudinal be** (uninflected *be* to denote habitual or regular action, as in "She be here everyday") and are more likely to delete forms of *be* in other uses (as in "She here now"). Most differences—whether of vocabulary, pronunciation, or grammar—tend, however, to be matters of degree rather than of kind. The differences between black and white speech are seldom of such magnitude as to impede communication, when a will to communicate exists.

The origin of black English has been attributed to two sources. On the one hand, it is said that blacks first acquired their English from the whites among whom they worked on the plantations of the New World, and therefore their present English reflects the kind of English their ancestors learned several hundred years ago, modified by generations of segregation. On the other hand, it is said that blacks, who spoke a number of different African for communication between those without a common tongue—perhaps based on Portuguese, African languages, and English. Because they had no other common language, the pidgin was **creolized**, that is, became the native and full language of the plantation blacks and eventually was assimilated to the English spoken by the whites around them, so that today there are few of the original **creole** features still remaining in black English. The difference between the two historical explanations is chiefly how they explain the divergent features between black and white speech. In the first explanation, those differences are supposed to be African features introduced by blacks into the English they learned from whites or else they are survivals of archaic features otherwise lost from the speech of whites. In the second explanation, they are supposed to be the remnants of the original creole, which over the years has been transformed gradually, by massive borrowing from white English, into a type of language much closer to the speech of whites than it originally was. The historical reality was certainly more complex than either view alone depicts, but both explanations doubtless have some truth in them. The passion with which one or the other view is often held is probably a consequence of emotional attitudes quite independent of the facts themselves.

STYLISTIC VARIATION

Stylistic variation is the major concern of those who write about language in the popular press, although such writers may not have much knowledge about language. A widespread suspicion among the laity that our language is somehow deteriorating becomes the opportunity for journalistic and other hucksters to peddle their nostrums. The usage huckster plays upon the insecurity and apprehensions of readers. ("Will America be the death of English?" ominously asked one guru.) Such linguistic alarmism does no good, other than making a buck for the alarmist, but it also does little harm; it is generally ineffectual.

The best-known and perhaps the best of the popular usage guides is the pleasantly magisterial *Dictionary of Modern English Usage* (1965) by H. W. Fowler. It enjoys considerable prestige in both England and America, doubtless because it makes such beguiling reading. Although Fowler's obiter dicta on usage are sometimes idiosyncratic, they are always well expressed and usually sensible. Those who write as Fowler recommends may occasionally sound a bit odd, but they will certainly write better than they would otherwise.

One stylistic variety that is of perennial interest is **slang**, primarily because it continually renews itself. Slang is a deliberately undignified form of speech whose use implies that the user is "in" or especially knowledgeable about the subject of the slang term; it may be irresponsible language (such as a sexual or scatological taboo term) signaling that the speaker is not part of the Establishment, or it may be protective language that disguises unpleasant reality (such as *waste* for 'kill') or saves the user from fuller explanation (such as *dig you* for 'like, love, desire, sympathize with you'). No single term will have all of these characteristics, but all slang shares several of them (Dumas and Lighter 1978). Because of its changeability, slang is hard to study; the best glossary of current slang is the *Dictionary of American Slang* (Wentworth and Flexner 1975). A new dictionary of slang on historical principles is under preparation by Jonathan Lighter at the University of Tennessee.

The Essential Oneness of All English

We have now come to an end of our comparative survey of the present state of English. What should have emerged from the treatment is a conception of the essential unity of the English language in all its national, regional, social, and stylistic manifestations. What, then, it may be asked, *is* the English language? Is it the speech of London, of Boston, of New York, of south Georgia, of Melbourne, of Montreal, of Calcutta? Is it the English of the metropolitan daily newspaper, of the bureaucratic memo, of the contemporary poet, of religious ritual, of football sportscasts, of political harangues, of loving whispers? A possible answer might be, none of these, but rather the sum of them all, along with all other blendings and developments that have taken place wherever what is thought of as the English language is spoken by those who have learned it as their mother tongue. The most important variety happens to be the standard English written by Britishers and Americans—and it should be clear by now that the importance of that language is due not to any inherent virtues it may possess, but wholly to the present importance in the affairs of the English-speaking world—some might go so far as to say of western European civilization—of those who write it.

For Further Reading

American and British English

Foster, *The Changing English Language*, 1968.
Foster, "Recent American Influence on Standard English," *Anglia*, 1956.
Marckwardt and Quirk, *A Common Language: British and American English*, 1964.
Moss, *What's the Difference? A British/American Dictionary*, 1973.
Schur, *English English*, 1980.
Zviadadze, *A Dictionary of Modern American and British English on a Contrastive Basis*, 1973.

British Dialects

Brook, *English Dialects*, 1965.
Hughes and Trudgill, *English Accents and Dialects: An Introduction to Social and Regional Varieties of British English*, 1979.
Wakelin, *English Dialects: An Introduction*, 1972.

Bailey and Robinson, *Varieties of Present-Day English*, 1973.
Ferguson and Heath, *Language in the USA*, 1981.
McDavid, *Varieties of American English*, 1980.
Mencken, *The American Language: The Fourth Edition and Two Supplements*, 1963.
Pederson, "Studies of American Pronunciation since 1945," *American Speech*, 1977.
Pyles, *Words and Ways of American English*, 1952.

American Regional Dialects

Allen, "Regional Dialects, 1945–1974," *American Speech*, 1977.
McDavid, "American English Dialects," in Francis, *The Structure of American English*, 1958.
Reed, *Dialects of American English*, 1977.
Shuy, *Discovering American Dialects*, 1967.
Williamson and Burke, *A Various Language: Perspectives on American Dialects*, 1971.

Sociolinguistics

Fasold, "The Relation between Black and White Speech in the South," *American Speech*, 1981.
Labov, *Language in the Inner City: Studies in the Black English Vernacular*, 1972.
Labov, *Sociolinguistic Patterns*, 1972.
Lakoff, *Language and Woman's Place*, 1975.
McDavid, *Dialects in Culture*, 1979.
Wolfram and Fasold, *The Study of Social Dialects in American English*, 1974.

Usage

Bryant, *Current American Usage*, 1962.
Creswell, *Usage in Dictionaries and Dictionaries of Usage*, 1975.
Fowler, *A Dictionary of Modern English Usage*, 1965.
Joos, *The Five Clocks*, 1967.
Pyles, *Thomas Pyles: Selected Essays on English Usage*, 1979
Quirk and Svartvik, *Investigating Linguistic Acceptability*, 1966.
Scargill, *Modern Canadian English Usage: Linguistic Change and Reconstruction*, 1974.

10 Words and Meanings

The sounds of a language change over a long period of time, so that even a familiar word like *night* comes to be quite different in its pronunciation from what our linguistic ancestors in the days of Alfred the Great would have regarded as normal. So too grammar has changed over a similar period, transforming English from a highly inflected language to one with few grammatical endings. Most English speakers probably have some awareness that sounds and grammar change, though they are likely to think of such change as deterioration, the lamentable effect of sloppy speech that indicates the language is going to the dogs. The kind of change that is most obvious, however, and that is consequently most interesting to the average person, is change in vocabulary. It is easy to observe, it is happening all the time, and it touches our daily lives with an unavoidable insistence.

Most people find the study of words and their meanings interesting and colorful. Witness in newspapers and magazines the numbers of letters to the editor, usually sadly misinformed, that are devoted to the uses and misuses of words. These are frequently etymological in nature, like the old and oft-recurring wheeze that sirloin is so called because King Henry VIII (or James I or Charles II) liked a loin of beef so well that he knighted one, saying "Arise, Sir Loin" at the conferring of the accolade. In reality, the term comes from

French *sur-* 'over, above' and *loin* and is thus a cut of meat from the top of the loin. It is likely, however, that the popular explanation of the knighting has influenced the modern spelling of the word.

Such fanciful tales appeal to our imagination and therefore are difficult to exorcise. The real history of words, however, is interesting enough to make unnecessary such fictions as that about the knighting of the steak. When the speakers of a language have need for a new word, they can make one up, borrow one from some other language, or adapt one of the words they already use by changing its meaning. The first two techniques for increasing the vocabulary will be the subjects of the next two chapters; the third will occupy our attention for the remainder of this one.

Semantics

Semantics, the study of meaning, is by no means limited to words and their histories. John Lyons (1977) and more briefly F. R. Palmer (1976) have usefully surveyed the field of semantics as it concerns linguistics, but it also concerns philosophy and, indeed, influences us in ways of which we are often quite unaware.

Some scholars have wondered whether the language we speak may not suggest or even determine the way we perceive the world. The idea that it may do so is known as the **Sapir-Whorf hypothesis**, after two linguists, Edward Sapir and Benjamin Lee Whorf, who proposed and popularized the concept (Sapir 1921; Whorf 1956). At the very least it seems probable that language calls our attention to some aspects of reality and away from others. Although the color spectrum is a continuum, we think of a rainbow as a series of stripes of red, orange, yellow, and so on, perhaps because we have names for those colors in our language; speakers of a language with different basic color terms might visualize the rainbow with different sorts of stripes, or in some other way altogether. A more extreme and far more interesting possibility is that our concepts of time, causation, agency, and the like owe something to the language we speak. It is certainly true that languages divide meaning into different semantic units, just as they divide sound into different phonological units. No two languages are pronounced in the same way, and none refer to experience in the same way. Yet how such differences influence thought is an open question. Linguists have generally given up trying to test the Sapir-Whorf hypothesis because they have not been able to devise satisfactory experiments, but the hypothesis remains an intriguing one.

On a more mundane and much firmer level is the influence of language on our daily activity and habits of thought. Because two persons can be referred to by the same word—for example, *Irishman*—we assume that they must be alike in certain stereotyped ways. (Thus we may unconsciously believe that all Irishmen have red hair, drink too much, and are quarrelsome.)

General Semantics, a study founded by Alfred Korzybski, is an effort to pay attention to such traps that language sets for us (Hayakawa 1978). Our concern in this chapter, however, is not with the studies of Korzybski and others, but rather with the ways in which the meanings of words change with time to allow us to talk about new things or about old things in a new light.

Why Meaning Varies

The attribution of some sort of meaning to combinations of distinctive speech sounds and in a few instances to single sounds is, in addition to being a natural process, a matter of social custom, and like other customs may vary with time, place, and situation: thus *tonic* may mean 'soft drink made with carbonated water' in parts of eastern New England, though elsewhere it usually means 'liquid medicinal preparation to invigorate the system' or in the phrase *gin and tonic* 'quinine water'; in the usage of musicians the same word may also mean the first tone of a musical scale. Moreover, many words in frequent use, like *nice*, *God*, and *democracy*, have, among speakers and writers of the same intellectual and social level, meanings that are more or less subjective and hence loose. All meanings of what is thought of as the same word, however, have certain elements in common—elements that may be said to operate within a certain field of meaning. If this were not true, there would be no communication.[1] But this is quite different from assuming the existence of "fixed," or "real," meanings.

Even though words do not have such inflexible meanings as we might prefer them to have, but only a field of meaning in which they operate and which may be extended in any direction or narrowed likewise, it is possible to be irritated at what we may consider a too imprecise use of words. For instance, after relating that he had seen a well-dressed man take the arm of a blind and ragged beggar and escort him across a crowded thoroughfare, a rather sentimental man remarked, "That was true democracy." It was, of course, only ordinary human decency, as likely to occur in a monarchy as in a democracy, and by no means impossible under an authoritarian government like, say, that of Oliver Cromwell or the Ayatollah Khomeini. The semantic element of the word *democracy* in the speaker's mind was kindness to those less fortunate than oneself. He approved of such kindness, as indeed we all do; it was "good," and "democracy" was also "good." Hence, as soft-minded people are quite prone to do, he equated democracy with goodness.

We are defeating the purpose of accurate communication when we use words so loosely. It is true that some words are by general consent used with a very loose meaning, and it is very likely that we could not get along without

---

[1] It is neither appropriate nor necessary here to go into the vexed philosophical question of what constitutes meaning—the "meaning" of *meaning*. C. K. Ogden and I. A. Richards (1946, pp. 185–208) recognized sixteen main and a number of subordinate senses.

a certain number of such words—*nice*, for instance, as in "She's a nice girl" (meaning that she has been well brought up, is kind, gracious, and generally well-mannered, or, with the word stressed, merely that she is chaste), in contrast to "That's a nice state of affairs" (meaning that it is a perfectly awful state of affairs). There is certainly nothing wrong with expressing pleasure and appreciation to a hostess by a heartfelt "I've had a very nice time," or even "I've had an awfully nice time." To seek for a more "accurate" word, one of more limited meaning, would be self-conscious and affected.

A large number of educated speakers and writers, for whatever reason, refuse to use *disinterested* in the sense 'uninterested, unconcerned,' a sense it previously had and lost for a while, and reserve the word for the meaning 'impartial, unprejudiced.' The criticized use has nevertheless gained ground at a terrific rate, and it is possible that before long it will completely drive out the other one. There will have been no great loss to language as communication. We shall merely have lost a synonym for *impartial* and acquired on all levels another way of saying 'uninterested' or 'unconcerned.' Educated readers of the future will be no more annoyed by the change than they are by similar changes that have given some of the words used in, say, the plays of Shakespeare and in the King James Bible different meanings for us from those that they had in early Modern English. Uneducated readers will be baffled and misled, to be sure; but simple people today frequently misinterpret the King James Bible (the only literature in early Modern English they are likely ever to read) with complete satisfaction to themselves. It is hardly feasible to expect language to stand still for the sake of ignorant people, who as a matter of fact manage quite well, as do the rest of us so long as our less informed fellows are restrained from forcibly imposing their interpretations of what they read, whether sacred or profane, on us.

Etymology and Meaning

The belief is widespread, even among some quite learned people, that the way to find out what a word means is to find out what it previously meant—or, preferably, if it were possible to do so, what it originally meant. That method is frequently used to deal with borrowed words, the mistaken idea being that the meaning of the word in current English and the meaning of the non-English word from which the English word is derived must be, or at any rate ought to be, one and the same. As a matter of fact, such an appeal to **etymology** to determine present meaning is as unreliable as would be an appeal to spelling to determine modern pronunciation. Change of meaning—**semantic change**, as it is called—may, and frequently does, alter the so-called **etymological sense**, which may have become altogether obsolete. (The etymological sense is only the earliest sense we can *discover*, not necessarily the very earliest.) The study of etymologies is, of course, richly rewarding. It may, for instance, throw a great deal of light on present meanings, and it frequently tells us something of the workings of the human mind in dealing with the phenomenon of meaning, but it is of very limited help in determining for us what a word "actually" means.

Certain popular writers, overeager to display their learning, have asserted that words are misused when they depart from their etymological meanings. Thus Ambrose Bierce once declared that *dilapidated*, because of its ultimate derivation from Latin *lapis* 'stone,' could appropriately be used only of a stone structure (Robertson 1954, p. 234). Such a notion, if true, would commit us to the parallel assertion that only what actually had roots could properly be eradicated, since *eradicate* is ultimately derived from Latin *rādix* 'root,' that *calculation* be restricted to counting pebbles (Lat. *calx* 'stone'), that *sinister* be applied only to leftists, and *dexterous* to rightists. By the same token we should have to insist that we could *admire* only what we could wonder at, inasmuch as the English word comes from Latin *ad* 'at' plus *mīrāri* 'to wonder';[2] or that *giddy* persons must be divinely inspired, inasmuch as *gid* is a derivative of *god* (*enthusiastic*, from the Greek, also had this meaning); or that only men may be virtuous, because *virtue* is derived from Latin *virtus* 'manliness,' itself a derivative of *vir* 'man.' Now, alas for the wicked times in which we live, *virtue* is applied to few men and not many women. *Virile*, also a derivative of *vir*, has retained all of its earlier meaning and has even added to it.

From these few examples, it must be obvious that we cannot ascribe anything like "fixed" meanings to words. What we actually encounter much of the time are meanings that are variable and that may have wandered from what their etymologies suggest. To suppose that invariable meanings exist, quite apart from context, is to be guilty of a type of naiveté that may vitiate all our thinking.

How Meaning Changes

Change of meaning—a phenomenon common to all languages—while frequently unpredictable, is not wholly chaotic. Rather, it follows certain paths that we might do well to familiarize ourselves with. First, it is necessary to distinguish between the **sense**, or literal meaning, of an expression and its **associations**. *Father, dad,* and *the old man* may all refer to the same person, but the associations of the three expressions are likely to be different, as are those of other synonymous terms like *pater, pops, daddy, sire, pappy, pa, dada, governor,* and *poppa.* Words change in both their senses and associations. A sense may expand to include more referents than it formerly had (**generalization**), contract to include fewer referents (**specialization**), or shift

---

[2] Compare Hamlet's use of *admiration* in the sense 'wonderment, amazement' in "Season your admiration for a while/With an attent eare" (1.2.192–93).

to include a quite different set of referents (**transfer of meaning**). The associations of a word may become worse (**pejoration**) or better (**amelioration**) and stronger or weaker than they formerly were. Each of these possibilities is examined below.[3]

Much, probably most, of the illustrative matter that follows, like that which precedes, has come from many books read over a long period of years. Some of the examples are by now more or less stock ones, but they make their point better than less familiar ones would do, and hence are used without apology, but with gratitude to whoever first dug them out. It is likely that many of them will be found in James Bradstreet Greenough and George Lyman Kittredge's old, but still good, *Words and Their Ways in English Speech* (1901).

Generalization and Specialization

An obvious classification of meaning is that based on the scope of things to which it can apply. That is to say, meaning may be generalized (extended, widened), or it may be specialized (restricted, narrowed). When we increase the scope of a word, we reduce the number of features in its definition that restrict its application. For instance, *tail* (from OE *tægl*) in earlier times seems to have meant 'hairy caudal appendage, as of a horse.' When we eliminated the hairiness (or the horsiness) from the meaning, we increased its scope, so that in Modern English the word means simply 'caudal appendage.' The same thing has happened to Danish *hale*, earlier 'tail of a cow.' In due course the cow was eliminated, and in present-day Danish the word means simply 'tail,' having undergone a semantic generalization precisely like that of the English word cited; the closely related Icelandic *hali* still keeps the cow in the picture.

Similarly, a *mill* was earlier a place for making things by the process of grinding, that is, for making meal. The words *meal* and *mill* are themselves related, as one might guess from their similarity. A mill is now simply a place for making things: the grinding has been eliminated, so that we may speak of a woolen mill, a steel mill, or even a gin mill. The word *corn* earlier meant 'grain' and is in fact related to the word *grain*. It is still used in this general sense in England, as in the "Corn Laws," but specifically it may there mean either oats (for animals) or wheat (for human beings). In American usage *corn* denotes 'maize,' which is of course not at all what Keats meant in his "Ode to a Nightingale" when he described Ruth as standing "in tears amid the alien corn." The building in which corn, regardless of its meaning, is stored is called a barn. *Barn* earlier denoted a storehouse for barley; the word is,

---

[3] Another kind of meaning change results from the use of a word as a new part of speech—for example, "When you write any committee member, be sure to *carbon* ['send a carbon copy to'] the executive secretary." Because a change of meaning like this creates a new part of speech and thus a new word, it will be considered in the next chapter.

in fact, a compound of two Old English words, *bere* 'barley' and *ærn* 'house.' By eliminating one of the features of its earlier sense, the scope of this word has been extended to mean a storehouse for any kind of grain. American English has still further generalized the term by eliminating the grain, so that *barn* may mean also a place for housing livestock.

The opposite of generalization is specialization, a process in which, by adding to the features of meaning, the referential scope of a word is reduced. *Deer*, for instance, used to mean simply 'animal' (OE *dēor*), as its German cognate *Tier* still does. Shakespeare writes of "Mice, and Rats, and such small Deare" (*King Lear* 3.4.144). By adding something particular (the family *Cervidae*) to the sense, the scope of the word has been reduced, and it has come to mean a specific kind of animal. Similarly *hound* used to mean 'dog,' as does its German cognate *Hund*. To this earlier meaning we have in the course of time added the idea of hunting and thereby restricted the scope of the word, which to us means a special sort of dog, a hunting dog. To the earlier content of *liquor* 'fluid' (compare *liquid*) we have added 'alcoholic.'

Meat once meant simply 'food,' a meaning that it retains in *sweetmeat* and throughout the King James Bible ("meat for the belly," "meat and drink"), though it acquired the meaning 'flesh' much earlier and had for a while both the general and the specialized meaning. *Starve* (OE *steorfan*) used to mean simply 'to die,' as its German cognate *sterben* still does. Chaucer writes, for instance, "But as hire man I wol ay lyve and sterve" (*Troilus and Criseyde* 1.427). A specific way of dying had to be expressed by a following phrase—for example, "of hunger, for cold." The *OED* cites "starving with the cold," presumably dialect, as late as 1867. The word came somehow to be associated primarily with death by hunger, and for a while there existed a compound verb *hunger-starve*. Usually nowadays we put the stress altogether on the added idea of hunger and lose the older meaning altogether. Although the usual meaning of *to starve* now is 'to die of hunger,' we also use the phrase "starve to death," which in earlier times would have been tautological. An additional, toned-down meaning grows out of **hyperbole**, so that "I'm starving" may mean only 'I'm very hungry.' The word, of course, is used figuratively, as in "starving for love," which, as we have seen, once meant 'dying for love.' This word furnishes a striking example of specialization and proliferation of meaning.

Transfer of Meaning

There are a good many special types of transfer of meaning. *Long* and *short*, for instance, are on occasion transferred from the spatial concepts to which they ordinarily refer and made to refer to temporal concepts, as in *a long time, a short while*; similarly with such nouns as *length* and *space*. **Metaphor** is involved when we extend the word *foot* 'lowest extremity of an animal' to all sorts of things, as in *foot of a mountain, tree,* and so forth. The meaning of the same word is shifted in a different way (by **metonymy**) when we add to its original sense something like 'approximate length of the human foot,' thereby making the word mean a unit of measure; we do much the same thing to *hand* when we use it as a unit of measure for the height of horses.

Meaning may be transferred from one sensory faculty to another (**synesthesia**), as when we apply *clear,* with principal reference to sight, to hearing, as in *clear-sounding. Loud* is transferred from hearing to sight when we speak of *loud colors. Sweet,* with primary reference to taste, may be extended to hearing (*sweet music*), smell ("The rose smells sweet"), and to all senses at once (*a sweet person*). *Sharp* may be transferred from feeling to taste, and so may *smooth. Warm* may shift its usual reference from feeling to sight, as in *warm colors,* and along with *cold* may refer in a general way to all senses, as in *a warm* (*cold*) *welcome.*

Abstract meanings may evolve from more **concrete** ones. Latin *cantus* 'the act of singing' came to acquire the more abstract meaning 'song.' In prehistoric Old English times the compound *understand,* as Leonard Bloomfield (1933, pp. 425, 429–30) points out, must have meant 'to stand among,' that is, 'close to'—*under* presumably having had the meaning 'among,' like its German and Latin cognates *unter* and *inter.* But this literal, concrete meaning gave way to the more abstract meaning that the word has today. Bloomfield cites parallel shifts from concrete to abstract in German *verstehen* ('to stand before'), Greek *epistamai* ('I stand upon'), Latin *comprehendere* ('to take hold of'), and Italian *capire,* based on Latin *capere* 'to grasp,' among others.

The first person to use *grasp* in an abstract sense, as in "He has a good grasp of his subject," was coining an interesting metaphor. But the shift from concrete to abstract, or from physical to mental, has been so complete that we no longer think of this usage as metaphorical: *grasp* has come to be synonymous with *comprehension* in contexts such as that cited, even though in other uses the word has retained its physical reference. It was similar with *glad,* earlier 'smooth,' though this word has completely lost the earlier meaning (except in the proper name *Gladstone,* if surnames may be thought of as having meaning) and may now refer only to a mental state. Likewise, meaning may shift from **subjective** to **objective**, as when *pitiful,* earlier 'full of pity, compassionate,' came to mean 'deserving of pity'; or the shift may be the other way round, as when *fear,* earlier 'danger,' something objective, came to mean 'terror,' a state of mind.

ASSOCIATION OF IDEAS

Change of meaning may be due simply to association of ideas. Latin *penna,* for instance, originally meant 'feather,' but came to be used to indicate an instrument for writing, whether made of a feather or not, because of the association of the quill with writing. Our word *pen* is ultimately derived from the Latin word, though it comes to us by way of Old French. Similarly, *paper* is from *papyrus*, a kind of plant, and the two were once invariably associated in people's minds, though paper is nowadays made from rags, wood, straw, and other fibrous materials, and this association has been completely lost. Sensational magazines used to be printed on paper of inferior quality made from wood pulp; they were referred to by writers, somewhat derisively, as wood-pulp magazines, or simply as the *pulps*, in contrast to the *slicks*, those printed on paper of better quality. Such "literature" has come up in the world, at least as far as its physical production is concerned, and many magazines whose reading matter is considered by serious-minded people to be of low quality are now printed on the slickest paper. They are nevertheless still referred to as "the pulps," and writers who keep the wolf from their door by supplying them with stories and articles are known as "pulp writers." Thus, because of an earlier association, the name of the physical product wood pulp has been applied to a type of periodical with reference to the literary quality of its contents. *Silver* has come to be used for eating utensils made of silver—an instance of **synecdoche**—and sometimes, by association, for the same articles when not made of silver, so that we may even speak of stainless steel silverware. The product derived from latex and earlier known as *caoutchouc* soon acquired a less difficult name, *rubber*, from association with one of its earliest uses, making erasures on paper by rubbing. *China* 'earthenware' originally designated porcelain of a type first manufactured in the country for which it is called, and the name of a native American bird, the *turkey*, derives from the fact that our ancestors somehow got the notion that it was of Turkish origin.[4] These names, like others that might be cited, arose out of associations long since lost.

THE EFFECT OF LATIN MEANINGS

In olden times, when every educated person knew Latin, Latin semantics might affect English word meanings. *Thing*, for example, meant in Old English 'assembly, sometimes for legal purposes,' a meaning that it had in the other Germanic languages and has retained in Icelandic, as in *Alþingi* 'all-assembly,' the name of the Icelandic parliament. English *thing* thus acquired from Latin *rēs*, which was used in much the same sense and was translated by *thing*, 'case at law' as one of its meanings. This meaning was subsequently lost, but because of the association, originally at one small point, the English word came to acquire every meaning that Latin *rēs* could have, which is to say, practically every other meaning of *thing* in present-day English. German *Ding* has had, quite independently, the same sense history. A word whose

---

[4] In French the same creature is called *dinde*, that is, *d'Inde* 'of or from India.' The French thought that America was India at the time when the name was conferred.

SOUND ASSOCIATIONS

Similarity or identity of sound may likewise influence meaning. *Fay*, from the Old French *fae* 'fairy' has influenced *fey*, from Old English *fǣge* 'fated, doomed to die' to such an extent that *fey* is practically always used nowadays in the sense 'spritely, fairylike.' The two words are pronounced alike, and there is an association of meaning at one small point: fairies are mysterious; so is being fated to die, even though we all are so fated. There are many other instances of such confusion through **clang association** (that is, association by sound rather than meaning). For example, in conservative use *fulsome* means 'offensively insincere' as in "fulsome praise," but it is often used in the sense 'extensive' because of the clang with *full*; *fruition* is from Latin *frui* 'to enjoy' by way of Old French, and the term originally meant 'enjoyment' but now usually means 'state of bearing fruit, completion' (Rex 1969); *fortuitous* earlier meant 'occurring by chance' but now is generally used as a synonym for *fortunate* because of its similarity to that word.

Pejoration and Amelioration

In addition to a change in its sense or literal meaning, a word may also undergo change in its associations. Such change is frequently due to ethical, or moral, considerations. A word may, as it were, go downhill, or it may rise in the world; there is no way of predicting what its career may be. *Politician* has had a downhill development in American English; in British English it is still not entirely without honor. *Knave* (OE *cnafa*), which used to mean simply 'boy'—it is cognate with German *Knabe*, which retains the earlier meaning—is another example of pejoration (from Lat. *pejor* 'worse'); it came to mean successively 'serving boy' (specialization), like that well-known knave of hearts[5] who was given to stealing tarts, and ultimately 'bad human being,' so that we may now speak of an old knave, or conceivably even of a knavish woman. On its journey downhill this word has thus undergone both specialization and generalization.

Boor, once meaning 'peasant,'[6] has had a similar pejorative development, as has *lewd*, earlier 'lay, as opposed to clerical,' and thereafter 'ignorant,' 'base,' and finally 'obscene,' which is the only meaning to survive. The same fate has befallen the Latin loanword *vulgar*, ultimately from *vulgus* 'the

---

[5] Actually a further specialization: the jacks in card games are called the knaves in upper-class British usage.

[6] Its cognate *Bauer* is the usual equivalent of *jack* or *knave* in German card playing, whence English *bower* (as in *right bower* and *left bower*) in certain card games such as euchre and five hundred.

common people'; the earlier meaning is retained in *Vulgar Latin*, the Latin that was spoken by the people up to the time of the early Middle Ages and was to develop into the various Romance languages. *Censure* earlier meant 'opinion.' In the course of time it has come to mean 'bad opinion'; *criticism* is well on its way to the same pejorative goal, ordinarily meaning nowadays 'adverse judgment.' The verbs *to censure* and *to criticize* have undergone a similar development. *Deserts* (as in *just deserts*) likewise started out indifferently to mean simply what one deserved, whether good or bad, but has come to mean 'punishment.' One other example of this tendency must suffice. *Silly* (OE *sǣlig*), earlier 'timely,' came to mean 'happy, blessed,' and subsequently 'innocent, simple'; then the simplicity, a desirable quality under most circumstances, was misunderstood (note the present ambiguity of *a simple man*), and the word took on its present meaning. Its German cognate *selig* progressed only to the second stage, though the word may be used facetiously to mean 'tipsy.'

Like *censure* and *criticize*, *praise* started out indifferently; it is simply *appraise* 'put a value on' with loss of its initial unstressed syllable (aphesis). But *praise* has come to mean 'value highly.' Here what has been added has ameliorated, or elevated, the semantic content of the word. The development of *nice*, going back to Latin *nescius* 'ignorant,' is similar. The Old French form used in English meant 'simple,' a meaning retained in Modern French *niais*. In the course of its career in English it has had the meanings 'foolishly particular' and then merely 'particular' (as in *a nice distinction*), among others. Now it often means no more than 'pleasant' or 'proper,' an all-purpose word of approbation.

Amelioration, the opposite of pejoration, is well illustrated by *knight*, which used to mean 'servant,' as its German relative *Knecht* still does. This particular word has obviously moved far from its earlier meaning, denoting as it usually now does a very special and exalted man who has been signally honored by his sovereign and who is entitled to prefix *Sir* to his name. *Earl* (OE *eorl*) once meant simply 'man,' though in ancient Germanic times it was specially applied to a warrior, who was almost invariably a man of good birth, in contrast to a *ceorl* (*churl*), or ordinary freeman. When under the Norman kings French titles were adopted in England, *earl* failed to be displaced but remained as the equivalent of the Continental *count*.

Taboo and Euphemism

Some words undergo pejoration because of a **taboo** against talking about the things they name; the replacement for a taboo term is a **euphemism** (from a Greek word meaning 'good-sounding'). Euphemisms, in their turn, are often subject to pejoration, eventually becoming taboo. Then the whole cycle starts again.

It is not surprising that superstition should play a part in change of meaning, as when *sinister*, the Latin word for 'left' (the unlucky side), acquired its present baleful significance. The verb *die*, of Germanic origin, is not once recorded in Old English. Its absence from surviving documents does not necessarily mean that it was not a part of the Old English word stock; however, in the writings that have come down to us, roundabout, toning-down expressions such as "go on a journey" are used instead, perhaps because of superstitions connected with the word itself—superstitions that survive into our own day, when people (at least those whom we know personally) "pass away," "go to sleep," or "go to their Great Reward." Louise Pound (1936) collected an imposing and—to the irreverent—amusing list of words and phrases used in referring to death in her article "American Euphemisms for Dying, Death, and Burial." She concluded that "one of mankind's gravest problems is to avoid a straightforward mention of dying or burial" (1936, p. 195).

Euphemism is especially frequent, and probably always has been, when we must come face to face with the less happy facts of our existence, for life holds even for the most fortunate of people experiences that are inartistic, violent, and hence shocking to contemplate in the full light of day—for instance, the first and last facts of human existence, birth and death, despite the sentimentality with which we have surrounded them. And it is certainly true that the sting of the latter is somewhat alleviated—for the survivors, anyway—by calling it by some other name, such as "the Great Adventure," "the flight to glory," and "the final sleep," which are among the many terms cited by Pound in the article just alluded to. *Mortician* is a much flossier word than *undertaker* (which is itself a euphemism with the earlier meanings 'helper,' 'contractor,' 'publisher,' and 'baptismal sponsor,' among others), but the *loved one* whom he prepares for public view and subsequent interment in a *casket* (earlier a 'jewel box,' as in *The Merchant of Venice*) is just as dead as a *corpse* in a *coffin*. Such verbal subterfuges are apparently thought to rob the grave of some of its victory; the notion of death is thus made more tolerable to human consciousness than it would otherwise be. Birth is much more plainly alluded to nowadays than it used to be, particularly by young married people. The free use of *pregnant* is not much older than World War II. A woman *with child, going to have a baby,* or *enceinte* used to deliver during her *confinement*, or, if one wanted to be really fancy about it, her *accouchement*.

Ideas of decency likewise profoundly affect language. All during the Victorian era, ladies and gentlemen were very sensitive about using the word *leg, limb* being almost invariably substituted, sometimes even if only the legs of a piano were being referred to. In the very year that marks the beginning of Queen Victoria's long reign, Captain Frederick Marryat noted in his *Diary in America* (1837) the American taboo on this word, when, having asked a young American lady who had taken a spill whether she had hurt her leg, she turned from him, "evidently much shocked, or much offended," later explaining to him that in America the word *leg* was never used in the presence of ladies. Later, the captain visited a school for young ladies where he saw, according to his own testimony, "a square pianoforte with four limbs," all dressed in little frilled pantalettes. For reasons that it would be difficult to analyze, a similar taboo was placed on *belly*, *stomach* being usually substituted for it, along with such nursery terms as *tummy* and *breadbasket* and the advertising copywriter's *midriff*.

   Toilet, a diminutive of French *toile* 'cloth,' in its earliest English uses meant a piece of cloth in which to wrap clothes; subsequently it came to be used for a cloth cover for a dressing table, and then the table itself, as when Lydia Languish in Sheridan's *The Rivals* says, "Here, my dear Lucy, hide these books. Quick, quick! Fling *Peregrine Pickle* under the toilet—throw *Roderick Random* into the closet."[7] There are other related meanings. The word came to be used in America as a euphemism for *privy*—itself, in turn, a euphemism, as are *latrine* (ultimately derived from Lat. *lavāre* 'to wash') and *lavatory* (note the euphemistic phrase "to wash one's hands"). But *toilet* is now frequently replaced by *rest room*, *comfort station*, *powder room*, or the coy *little boys'* (or *girls'*) *room*, and younger-generation speakers minding their manners invariably use *bathroom*, even though there may be no tub and no occasion for taking a bath. One may even hear of a dog's "going to the bathroom" in the living room. It is safe to predict that these evasions will in their turn come to be regarded as indecorous, and other expressions will be substituted for them.

   Euphemism is likewise resorted to in reference to certain diseases. Like that which attempts to prettify, or at least to mollify, birth, death, and excretion, this type of verbal subterfuge is doubtless deeply rooted in fear and superstition. An ailment of almost any sort, for instance, is nowadays often referred to as a *condition* (*heart condition*, *kidney condition*, *malignant condition*, and so forth), so that *condition*, hitherto a more or less neutral word, has thus had a pejorative development, coming to mean 'bad condition.'[8] *Leprosy* is no longer used by the American Medical Association because of its repulsive connotations; it is now replaced by the colorless *Hansen's disease*. *Cancer* may be openly referred to, though it is notable that a Hollywood astrologer, Carroll Righter, abandoned the term as a sign of the zodiac, referring instead to those born under Cancer as "Moon Children." The taboo has been removed from reference to the various specific venereal diseases, formerly *blood diseases* or *social diseases*.

   Old age and its attendant decay have probably been made more bearable

[7] Early in this century the direction for the disposal of *Roderick Random* would have been as risible as that for *Peregrine Pickle*, when *closet* was frequently used for *water closet*, now practically obsolete.

[8] Although *to have a condition* means 'to be in bad health,' *to be in condition* continues, confusingly enough, to mean 'to be in good health.'

for many elderly and decrepit people by calling them *senior citizens*. A similar verbal humanitarianism is responsible for *underprivileged* 'poor,' now largely supplanted by *disadvantaged*; *sick* 'insane'; *exceptional child* 'a pupil of subnormal mentality';[9] and a good many other voguish euphemisms. In the last cited example, pejoration has also operated—unless it can be conceived generally that being below par intellectually is a desirable thing, as the schools would seem to have supposed. One wonders whether to the next generation an "exceptional person" will be thought of as a dull and stupid one, that is, an exceptional child grown to maturity, and whether the "exceptional bargains" offered by the stores had not better be passed up in favor of merely average ones.

Sentimental equalitarianism has led us to attempt to dignify humble occupations by giving them high-sounding titles: thus a *janitor* (originally a doorkeeper, from *Janus*, the doorkeeper of heaven in Roman mythology) has in many parts of America become a *custodian*, and there are many engineers who would not know the difference between a calculator and a cantilever. H. L. Mencken (1936, pp. 289–91) cites, among a good many others, *demolition engineer* 'house wrecker,' *sanitary engineer* 'garbage man,' and *extermination engineer* 'rat catcher.' The meaning of *profession* has been generalized to such an extent that it may include practically any trade or vocation. *Webster's Third* illustrates the extended sense of the word with quotations referring to the "old profession of farming" and "men who make it their profession to hunt the hippopotamus." The term has also been applied to plumbing, waiting on tables, and almost any other gainful occupation. Such occupations may be both useful and honorable, but they are not professions according to the undemocratic and now perhaps outmoded sense of the term. As long ago as 1838 James Fenimore Cooper in *The American Democrat* denounced such democratic subterfuges as *boss* for *master* and *help* for *servant*, but these seem very mild nowadays. One of the great concerns of the democratic and progressive age in which we live would seem to be to ensure that nobody's feelings shall ever be hurt—at least not by words.

It is characteristic of the human mind, in varying degrees of course, to identify words with objects, persons, and ideas—to think much of the time not in terms of the actual situations of flesh-and-blood life, but in relation to words, like that oft-quoted little girl who, upon first seeing a pig, remarked that it was certainly rightly named, for it was a very dirty animal. But a pig by any other name—even if it were called a rose—would smell as bad. What one happens to call it—*Schwein, lechón, porco*, or *pig*—makes no difference in the nature of the creature, nor is one name any more appropriate than another. To suppose that our term is superior—that a pig really *is* a pig and hence that we who speak English are more perceptive than foreigners in

[9] Although children who exceed expectations have been stigmatized by the schools as *overachievers*, they are also sometimes called *exceptional*, apparently because of an assumption that any departure from the average is disabling.

calling it by its "right" name—is so naive that no one would own to such a belief. Yet it is certainly true that in their everyday lives people frequently act as though they thought words were identical with what they designate.

During World War II the name of a widely known and highly satisfactory pencil was changed from Mikado to Mirado—a hardly noticeable change, involving a single letter. Yet it is doubtful that the manufacturer would have gone to so much trouble and expense in making that little change had he not been convinced that, with Japan as our enemy, many patriots would refuse to buy a pencil named for its emperor, although no sane person could imagine that the pencil was a whit superior because of the change of name.

The Fate of Intensifying Words

Words rise and fall not only on a scale of goodness, by amelioration and pejoration, but also on a scale of strength. **Intensifiers** constantly stand in need of replacement, because they are so frequently used that their intensifying force is worn down. As an adverb of degree, *very* has only an intensifying function; it has altogether lost its independent meaning 'truly,' though as an adjective it survives with older meanings in phrases like "the very heart of the matter" and "the very thought of you." Chaucer does not use *very* as an intensifying adverb; the usage was doubtless beginning to be current in his day, though the *OED* has no contemporary citations. The *verray* in Chaucer's description of his ideal soldier, "He was a verray, parfit gentil knyght," is an adjective; the meaning of the line is approximately 'He was a true, perfect, gentle knight.'

For Chaucer and his contemporaries, *full* seems to have been the usual intensifying adverb, though Old English *swīðe* (the adverbial form of *swīð* 'strong') retained its intensifying function until the middle of the fifteenth century, with independent meanings 'rapidly' and 'instantly' surviving much longer. *Right* was also widely used as an intensifier in Middle English times, as in Chaucer's description of the Clerk of Oxenford: "he nas [that is, *ne was*] nat right fat," which is to say, 'He wasn't very fat.' This usage survives formally in *Right Reverend*, the title of a bishop; in *Right Honourable*, that of members of the Privy Council and a few other dignitaries; and in *Right Worshipful*, that of most lord mayors; as also in the more or less informal usages *right smart*, *right well*, *right away*, *right there*, and the like.

Sore, as in *sore afraid*, was similarly long used as an intensifier for adjectives and adverbs; its use to modify verbs is even older. Its cognate *sehr* is still the usual intensifier in German, in which language it has completely lost its independent use.

In view of the very understandable tendency of such intensifying words to become dulled, it is not surprising that we should cast about for other words to replace them when we really want to be emphatic. "It's been a very pleasant instead say, "It's been an *awfully* pleasant evening"; "*very* nice" may likewise become "*terribly* nice." In negative utterances, *too* is coming to be widely used as an intensifier: "Newberry's not *too* far from here"; "Juvenile-court law practice is not *too* lucrative." Also common in negative statements and in questions are *that* and *all that*: "I'm not *that* tired"; "Is he *all that* eager to go to Daytona?"

Prodigiously was for a while a voguish substitute for *very*, so that a Regency "blood" like Thackeray's Jos Sedley might speak admiringly of a shapely woman as "a prodigiously fine gel" or even a "monstrous fine" one. The first of these now-forgotten intensifiers dates approximately from the second half of the seventeenth century; the second is about a century earlier. An anonymous contributor to the periodical *The World* in 1756 deplored the "pomp of utterance of our present women of fashion; which, though it may tend to spoil many a pretty mouth, can never recommend an indifferent one"; the writer cited in support of his statement the overuse by fashionable women of *vastly, horridly, abominably, immensely,* and *excessively* as intensifiers (Tucker 1974, p. 96).

Some Circumstances of Semantic Change

The meaning of a word may vary even with the group in which it is used. For all speakers *smart* has the meaning 'intelligent,' but there is a specialized class usage in which it means 'fashionable.' The meaning of *a smart woman* may thus vary with the social group of the speaker; it may indeed have to be inferred from the context. The earliest meaning of this word seems to have been 'sharp,' as in *a smart blow. Sharp* has also been used in the sense 'up-to-date, fashionable,' as in *a sharp dresser*, by speakers who admire a particular type of "sharpness."

Similarly, a word's meaning may vary according to changes in the thing to which it refers. *Hall* (OE *heall*), for instance, once meant a very large roofed place, like the splendid royal dwelling place Heorot in which Beowulf fought Grendel. Such buildings were usually without smaller attached rooms, though Heorot had a "bower" (*būr*), earlier a separate cottage, but in *Beowulf* a bedroom to which the king and queen retired. (This word survives only in the sense 'arbor, enclosure formed by vegetation.') For retainers the hall served as meeting room, feasting room, and sleeping room. Later *hall* came to mean 'the largest room in a great house,' used for large gatherings such as receptions and feasts, though the use of the word for the entire structure survives in the names of a number of manor houses such as Little Wenham Hall and Speke Hall in England. There are a number of other meanings, all connoting size and some degree of splendor, and all a far cry from the modern American use of *hall* as a narrow passageway leading to rooms or the modern British use as a vestibule or entrance passage immediately inside the front door of a small house. The meaning of *hall* must be determined by the context in which it occurs.

Akin to what we have been considering is modification of meaning as the result of a shift in point of view. *Crescent*, from the present participial form of Latin *cresco*, used to mean simply 'growing, increasing,' as in Pompey's "My powers are Cressent, and my Auguring hope/Sayes it will come to'th'full" (*Antony and Cleopatra* 2.1.10–11). The new, or growing, moon was thus called the crescent moon. There has been a shift, however, in the dominant element of meaning, the emphasis coming to be put entirely on shape, specifically on a particular shape of the moon, rather than upon growth. *Crescent* thus came to denote the moon between its new and quarter phases, whether increasing or decreasing, and then any similar shape. Similarly, in *veteran* (Lat. *veterānus*, a derivative of *vetus* 'old'), the emphasis has shifted from age to military service, though not necessarily long service: a veteran need not have grown old in service, and we may in fact speak of a *young veteran*. The fact that etymologically the phrase is self-contradictory is of no significance as far as present usage is concerned. The word is, of course, extended to other areas—for instance, *veteran politician*; in its extended meanings it continues to connote long experience and usually mature years as well.

THE VOGUE FOR WORDS OF LEARNED ORIGIN

When learned words acquire popular currency, they almost inevitably acquire at the same time new, less exact, meanings, or at least new shades of meaning. *Philosophy*, for instance, earlier 'love of wisdom,' has now a popular sense 'practical opinion or body of opinions,' as in "the philosophy of salesmanship," "the philosophy of Will Rogers," and "homespun philosophy." An error in translation from a foreign language may result in a useful new meaning—for example, *psychological moment*, now 'most opportune time' rather than 'psychological momentum,' which is the proper translation of German *psychologisches Moment*, the ultimate source of the phrase. The popular misunderstanding of *inferiority complex*, first used to designate an unconscious sense of inferiority manifesting itself in assertive behavior, has given us a synonym for *diffidence, shyness*. It is similar with *guilt complex*, now used to denote nothing more psychopathic than a feeling of guilt. The term *complex*, as first used by psychoanalysts more than half a century ago, designated a type of aberration resulting from the unconscious suppression of more or less related attitudes. The word soon passed into voguish and subsequently into general use to designate an obsession of any kind—a bee in the bonnet, as it were. Among its progeny are *Oedipus complex*, *herd complex*, and *sex complex*. The odds on its increasing fecundity would seem to be rather high.

Other fashionable terms from psychoanalysis and psychology, with which our times are so intensely preoccupied, are *subliminal* 'influencing behavior below the level of awareness,' with reference to a very sneaky kind of advertising technique; *behavior pattern*, meaning simply 'behavior'; *neurotic*, with a wide range of meaning, including 'nervous, highstrung, artistic by temperament, eccentric, or given to worrying'; *compulsive* 'habitual,' as in *compulsive drinker* and *compulsive criminal*; and *schizophrenia* 'practically any mental or emotional disorder.'

It is not surprising that the newer, popular meanings of what were once more or less technical terms should generally show a considerable extension of the earlier, technical meanings. Thus, *sadism* has come to mean simply 'cruelty' and *exhibitionism* merely 'showing off,' without any of the earlier connotations of sexual perversion, as in fact the word *psychology* itself may mean nothing more than 'mental processes' in a vague sort of way. An intense preoccupation in the mid-twentieth century with what is fashionably and doubtless humanely referred to as *mental illness*—a less enlightened age than ours called it *insanity*, and people afflicted with it were said to be *crazy*—must to a large extent be responsible for the use of such terms as have been cited. Also notable is the already mentioned specialization of *sick* to refer to mental imbalance.

A great darling among the loosely used pseudoscientific **vogue words** of recent years is *image* in the sense 'impression that others subconsciously have of someone.' A jaundiced observer of modern life might well suppose that what one actually is is not nearly so important as the image of oneself that one is able—to use another vogue word—to *project*. If the "image" is phony, what difference does it make? In a time when political campaigns are won or lost by the impression a candidate makes on the television screen and therefore in opinion polls, *image* is all-important.

A particularly important kind of image to convey, especially for politicians, is the *father image*. Young people are apparently in great need of a *father figure* to *relate to*, just as they require a *role model* to achieve the most successful *life style*. The last-mentioned expression, which has all but replaced the earlier voguish *way of life*, may refer to casual dress, jogging, homosexuality, the use of a Jacuzzi hot tub, or a great many other forms of behavior that have little to do with what has traditionally been thought of as style. *Peer pressure* from one's *peer group* is often responsible for the adoption of one "style" or another; the voguish use of *peer* has doubtless seeped down from educationists, whose *expertise* in this, as in many other matters, is greatly admired, although not always richly rewarded, by the "sponsoring society."

Among the more impressive vogue words of the 1970s and early 1980s are *charisma* and *charismatic* '(having) popular appeal' (earlier, 'a spiritual gift, such as that of tongues or prophesy'). The original sense of *ambience* or *ambiance* 'surrounding atmosphere, environment' is still apparent in a report of "major changes in the social ambience of Wall Street" (*Time*, 29 October 1973, p. 121), but that meaning has shifted considerably in the description of a chair as "crafted with a Spanish ambience" (*Family Weekly*, 26 November 1972, p. 16) and has slipped away altogether in the puffery of a restaurant said to have "great food, served professionally in an atmosphere of ambiance" (*Manhattan East*, cited in *New Yorker*, 17 June 1974, p. 91). Other popular expressions of recent years are *scenario, paradigm,* and *bottom line*—the last was originally an accounting term referring to the final line of a financial report but has come to mean 'conclusion, clincher' (Russell and Porter 1973, pp. 251–54).

Computer jargon has been a rich source of vogue words in recent years. Although *input* and *output* have been around since the mid-eighteenth and nineteenth centuries, respectively, their current fashionableness results from an extension of their use for information fed into and spewed out of a computer. *Interface* is another nineteenth-century term for the touching surface between any two substances—for example, oil floating on the top of a pan of water; it was taken up in computer use to denote the equipment that presents the computer's work for human inspection, such as a typewriter printout or a CRT display. Now the word is used as a noun to mean just 'connection' and as a verb to mean 'connect' or 'work together smoothly.' It often takes dictionaries longer to catch up with such extended meanings of technical terms than it does to report wholly new words; among the voguish and semantically altered technical vocabulary that lexicographers have been slow to report are *catalyst, osmosis, out of synch, parameter,* and *syndrome* (Landau 1980).

DESEXED LANGUAGE

One of the awkward problems of English, and indeed of many languages, is a lack of means for talking about persons without specifying their sex. Apparently sexual differences have been so important for the human species and the societies its members have formed that most languages make obligatory distinctions between males and females in both vocabulary and grammar. On those occasions, however, when one wishes to discuss human beings without reference to their sex, the obligatory distinctions are bothersome and may be prejudicial. Consequently, in recent years many publishers and editors have tried to eliminate both lexical and grammatical bias toward the male sex.

The bias in question arises because of the phenomenon of **semantic marking**. A word like *sheep* is **unmarked** for sex, since it is applicable to either males or females of the species; there are separate terms **marked** for maleness (*ram*) and femaleness (*ewe*) when they are needed. If terms for all species followed this model, no problems would arise, but unfortunately they do not. *Duck* is like *sheep* in being unmarked for sex, but it has only one marked companion, namely, *drake* for the male. Because we lack a single term for talking about the female bird, we must make do with an ambiguity in the term *duck*, which refers either to a member of the species without consideration of sex or to a female. An opposite sort of problem arises with *lion* and *lioness*; the latter term is marked for femaleness, and the former is unmarked and therefore used either for felines without consideration of sex or for males of the species. The semantic features of these terms, as they relate to sex, can be shown as follows (+ means 'present,' − 'absent,' and ± 'unmarked'):

	SHEEP	RAM	EWE	DUCK	DRAKE	LION	LIONESS
Male	±	+	−	±	+	±	−
Female	±	−	+	±	−	±	+

Lions and ducks are quite unconcerned with what we call them, but as human beings we are very much concerned with what we call ourselves. Consequently, the linguistic problem of referring to men and women is both complex and emotional. *Woman* is clearly marked for femaleness, like *lioness*. Some persons interpret *man* as unmarked for sex, like *lion*. Others point out that it is so often used for males in contrast to females that it must be regarded as marked for maleness, like *drake*; they also observe that because of the male connotations of *man*, women are often by implication excluded from statements in which the word is used generically—for example, "Men have achieved great discoveries in science during the last hundred years." By such language we may be led unconsciously to assume that males rather than females are the achievers of our species. If, as some etymologists believe, the word *man* is historically related to the word *mind*, its original sense was probably something like 'the thinker,' and it clearly denoted the species rather than the sex. In present use, however, the word often is ambiguous, as in the example cited a few lines above. The ambiguity can be resolved by context: "Men (the species) are mortal" versus "Men (the sex) are at present shorter-lived than women." Nevertheless, ambiguity is sometimes awkward and often annoying to the linguistically sensitive.

By linguistic engineering editors and others have attempted to eliminate the ambiguity in recent years by substituting other words (such as *person*) whenever *man* might be used of both sexes. Thus we have *chairperson, anchor person* (for the one who anchors a TV news program), *layperson*, and even *straw person*. The new forms were bound to call forth some heavy-handed humor in the form of *woperson* and even more bizarre concoctions. But not all the new gaucheries have been created by jokesters; some are the products of humorless bureaucrats, such as the civil rights director for the Department of Health, Education and Welfare who complained that he could not enforce anti–sex discrimination laws because of "limited person power in the Office for Civil Rights" (quoted in the *Athens* [Ga.] *Banner-Herald*, 6 July 1975, p. 2).

Some Circumstances of Semantic Change

Other efforts to avoid sexual reference, such as *supervisor* in place of *foreman* and *flight attendant* in place of both *steward* and *stewardess*, are unfortunately pompous. On the other hand, *housespouse* as a replacement for both *housewife* and its newfound mate, *househusband*, has a lilt and a swagger that make it appealing.

The grammatical problems of sexual reference are especially great in the choice of a pronoun after indefinite pronouns like *everyone, anyone,* and *someone.* Following the model of unmarked *man,* handbooks have recommended unmarked *he* in expressions like "Everyone tried his best," with reference to a mixed group. The other generally approved option, "Everyone tried his or her best," is wordy and can become intolerably so with repetition, as in "Everyone who has not finished writing his or her paper before he or she is required to move to his or her next class can take it with him or her."

In colloquial English speakers long ago solved that problem by using the plural pronouns *they, them, their,* and *theirs* after indefinites: "Somebody's lost their book." Although still abjured by fastidious writers, such use of *they* and its forms is increasing in standard English and has in fact been recommended by progressive groups like the National Council of Teachers of English. Idealists have also proposed a number of invented forms to fill the gap, such as *thon* (from *that one*), *he'er, he/she,* and *shem* (Baron 1981), but almost no one has taken them seriously.

Language reformers in the past have not been notably successful in remodeling English nearer to their hearts' desire. The language has a way of following its own course and leaving would-be guides behind. Whether the current interest in desexing language will have more lasting results than other changes previously proposed and labored for is an open question. Unselfconscious speech has already partly solved the grammatical problem with the *everybody . . . they* construction. If the lexical problem is solved by the extended use of *person* and other epicene alternatives, we will have witnessed a remarkable influence by those who edit books and periodicals. Whatever the upshot, the contemporary concern is testimony to one kind of semantic sensibility among present-day English speakers.

Semantic Change Is Inevitable

It is a great pity that language cannot be the exact, finely attuned instrument that deep thinkers wish it to be. But the facts are, as we have seen, that the meaning of practically any word is susceptible to change of one sort or another, and some words have so many individual meanings that we cannot really hope to be absolutely certain of the sum of these meanings. But it is probably quite safe to predict that the members of the human race, *homines sapientes* more or less, will go on making absurd noises with their mouths at one another in what idealists among them will go on considering a deplorably sloppy and inadequate manner, and yet manage to understand one another well enough for their own purposes.

The idealists may, if they wish, settle upon Esperanto, Ido, Ro, Volapük, or any other of the excellent scientific languages that have been laboriously constructed. The game of constructing such languages is still going on. Some naively suppose that, should one of these ever become generally used, there would be an end to misunderstanding, followed by an age of universal brotherhood—the assumption being that we always agree with and love those whom we understand, though the fact is that we frequently disagree violently with those whom we understand very well. (Cain doubtless understood Abel well enough.)

But be that as it may, it should be obvious that, if such an artificial language were by some miracle ever to be accepted and generally used, it would be susceptible to precisely the kind of changes in meaning that have been our concern in this chapter as well as to such changes in structure as have been our concern throughout—the kind of changes undergone by those natural languages that have evolved over the eons. And most of the manifold phenomena of life—hatred, disease, famine, birth, death, sex, war, atoms, isms, and people, to name only a few—would remain as messy and hence as unsatisfactory to those unwilling to accept them as they have always been, no matter what words we use in referring to them.

For Further Reading

Bréal, *Semantics: Studies in the Science of Language*, 1900.

ETC.: A Review of General Semantics, various issues.

Hayakawa, *Language in Thought and Action*, 1978.

Lyons, *Semantics*, 1977.

Palmer, *Semantics: A New Outline*, 1976.

Pyles and Algeo, "Meaning," ch. 6 of *English: An Introduction to Language*, 1970.

Stern, *Meaning and Change of Meaning, with Special Reference to the English Language*, 1931.

Whorf, *Language, Thought, and Reality*, 1956.

Williams, *The Conflict of Homonyms in English*, 1944

11 New Words from Old

In the present state of our knowledge, there is, as we have seen, little point in speculating about the ultimate origins of words. But we can know with varying degrees of certainty a good deal about the making of words in historical times, and our principal concern in this chapter will be an examination of the various processes involved in the making. Those processes can be grouped into five major kinds, as new words are made by **creating** or by **combining**, **shortening**, **blending**, or **shifting** the uses of old words and morphemes.

Creating Words

ROOT CREATIONS

It is unlikely that very many words have come into being during an historical period that have not been suggested in one way or another by previously existing words.[1] An oft-cited example of a word completely without associations with any existing word or words (a **root creation**) is *Kodak*,

[1] A good many given names, encountered primarily in the American Deep South and the Southwest, but of a type current all over the United States, are doubtless pure root creations—for example, *Lugen, Zedro* (suggested by *Pedro*?), *Velpo, Phalla, Morta* (*Marta*?), and *Venrean*. These and scores of others are cited in "Onomastic Individualism in Oklahoma" (Pyles 1947) and in "Bible Belt Onomastics, or Some Curiosities of Anti-Pedobaptist Nomenclature" (Pyles 1959).

which made its first appearance in print in the *U.S. Patent Office Gazette* in 1888 and was, according to George Eastman, who invented the word as well as the device it names, "a purely arbitrary combination of letters, not derived in whole or in part from any existing word,"[2] though according to his biographer a very slight association was in fact involved in his use of the letter *k*, for his mother's family name began with that letter. *Nylon, Dacron,* and *Orlon* are similarly etymologyless words.[3]

ECHOIC WORDS

Sound alone is the basis of a limited number of words, called **echoic** or **onomatopoeic**, like *bang, burp, splash, tinkle, ping, bobwhite,* and *cuckoo*. Leonard Bloomfield (1933, p. 156) distinguished between words that are actually imitative of sound, like *meow, moo, bowwow,* and *vroom*—though as we have seen these differ from language to language—and those he called **symbolic** ("somehow illustrating the meaning more immediately than do ordinary speech-forms. . . . To the speaker it seems as if the sounds were especially suited to the meaning"), like *bump* and *flick*. Symbolic words regularly come in sets that rime (*bump, lump, clump, hump*) or alliterate (*flick, flash, flip, flop*). Both imitative and symbolic words frequently show doubling, sometimes with slight variation, as in *bowwow, choo-choo,* and *pe(e)wee*.

EJACULATIONS

Some words imitate more or less instinctive vocal responses to emotional situations. One of these **ejaculations**, *ouch*, is something of a mystery: it does not appear in British writing except as an Americanism. The *OED* derives it from German *autsch*, an exclamation presumably imitative of what a

---

[2] From a letter written by Eastman to the late John Matthews Manly in 1906, quoted by H. L. Mencken (1945, p. 342, n. 1).

[3] *Nylon* may not be quite etymologyless. According to *Context*, a Du Pont company publication (vol. 7, no. 2, 1978), when the material was first developed, it was called *polyhexamethyleneadipamide*. Realizing the stuff needed a catchier name than that, the company thought of *duprooh*, an acronym for "Du Pont pulls rabbit out of hat," but instead settled on *no-run* until it was pointed out that stockings made of the material were not really run-proof. So the spelling of that word was reversed to *nuron*, which was modified to *nilon* to make it sound less like a nerve tonic. Then, to prevent a pronunciation like "nillon," the company changed the *i* to *y*, producing *nylon*. Thus beneath that apparently quite arbitrary word lurks the English expression *no-run*. Most trade names are clearly suggested by already existing words. *Vaseline*, for instance, was made from German *Wasser* 'water' plus Greek *elaion* 'oil' (Mencken 1936, p. 172, n. 3); *Kleenex* was made from *clean*, and *Cutex* from *cuticle*, both with the addition of a rather widely used but quite meaningless pseudoscientific suffix *-ex*.

German exclaims at fairly mild pain, such as stubbing a toe or hitting a thumb with a tack hammer—hardly anything more severe, for when one is suffering really rigorous pain one is not likely to have the presence of mind to remember to say "Ouch!" The vocal reaction, if any, is likely to be a shriek or a scream. *Ouch* may be regarded as a conventional representation of the sounds actually made when one is in pain. The interesting thing is that the written form has become so familiar, so completely conventionalized, that Americans (and Germans) do actually say "Ouch!" when they have hurt themselves so slightly as to be able to remember what they *ought* to say under the circumstances.

Other such written representations, all of them highly conventionalized, of what are thought to be "natural utterances" have also become actual words—for instance, *ha-ha*, with the variant *ho-ho* for Santa Claus and other jolly fat men, and the girlish *tehee*, which the naughty but nonetheless delectable Alison gives utterance to in Chaucer's *Miller's Tale*, in what is perhaps the most indecorously funny line in English poetry. Now, it is likely that, if Alison were a real-life girl (rather than better-than-life, as she is by virtue of being the creation of a superb artist), upon receipt of the misdirected kiss she might have tittered, twittered, giggled, or gurgled under the decidedly improper circumstances in which she had placed herself. But how to write a titter, a twitter, a giggle, or a gurgle? Chaucer was confronted with the problem of representing by alphabetical symbols whatever the appropriate vocal response might have been, and *tehee*, which was doubtless more or less conventional in his day, was certainly as good a choice as he could have made. The form with which he chose to represent girlish glee has remained conventional. When we encounter it in reading, we think—and, if reading aloud, we actually say—[tihí],[4] and the effect seems perfectly realistic to us. But it is highly doubtful that anyone ever uttered *tehee*, or *ha-ha*, or *ho-ho*, except as a reflection of the written form. Laughter, like pain, is too paroxysmal in nature, too varying from individual to individual, and too unspeechlike to be represented accurately by symbols that are not even altogether adequate for the representation of speech sounds.

It is somewhat different with a vocal manifestation of disgust, contempt, or annoyance, which might be represented phonetically (but only approximately) as [č]. This was, as early as the mid-fifteenth century, represented as *tush*, and somewhat later less realistically as *twish*. *Twish* became archaic as a written form, but [təš] survives as a spoken interpretation of *tush*. As in the instances cited, and in others to be cited, sounds came first; then the graphic representation, always somewhat inadequate; then finally a new word in the language based on an interpretation of the graphic representation of what was in the beginning not a word at all, but—to use a modern term in describing it—merely something in the nature of a sound effect.

[4] It was presumably [tehé] in Alison's pre-vowel-shift pronunciation.

New Words from Old

Pish and *pshaw* likewise represent "natural" emotional utterances of disdain, contempt, impatience, irritation, and the like, and have become so conventionalized as to have been used as verbs.[5] Both began as something like [pš]. W. S. Gilbert combined two such utterances to form the name of a "noble lord," Pish-Tush, in *The Mikado*, with two similarly expressive ones, Pooh-Bah, for the overweeningly aristocratic "Lord High Everything Else."[6]

Pugh is imitative of the disdainful sniff with which many persons react to a bad smell, resembling a vigorously articulated [p]. But, as with the examples previously cited, it has been conventionalized because of the written form into an actual word pronounced [pyu] or prolongedly as [píyú]. *Pooh* (sometimes with reduplication as *pooh-pooh*) is a variant, with somewhat milder implications. The reduplicated form may be used as a verb, as in "He pooh-poohed my suggestion." *Fie*, used for much the same purposes as *pugh*, is now archaic; it likewise represents an attempt at imitation. *Faugh* is probably a variant of *fie*; so, doubtless, is *phew*. *Ugh*, in its purest form a tensing of the stomach muscles followed by a glottal stop, has not been conventionalized to quite the same extent when used as an exclamation of disgust or horror. As a grunt supposedly made by a comedy Indian it is, one hopes only facetiously, pronounced [əg].

The palatal click, articulated by placing the tongue against the palate and then withdrawing it, sucking in the breath, is an expression of impatience or contempt. It is also sometimes used in reduplicated form (there may in fact be three or more such clicks) in scolding children, as if to express shock and regret at some antisocial act. Its best-known written form nowadays is *tut(-tut)*, which has become a word in its own right, pronounced not as a click but according to the spelling. However, *tsk-tsk*, which is intended to represent the same click, is gaining ground with the pronunciation [tísktísk]. Older written forms are *tchick* and *tck* (with or without reduplication). *Tut(-tut)* has long been used as a verb, as in Bulwer-Lytton's "pishing and tutting" (1849) and Hall Caine's "He laughed and tut-tutted" (1894), both cited by the *OED*.

A sound we frequently make to signify agreement may be represented approximately as [m̀hḿ]. This is written as *uh-huh*, and the written form is altogether responsible for the pronunciation [əhə́]. The *p* of *yep* and *nope* was probably intended to represent the glottal stop frequently heard in the pronunciation of *yes*·(without -*s*) and *no*, but one also frequently hears [yɛp] and [nop], which may be pronunciations based on the written forms.

The form *brack* or *braak* is sometimes used to represent the so-called

---

[5] See the citation in *Webster's Third New International Dictionary* (1961), which combines both, s.v. *pish* ("pished and pshawed a little at what had happened").

[6] Yum-Yum, the name of the delightful heroine of the same opera, is similarly a conventionalized representation of sounds supposedly made as a sign of pleasure in eating. These have given us a new adjective, *yummy*, as yet more or less confined to juvenile use—but give it time.

Bronx cheer. Eric Partridge (1948, pp. 12, 83) has suggested, however, that Hamlet's "Buz, buz!" (2.2.396), spoken impatiently to Polonius, is intended to represent the vulgar noise also known as "the raspberry."[7]

Combining Words: Affixing

AFFIXES FROM OLD ENGLISH

New words are, however, much more commonly acquired by other processes, the most common of these being **affixation**, the use of prefixes and suffixes. Many affixes were at one time independent words, like the insignificant-seeming *a-* of *aside, alive, aboard*, and *a-hunting*, which was earlier *on*, with the usual old loss of *-n* in this word when unstressed and followed by a consonant (see p. 146), and the *-ly* of many adjectives, like *manly, godly*, and *homely*, which has developed from Old English *līc* 'body.' When so used, *līc* (which became *lic* and eventually *-ly* through lack of stress) originally meant something like 'having the body or appearance of': thus the literal meaning of, say, *manly* is 'having the body or form of a man.' Old English regularly added *-e* to adjectives to make adverbs of them (p. 119)—thus *riht* 'right,' *rihte* 'rightly.' Adjectives formed with *-lic* acquired adverbial forms in exactly the same way—thus *cræftlic* 'skillful,' *cræftlice* 'skillfully.' With the late Middle English loss of both final *-e* and final unstressed *-ch*, earlier Middle English *-lich* and *-liche* fell together as *-li* (*-ly*). Because of these losses, we do not ordinarily associate Modern English *-ly* with *like*, the Northern dialect form of the full word that ultimately was to prevail in all dialects of English. In Modern English the full form has been used again as a suffix— history thus repeating itself—as in *gentlemanlike* and *godlike*, which are quite distinct creations from *gentlemanly* and *godly*.

Other prefixes surviving from Old English times include the following:

AFTER-: as in *aftermath, aftereffect, afternoon*

BE-: the unstressed form of *by* (OE *bī*), as in *believe, beneath, beyond, behalf, between*

FOR-: either intensifying, as in *forlorn*, or negating, as in *forbid, forswear*

MIS-: as in *misdeed, misalign, mispronounce*

OUT-: Old English *ūt-*, as in *outside, outfield, outgo*

UN-: for an opposite or negative meaning, as in *undress, unafraid, un-English*

UNDER-: as in *understand, undertake, underworld*

---

[7] Julian Franklyn in his *Dictionary of Rhyming Slang* (1960) plausibly states that *raspberry* in this sense comes from the Cockney "rhyming slang" phrase *raspberry tart* for *fart*.

WITH-: 'against,' as in *withhold, withstand, withdraw*

Other suffixes that go back at least to Old English times are the following:

-DOM: Old English *dōm*, earlier an independent word that has developed into *doom*, in Old English meaning 'judgment, statute,' that is, 'what is set,' and related to *do*; as in *freedom, filmdom, gangsterdom*

-ED: used to form adjectives from nouns, as in *storied, crabbed, bowlegged*

-EN: also to form adjectives, as in *golden, oaken, leaden*

-ER: Old English *-ere*, to form nouns of agency, as in *singer, baby sitter, do-gooder*, a suffix that, when it occurs in loanwords—for instance, *butler* (from Anglo-French *butuiller* 'bottler, manservant having to do with wines and liquors') and *butcher* (from Old French, literally 'dealer in flesh of billy goats')—goes back to Latin *-ārius*, but that is nevertheless cognate with the English ending

-FUL: to form adjectives, as in *baleful, sinful, wonderful*, and, with secondary stress, to form nouns as well, as in *handful, mouthful, spoonful*

-HOOD: Old English *-hād*, as in *manhood* and *priesthood*, earlier an independent word meaning 'condition, quality'

-ING: Old English *-ung* or *-ing*, to form verbal nouns, as in *reading*

-ISH: Old English *-isc*, to form adjectives, as in *English* and *womanish*

-LESS: Old English *-lēas* 'free from,' also used independently and cognate with *loose*, as in *wordless, reckless, hopeless*

-NESS: to form abstract nouns from many adjectives (and some participles), as in *manliness, learnedness, obligingness*

-SHIP: Old English *-scipe*, to form abstract nouns, as in *lordship, fellowship, worship* (that is, 'worth-ship')

-SOME: Old English *-sum*, to form adjectives, as in *lonesome, wholesome, winsome* (OE *wynn* 'joy' plus *sum*)

-STER: Old English *-estre*, originally feminine, as in *spinster* 'female spinner' and *webster* 'female weaver,' but later losing all sexual connotation, as in *gangster* and *speedster*

-TH: to form abstract nouns, as in *health, depth, sloth*

-WARD: as in *homeward, toward, outward*

-Y: Old English *-ig*, to form adjectives as in *thirsty, greedy, bloody*[8]

---

[8] The **diminutive** *-y* (or *-ie*) of *Kitty, Jackie, baby*, and *hippie* (or *hippy*) is from another source and occurs first in Middle English times. The *-y* occurring in loanwords of Greek (*phlebotomy*), Latin (*century*), and French (*contrary*) origin may represent Greek *-ia* (*hysteria*), Latin *-ius, -ium, -ia* (*radius, medium, militia*), or French *-ie* (*perjury*), *-ee* (*army*). This *-y* is not a living suffix. Diminutive *-y* is living; that is, it is still available for forming new diminutives. Similarly, we continue to form adjectives with the *-y* from Old English *-ig*—for example, *jazzy, loony, tubby, iffy*.

Many of these affixes are still living, in that they may be used for the creation of new words. Most have been affixed to nonnative words, as in some of the examples cited—for instance, *mispronounce, obligingness,* and also *czardom, pocketful, Romish, coffeeless, orderly* (*-liness*), and *sugary* (*-ish*). A number of others very common in Old English times either have not survived at all or survive only as fossils, like *ge-* in *enough* (OE *genōg, genōh*), *afford* (OE *geforðian*), *aware* (OE *gewær*), *handiwork* (OE *handgeweorc*), and *either* (OE *ægðer,* a contracted form of *æg[e]hwæðer*). *And-* 'against, toward,' the English cognate of Latin *anti-,* survives only in *answer* (OE *andswaru,* literally 'a swearing against') and, in unstressed form with loss of both *n* and *d,* in *along* (OE *andlang*).

AFFIXES FROM OTHER LANGUAGES

Those languages with which English has had the closest cultural contacts —Latin, Greek, and French—have furnished a number of freely used affixes for English words. The combination of native and foreign morphemes began quite early and has never ceased, though in earlier times it was the English suffix that was joined to the borrowed word rather than the other way round, as in Old English *grammatisc* 'grammatish,' later supplanted by *grammatical.*[9] Since English has a lexicon culled from many sources, it is not surprising that one finds a good many **hybrid forms**.

One of the most commonly used prefixes of nonnative origin is Greek *anti-* 'against,' which, in addition to its occurrence in long-established learned words like *antipathy, antidote,* and *anticlimax,* has been freely used since the seventeenth century for new, mostly American, creations—for instance, *anti-Federalist, anti-Catholic, antitobacco, antislavery, antisaloon, antiaircraft,* and *antiabortion. Pro-* 'for' has been somewhat less productive. *Super-,* as in *superman, supermarket,* and *superhighway,* has even become an independent adjective in childish and familiar usage, as in "Our new car's super"; there is also a reduplicated form *superduper* 'very super.' Other foreign prefixes are *ante-, de-, dis-, ex-, inter-, multi-, neo-, non-, post-, pre-, pseudo-, re-, semi-, sub-,* and *ultra-.*

Borrowed suffixes that have been added to English words (whatever their ultimate origin) include, but are by no means limited to, the following:

-ESE: Latin *-ēnsis* by way of Old French, as in *federalese, journalese, educationese*

-(I)AN: Latin *-(i)ānus,* used to form adjectives from nouns, as in *Nebraskan, Miltonian*

-(I)ANA: from the neuter plural of the same Latin ending, which has a limited use nowadays in forming nouns from other nouns, as in *Americana, Menckeniana*

---

[9] For other examples, see Alistair Campbell (1959, pp. 206–07).

New Words from Old

-ICIAN: Latin -ic- plus -iānus, as in *beautician, mortician*, which, although linguistic pomposities, at least indicate the viability of the suffix

-IZE: Greek -izein, a very popular suffix for making verbs, as in *pasteurize, criticize, harmonize*

-OR: Latin, as in *chiropractor* and *realtor*, words never known to the ancients

-ORIUM: Latin, as in *pastorium* 'Baptist parsonage,' *crematorium* 'place used for cremation,' *cryotorium* 'place where frozen dead are stored until science can reanimate them'

One of the most used of borrowed suffixes is -al (Lat. -alis), which makes adjectives from nouns, as in *doctoral, fusional, harmonal*, and *tidal*. The continued productivity of that suffix can be seen in the decree of the chief censor for the NBC television network: "No frontal nudity, no backal nudity, and no sidal nudity" (quoted in the *Atlanta Constitution*, 19 June 1974, p. B-12).

VOGUISH AFFIXES

Though no one can say why—fashion would seem to be the principal determinant—certain affixes have been particularly popular during certain periods. For instance, -wise affixed to nouns and adjectives to form adverbs was practically archaic until approximately the 1940s, occurring only in a comparatively few well-established words, such as *likewise, lengthwise, otherwise*, and *crosswise*. The *OED* cites a few examples of its free use in modern times—for instance, *Cardinal-wise* (1677), *festoon-wise* (1743), and *Timothy* or *Titus-wise* (1876). But around 1940 a mighty proliferation of words in -wise began—for instance, *budgetwise, saleswise, weatherwise, healthwise*—and literally hundreds of others have continued to be invented: *drugwise, personalitywise, securitywise, timewise, salarywise*, and *fringe benefitwise*. Such use of -wise can hardly be written off as ephemeral. Because of their economy in circumventing such phrases as *in respect of* and *in the manner of*, many such new coinages are likely to become permanent additions to the language, despite all the objurgations of older-generation speakers. The sudden resuscitation of this suffix—an independent word so used even in Old English times, as in *rihtwīs* 'rightwise'—is incapable of explanation. There are no inhibitions whatever on its free employment in either American or British English, as in the winning coinage of Mrs. Lyndon B. (Lady Bird) Johnson: "Fabric-wise, I like this room best" (quoted in *Time*, 17 November 1961, p. 34).

Type has enjoyed a similar vogue and is well on its way to being a freely used suffix. With it, adjectives may be formed from nouns, as in "Both Methodists and Episcopalians have Catholic-type bishops with considerable authority" (Jacksonville *Florida Times-Union*, 5 December 1960, p. 1) and "undraped girls, in a 'Las Vegas-type revue'" (*Time*, 29 December 1961, p. 13).

Combining Words: Affixing

Like -*wise*, -*type* is also economical, enabling us to shortcut such locutions as *bishops of the Catholic type* and *a revue of the Las Vegas type.*

The suffix -*ize* has already been mentioned. Ultimately from Greek -*izein*, it has had a centuries-old life as a means of making verbs from nouns and adjectives, not only in English, but in other languages as well—for instance, French -*iser*, Italian -*izare*, Spanish -*izar*, and German -*isieren*. Many English words with this suffix are borrowings from French—for instance (with *z* for French *s*), *authorize*, *moralize*, *naturalize*; others are English formations (though some of them may have parallel formations in French)—for instance, *concertize*, *patronize*, *fertilize*; still others are formed from proper names—for instance, *bowdlerize*, *mesmerize*, *Americanize.*

This suffix became very productive around 1950, and dozens of new creations have come into being: *accessorize*, *moisturize*, *sanitize*, *glamorize*, *personalize* 'to mark with name, initials, or monogram,'[10] *tenderize*, and a good many others. The most widely discussed of all these creations, however, must surely be *finalize*, which descended to general usage from the celestial mists of bureaucracy, business, and industry, where nothing is merely ended, finished, or concluded. It is a great favorite of administrators of all kinds and sizes—including the academic. When *Webster's Third* quite properly listed the word, bellows of anger and groans of outraged propriety issued from editorial writers (notably of the *New York Times* and of *Life*), who seem with a few honorable exceptions to regard themselves as custodians of the English language.

Greek formed nouns of action from verbs in -*izein* by modifying the ending to -*ismos* or -*isma*, as reflected in many pairs of loanwords in English, such as *ostracize–ostracism* and *criticize–criticism*. Several new uses of the suffix -*ism* have developed. The prejudice implied in *racism* has extended to *sexism*, *ageism*, and *speciesism* 'human treatment of other animals as mere objects.' Other recently popular derivatives are *Me-ism* 'selfishness,' *foodism* 'gluttony,' *volunteerism* 'donated service,' and *presidentialism* 'respect for and confidence in the office of president.' The suffix -*ism* also may be used as an independent word, as in *creeds and isms*. Such use of suffixes must be rather rare, though -*ology* has also been so used to mean 'science,' as in "Chemistry, Geology, Philology, and a hundred other ologies."[11] Prefixes have fared somewhat better; *anti-*, *pro-*, *con-*, and *ex-*, are all used as nouns.

De-, a prefix of Latin origin with negative force, is still much alive. Though many words beginning with it are from Latin or French, it has for centuries been used for the formation of new words. *Demoralize* was claimed by Noah Webster as his only coinage, and it is a fact that he was the first to use it in English; but it could just as well be from French *démoraliser*. The

[10] In other senses—for example, 'personify'—this word is considerably older but is almost certainly a new creation in the sense specified.

[11] Cited from 1811 in the *OED*, whose latest citation is from 1884. An extensive, though still incomplete, list of words with these endings is -*Ologies & -Isms* (Zettler 1978).

New Words from Old

prefix is used before words of whatever origin, as in *defrost, dewax,* and *debunk.* Sir Ernest Gowers (1954, p. 54) cites, from a collection of "septic verbs" made by Sir Alan Herbert, such poisonous specimens as *debureaucratise, dewater, deinsectize,* and *deratizate* 'get rid of rats,' and he reports *defeathered geese* from a directive issued by the British Ministry of Food. Two other *de-* words from Herbert's Index seem considerably less septic nowadays than they must have when the list was made—*decontaminate* and *dehumidify,* which we have learned to take in our stride, though they seem to be merely pompous ways of saying 'purify' and 'dry out.' A somewhat different sense of the prefix in *debark* has led to *debus, detrain,* and *deplane. Dis-,* likewise from Latin, is also freely used in a negative function, particularly in officialese, as in *disincentive* 'deterrent,' *disassemble* 'take apart,' and *dissaver* 'one who does not save money.'

Perhaps as a result of the decision during the 1970s that smaller is better, the prefix *mini-* enjoyed maxi use. Among the new combinations into which it entered were *minibikini, mini–black holes, minicar* and *minibus, minicam* 'miniature camera,' *minicinema* and *minimovie,* the seemingly contradictory *miniconglomerate* and *minimogul, minilecture, minimall,* and *minirevolution.* The form *mini,* which is a short version of *miniature,* came to be used as an independent adjective, and even acquired a comparative form, as in "Fortunately, the curator of ornithology decided to give another talk, mini-er than the first" (*New Yorker,* 17 February 1975, p. 27).

Other voguish affixes are *non-,* from Latin, used according to Gowers (1954, p. 57) "to turn any word upside-down," as in *nonsick* 'healthy' and *nonavailability* 'lack';[12] *-ee,* from French, as in *hijackee, hiree* 'new employee,' *integratee, mentee* 'person receiving the attention of a mentor,' *returnee* 'returner,' and *trustee;* and *re-,* from Latin, as in *re-decontaminate* 'purify again,' *recivilianize* 'return to civilian life,' and *recondition* 'repair, restore.' The scientific suffix *-on,* from Greek, has been widely used in recent years to name newly discovered substances like *interferon* in the human bloodstream and newly posited subatomic particles like the *gluon* and the *graviton.* Perhaps an extension of the *-s* in disease names like *measles* and *shingles* has supplied the ending of words like *dumbs* and *smarts,* as in "The administration has been stricken with a long-term case of dumbs" and "He's got street-smarts" (that is, 'is knowledgeable about the ways of life in the streets')

New suffixes are still being introduced into English. From such Yiddishisms as *nudnik,* but reinforced by the Russian *sputnik,* comes *-nik,* generally used in a derogatory way: *beatnik, no-goodnik, peacenik* 'pacifist,' *foundationnik* 'officer of a foundation,' and *refusednik* 'person denied a visa to enter or

---

[12] *Non-* has also developed two new uses: first, to indicate a scornful attitude toward the thing denoted by the main word, as in *nonbook* 'book not intended for normal reading, such as a coffee-table art book'; and second, to indicate that the person or object denoted by the main word is dissimulating or has been disguised, as in *noncandidate* 'candidate who pretends not to be running for office' (Algeo 1971).

leave Russia.' Of uncertain origin, but perhaps combining the ending of such Spanish words as *amigo, chicano,* and *gringo* with the English exclamation *oh,* is a relatively new suffix used to form nouns like *ammo, cheapo* 'stingy person,' *combo, daddy-o, kiddo, politico, saccharino* 'flattery,' *sicko* 'psychologically unstable person,' *supremo* 'leader,' *weirdo, wrongo* 'mistake'; adjectives like *bizarro* 'bizarre,' *blotto* 'drunk,' *sleazo* 'sleazy,' *socko* and *boffo* 'highly successful,' and *stinko*; and exclamations like *cheerio* and *righto.* Equally voguish are a number of affixes that have been created in English by a process of blending: *agri-, docu-, Euro-, petro-,* and *syn-*; *-aholic, -ateria, -gate, -rama,* and *-thon.* These new affixes and the process through which they come into being are discussed below (pp. 280–81).

Combining Words: Compounding

A **compound** is made by putting two or more words together to form a new word with a meaning in some way different, if only in being more specific, from that of its elements—for instance, a *blackboard* is not the same thing as a *black board*; indeed, nowadays many blackboards are green, or some other color. Compounds may be variably spelled solid, hyphenated, or open (*hatchback, laid-back, call back*), as explained below.

Compounding has been very common in English, as in other Germanic languages as well, from earliest times. Old English has *blīðheort* 'blithe-heart(ed),' *eaxlgestella* 'shoulder-companion, that is, comrade,' *brēostnet* 'breast-net, that is, corslet,' *leornungcniht* 'learning retainer (knight), that is, disciple,' *wǣrloga* 'oath-breaker, devil (warlock),' *woroldcyning* 'world, that is, earthly-king,' *fullfyllan* 'to fulfill,' and many other such compound words.

The compounding process has gone on continuously. During the 1970s, for instance, the American people heard and read such new nouns as *role model* 'person whose behavior is to be imitated,' *test-tube baby* 'baby conceived by fertilization of an egg outside the womb,' *boat people* 'refugees, especially from Southeast Asia, who travel by boat,' *cooktop* 'plate with embedded heating elements,' and *gas guzzler* 'automobile requiring large amounts of gasoline.' They encountered such new verbs as *blow-dry* 'style hair with a blow dryer,' *downsize* 'design on a smaller scale,' *tailgate* 'have a picnic on the tailgate of a station wagon,' and *mainstream* 'integrate the handicapped with other children in regular classes.' They used such new adjectives as *off-the-wall* 'unconventional,' *born-again* 'evangelical,' *no-frills* 'without nonessentials,' *pro-life* 'antiabortionist,' and *upscale* 'above average in income and education.'[13] Although some of those compounds are older than the 1970s, they all came into widespread use during that decade.

[13] These words are all from the annual editorial lists of "New Words and Meanings" for the 1975–80 revisions of *The World Book Dictionary,* ed. Clarence L. Barnhart and Robert K. Barnhart.

As far as writing is concerned, compound adjectives are usually hyphenated, like *one-horse, loose-jointed,* and *front-page,* though some that are particularly well established, such as *outgoing, overgrown, underbred,* and *forthcoming,* are solid. It is similar with compound verbs, like *overdo, broadcast, sidestep,* beside *double-date, baby-sit,* and *goose-step,* though these sometimes occur as two words. With the writing of compound nouns the situation is likewise somewhat inconsistent: we write *ice cream, Boy Scout, real estate, post office, high school* as two words; we hyphenate *sit-in, go-between, fire-eater, higher-up;* we write solid *firearm, icebox, postmaster, highball.* But hyphenation varies to some extent with the dictionary one consults, the style books of editors and publishers, and individual whim, among other things. Many compound prepositions like *upon, throughout, into,* and *within* are written solid, but others like *out of* have a space. Also written solid are compound adverbs such as *nevertheless, moreover,* and *henceforth* and compound pronouns like *whoever* and *myself.*[14]

A more significant characteristic of compounds—one that tells us whether we are dealing with two or more words used independently or as a unit—is their tendency to be more strongly stressed on one or the other of their elements, in contrast to the more or less even stresses characteristic of phrases. A *man-eating shrimp* would be a quite alarming marine phenomenon; nevertheless, the sharply contrasting primary and secondary stresses of *man* and *eat* (symbolized by the hyphen) make it perfectly clear that we are here concerned with a hitherto unheard-of anthropophagous decapod. There is, however, nothing in the least alarming about a *man eating shrimp,* with approximately even stresses on *man* and *eat.*

This type of stress in compounds marks the close connection between the constituents that gives them their special meanings. In effect, it welds together the elements and thus makes the difference between the members of the following pairs:

HÓTBÈD: 'place that encourages rapid growth'	HOT BED: 'warm sleeping place'
HÍGHBRÒW: 'intellectual'	HIGH BROW: 'result of receding hair'
BLÁCKBÀLL: 'vote against'	BLACK BALL: 'ball colored black'
GRÉENHÒUSE: 'heated structure for growing plants'	GREEN HOUSE: 'house painted green'
MÁKEÙP: 'cosmetics'	MAKE UP: 'reconcile'
HÉADHÙNTER: 'savage'	HEAD HUNTER: 'top man on a safari'
LÓUDSPÈAKER: 'sound amplifier'	LOUD SPEAKER: 'noisy talker'

[14] For a very careful study of the writing of compounds, see *Webster's Third New International Dictionary,* pp. 30a–31a.

Combining Words: Compounding

In compound nouns it is usually the first element that gets the primary stress, as in all the examples of compound nouns given above, and in adverbs and prepositions the last (*nèverthelèss, withóut*). For verbs and pronouns it is impossible to generalize (*bróadcàst, fulfíll; sómebody* [or *sómebòdy*], *whoéver*). The important thing is the unifying function of contrasting stress in the formation of compounds of whatever sort.

Generally when complete loss of secondary stress occurs, phonetic change occurs as well. For instance, *Énglish mán*, having in the course of compounding become *Énglish-màn*, proceeded to become *Énglishman* [-mən]. The same vowel reduction has occurred in *highwayman* 'robber,' but not in *businessman*; in *gentleman, horseman,* and *postman,* but not in *milkman* and *iceman*. It is similar with the [-lənd] of *Maryland, Iceland, woodland,* and *highland* as contrasted with the secondarily stressed final syllables of such newer compounds as *wonderland, movieland,* and *Disneyland*; with the *-folk* of *Norfolk* and *Suffolk* (there is a common American pronunciation of the former with [-fòk] and, by assimilation, with [-fòrk]); and with the *-mouth* of *Portsmouth,* the *-combe* of *Wyecombe,* the *-burgh* of *Edinburgh* (usually [-brə]), and the *-stone* of *Folkestone*. Even more drastic changes occur in the final syllables of *coxswain* [káksən], *Keswick* [kézɪk], and *Durham* [dɚəm] (though in *Birmingham,* as the name of a city in Alabama, the *-ham* is pronounced as the spelling suggests it "should" be), and in both syllables of *boatswain* [bósən], *forecastle* [fóksəl], *breakfast, Christmas* (that is, Christ's mass), *cupboard,* and *Greenwich,*[15] to cite only a few of many examples. Perhaps it is lack of familiarity with the word—just as the landlubber might pronounce *boatswain* as [bótswèn]—that has given rise to an analytical pronunciation of *clapboard,* traditionally [klǽbərd]. *Grindstone* and *wristband* used to be respectively [grínstən] and [rízbənd]. Not many people have much occasion to use either word nowadays; consequently, the older tradition has been lost, and the words now have secondary stress and full vowels instead of [ə] in their last elements. The same thing has happened to *waistcoat,* now usually [wéstkòt]; the traditional [wéskət] has become old-fashioned. Lack of familiarity can hardly explain the new analysis of *forehead* as [fórhèd] rather than the traditional [fórəd]; a consciousness of the spelling of the word is responsible.

AMALGAMATED COMPOUNDS

The phonetic changes we have been considering have the effect of welding the elements of certain compounds so closely together that, judging from sound (and frequently also from their appearances when written), one would sometimes not suspect that they were indeed compounds. In *daisy,* for

[15] Except for Greenwich Village in New York and Greenwich, Connecticut, this is as an American place name usually pronounced as spelled, rather than as [grénɪč] or [grénɪj]. The usual English pronunciation is [grínɪj].

instance, phonetic reduction of the final element has caused that element to be identical with a suffix. Geoffrey Chaucer was quite correct when he referred to "The dayesyë, or elles the yë (eye) of day" in the Prologue to *The Legend of Good Women*, for the word is really from the Old English compound *dægesēage* 'day's eye.' The *-y* of *daisy* is thus not an affix like the diminutive *-y* of *Katy* or the *-y* from Old English *-ig* of *hazy*; instead, the word is from a historical point of view a compound.

Such closely welded compounds have been called **amalgamated** by Arthur G. Kennedy (1935, p. 350), who lists, among a good many others, *as* (OE *ul* 'all' plus *swā* 'so'), *garlic* (OE *gār* 'spear' plus *lēac* 'leek'), *hussy* (OE *hūs* 'house' plus *wīf* 'woman, wife'), *lord* (OE *hlāf* 'loaf' plus *weard* 'guardian'), *marshal* (OE *mearh* 'horse' plus *scealc* 'servant'), *nostril* (OE *nosu* 'nose' plus *þyrel* 'hole'), and *sheriff* (OE *scīr* 'shire' plus *(ge)rēfa* 'reeve'). Many proper names are such amalgamated compounds—for instance, among place names, *Boston* ('Botulf's stone'), *Sussex* (OE *sūð* 'south' plus *Seaxe* 'Saxons'; compare *Essex* and *Middlesex*), *Norwich*[16] (OE *norð* 'north' plus *wīc* 'village'), and *Bewley* (Fr. *beau* 'beautiful' plus *lieu* 'place'). The reader will find plenty of other interesting examples in Eilert Ekwall's *The Concise Oxford Dictionary of English Place-Names* (1960). It is similar with surnames (which are, of course, sometimes place names as well)—for instance, *Durward* (OE *duru* 'door' plus *weard* 'keeper'), *Purdue* (Fr. *pour* 'for' plus *Dieu* 'God'), and *Thurston* ('Thor's stone,' ultimately Scandinavian); and with a good many given names as well—for instance, *Ethelbert* (OE *æðel* 'noble' plus *beorht* 'bright'), *Alfred* (OE *ælf* 'elf' plus *rēd* 'counsel'), and *Mildred* (OE *milde* 'mild' plus *þryð* 'strength').

FUNCTION AND FORM OF COMPOUNDS

The making of a compound is inhibited by few considerations other than those dictated by meaning. A compound may be used in any grammatical function: as noun (*wishbone*), pronoun (*anyone*), adjective (*foolproof*), adverb (*overhead*), verb (*gainsay*), conjunction (*whenever*), or preposition (*without*). It may be made up of two nouns (*baseball, mudguard, manhole*); of an adjective followed by a noun (*bluegrass, madman, first-rate*); of a noun followed by an adjective or a participle (*bloodthirsty, trigger-happy, homemade, heartbreaking, time-honored*); of a verb followed by an adverb (*pinup, breakdown, setback, cookout, sit-in*); of an adverb followed by a verb form (*upset, downcast, forerun*); of a verb followed by a noun that is its object (*daredevil, blowgun, touch-me-not*); of a noun followed by a verb (*hemstitch, pan-fry, typeset*); of an adverb followed by an adjective or a participle (*overanxious, oncoming, well-known, uptight*); of a preposition followed by

---

[16] Traditionally pronounced to rime with *porridge*, as in the old nursery jingle about the man from Norwich who ate some porridge. The name of the city in Connecticut is, however, pronounced as the spelling seems to indicate.

274   its object (*overland, indoors*); and of a participle followed by an adverb (*washed-up, carryings-on, worn-out*). There are in addition a number of phrases that have become welded into compounds—for example, *will-o'-the-wisp, happy-go-lucky, mother-in-law, tongue-in-cheek, hand-to-mouth, lighter-than-air*. Many compounds are made up of adjective plus noun plus the ending *-ed*—for example, *bald-headed, dimwitted,* and *hairy-chested*—and some of noun plus noun plus *-ed*—for example, *pigheaded* and *snowcapped*.

Shortening Words

CLIPPED FORMS

A **clipped form** must be regarded as a new word, particularly when, as it frequently does, it supplants the longer form altogether. Thus, *mob* can be said to have supplanted *mobile vulgus* 'movable, or fickle, common people'; and *omnibus*, in the sense 'motor vehicle for paying passengers,' is almost as archaic as *mobile vulgus,* having been clipped to *bus*. The clipping of *omnibus*, literally 'for all,' is a strange one because *bus* is no root but merely part of the dative plural ending *-ibus* of the Latin noun *omnis* 'all'; but there is really no reason why English usage should reflect the grammatical features of other languages from which it has borrowed words. *Periwig*, like the form *peruke* (Fr. *perruque*), of which it is a modification, is completely gone; only the abbreviated *wig* survives, and those who use it are not likely to be even slightly aware of the full form. *Taxicab* has completely superseded *taximeter cabriolet* and has, in turn, supplied us with two new words, *taxi* and *cab*.[17] *Pantaloons* seems quite archaic. The clipped form *pants* may be said to have won the day completely. *Bra* seems similarly to be pushing out *brassière,* which in French means a shoulder strap (derived from *bras* 'arm') or a bodice fitted with such straps.

Other abbreviated forms more commonly used than the longer ones include *phone, zoo, extra, flu, auto,* and *ad*. *Zoo* is, of course, from *zoological garden* with the sound change from [zoə-] to [zu-] because of the spelling. *Extra*, which is probably a clipping from *extraordinary*, has become a separate word. *Auto*, like the full form *automobile*, is rapidly losing ground to *car*, an abbreviated form of *motorcar*. In time *auto* may become archaic. *Advertisement* has become *ad* in American English but was clipped less drastically to *advert* in British English, though *ad* is rapidly gaining ground in England. *Razz*, a clipped form of *raspberry* 'Bronx cheer' (see above, p. 264) used as either noun or verb, is doubtless more frequent than the full form.

Recent clippings have included the nouns *bio* from *biography* or *biographical sketch, high tech* 'use of industrial materials for interior decoration in private residences,' from *high technology, perk* from *perquisite, soap* from

---

[17] As a shortening of *cabriolet, cab* is almost a century older than *taxicab*.

soap opera, and *kidvid* 'children's television,' concocted from *video* with the aid of the riming *kid.* Clipped adjectives are *op-ed* 'pertaining to the page opposite the editorial page, on which syndicated columns and other "think pieces" are printed' and *pop,* derived from *popular,* as in "pop culture," "pop art," and "pop sociology." *Hype* is used as either a noun 'advertising, publicity stunt' or a verb 'stimulate artificially, promote'; apparently it is a clipping of *hypo,* which, in turn, is a clipping of *hypodermic needle,* thus reflecting the influence of the drug subculture on Madison Avenue and hence on the rest of us. Another clipped verb is *rehab,* from *rehabilitate,* as in "Young people are rehabbing a lot of the old houses in the inner city."

As the foregoing examples illustrate, clipping can shorten a form by cutting between words (*soap opera > soap*) or between morphemes (*biography > bio*). But it often ignores lexical and morphemic boundaries and cuts instead in the middle of a morpheme (*popular > pop, rehabilitate > rehab*). In so doing, it creates new morphemes and thus enriches the stock of potential building material for making other words. In *helicopter,* the *-o-* is the combining element between Greek *helic-* (the stem of *helix*) 'spiral' and *pter(on)* 'wing,' but the word has been mistakenly analyzed as *heli-copter* rather than as *helico-pter* and, in addition to the independent *copter,* such combinations as *gyrocopter* and *hoppicopter* have come into being (Stubelius 1958, pp. 268–70), as well as *heliport,* 'a terminal for helicopters.'

ACRONYMS

An extreme kind of clipping is the use of the initial letters of words (*KO, YMCA*), or sometimes of syllables (*TB, TV, PJs* 'pajamas'), as if these were words. Usually the motive for this clipping is either brevity or catchiness, though sometimes euphemism may be involved, as with *BO, BM,* and *VD.* Perhaps *TB* also was euphemistic in the beginning, when the disease was a much direr threat to life than it now is and its very name was uttered in hushed tones.

One of the oldest, and by far most successful, initial clippings is *OK.* Allen Walker Read (in six articles published in 1963 and 1964) traced the history of the form to 1839, showing that it originated as a clipping of *oll korrect,* a playful misspelling that was part of a fad for orthographic jokes and abbreviations. It was then used as a pun on *Old Kinderhook,* the nickname of Martin Van Buren during his political campaign of 1840. Efforts to trace the word to more exotic sources—including Finnish, Choctaw, Burmese, Greek, and more recently African languages—have been unsuccessful (Cassidy 1981) but will doubtless continue to challenge the ingenuity of amateur etymologists.

It is inevitable that it should have dawned on some waggish genius that the initial letters of words in certain combinations frequently made pronounceable sequences of letters. Thus, the abbreviation for the military phrase *absent without official leave, AWOL,* came to be pronounced not only as a sequence of the four letter names, but also as though they were the spelling for an ordinary word, *awol* [éwòl]. It was, of course, even better if the initials spelled out an already existing word, as those of *white Anglo-Saxon Protestant* spell out *Wasp.* There had to be a learned term to designate such words, and *acronym* was coined from Greek *akros* 'tip' and *onyma* 'name,' by analogy with *homonym.* Thus two main kinds of clippings can be called **acronyms**: those pronounced with letter names, like *TV,* and those pronounced according to ordinary spelling rules, like *Wasp.* Some authorities restrict the term *acronym* to the second kind, but in fact there is a good deal of latitude in how the label is applied (Algeo 1975). There are even mixed examples in which the two systems of pronunciation are combined—for example, *VP* (for *v*ice *p*resident) pronounced like *veep* and *ROTC* (for *R*eserve *O*fficers *T*raining *C*orps) pronounced like *rotcy.*

The British seem to have beaten us to the discovery of the joys of making acronyms that can be pronounced as words, even though the impressively learned term to designate what is essentially a letters game was probably born in America. In any case, as early as World War I days the *D*efence [*sic*, in British spelling] *o*f the *R*ealm *A*ct had come to be called *Dora* and a member of the *W*omen's *R*oyal *N*aval Service had come to be called (with the insertion of a vowel) a *Wren. Wren* furnished the pattern in World War II for *Wac* (*W*omen's *A*rmy *C*orps) and a number of others—our happiest being *Spar* 'woman Coast Guard,' from the motto of the U.S. Coast Guard, *S*emper *Par*atus. The euphemistic *fu* words—the most widely known is *snafu*[18]—are also among the acronymic progeny of World War II. The process has in some instances been reversed; for example, *Waves,* which resembles a genuine acronym, most likely preceded the phony-sounding supposed source, *W*omen *A*ccepted for *V*olunteer *E*mergency *S*ervice. The following are also probably reverse acronyms: *CORE* (*C*ongress *o*f *R*acial *E*quality), *JOBS* (*J*ob *O*pportunities in the *B*usiness *S*ector), *NOW* (*N*ational *O*rganization of *W*omen), and *ZIP* (*Z*one *I*mprovement *P*lan).

Acronyms lend themselves to humorous uses. *Bomfog* has been coined as a term for the platitudes and pieties that candidates for public office are wont to utter; it stands for *B*rotherhood *o*f *M*an, *F*atherhood *o*f *G*od. But other acronyms are used in full seriousness and have become part of the everyday lives of millions of Americans. For example, *CB* for *c*itizens' *b*and radio is used by countless CBers while driving their *RVs* (*r*ecreational *v*ehicles, such as "motor homes"). Even more serious is the *swat* team or force (from *s*pecial *w*eapons *a*nd *t*actics), which is deployed in highly dangerous police assignments such as flushing out snipers. When men first reached the moon, they traveled across its surface in a *lem,* or *l*unar *e*xcursion *m*odule. The

---

[18] Less well known today are *snafu*'s humorous comparative, *tarfu* 'things are really fouled up,' and superlative, *fubar* 'fouled up beyond all recognition' (to use the euphemism to which *Webster's Third New International Dictionary* had recourse in etymologizing *snafu*).

New Words from Old

best-known scientific acronym is *radar*, from *r*adio *d*etecting *a*nd *r*anging,
but there are a good many others, like the more recent *laser* (*l*ight *a*mplification by *s*timulated *e*mission of *r*adiation). *Laser* was obviously suggested by an earlier acronym *maser* (*m*icrowave *a*mplification by *s*timulated *e*mission of *r*adiation).

APHETIC FORMS

A special type of shortening consists of what is left over after an initial unstressed syllable has been lost, as in childish "'Scuse me" and "I did it 'cause I wanted to." Frequently this phenomenon has resulted in two different words—for instance, *fender–defender*, *fence–defense*, *cute–acute*, *squire–esquire*, and *sport–disport*—in which the first member of each pair is simply an **aphetic form** of the second. The meanings of *etiquette* and its aphetic form *ticket* have become rather sharply differentiated; the primary meaning of French *étiquette* is preserved in the English shortening. Sometimes, however, an aphetic form is merely a variant of the longer form—for instance, *possum–opossum* and *coon–raccoon*.

Aphesis is a sound change, a special variety of what is called ellipsis in chapter 2 (p. 38). It is quite different from the process of clipping, although the results of the two kinds of shortening may look similar. Perhaps the best way to distinguish between them is with an example. When the word *professor* is pronounced casually, the first, unstressed syllable may be omitted, shortening it to *'fessor*, an aphetic form. When students want to shorten the word, however, they are likely to clip it to *prof*, a more or less deliberate shortening that eliminates, in this case, even the originally stressed vowel of the word. The shortening of *professor* to *prof* is probably based on the written abbreviation "Prof."; but what makes it different from aphesis is that it does not result from the general rule that unstressed syllables tend to be omitted. All aphetic forms are the consequences of that rule.

BACK FORMATIONS

Back formation is the making of a new word from an older word that is mistakenly assumed to be a derivative of it, as in *to burgle* from *burglar*, the final *ar* of which suggests that the word is a noun of agency and hence *ought* to mean 'one who burgles.' The facetious *to ush* from *usher* and *to buttle* from *butler* are similar.

In origin the final consonant [-z] of *pease* is not, as it seems to the ear to be, the English plural suffix -*s*; it is, in fact, not a suffix at all. But by the seventeenth century *pease* was mistaken for a plural, and a new singular, *pea*, was derived from a word that was itself singular, precisely as if we were to derive a form **chee* from *cheese* under the impression that *cheese* was plural; then we should have *one chee, two chees*, just as we now have *one pea*, *two peas. Cherry* has been derived by an identical process from Old English *ciris*, a Latin loanword (compare Fr. *cerise*), the final *s* having been assumed to be the plural suffix. Similarly, *sherry wine* was once *sherris wine*, to cite one of the English spellings for Xeres[19] (now Jerez), the city in Spain where the wine was originally made. The wonderful one-hoss *shay* of Oliver Wendell Holmes's poem was so called because of the notion that *chaise* was a plural form, and the heathen *Chinee* of Bret Harte's poem is similarly explained.

Other nouns in the singular that look like plural forms are *alms* (OE *ælmysse*, from Lat. *eleēmosyna*), *riches* (ME *richesse* 'wealth'), and *molasses*. The first two are in fact now construed as plurals. Nonstandard *those molasses* assumes the existence of a singular *that *molass*, though such a form is not indeed heard. People who sell women's hose, however, sometimes refer to a single stocking, or perhaps to a pair collectively, as a "very nice hoe," and salesclerks for men's clothing have been reported as speaking of "a fine pant" instead of "a pair of pants." When television talk-show host Johnny Carson responds to a single handclap with, "That was a wonderful applaw," his joke reflects the same tendency in English that leads to the serious use of *kudo* as a new singular for *kudos*, although the latter, a loanword from Greek, is singular itself.

The adverb *darkling* 'in the darkness' (*dark* plus adverbial *-ling*, a suffix that in Old English denoted direction, extent, or something of the sort) has been misunderstood as a present participial form, giving rise to a new verb *darkle*, as in Lord Byron's "Her cheek began to flush, her eyes to sparkle,/And her proud brow's blue veins to swell and darkle" (*Don Juan* 6.101), in which *darkle* is construed to mean 'to grow dark.' A few years previously, in his "Ode to a Nightingale," Keats had used *darkling* in "Darkling I listen; and, for many a time,/I have been half in love with easeful Death," where it presumably has the historical adverbial sense. It is not here implied that Byron misunderstood Keats's line; the examples merely show how easily the verb might have developed as a back formation from the adverb. *Grovel*, first used by Shakespeare (*OED*), comes to us by way of a similar misconception of *groveling* (*grufe* 'face down' plus *-ling*), and *sidle* is likewise from *sideling* 'sidelong.'[20]

There is another species of back formation, in which the secondary form could just as well have been the primary one, and in which no misunderstanding is involved. *Typewriter*, of American origin, came before the verb *typewrite*; nevertheless, the ending *-er* of *typewriter* is actually the noun-of-agency ending, so that the verb could just as well have come first, only it

[19] In Spanish *x* formerly had the value [š], so that the English spelling was perfectly sound phonetically.

[20] An intentional humorous assumption of *-ing* as a participial ending occurs in J. K. Stephen's immortal "When the Rudyards cease from Kipling,/And the Haggards ride no more." There is a similar play in the popular joke "Do you like Kipling?" "I don't know—I've never kippled" (Nilsen 1980, p. 235).

New Words from Old

didn't. It is similar with *housekeep* from *housekeeper* (or *housekeeping*), *baby-sit* from *baby sitter*, and *bargain-hunt* from *bargain hunter*. The adjective *housebroken* 'excretorily adapted to the indoors' is older than the verb *house-break*; but, since *housebroken* is actually a compounding of *house* and the past participle *broken*, the process might just as well have been the other way around—the usual way—except that it wasn't.

Blending Words

The blending of two existing words to make a new word was doubtless an unconscious process in the oldest periods of our language. The *haþel* 'nobleman' in line 1138 of the late fourteenth-century masterpiece *Sir Gawain and the Green Knight* is apparently a blend of *aþel* (OE æðele 'noble') and *haleþ* (OE hæleð 'man'). Other early examples, with the dates of their earliest occurrence as given in the *OED*, are *flush* (*flash* plus *gush*; The *Random House Dictionary* says "in some senses, further blended with *blush*") [1548]; *twirl* (*twist* plus *whirl*) [1598]; *dumfound* (apparently *dumb* plus *confound*) [1653]; and *flurry* (*flutter* plus *hurry*) [1698].

Lewis Carroll (Charles Lutwidge Dodgson[21]) made a great thing of such **blends**, which he called **portmanteau words**, particularly in his "Jabberwocky" poem. Two of his creations, *chortle* (*chuckle* plus *snort*) and, to a lesser degree, *galumph* (*gallop* plus *triumph*), have become established in the language. His *snark*, a blend of *snake* and *shark*, though widely known, failed to find a place because there was no need for it.

Recent years have seen a mighty proliferation of conscious blendings. Perhaps the most successful of these are *smog* (*smoke* plus *fog*) and *motel* (*motor* plus *hotel*).[22] *Urinalysis* (*urine* plus *analysis*), of American origin also, first appeared in 1889 and has since attained to scientific respectability, as have the much more recent *quasar* (*quasi* plus *stellar*) and *pulsar* (*pulse* plus *quasar*). *Cafetorium* (*cafeteria* plus *auditorium*) has made a great deal of headway in the American public school systems and would seem to be a useful term for a large room planned for the double purpose indicated by it. Boy Scouts frequently have *camporees* (*camp* plus *jamboree*[23]). A number of eating establishments now feature *broasted* (*broiled* plus *roasted*) chicken, which those of hearty appetite might conceivably order for *brunch* (*breakfast* plus *lunch*).

[21] His endearing passion for "fooling around" with language is indicated by his pen name: *Carolus* is the Latin equivalent of *Charles*, and *Lutwidge* must have suggested to him German *Ludwig*, the equivalent of English *Lewis*. *Charles Lutwidge* thus became (in reverse) *Lewis Carroll*.

[22] There are also, at least in Florida, *botels* for those who arrive in boats.

[23] According to *The Random House Dictionary*, this word is itself "apparently" a blend of *jabber* and *shivaree*, with the *m* from *jam* 'crowd.'

Blends are easy to create, which is doubtless why there are so very many of them, and they are at the moment very popular. They can be found in discussions of almost every subject. Science fiction readers and writers are in touch with one another through the *fanzine* (*fan* plus *magazine*). Those with less exotic tastes in literature have available *faction* (*fact* plus *fiction*), a mixture of historically accurate writing with imaginative invention. Changes in sexual mores have given rise to *palimony* (*pal* plus *alimony*) for unmarried ex-partners and *equalimony* 'support by a woman of her ex-husband.' Those decrying the commercialization of Christmas promote the use of the *chrismon* (*Christ*[*mas*] plus *monogram*) 'white and gold religious symbols used as decorations on a Christmas tree.'

NEW MORPHEMES FROM BLENDING

Blending can, and frequently does, create new morphemes or give new meanings to old ones. For instance, in German *Hamburger* 'pertaining to, or associated with, Hamburg,' the *-er* is affixed to the name of the city. This adjectival suffix may be joined to any place name in German—for example, *Braunschweiger Wurst* 'Brunswick sausage,' *Wiener Schnitzel* 'Vienna cutlet,' and the like. In English, however, the word *hamburger* was blended so often with other words (*cheeseburger* being the chief example, but also *steakburger*, *chickenburger*, *vegeburger*, and a host of others) that the form *burger* came to be used as an independent word. Compounds of it now denote a sandwich containing a patty of meat or some other food (*any* other food, in fact) capable of being made into a patty. A similar culinary example is the *eggwich* and the commercially promoted *Spamwich*, which have not so far, however, made *-wich* into an independent word.

Automobile, taken from French, was originally a combination of Greek *autos* 'self' and Latin *mobilis* 'movable.' *Auto-* is thus a combining form that can be seen with the same meaning in *autohypnosis*, *autograph*, *autobiography*, and a great many other words. But *automobile* was blended to produce new forms like *autocar*, *autobus*, and *autocamp*. The result is a new word, *auto*, with a meaning quite different from that of the original combining form. One of the new blendings, *autocade*, has the ending of *cavalcade*, which also appears in *aquacade*, *musicade*, *motorcade*, and *tractorcade*, with the sense of *-cade* as either 'pageant' or 'procession.' The second element of *automobile* has acquired a combining function as well, as in *bookmobile* 'library on wheels' and *bloodmobile* 'blood bank on wheels.'

Other new morphemes formed by blending are *-holic* 'addict, one who habitually does or uses' whatever the first part of the word denotes, and *-thon* 'group activity lasting for an extended time and designed to raise money for a charitable cause.' The first results from blending *alcoholic* with other words—for example, *credaholic* (from *credit*), *chocoholic* (from *chocolate*), *pokerholic, potatochipoholic, punaholic, sexaholic, sleepaholic, spendaholic*, and the most frequent of such trivia, *workaholic*.[24] The second is the tail end of *marathon*, whence the notion of endurance in such charitable affairs as a *showerthon* (during which students took turns showering for 360 continuous hours to raise money for the American Cancer Society), a *fastathon* (in which young people all fasted for 30 hours to raise money for the needy), and a *cakethon* (a five-hour auction of homemade cakes for the Heart Association); other examples are *bikeathon, Putt-Putt-athon* (from *Putt-Putt* 'commercial miniature golf'), *quiltathon, radiothon, teeter-totter-athon*, and *wakeathon*.

Another old morpheme given a new sense by blending is *gate*. After the forced resignation of Richard Nixon from the presidency, the term *Watergate* (the name of the apartment-house and office complex where the events began that led to his downfall) became a symbol for scandal and corruption, usually involving some branch of government and often attended by official efforts to cover up the facts. In that sense the word was blended with a variety of other terms to produce such new words as *Info-gate, Irangate, Koreagate, Oilgate, Peanutgate, Prisongate*, and *Winegate*.[25] Word making that depends, as here, on topical allusion is not likely to endure. The spate of words ending in *-gate* that flowed during the 1970s will probably dry up as the memory of the Nixon years fades and old political animosities die out. However, even if *-gate* words prove to be ephemeral, as seems probable, they illustrate a lively kind of word making and the fecundity of the process.

FOLK ETYMOLOGY

Folk etymology—the naive misunderstanding of a more or less esoteric word that makes it into something more familiar and hence seems to give it a new etymology, false though it be—is a minor kind of blending. Spanish *cucaracha* 'wood louse' has thus been modified to *cockroach*, though the justly unpopular creature so named is neither a cock nor a roach in the earlier sense of the word (that is, a freshwater fish). Notions of verbal delicacy have largely done away with what looks like the first element of an English compound (but which, as we have just seen, really isn't anything of the sort), with the consequence that *roach* has come to mean what *cucaracha* originally meant.

A very neat example of how the folk-etymological process works is furnished by the experience of a German teacher of ballet who attended classes in modern dance at an American university in order to observe American teaching techniques. During one of these classes, she heard a

---

[24] A good many other examples are cited by Philip C. Kolin (1979).

[25] Other examples are cited by I. Willis Russell and Mary Gray Porter in "Among the New Words" (1978, pp. 215–17) and by David K. Barnhart (1980).

student describe a certain ballet jump, which he referred to as a "soda box." Genuinely mystified, she inquired about the term. The student who had used it and other members of the class averred that it was precisely what they always said and that it was spelled as they pronounced it—*soda box*. What they had misheard from their instructor was the practically universal ballet term *saut de basque* 'Basque leap.' One cannot but wonder how widespread the folk-etymologized term is in American schools of the dance.[26]

All of us sometimes hear a new word imperfectly, and frequently when among friends we ask, "How do you spell it?"—as if such knowledge were necessarily a sure clue to either its standard pronunciation or its meaning. But often we think that we have understood and go on thinking so, perhaps for years, like the woman who confessed with considerable amusement at her own naiveté that it was only after her marriage that she realized that the name of a certain piece of furniture that she thought of as a *Chester drawers* was really a *chest of drawers*.[27] Sometimes our misunderstanding is aided by sheer and amazing coincidence. As a child too young to read, one of the authors of this book misheard *artificial snow* as *Archie Fisher snow*, a plausible enough boner for one who lived in a town in which a prominent merchant was named Archie Fisher. In any case, Mr. Fisher displayed the stuff in his window, and for all an innocent child knew he might even have invented it.

When this sort of misunderstanding of a word becomes widespread, we have acquired a new item in the English lexicon—one that usually completely displaces the old one and frequently seems far more appropriate than the displaced word. Thus *crayfish* seems more fitting than would the normal modern phonetic development of its source, Middle English *crevice*, taken from Old French, which language in turn took it from Old High German *krebiz* 'crab' (Modern *Krebs*). Other examples of folk etymology follow, many of them well known and often cited in other works (particularly by Greenough and Kittredge 1901, ch. 23, and McKnight 1923, ch. 13).

ACORN: Middle English *akern*, Old English *æcern* 'oak or beech mast' —nothing to do with *corn*
BELFRY: Middle English *berfrey* 'tower'—nothing to do with *bell*
BRIDEGROOM: Middle English *bridegome*, Old English *brȳd* 'bride' plus *guma* 'man'—nothing to do with *groom*
CARRYALL: French *cariole*—nothing to do with *carry* or *all*
COLDSLAW: Dutch *koolsla*, compound of *kool* 'cabbage' plus *sla* 'salad'—nothing to do with *cold*

[26] For this example, which is fresh as far as we know, we are indebted to our former colleague, Ernest H. Cox, who got it from the American husband of the baffled *Ballett-meisterin*.

[27] This misunderstood form is widespread. Witness the classified advertisement reading in part "Stove, table & chairs, bed and chester drawers" (*Athens* [Ga.] *Observer*, 12 September 1974, p. 11).

CONTREDANSE, CONTRADANCE: French mistranslation of English *country dance*, reborrowed by English—nothing to do with French *contre* 'counter'

CURTAIL: older *curtal*, from French *courtault* 'shortened'—nothing to do with *tail*

CUTLASS: French *coutelas*, ultimately Latin *cultellus* 'little knife'—nothing to do with either *cut* or *lass*

CUTLET: French *côtelette* 'little rib,' ultimately Latin *costa* 'rib'—nothing to do with *cut*

FEMALE: Old French *femelle* 'little woman'—nothing to do with *male*

GREYHOUND: Scandinavian *grey* 'dog, bitch' plus *hound*—nothing to do with *grey* 'color'

HANGNAIL: earlier *angnail*, from Old English *ange* 'painful' plus *nægl* 'nail'—nothing to do with *hanging*

HELPMATE: *help* plus *meet* 'fitting,' misunderstood as a compound in two occurrences in Genesis 2 as "an help meet for him," subsequently influenced by *mate*, with which it has nothing to do

HICCOUGH: variant spelling of imitative *hiccup* showing influence of *cough*

JERUSALEM ARTICHOKE: from Italian *girasole* 'sunflower'—nothing to do with *Jerusalem*

MANDRAKE: from the herb *mandragora*—nothing to do with *man* or *drake*

MISTLETOE: Old English *mistel* 'mistletoe' plus *tān* 'twig'—nothing to do with *toe*

MONOKINI: a one-piece version of the bikini, name of an atoll of the Marshall Islands in the Pacific Ocean—nothing to do with *bi-* 'two'

MUSKRAT: Algonquian *musquash*—nothing to do with either *musk* or *rat*

PENTHOUSE: Middle English *pentis*, aphetic form of Old French *apentis*, connected with *pend* 'hang'—nothing to do with either *pent* 'confined' or *house*

PICKAX: Middle English *picois*, from Old French—nothing to do with *ax*

REINDEER: Scandinavian *hreinn*, the name of the animal, plus *deer* 'animal'—nothing to do with *rein*

SALTCELLAR: Middle English *saltsaler*, the second element from Old French *saliere* 'pertaining to salt'—nothing to do with *cellar* 'basement'

SHAMEFACED: earlier *shamefast*, Old English *sceamfæst*, that is, 'bound by shame'—nothing to do with *face*

SIRLOIN: French *sur* 'above' plus *loin*—nothing to do with *sir*

TITMOUSE: Middle English *titmose*—nothing to do with *mouse*

TUBEROSE: Latin *tūberōsa* 'tuberous,' misinterpreted as *tube* plus *rose*

Blending Words

WELSH RAREBIT: originally *Welsh rabbit* (a joke, like calling Coca-Cola "Confederate champagne")—nothing to do with a *rare bit*

WOODCHUCK: Algonquian *otchek*—nothing to do with either *wood* or *chucking*

WORMWOOD: Old English *wermōd* 'absinthe'—nothing to do with *worm* or *wood*

Note that all of the forms that have just been cited, with the possible exception of *coldslaw*, are standard, even though they are the results of what were once blunders. *Chaise lounge* for *chaise longue* 'long chair' is listed as a variant in *Webster's Third*, and seems to be on the way to full social respectability. A dealer says that the prevailing pronunciation, both of those who buy and of those who sell, is either [šɛz laʊnǰ] or [čes laʊnǰ], the first of these in some circles being considered somewhat elite, not to say snobbish, in that it indicates that the user has "had" French. In any case, as far as speakers of English are concerned, the boner is remarkably apt, as indeed are many of the folk-etymologized forms that have been cited. And there can be little doubt that the aptness of a blunder has much to do with its ultimate acceptance.

Shifting Words to New Uses

ONE PART OF SPEECH TO ANOTHER

A very prolific source of new words from old is the facility of Modern English, because of its paucity of inflection, for converting words from one grammatical function to another with no change in form, a process known as **functional shift**. Thus, the name of practically every part of the body has been converted to use as a verb—one may *head* a committee, *shoulder* or *elbow* one's way through a crowd, *hand* in one's papers, *finger* one's tie, *thumb* a ride, *back* one's car, *leg* it along, *shin* up a tree, *foot* a bill, *toe* a mark, and *tiptoe* through the tulips—without any modification of form such as would be necessary in other languages, such as German, in which the suffix -*(e)n* is a necessary part of all infinitives. It would not have been possible to shift words thus in Old English times either, when infinitives ended in -*(a)n* or -*ian*. But Modern English does it with the greatest ease; to cite a few nonanatomical examples, *to contact*, *to chair* (a meeting), *to telephone*, *to date*, *to park*, *to proposition*, and *to M.C.* (or *emcee*).

Verbs may also be used as nouns. One may, for instance, take a *walk*, a *run*, a *drive*, a *spin*, a *cut*, a *stand*, a *break*, a *turn*, or a *look*. Nouns are just as freely used as adjectives, or practically so as attributives (*head bookkeeper*, *handlebar mustache*, *stone wall*), and adjectives and participles are used as nouns—for instance, *commercial* 'sales spiel on a television or radio show,' *formals* 'evening clothes,' *clericals* 'clergyman's street costume,' *devotional* 'short prayer service subsidiary to some other activity,' *private* 'noncommissioned soldier,' *elder, painting,* and *earnings.*

Adjectives may also be converted into verbs, as with *better, round, tame,* and *rough.* Even adverbs and conjunctions are capable of conversion, as in "the *whys* and the *wherefores,*" "*but* me no *buts*" (in which *but* is first used as a verb, then as a pluralized noun), and "*ins* and *outs.*" The attributive use of *in* and *out,* as in *inpatient* and *outpatient,* is quite old, as is their use as nouns just cited. The adjectival use of *in* meaning 'fashionable' or 'influential,' as in "the *in* thing" and "the *in* group," is recent, however. The adjectival use of the adverb *now* meaning 'of the present time,' as in "the *now* king," dates from the fifteenth century, whereas the meaning 'modern, and hence fashionable,' as in "the *now* generation," is a product of our own times. Transitive verbs may be made from older intransitive ones, as has happened fairly recently with *to shop* ("Shop Our Fabulous Sale Now in Progress"; "It's smart for all/To shop Duvall") and *to sleep* ("Her [a cruising yacht's] designer has claimed that she can sleep six"[28]).

A good many combinations of verbs and adverbs—for instance, *slow down, check up, fill in* 'furnish with a background sketch,' *break down* 'analyze,' and *set up*—are easily convertible into nouns, though usually with shifted stress, as in *to check úp* contrasted with *a chéckup.* Some such combinations are also used as adjectives, as in *sit-down strike, sit-in demonstration,* and *drive-in theater.*

As with the verb-adverb combinations, change of form is sometimes involved when verbs, adjectives, and nouns shift functions, the functional shift often being indicated by a shift of stress: compare *upsét* (verb) and *úpset* (noun), *prodúce* (verb) and *próduce* (noun), *pérfect* (adjective) and *perféct* (verb).[29] Not all speakers make the functional stress distinction in words like *ally* and *address,* but many do. Some words whose functions used to be distinguished by shift of stress seem to be losing the distinction. *Perfume* as a noun is now often stressed on the second syllable, and a building contractor regularly *cóntràcts* to build a house.

COMMON WORDS FROM PROPER NAMES

A large number of words have come to us from proper names—a kind of functional shift known as **commonization**. From names of persons, to begin with, the three best-known examples are probably *lynch* (by way of *Lynch's law,* from the Virginian Captain William Lynch [1742–1820], who led a campaign of "corporeal punishment" against those "unlawful and

---

[28] Let this not be supposed an instance of peculiarly American linguistic depravity; the citation is from the London *Daily Telegraph and Morning Post,* 13 August 1956, p. 3.

[29] Otto Jespersen (1909–49, 1: 173–84) cites the varying stress according to grammatical function in *affix, absent, compact, conduct, content, insult, minute, object, perfume, progress, rebel, record, subject,* along with a good many others.

abandoned wretches" who were harassing the good people of Pittsylvania County, such as "to us shall seem adequate to the crime committed or the damage sustained"),[30] *boycott* (from another captain, Charles Cunningham Boycott [1832–97], who, because as a land agent he refused to accept rents at figures fixed by the tenants, was the best-known victim of the policy of ostracization of the Irish Land League agitators), and *sandwich* (from the fourth Earl of Sandwich [1718–92], said to have spent twenty-four hours at the gaming table with no other refreshment than slices of meat between slices of bread). The following words are also the unchanged names of actual people: *ampere, bloomer,*[31] *bowie* (knife), *cardigan, chesterfield* (overcoat or sofa), *davenport, derby, derrick, derringer, graham* (flour), *guy, lavaliere, macintosh, maudlin,*[32] *maverick, ohm, pompadour, pullman, shrapnel, solon* (legislator), *valentine, vandyke* (beard or collar), *watt, zeppelin. Bobby* 'British policeman' is from the pet form of the name of Sir Robert Peel, who made certain reforms in the London police system. It has almost driven out the synonymous *peeler.*

Comparatively slight spelling modifications occur in *dunce* (from John Duns[33] Scotus [d. *ca.* 1308], who was in reality anything but a dunce—to his admirers he was *Doctor Subtilis*) and *praline* (from Maréchal Duplessis-Praslin [d. 1675]). *Tawdry* is a clipped form of *Saint Audrey* and first referred to the lace bought at St. Audrey's Fair in Ely. *Epicure* is an anglicized form of *Epicurus. Kaiser* and *czar* are from *Caesar. Volt* is a clipped form of the surname of Count Alessandro Volta (d. 1827), and *farad* is derived likewise from the name of Michael Faraday (d. 1867). The name of an early American politician, Elbridge Gerry, is blended with *salamander* in the coinage *gerrymander. Pantaloon,* in the plural an old-fashioned name for trousers, is only a slight modification of French *pantalon,* which, in turn, is from Italian *Pantalone,* the name of a silly senile Venetian of early Italian comedy who wore such close-fitting nether coverings.

The following are derivatives of personal names: *begonia, bougainvillea, bowdlerize, camellia, chauvinism, comstockery, dahlia, jeremiad, masochism, mesmerism, nicotine, onanism, pasteurize, platonic, poinsettia, sadism, spoonerism, wisteria, zinnia.* Derivatives of the names of two writers—*Machiavellian*

[30] From the compact drawn up by Captain Lynch and his neighbors, cited by M. M. Mathews (1951, s.v. *lynch law*).

[31] Usually in the plural, from Mrs. Amelia Jenks Bloomer (1818–94), who publicized the garb. One could devise no more appropriate name for voluminous drawers for women than the surname of the lady's unfortunate husband, though since he had nothing to do with their design or with advocating their adoption it would be more just to call them *jenkses.* But the innocent must suffer with the guilty.

[32] Long an English spelling for Old French *Madelaine,* ultimately from Latin *Magdalen,* that is, Mary Magdalene, who was frequently represented as tearfully melancholy by painters.

[33] Like many personal names, this is from a place name—Duns, Scotland, the birthplace of John, whose full name means 'John of Duns the Scotsman.'

and *Rabelaisian*—are of such wide application that capitalizing them hardly seems necessary, any more than *platonic*.

The names of the following persons in literature and mythology (if gods, goddesses, and muses may be considered persons) are used unchanged: *atlas, babbitt, calliope, hector, hermaphrodite, mentor, mercury, nemesis, pander, psyche, simon-pure, volcano. Benedick*, the name of Shakespeare's bachelor *par excellence* who finally succumbed to the charms of Beatrice, has undergone only very slight modification in *benedict* '(newly) married man.' *Don Juan, Lothario, Lady Bountiful, Mrs. Grundy, man Friday*, and *Pollyanna* (which even has a derivative, *Pollyannaism*), though written with initial capitals, probably belong here also.

The following are derivatives of personal names from literature and mythology: *aphrodisiac, bacchanal, herculean, jovial, malapropism, morphine, odyssey, panic, quixotic, saturnine, simony, stentorian, tantalize, terpsichorean, venereal, vulcanize*. Despite their capitals, *Gargantuan* and *Pickwickian* should doubtless be included here also.

Names may be used generically or because of some supposed appropriateness, like *billy* (in *billycock, hillbilly, silly billy*, and alone as the name of a policeman's club), *tom(my)* (in *tomcat, tomtit, tomboy, tommyrot, tomfool*), *john* 'toilet' (compare older *jakes*), *johnny* (in *stagedoor johnny, johnny-on-the-spot*, and perhaps *johnnycake*, though this may come from American Indian *jonikin* 'type of griddlecake' plus *cake*), *jack* (in *jackass, cheapjack, steeplejack, lumberjack, jack-in-the-box, jack-of-all-trades*, and alone as the name of a small metal piece used in a children's game known as *jacks*), *rube* (from *Reuben*), *hick* (from *Richard*), and *toby* 'jug' (from *Tobias*).

Place names have also furnished a good many common words. The following, the last of which exists only in the mind, are unchanged in form: *arras, babel, bourbon, billingsgate, blarney, buncombe* (see below), *champagne, cheddar, china, cologne, grubstreet, guinea, homburg, java* 'coffee,' *limerick, mackinaw, madeira, madras, magnesia, meander, morocco, oxford* (shoe or basket-weave cotton shirting), *panama, sauterne, shanghai, shantung, suède* (French name of Sweden), *tabasco, turkey, tuxedo*, and *utopia*.

The following are either derivatives of place names or place names that have different forms from those known to us today: *bayonet, bedlam, calico, canter, cashmere, copper, damascene, damask, damson, denim, frankfurter, gauze, hamburger, italic, jeans* (pants), *laconic, limousine, mayonnaise, milliner, roman* (type), *romance, sardonic, sherry* (see p. 278), *sodomy, spaniel, spartan, stogy, stygian, wiener, worsted. Damascene, damask*, and *damson* all three come from *Damascus. Canter* is a clipping of *Canterbury* (gallop), the easy-going pace of pilgrims to the tomb of St. Thomas à Becket in Canterbury, the most famous and certainly the "realest" of whom are a group of people who never lived at all save in the poetic imagination of Geoffrey Chaucer and everlastingly in the hearts and minds of those who know his *Canterbury Tales*.

Shifting Words to New Uses

VERNACULAR, SLANG, AND ARGOT

The specialized languages of games, trades, criminal activities, and the like have contributed a number of new words and phrases, or at least new uses of old ones, like *roughneck, roustabout, wildcatter, logrolling, crestfallen, to tilt at, to fence, fair play, to cross swords, to ante up, knockout, below the belt, mark* 'dupe,' *to bowl over, in the chips, on the lam, to take the rap,* and many others. The line between these and slang would be difficult to draw. In any case, slang has been for a long time one of the most productive forms of language. Among its contributions to more or less general language are *hip* (formerly *hep*); *far out* 'eccentric, extreme'; *split* 'leave'; *cool* 'superior, sophisticated'; *straight* (formerly 'heterosexual,' but now extended to include many of the "Establishment" connotations of older *square*); the reduplicated *no-no* 'something taboo, as in "That's a no-no"'; a number of verb-adverb combinations such as *cop-out* (used as verb and noun, with differentiating stress) and *hang-up* 'inconvenience, inhibition' (also used as a verb, as in "I was hung up"). There are a limited number of what are doubtless pure root creations—for example, *snide, bazooka* (which may owe something to both *bazoo* and *kazoo*), and the reduplicated *heebie-jeebies.*

A good many slang terms are merely clipped forms, like the afore-mentioned once slangy *mob*, which was pilloried, along with a number of other such abbreviations, by Jonathan Swift in a famous paper printed in the *Tatler* of 28 September 1710. *Bunk* is an abbreviation of *Buncombe*, the name of a county in North Carolina, whose representative in Congress in the early 1800s once remarked in the course of a particularly dull and windy speech that he was "only talking for Buncombe." *Kook* 'eccentric person' is a shortening of *cuckoo*, which with the same meaning or used as an adjective meaning 'crazy' is also slang.

LITERARY COINAGES

At what would seem to be another extreme, but is not necessarily so, writers have also coined new terms, like Gelett Burgess's *blurb*, Will Irwin's *highbrow*, and H. L. Mencken's *Bible Belt* and the less viable *booboisie* and *ecdysiast.* Henry Bradley, in his still valuable *The Making of English* (1904, p. 215), points out that "it is a truth often overlooked, but not unimportant, that every addition to the resources of a language must in the first instance have been due to an act (though not necessarily a voluntary or conscious act) of some one person," and devotes an entire chapter, entitled "Some Makers of English," to illustrating this truth. He cites among others *loving-kindness* (Coverdale), *peacemaker* (Tindale), *braggadocio* and *derring-do* 'chivalry' (Spenser), *lonely, dwindle,* and *orb* 'globe' (Shakespeare), *pande-monium, irresponsible,* and *impassive* (Milton), and *raid, gruesome, uncanny,*

New Words from Old

and *glamour* (Scott). Bradley makes it clear that the first *known* occurrences are in the works of the authors named; there may have been earlier ones.

Two literary examples that have been very popular are *Catch-22*, from the novel of the same name by Joseph Heller, and *1984*, also from a novel of the same name by George Orwell. *Catch-22* denotes a dilemma in which each alternative is blocked by the other. In the novel, the only way for a combat pilot to get a transfer out of the war zone is to ask for one on the ground that he is insane, but anyone who seeks to be transferred is clearly sane, since only an insane person would want to stay in combat. The rules provide for a transfer, but Catch-22 prevents one from ever getting it. Orwell's dystopian novel is set in the year 1984, and its title has come to denote the kind of society the novel depicts—one in which individual freedom has been lost, people are manipulated through cynical television propaganda by the government, and life is a grey and hopeless affair.

Another literary contribution that has come into the language less directly is *quark*. As used in theoretical physics, the term denotes a hypothetical particle, the fundamental building block of all matter, originally thought to be of three kinds. The theory of these threefold fundamental particles was developed by a Nobel Prize winner, Murray Gell-Mann, of the California Institute of Technology; he called them *quarks* and then discovered the word in James Joyce's novel *Finnegans Wake* in the phrase "Three quarks for Muster Mark!" Doubtless Gell-Mann had seen the word in his earlier readings of the novel, and it had stuck in the back of his mind until he needed a term for his new particles. It is not often that we know so much about the origin of a word in English.

DISTRIBUTION OF NEW WORDS

Which of the kinds of word making discussed in this chapter are the most prolific sources of new words today? Two studies of that question, based on different materials but covering similar periods of time, have reached remarkably similar conclusions.[34] The most productive source of new words is affixing, which accounts for 30 to 34 percent of the innovations in recent English. It is closely followed by compounding (28 to 30 percent of the new words). Thus these two ways of combining morphemes and words already in the language together account for 58 to 64 percent of the additions to our

---

[34] Garland Cannon's study "Statistical Etymologies of New Words in American English" (1978) is based on *6,000 Words: A Supplement to Webster's Third New International Dictionary*, which lists words collected by the editors of that dictionary between 1961 and 1976. "Where Do All the New Words Come From?" (Algeo 1980) is based on *The Barnhart Dictionary of New English since 1963*, which lists words collected by Clarence L. Barnhart, Inc., as having entered the working vocabulary of English between 1963 and 1972. In the statistics cited in the text, the first figure in each case is from Cannon's study and the second from Algeo's.

vocabulary. The next most productive process is shifting the use of already existing words; it accounts for 26 to 14 percent of the new items. The remaining types of word making are of relatively minor importance: shortening (8 to 10 percent), borrowing—to be discussed in the next chapter—(6 to 7 percent), blending (1 to 5 percent), and creating quite new words (less than 1 percent).[35]

It is obvious from the two studies that present-day English speakers prefer, as their linguistic ancestors have doubtless always done, to make new words by putting together the basic building blocks of the vocabulary (words and morphemes) already available to them, or to shift the uses of old words without changing their forms. Between them, combining and shifting account for 84 to 78 percent of the new words in recent English—roughly four-fifths of them. The remaining 16 to 22 percent are distributed among the other processes—shortening, borrowing, blending, and creating—which may add completely new morphemic shapes to the language, as combining cannot and shifting usually does not. English speakers (and probably the speakers of all languages, for that matter) prefer to make use of the resources they have rather than concoct new basic materials. If language were not thus fundamentally conservative, it would be less well suited to performing its principal function—allowing human beings to communicate with one another. On the other hand, if language did not permit both novel uses of old forms and the introduction of new ones, it could not adapt to changes in the lives of its speakers. But language is adaptive, and therefore vocabulary continues to grow, as this chapter has abundantly demonstrated.

For Further Reading

Word Making: General Works

American Speech: A Quarterly of Linguistic Usage, various issues.
Barnhart, Steinmetz, and Barnhart, The Barnhart Dictionary of New English since 1963, 1973.
Barnhart, Steinmetz, and Barnhart, The Second Barnhart Dictionary of New English, 1980.
Onions, The Oxford Dictionary of English Etymology, 1966.
The Oxford English Dictionary, and Supplement, 1933, 1972–.
Ross, Etymology, 1958.
Russell and Porter, "Among the New Words," American Speech, various issues.

[35] A third study, "The Production of New Scientific Terms," by Arthur Lewis Caso (1980) concentrates upon a specialized vocabulary—technical terms from physics and the earth sciences—and arrives at conclusions that differ in two significant respects: the most productive processes for these scientific terms are shifting (39 percent) and borrowing (22 percent). The remaining processes have the same relative order as in the Cannon and Algeo studies, but generally reduced productivity: affixing (20 percent), compounding (12 percent), shortening (4 percent), blending (2 percent), and creating (less than 1 percent).

6,000 Words: A Supplement to Webster's Third New International Dictionary, 1976.
Skeat, *An Etymological Dictionary of the English Language*, 1910.
"Words and Meanings, New," *Britannica Book of the Year*, various years.

Word Formation

Adams, *An Introduction to Modern English Word-Formation*, 1973.
Algeo, "The Taxonomy of Word Making," *Word*, 1978.
Algeo, "Where Do All the New Words Come From?" *American Speech*, 1980.
Cannon, "Statistical Etymologies of New Words in American English," *Journal of English Linguistics*, 1978.
Caso, "The Production of New Scientific Terms," *American Speech*, 1980.
Kreidler, "Creating New Words by Shortening," *Journal of English Linguistics*, 1979.
Lees, *The Grammar of English Nominalizations*, 1963.
Marchand, *The Categories and Types of Present-Day English Word-Formation*, 1969.
Matthews, *Morphology: An Introduction to the Theory of Word-Structure*, 1974.
Seymour, *A Bibliography of Word Formation in the Germanic Languages*, 1968.
Soudek, *Structure of Substandard Words in British and American English*, 1967.

Slang

Berrey and Van den Bark, *The American Thesaurus of Slang*, 1953.
Dumas and Lighter, "Is *Slang* a Word for Linguists?" *American Speech*, 1978.
Farmer and Henley, *Dictionary of Slang and Its Analogues*, 1890–1904.
Franklyn, *A Dictionary of Rhyming Slang*, 1960.
Partridge, *A Dictionary of Slang and Unconventional English*, 1970.
Partridge, *Slang Today and Yesterday*, 1970.
Wentworth and Flexner, *Dictionary of American Slang*, 1975.

Special Vocabularies

Adams, *Western Words: A Dictionary of the Range, Cow Camp, and Trail*, 1968.
Boone, *The Petroleum Dictionary*, 1952.
Maurer, *The Argot of the Racetrack*, 1951.
Maurer, *Whiz Mob: A Correlation of the Technical Argot of Pickpockets with Their Behavior Pattern*, 1955.
Mueller, *Buzzwords: A Guide to the Language of Leadership*, 1974.
Partridge, *A Dictionary of the Underworld*, 1964.

12 Foreign Elements in the English Word Stock

Thus far we have dealt only incidentally with the non-English elements in the English lexicon. In the present chapter we shall make a rapid survey of these, along with some examination of the various circumstances—cultural, religious, military, and political—surrounding their adoption.

When speakers imitate a word from a foreign language and at least partly adapt it in sound or grammar to their native speechways, the process is known as **borrowing**, and the word thus borrowed is a **loanword**. The history of a loanword may be quite complex because such words have often passed through a series of languages before reaching English. For example, *chess* was borrowed from Old French in the thirteenth century. The Old French word (pl. *esches*, sing. *eschec*) was, in turn, a normal development of the Medieval Latin form *scaccus*, borrowed from Arabic, which had earlier borrowed it from Persian *shāh* 'king.' Thus the etymology of the word reaches from Persian, through Arabic, Latin, and Old French, to English. The **direct** or **immediate source** of *chess* is Old French, but its **ultimate source** (as far back as we can trace its history) is Persian. Similarly, the **etymon** of *chess*, that is, the word from which it has been derived, is immediately *esches* and

292

Latin Loanwords

LATIN INFLUENCE IN THE GERMANIC PERIOD

Long before English began its separate existence, while it was merely a regional type of Germanic, those who spoke it had acquired a number of Latin words—loanwords that are common to several or to all of the Germanic languages to this day. Unlike a good many later borrowings, they are mostly concerned with military affairs, commerce, agriculture, or with refinements of living that the Germanic peoples had acquired through a fairly close contact with the Romans since at least the beginning of the Christian era. *Wine* (OE *wīn*, Lat. *vīnum*), for instance, is a word that denotes a thing the Germanic peoples learned about from the Romans. It is to be found in one form or another in all the Germanic languages—the same form as the Old English in Old Frisian and Old Saxon, *Wein* in Modern German, *wijn* in Modern Dutch, *vin* in Danish and Swedish. The Baltic, Slavic, and Celtic peoples also acquired the same word from Latin. It was brought to Britain by the Germanic warrior-adventurers who in the mid-fifth century, as we have seen, became the first English people. Their not-so-remote ancestors had known malt drinks very well—*beer* and *ale* are both Germanic words, and mead was known to the Indo-Europeans—but apparently the principle of fermentation of fruit juices was a specialty of the Mediterranean peoples. Roman merchants had penetrated into the Germania of these early centuries, Roman farmers had settled in the Rhineland and the valley of the Moselle, and Germanic soldiers had marched with the Roman legions (Priebsch and Collinson 1966, pp. 264–65).

There are about 175 early loanwords from Latin, most of them indicating special spheres in which the Romans excelled, or were thought to do so by the Germanic peoples (Serjeantson 1935, pp. 271–77). Many of these words have survived into Modern English. They include *ancor* 'anchor' (Lat. *ancora*), *butere* 'butter' (Lat. *būtyrum*), *cealc* 'chalk' (Lat. *calc-*), *cēap*[1] 'marketplace, wares, price' (Lat. *caupō* 'tradesman,' more specifically 'wine-seller'), *cēse* 'cheese' (Lat. *cāseus*), *cetel* 'kettle' (Lat. *catillus* 'little pot'), *cycene* 'kitchen' (Lat. *coquīna*), *disc* 'dish' (Lat. *discus*), *mangere* '-monger, trader' (Lat. *mungō*), *mīl* 'mile' (Lat. *mīlia* [*passuum*] 'a thousand [paces]'), *mynet* 'coin,' coinage, Modern English *mint* (Lat. *monēta*), *piper* 'pepper'

---

[1] Obsolete as a noun except in proper names such as *Chapman, Cheapside* (once simply *Cheap*, then *Westcheap*), *Eastcheap*, and *Chepstow*. The adjectival and adverbial use of *cheap* is of early Modern English origin and is, according to the *OED*, a shortening of *good cheap* 'what can be purchased on advantageous terms.' *To cheapen* is likewise of early Modern English origin and used to mean 'to bargain for, ask the price of,' as when Defoe's Moll Flanders went out to "cheapen some laces."

(Lat. *piper*), *pund* 'pound' (Lat. *pondō* 'measure of weight'), *sacc* 'sack' (Lat. *saccus*), *sicol* 'sickle' (Lat. *secula*), *strǣt* 'paved road, street' (Lat. [*via*] *strāta* '[road] paved'), and *weall* 'wall' (Lat. *vallum*).

POPULAR AND LEARNED LOANWORDS

It is useful at this point to make a distinction between popular and learned loanwords. **Popular loanwords** are of oral transmission and are part of the vocabulary of everyday communication, like those words that have been cited. For the most part they are not felt to be in any way different from English words; in fact, those who use them are seldom aware that they are of foreign origin. **Learned loanwords**, on the other hand, owe their adoption to more or less scholarly influences. The principal influence in Old English times was, as we should expect, the church.

Learned words may in time become part of the living vocabulary, even though their use may be confined to a certain class or group; or they may, as with *clerk* (OE *cleric, clerc* from Lat. *clēricus*), pass into general usage. *Cleric* was once more taken from Latin as a learned word to denote a clergyman, since *clerk* had acquired other meanings, including 'scholar,' 'scribe,' 'one in charge of records and accounts in an organization,' and 'bookkeeper.' It was later to acquire yet another meaning, 'one who waits upon customers in a retail establishment,' in American English, the equivalent of the British 'shop assistant.' The earliest English meaning has survived in legal usage, in which a priest of the Church of England is described as a "clerk in holy orders."

The approximate time at which a word was borrowed is often indicated by its form: thus, as Mary Serjeantson points out (1935, p. 13), Old English *scōl* 'school' (Lat. *schola*, ultimately Greek) is obviously a later borrowing than *scrīn* 'shrine' (Lat. *scrīnium*), which must have been adopted before the Old English change of [sk-] to [š-] in order for it to have acquired the later sound. At the time when *scōl* was borrowed, this sound change was no longer operative. Had the word been borrowed earlier, it would have developed into Modern English **shool*.[2]

---

[2] Since all the early borrowings from Latin are popular loanwords, they have gone through all phonological developments that occurred subsequent to their adoption in the various Germanic languages. *Chalk, dish,* and *kitchen,* for instance, show, respectively, in their initial, final, and medial consonants the Old English palatalization of *k*; in addition, the last-cited word in its Old English form *cycene* shows mutation of Vulgar Latin *u* in the vowel of its stressed syllable. German *Küche* and *Münze* (corresponding to OE *mynet*) show the same mutation. An earlier *a* has been mutated by *i* in a following syllable in *cetel* (compare Ger. *Kessel*). It is similar with the German development of the same words. All have undergone the High German sound shift (see above, p. 95), the *d* of Latin *discus* occurring as *t* in *Tisch,* the medial *t* of *monēta* and *strāta* as *z* [ts] and *ss* in German *Münze* and *Strasse,* the *p* of Latin *pondō* and *piper* as *pf* and *ff* in German *Pfund* and *Pfeffer,* and the postvocalic *k* of Latin *secula* as *ch* in German *Sichel.* The fact that none of these early loanwords has been affected by the First Sound Shift (see pp. 89–94) indicates that they were borrowed after this shift had been completed.

Among the early English loanwords from Latin, some of which were acquired not directly, but from the British Celts, are *candel* 'candle' (Lat. *candēla*), *ceaster* 'city' (Lat. *castra* 'camp'),[3] *cest* 'chest' (Lat. *cista*, later *cesta*), *crisp* 'curly' (Lat. *crispus*), *earc* 'ark' (Lat. *arca*), *mægester* 'master' (Lat. *magister*), *mynster* 'monastery' (Lat. *monastērium*), *peru* 'pear' (Lat. *pirum*), *port* 'harbor' (Lat. *portus*), *sealm* 'psalm' (Lat. *psalmus*, taken from Gr.), and *tīgle* 'tile' (Lat. *tēgula*).

Somewhat later, after approximately A.D. 650, and hence not showing early English sound changes, such learned loanwords as the following occur: *alter* 'altar' (Lat. *altar*), *(a)postol* 'apostle' (Lat. *apostolus*), *balsam* (Lat. *balsamum*), *circul* 'circle' (Lat. *circulus*), *comēta* 'comet,' *cristalla* 'crystal' (Lat. *crystallum*), *dēmon* (Lat. *daemon*), *fers* 'verse' (Lat. *versus*), *mæsse*, *messe* 'mass' (Lat. *missa*, later *messa*), *martir* 'martyr' (Lat. *martyr*), *paper* (Lat. *papȳrus*), *plaster* (medical) (Lat. *emplastrum*), and *templ* 'temple' (Lat. *templum*). Since Latin borrowed freely from Greek, it is not surprising that some of the loans cited are of Greek origin; examples (to cite their Modern English forms) include *apostle, balsam, comet, crystal, demon,* and *paper.* This is the merest sampling of Latin loanwords in Old English. Somewhat more than 500 in all occur in the entire Old English period up to the Conquest. Serjeantson (1935, pp. 277–88) lists, aside from the words from the Continental period, 111 from the period from approximately A.D. 450 to 650, and 242 from approximately A.D. 650 to the time of the Norman Conquest. These numbers, of course, are not actually large as compared with the Latin borrowings in later times.

Many Latin loanwords, particularly those from the later period, were certainly never widely used, or even known. Some occur only a single time, or in only a single manuscript. Many were subsequently lost, some to be reborrowed, often with changes of meaning, at a later period from French or from Classical Latin. For instance, our words *sign* and *giant* are not from Old English *segn* and *gīgant* but are later borrowings from Old French *signe* and *geant.* In addition, a learned and a popular form of the same word might coexist in Old English—for instance, *Latin* and *Læden*, the second of which might also mean 'any foreign language.'

These loanwords, the later learned ones as well as the earlier popular ones, were usually made to conform to Old English declensional patterns, though occasionally, in translations from Latin into Old English, Latin case forms, particularly of proper names, may be retained (for example, "fram Agustō þām cāsere" from the translation of Bede's account of the departure

---

[3] This survives in *Chester, Castor, Caister*, and as an element in the names of a good many English places, many of which were once in fact Roman stations—for instance, *Casterton, Chesterfield, Exeter* (earlier *Execestre*), *Gloucester, Lancaster, Manchester,* and *Worcester.* The differences in form are mostly dialectal.

of the Romans from Britain: 'from Augustus the emperor,' with the Latin ending -ō in close apposition with the Old English dative endings in -m and -e). As with earlier borrowings, there came into being a good many **hybrid formations**: that is, native endings were affixed to foreign words—for example, -isc in *mechanisc* 'mechanical,' -dōm in *pāpdōm* 'papacy,' and -ere in *grammaticere* 'grammarian'—and hybrid compounds arose, such as *sealmscop* (Lat. *psalma* and OE *scop* 'singer, bard'). Infinitives took the Old English ending -ian, as in the grammatical term *declīnian* 'to decline.'

LATIN WORDS BORROWED IN MIDDLE ENGLISH TIMES

Many borrowings from Latin occurred during the Middle English period. Frequently it is impossible to tell whether a word is from French or from Latin—for instance, *complex*, *miserable*, *nature*, *register*, *relation*, *rubric*, and *social*, which might be from either language, judging by form alone. Depending on its meaning, the single form *port* may come from Latin *portus* 'harbor,' French *porter* 'to carry,' Latin *porta* 'gate,' or Portuguese *Oporto* (that is, *o porto* 'the port,' the city where "port" wine came from originally)—not to mention the nautical use of the word for one side of a ship, the origin of which is uncertain.

In the period between the Norman Conquest and 1500, many Latin words having to do with religion appeared in English, among them *collect* 'short prayer,' *dirge*, *mediator*, and *Redeemer* (first used with reference to Christ: the synonymous *redemptor* occurs earlier). To these, might be added legal terms—for instance, *client*, *conviction*, and *subpoena*; words having to do with scholastic activities—for instance, *index*, *library*, *scribe*, and *simile*; and words having to do with science—for instance, *dissolve*, *equal*, *essence*, *medicine*, *mercury*, *opaque*, *orbit*, *quadrant*, and *recipe*. These are only a few out of hundreds of Latin words that were adopted before 1500: a longer list would include verbs (for example, *admit*, *commit*, *discuss*, *interest*, *mediate*, *seclude*) and adjectives (for example, *complete*, *imaginary*, *instant*, *legitimate*, *obdurate*, *populous*).

LATIN WORDS BORROWED IN MODERN ENGLISH TIMES

The great period of borrowings from Latin and from Greek by way of Latin is the Modern English period. The century or so after 1500 saw the introduction of, among many others, the words *abdomen*, *area*, *compensate*, *data*, *decorum*, *delirium*, *denominate*, *digress*, *editor*, *fictitious*, *folio*, *gradual*, *imitate*, *janitor*, *jocose*, *lapse*, *medium*, *notorious*, *orbit*, *peninsula*, *querulous*, *quota*, *resuscitate*, *series*, *sinecure*, *strict*, *superintendent*, *transient*, *ultimate*, *urban*, *urge*, and *vindicate*.

Present-day loanwords with Latin etymologies are often terms that have been concocted from Latin morphemes but that were unknown as units to the ancients. The international vocabulary of science draws heavily on such **neo-Latin** forms, but so do the vocabularies of other areas of modern life. Among the recent classical contributions to English (with definitions from *The Barnhart Dictionary of New English since 1963*) are *aleatoric* 'dependent on chance' (from *āleātor* 'gambler, dice player'); *circadian* 'functioning or recurring in 24-hour cycles' (from *circā diēm* 'around the day'); *Homo habilis* 'extinct species of man believed to have been the earliest toolmaker' (literally 'skillful man'); *militaria* 'collection of objects having to do with the military, such as firearms, decorations, uniforms, etc.' (neut. pl. of *mīlitāris* 'military'); *Pax Americana* 'peace enforced by American power' (modeled on *Pax Romana*); and *vexillology* 'study of flags' (from *vexillum* 'flag' or 'banner'). Latin was the first major contributor of loanwords to English, and it remains one of our most important resources.

Greek Loanwords

Even before the Conquest a number of Greek words had entered English by way of Latin, in addition to some very early loans that may have come into Germanic directly from Greek, such as *church*. From the Middle English period on, Latin and French are the immediate sources of most loanwords ultimately Greek—for instance (from Latin), *allegory, anemia, anesthesia,*[4] *aristocracy, barbarous, chaos, comedy, cycle, dilemma, drama, electric, enthusiasm, epithet, epoch, history, homonym, metaphor, mystery, paradox, pharynx, phenomenon, rhapsody, rhythm, theory,* and *zone*; (from French) *center, character, chronicle, democracy, diet, dragon, ecstasy, fantasy, harmony, lyre, machine, nymph, pause, rheum,* and *tyrant*. Straight from Greek (though some are combinations unknown in classical times) come *acronym, agnostic, anthropoid, autocracy, chlorine, idiosyncrasy, kudos, oligarchy, pathos, phone, telegram,* and *xylophone*, among many others.

The richest foreign sources of our present English word stock are Latin, French, and Greek (including those words of Greek origin that have come to us by way of Latin and French). Many of the Latin and Greek words were in the beginning confined to the language of erudition, and some of them still are; others have passed into the stock of more or less everyday speech. It must be remembered in this connection that in earlier periods Latin was to the English the language of literature, science, and religion. Although Greek had tremendous prestige as a classical language, there was comparatively little firsthand knowledge of it in western Europe until the advent of refugee Greek scholars from Constantinople after the conquest of that city by the

---

[4] In its usual modern sense 'drug-induced insensibility,' this word was first used in 1846 by Oliver Wendell Holmes, who was a physician as well as a poet.

Turks in 1453. Hence, most of the Greek words that appear first in early Modern English occurred, as far as the English were concerned, in Latin works, though their Greek provenience usually would have been recognized. Latin was, in fact, freely used in both written and spoken forms by the learned all over Europe throughout the medieval and early modern periods. Petrarch translated Boccaccio's story of the patient Griselda into Latin to ensure that such a highly moral tale should have a wider circulation than it would have had in Boccaccio's Italian, and it was this Latin translation that Chaucer used as the source of his *Clerk's Tale*. More, Bacon, and Milton all wrote in Latin, just as the Venerable Bede and other learned men had done centuries earlier.

Celtic Loanwords

It is likely that even before the beginning of Latin borrowing in England, the English must have acquired some words from the Celts. As has been pointed out, some of the Latin loans of the period up to approximately A.D. 650 were acquired by the English indirectly through the Celts. It is likely that *ceaster* and *-coln*, as in *Lincoln* (Lat. *colōnia*), were so acquired. Phonology is not much help to us as far as such words are concerned, since they underwent the same prehistoric Old English sound changes as the words that the English brought with them from the Continent.

There are, however, a number of genuinely Celtic words acquired during the early years of the English settlement. We should not expect to find many, for the British Celts were a subject people, and a conquering people are unlikely to adopt many words from those whom they have supplanted. The very insignificant number of words from American Indian languages that have found a permanent place in American English strikingly illustrates this fact. The Normans are exceptional in that they ultimately gave up their own language altogether and became English, in a way in which the English never became Celts. Probably no more than a dozen or so Celtic words other than place names were adopted by the English up to the time of the Conquest.[5] These include *bannuc* 'a bit,' *bratt* 'cloak,' *brocc* 'badger,' *cumb* 'combe, valley,' and *torr* 'peak.' Just as many American place names are of Indian origin, so many English place names are of Celtic provenience: *Avon, Carlisle, Cornwall, Devon, Dover, London, Usk*, and scores more.

In more recent times a few more Celtic words have been introduced into English: from Irish Gaelic in the seventeenth century *brogue, galore, lepre-chaun, shamrock, tory*, and subsequently *banshee, blarney, colleen*, and

[5] There were, however, doubtless some Celtic loanwords in common Germanic and also in Latin: Old English *rīce* as a noun meaning 'kingdom' and as an adjective 'rich, powerful' (cf. Ger. *Reich*) is almost certainly of Celtic origin, borrowed before the settlement of the English in Britain. The Celtic origin of a few others (for example, OE *ambeht* 'servant,' *dūn* 'hill, down') has been seriously questioned.

shillelagh; from Scots Gaelic, in addition to *clan*, *loch*, and a few rarely used words that entered English in late Middle English times, *bog*, *cairn*, *plaid*, *slogan*, *whiskey*, and some others less familiar; from Welsh, *crag*, occurring first in Middle English, is the best known; others of more recent introduction include *cromlech* 'circle of large stones' and *eisteddfod* 'Welsh festival.'

Scandinavian Loanwords

OLD AND MIDDLE ENGLISH BORROWINGS

Most of the Scandinavian words in Old English do not actually occur in written records until the Middle English period, though undoubtedly they were current long before the beginning of that period. Practically all of the extant documents of the late Old English period come from the south of England, specifically from Wessex. It is likely that Scandinavian words were recorded in nonextant documents written in that part of the country to which Alfred the Great by force of arms and diplomacy had persuaded the Scandinavians to confine themselves—the Danelaw, comprising all of Northumbria and East Anglia and half of Mercia.

In the later part of the eleventh century the Scandinavians became gradually assimilated to English ways, though Scandinavian words had been in the meanwhile introduced into English. As we have seen, many Scandinavian words closely resembled their English cognates; sometimes, indeed, they were so nearly identical that it would be impossible to tell whether a given word was Scandinavian or English. Sometimes, however, if the meanings of obviously related words differed, **semantic contamination** might result, as when Old English *drēam* 'joy' acquired the meaning of the related Scandinavian *draumr* 'vision in sleep.' Otto Jespersen (1954, pp. 64–65) cites also *brēad* 'fragment,'[6] *blōma* 'lump of metal,' and poetic *eorl* 'warrior, noble' (ModE *bread*, *bloom* 'flower,' *earl*). The last of these words acquired the meaning of the related Scandinavian *jarl* 'underking, governor.' Similarly, the later meanings of *dwell* (OE *dwellan*, *dwelian*), *holm* 'islet' (same form in Old English), and *plow* (OE *plōh*) coincide precisely with the Scandinavian meanings, though in Old English these words meant, respectively, 'to lead astray, hinder,' 'ocean,' and 'measure of land.'

Late Old English and early Middle English loans from Scandinavian were made to conform wholly or in part with the English sound and inflectional system. These include (in modern form) *by* 'town, homestead,'[7] *carl* 'man' (cognate with OE *ceorl*, the source of *churl*), *fellow*, *hit* (first 'meet

---

[6] The usual Old English word for the food made from flour or meal was *hlāf*, as in "Ūrne gedæghwāmlīcan hlāf syle ūs tō dæg" 'Our daily bread give us today.'

[7] As in *bylaw* 'town ordinance.' The word also occurs in place names, as in *Derby*, *Grimsby*, and *Rigsby*.

with,' later 'strike'), *law, rag, sly, swain, take* (completely displacing *nim,* from OE *niman*), *thrall,* and *want.* The Scandinavian provenience of *sister* has already been alluded to (p. 104).

A good many words with [sk] are of Scandinavian origin, for, as we have seen, early Old English [sk], written *sc,* came to be pronounced [š]. Such words as *scathe, scorch, score, scot* 'tax' (as in *scot-free* and *scot and lot*), *scowl, scrape, scrub, skill, skin, skirt* (compare native *shirt*), and *sky* thus show by their initial consonant sequence that they entered the language after this change had ceased to be operative. All have been taken from Scandinavian.

Similarly the [g] and [k] before front vowels in *gear, geld, gill* (of a fish), *kick, kilt,* and *kindle* point to Scandinavian origins for these words, since the velar stops became in Old English under such circumstances [y] and [č], respectively. The very common verbs *get* and *give* come to us not from Old English *gitan* and *gifan,* which began with [y], but instead from cognate Scandinavian forms in which the palatalization of [g] in the neighborhood of front vowels did not occur. Native forms of these verbs with [y-] occur throughout the Middle English period side by side with the Scandinavian forms with [g-], which were ultimately to supplant them. Chaucer consistently used *yive, yeve,* and preterit *yaf.*

As a rule the Scandinavian loans involve little more than the substitution of one word for another (such as *window,* from *vindauga,* literally 'wind-eye,' replacing *eyethurl,* literally 'eyehole,' from OE *ēagþyrl*), the acquisition of new words for new concepts (such as certain Scandinavian legal terms) or new things (such as words for various kinds of warships with which the Scandinavians made the English acquainted), or the more or less sporadic and invariably slight modification in the form of an English word due to Scandinavian influence (like *sister*). More important and more fundamental is what happened to the Old English pronominal forms of the third person plural: all the *th-* forms, as we have seen (pp. 145 and 157), are of Scandinavian origin. Of the native forms in *h-* (p. 121), only *'em* (ME *hem;* OE *him*) survives, and it is commonly but mistakenly thought of as a reduced form of *them.*

SCANDINAVIAN LOANWORDS IN MODERN ENGLISH

A number of Scandinavian words have entered English during the modern period. The best known of them are *muggy, rug, scud,* and *ski,* the last of these dating from the later years of the nineteenth century. *Skoal* (Danish *skaal*) has had a recent alcoholic vogue. It comes as a surprise to learn that it first appears in English as early as 1600, though its early use seems to have been confined to Scotland. The *OED* reasonably suggests that it may have been introduced through the visit of James VI of Scotland (afterward James I of England) to Denmark, whither he journeyed in 1589 to meet his bride.

Geyser (1763), *rune* (1685), *saga* (1709), and *skald* (*ca.* 1763) are all from Icelandic. *Smörgåsbord* entered English from Swedish around the mid-1920s. It is usually written in English without the Swedish diacritics. Swedish *ombudsman* 'official who looks into citizens' complaints against government bureaus and against other officials' has as yet only limited currency, though it is entered in recent dictionaries.

French Loanwords

MIDDLE ENGLISH BORROWINGS

No loanwords unquestionably of French origin occur in English earlier than 1066. Leaving out of the question doubtful cases, some of the earliest loans that are unquestionably French are (to cite their Modern English forms) *castle, juggler, prison*, and *service*. *Capon* could be French but was most likely taken directly from Latin. As Alistair Campbell (1959, p. 221) observes, "Even after 1066 French words flow into the literary language more slowly than Norse ones, and they do not occur frequently until [after 1132]."

The Norman Conquest made French the language of the official class in England. Hence it is not surprising that many words having to do with government and administration, lay and spiritual, are of French origin: the word *government* itself, along with Middle English *amynistre*, later replaced by the Latin-derived *administer* with its derivative *administration*. Others include *attorney, chancellor, country, court, crime* (replacing English *sin*, which thereafter came to designate the proper business of the Church, though the State has from time to time tried to take it over), *(e)state*,[8] *judge, jury, noble*, and *royal*; in the religious sphere, *abbot, clergy, preach, sacrament*, and *vestment*, among a good many others. Words designating English titles of nobility except for *king, queen, earl, lord*, and *lady*—namely, *prince, duke, marquess, viscount, baron*, and their feminine equivalents—date from the period when England was in the hands of a Norman French ruling class. Even the earl's wife is a *countess*, and the peer immediately below him in rank is a *viscount* (that is, 'vice-count'), indicating that the earl corresponds in rank with the Continental count. In military usage, *army, captain, corporal, lieutenant* (literally 'place holding'), *sergeant* (originally a serving man or attendant), and *soldier* are all of French origin.[9]

---

[8] *State* is an aphetic form. Both it and the full form *estate* were obviously borrowed before French loss of *s* before *t* (Mod. Fr. *état*).

[9] *Colonel* does not occur in English until the sixteenth century (as *coronnel*, whence the pronunciation). French *brigade* and its derivative *brigadier* were introduced in the seventeenth century. *Major* is Latin, occurring first (as an adjective) in *sergeant major* in the later years of the sixteenth century; the nonmilitary adjectival use in English is somewhat earlier. The French equivalent has occurred in English since the end of the thirteenth century, its Modern English form being *mayor*.

French names were given not only to various animals when served up as food at Norman tables—*beef*, *mutton*, *pork*, and *veal*, for instance—but also to the culinary processes by which the English cow, sheep, pig, and calf were prepared for human consumption, for instance, *boil*, *broil*, *fry*, *roast*, and *stew*. Native English *seethe* is now used mostly metaphorically, as in *to seethe with rage* and *sodden in drink* (*sodden* being the old past participle of the strong verb *seethe* 'boil, stew'). Other French loans from the Middle English period, chosen more or less at random, are *dignity*, *enamor*, *feign*, *fool*, *fruit*, *horrible*, *letter*, *literature*, *magic*, *male*, *marvel*, *mirror*, *oppose*, *question*, *regard*, *remember*, *sacrifice*, *safe*, *salary*, *search*, *second* (replacing OE *ōðer*, as an ordinal number), *secret*, *seize*, *sentence*, *single*, *sober*, and *solace*.

French words have come into English from two dialects of French, the Norman spoken in England (Anglo-Norman) and the Central French (that of Paris, later standard French). We can frequently tell by the form of a word whether it is of Norman or of Central French provenience. For instance, Latin *c* [k] before *a* developed into *ch* [č] in Central French, but remained in the Norman dialect; hence *chapter*, from Middle English *chapitre* (from Old French), ultimately going back to Latin *capitulum* 'little head,' a diminutive of *caput*, is from the Central dialect. Compare also the **doublets** *chattel* and *cattle*, from Central French and Norman, respectively, both going back to Latin *capitāle* 'possession, stock,' *capital* in this sense being a Latin loan. Similarly, Old French *w* was retained in Norman French, but elsewhere became [gw] and then [g]: this development is shown in such doublets as *wage–gage* and *warranty–guarantee*. There are a good many other phonological criteria.

The century and a half between 1250 and the death of Chaucer was a period during which the rate of adoption of French words by English was greater than it had ever been before or has ever been since. A statistical study by Jespersen (1954, pp. 86–87) of a thousand French loanwords in those volumes of the *OED* available to him at the time of his investigation shows that nearly half were adopted during the period in question. Jespersen's estimate is based on the dates of earliest occurrence of these French words in writing, as supplied by the dated quotations in the *OED*. He was aware, of course, that the first written occurrence of a word, particularly of a popular word, is almost inevitably somewhat later than its actual first use. His table of the numbers of French loanwords grouped by the half centuries of their first known written appearance in English, remains nevertheless a striking demonstration of the chronology of French borrowing in English.

Let us pause to examine the opening lines of the *Canterbury Tales*, written toward the end of this period. The italicized words are of French origin:

> Whan that Aprille with hise shoures soote
> The droghte of *March* hath *perced* to the roote

And bathed every *veyne* in swich *licour*
Of which *vertu engendred* is the *flour*;
Whan Zephirus eek with his swete breeth   5
Inspired hath in every holt and heeth
The *tendre* croppes, and the yonge sonne
Hath in the Ram his half[e] *cours* yronne,
And smale foweles maken *melodye*,
That slepen al the nyght with open eye—   10
So priketh hem *nature* in hir *corages*—
Thanne longen folk to goon on *pilgrimage*[*s*],
And *Palmeres* for to seken *straunge* strondes,
To ferne halwes kowthe in sondry londes
And *specially* from every shires ende   15
Of Engelond to Caunturbury they wende
The hooly blisful martir for to seke
That hem hath holpen whan þat they were seeke.
Bifil that in that *seson* on a day,
In Southwerk at the *Tabard* as I lay   20
Redy to wenden on my *pilgrymage*
To Caunterbury with ful *devout corage*,
At nyght were come in to that *hostelrye*
Wel nyne and twenty in a *compaignye*
Of sondry folk by *aventure* y-falle   25
In felaweshipe, and *pilgrimes* were they alle
That toward Caunterbury wolden ryde.

[Ellesmere MS, ed. Furnivall 1868, pt. 1, p. 1]

In these 27 lines there are 189 words. Counting *pilgrimage* and *corage* only once, 24 of these words come from French. Such a percentage is doubtless also fairly typical of cultivated London usage in Chaucer's time. According to Serjeantson (1935, p. 151), between 10 and 15 percent of the words Chaucer used were of French origin. It will be noted, as has been pointed out before, that the indispensable, often used, everyday words—auxiliary verbs, pronouns, and particles—are of native origin. To the fourteenth century, as Serjeantson points out (p. 136), we owe most of the large number of still current abstract terms from French ending in -*ance*, -*ant*, -*ence*, -*ent*, -*ity*, -*ment*, -*tion*, and those beginning in *con*-, *de*-, *dis*-, *ex*-, *pre*-, and the like, though some of them do not actually show up in writing for another century or so.

LATER FRENCH LOANWORDS

Borrowing from French has gone on ever since the Middle Ages, though never on so large a scale. It is interesting to note that the same French word may be borrowed at various periods in the history of English, like *gentle*, *genteel,* and *jaunty,*[10] all from French *gentil*—the last two of seventeenth-century introduction. It is similar with *chief,* first occurring in English in the fourteenth century, and *chef,* in the nineteenth—the doublets show by their pronunciation the approximate time of their adoption: the Old French affricate [č] survives in *chief,* in which the vowel has undergone the expected shift from [ē] to [ī]; *chef* shows the Modern French shift of the affricate to the fricative [š]. In words of French origin spelled with *ch,* the pronunciation is usually indicative of the time of adoption: thus *chamber, champion, chance, change, chant, charge, chase, chaste, chattel, check,* and *choice* were borrowed in Middle English times, whereas *chamois, chauffeur, chevron, chic, chiffon, chignon, douche,* and *machine* have been taken over in Modern English times. Since *chivalry* was widely current in Middle English, one would expect it to begin in Modern English with [č]; the word has, as it were, been re-Frenchified, perhaps because with the decay of the institution it became more of an eye word than an ear word. Daniel Jones and A. C. Gimson (1977) record [č] as current but label such pronunciation old-fashioned.

Carriage, courage, language, savage, viage (later modernized as *voyage*), and *village,* came into English in Middle English times and have come to have initial stress in accordance with English patterns. Chaucer and his contemporaries could have it both ways in their poetry—for instance, either *couráge* or *cóurage,* as also with other French loans—for instance, *colour, figure, honour, pitee, valour, vertu.* This practice is still evidenced by such doublets as *dívers* and *divérse* (showing influence of Lat. *dīversus*). The position of the stress is frequently evidence of the period of borrowing: compare, for instance, older *cárriage* with newer *garáge, válour* with *velóur,* or *véstige* with *prestíge.*

Loans from French since the late seventeenth century are, as we should expect, less completely naturalized by and large than most of the older loans that have been cited, though some, like *cigarette, picnic, police,* and *soup,* seem commonplace enough. These later loans[11] also include *aide-de-camp, amateur, ballet, baton, beau, bouillon, boulevard, brochure, brunette, bureau, café, camouflage, chaise longue, champagne, chaperon* (in French, a hood or cap formerly worn by women),[12] *chi-chi* 'chic gone haywire,' *chiffonier* (in France, a ragpicker), *chute, cliché, commandant, communiqué, connoisseur, coupé* ('cut off,' past participle of *couper,* used of a closed car with short body and practically always pronounced [kup] in American English), *coupon, crêpe, crochet, débris, début(ante), décor, de luxe, dénouement, détour, élite,*

[10] *Gentile* was taken straight from Latin *gentīlis,* meaning 'foreign' in post–Classical Latin.

[11] In the forms cited, the French accents and other diacritics have been used, though many of the words cited with such markings are now printed without them in English.

[12] The English meaning is explained, doubtless correctly, as deriving from the notion that a married woman shields the younger girl as a hood shields the face. (See *OED,* s.v. *chaperon* 3, quotation for 1864.)

embonpoint,[13] *encore, ensemble, entrée, envoy, etiquette, fiancé(e), flair, foyer* (British [fwáje] or [fɔ́ɪje]; American [fɔ́ɪər]), *fuselage, genre, glacier, grippe, hangar, hors d'oeuvre, impasse, invalid, laissez faire, liaison, limousine, lingerie, massage, matinée*,[14] *mêlée, ménage, menu, morale, morgue, naïve, négligé* (as *negligee), nuance, passé, penchant, plateau, première, protégé, rapport, ration*,[15] *ravine, repartee, repertoire, reservoir, restaurant, reveille* (British [rɪvǽlɪ]; American [révəli]), *revue, risqué, roué, rouge, saloon* (and its less thoroughly Anglicized variant *salon), savant, savoir faire, souvenir, suède, surveillance, svelte, tête-à-tête, vignette,* and *vis-à-vis.*

There are also a fairish number of **loan translations** from French, such as *marriage of convenience (mariage de convenance), that goes without saying (ça va sans dire),* and *trial balloon (ballon d'essai).* In loan translation the parts of a foreign expression are translated, thus producing a new idiom in the native language, as in (to cite another French example) *reason of state* from *raison d'état.* Such forms are a kind of **calque.**

The suffix -*ville* in the names of so many American towns is, of course, of French origin. Of the American love for it, Matthew Arnold declared, with some justice: "The mere nomenclature of the country acts upon a cultivated person like the incessant pricking of pins. What people in whom the sense of beauty and fitness was quick could have invented, or could tolerate, the hideous names ending in *ville,* the Briggsvilles, Higginsvilles, Jacksonvilles, rife from Maine to Florida; the jumble of unnatural and inappropriate names everywhere?"[16] *Chowder, depot* 'railway station,' *gopher, levee* 'embankment,' *picayune, prairie, praline, shivaree (charivari),* and *voyageur* are Americanisms of French origin.

Spanish and Portuguese Loanwords

English has taken words from various other European languages as well, as we should expect in the light of the external history of the language, involving as this does the contact of English-speaking people with Continental Europeans as a result of cultural exchanges of one sort or another, of trade,

---

[13] Compare the loan translation *in good point,* which occurs much earlier, such as in Chaucer's description of the Monk in line 200 of the General Prologue of the *Canterbury Tales:* "He was a lord ful fat and in good poynt."

[14] Earlier, as its derivation from *matin* implies, a morning performance.

[15] The traditional pronunciation, riming with *fashion,* indicates the Modern French origin of this word, meaning originally 'portion of food given to a soldier.' It has acquired within the past 50 years or so a pronunciation on the analogy of *nation* and *station,* which came into English during the medieval period.

[16] *Civilization in the United States* (1888, reprinted by Nevins 1923, p. 509). Pylesville, in Harford County, Maryland, would really have set the pins to pricking in Arnold's soul. Fortunately, he seems not to have encountered this seat of American culture and fashion.

of exploration, and of colonization. Moreover, a good many non-European words entered English by way of Spanish, and to a smaller extent by way of Portuguese, mostly from the sixteenth century on. Spanish words and words of Spanish transmission, many coming from the New World, include *alligator* (*el lagarto* 'the lizard'), *anchovy, armada, armadillo* (literally 'little armed one'), *avocado* (ultimately Nahuatl *ahuacatl*, confused with Sp. *abogado* 'advocate, lawyer'), *barbecue, barracuda, bolero, cannibal* (*Caribal* 'Caribbean'), *cargo, cask* (*casque*), *castanet, chocolate* (ultimately Nahuatl), *cigar, cockroach, cocoa, cordovan* (leather; an older form, *cordwain*, comes through French), *corral, desperado, domino* 'cloak or mask,' *embargo, flotilla, galleon, guitar, junta, key* 'reef' (*cayo*), *maize* (ultimately Arawak), *mantilla, mescal* (ultimately Nahuatl), *mosquito* 'little fly,' *mulatto, negro, palmetto, peccadillo, plaza,*[17] *potato* (ultimately Arawak), *punctilio, sherry, silo, sombrero, tango, tomato* (ultimately Nahuatl), *tornado,*[18] *tortilla,* and *vanilla.* Many of these— for instance, *barbecue, barracuda,* and *tortilla*—are more familiar to Americans than to the English, though they may have occurred first in British sources.

A good many words were adopted from Spanish in the nineteenth century by Americans: *adobe, bonanza, bronco, buckaroo* (*vaquero*), *calaboose* (*calabozo*), *canyon, chaparral* 'scrub oak' (whence *chaps,* or *shaps,* 'leather pants worn by cowboys as protection against such vegetation'), *cinch, frijoles, hacienda, hoosegow* (*juzgado,* in Mexican Spanish 'jail'), *lariat* (*la reata* 'the rope'), *lasso, mesa, mustang, patio, pinto, poncho, pueblo, ranch, rodeo, sierra, siesta, stampede* (*estampida*), *stevedore* (*estivador* 'packer'), and *vamoose* (*vamos* 'let's go'). *Mescal, mesquite,* and *tamale* are ultimately Nahuatl, entering American English before the nineteenth century, like similar loans in British English, by way of Spanish. *Chili,* also of Nahuatl origin, entered British English in the seventeenth century, but it is likely, as M. M. Mathews (1948, p. 18) points out, that its occurrence in American English in the nineteenth century—"at the time we began to make first hand acquaintance with the Spanish speakers on our Southwestern border"— is not a continuation of the British tradition but represents an independent borrowing of a word for which Americans had had till that time very little if any use.

Twentieth-century borrowings include another food term—*frijoles refritos* and its loan translation, *refried beans*—as well as terms for drinks, such as *margarita* and *sangria. Chicano, macho,* and *machismo* reflect social phenomena of recent years. *Moment of truth* 'critical time for reaching a decision or taking action' is a translation of *momento de la verdad,* which refers to the moment of the kill, when a matador faces the charging bull; the term was

[17] From Latin *platēa,* also the ultimate source of the English loanword *place,* which occurs in Old English times, and of the Italian loanword *piazza.*
[18] A blend of *tronada* 'thunderstorm' and *tornar* 'to turn.'

popularized by Hemingway's novel *Death in the Afternoon*, though persons who use the expression now may be unaware of its origin in bullfighting.

No words came into English directly from Portuguese until the Modern English period; those that have been adopted include *albino, bossa nova, flamingo, madeira* (from the place), *molasses, pagoda, palaver,* and *pickaninny* (*pequenino* 'very small'). There are a few others considerably less familiar.

Italian Loanwords

From yet another Romance language, Italian, English has acquired a good many words, including much of our musical terminology. As early as the sixteenth century *duo, fugue, madrigal, viola da gamba* 'viol for the leg,' and *violin* appear in English; in the seventeenth century, *allegro, largo, opera, piano*[19] 'soft,' *presto, recitative, solo,* and *sonata;*[20] in the eighteenth, when interest in Italian music reached its apogee in England, *adagio, andante, aria, cantata, concerto, contralto, crescendo, diminuendo, duet, falsetto, finale, forte*[21] 'loud,' *libretto, maestro, obbligato, oratorio, rondo, soprano, staccato, tempo, trio, trombone, viola,* and *violoncello;* and in the nineteenth, *alto, cadenza, diva, legato, piccolo, pizzicato, prima donna,* and *vibrato.*

Other loanwords from Italian include *artichoke, balcony, balloon, bandit, bravo, broccoli, cameo, canto, carnival, casino, cupola, dilettante,*[22] *firm* 'business association,' *fresco, ghetto, gondola, grotto, incognito, inferno, influenza, lagoon, lava, malaria* (*mala aria* 'bad air'), *maraschino, miniature, motto, pergola, piazza, portico, regatta, replica, scope, stanza, stiletto, studio, torso, umbrella, vendetta,* and *volcano,* not to mention those words of ultimate Italian origin, like *cartoon, citron, corridor, gazette,* and *porcelain,* which have entered English by way of French. An expression of farewell, *ciao* [čaʊ], has enjoyed a period of great, although perhaps brief, popularity in trendy circles. The term *la dolce vita* was popularized by an Italian motion picture of that name; a *paparazzo* is a free-lance photographer who specializes in candid shots of beautiful people indulging in *la dolce vita.* Another kind of influence is attested by *Cosa Nostra* and *mafioso,* as well as the translation *godfather* for the head of a crime syndicate.

Macaroni (Mod. Italian *maccheroni*) came into English in the sixteenth

[19] As the name of the instrument, a clipped form of eighteenth-century *pianoforte,* the earliest occurrence cited by the *OED* is in 1803.

[20] In regard to this word the *OED* manages to antedate itself by eleven years. Its first citation is from 1694, though elsewhere (s.v. *piano* 'soft') there is a citation of Purcell's *Sonnatas* [sic] *in Three Parts,* the date of which is 1683.

[21] The identically written word pronounced with final *e* silent and meaning 'strong point' is from French.

[22] Frequently pronounced as if French, by analogy with *debutante.*

century,[23] *vermicelli* in the seventeenth, and *spaghetti* and *gorgonzola* (from the town) in the nineteenth. *Ravioli* (as *rafiol*) occurs in English in the fifteenth century, and later as *raviol* in the seventeenth century. Both forms are labeled obsolete and rare; it is indeed likely that the single occurrence of each form cited by the *OED* is the only one. The modern form thus can hardly be considered as continuing an older tradition but is instead a reborrowing, perhaps by way of American English in the twentieth century. *Al dente*, *lasagna*, *linguine*, *manicotti*, *pizza*, and *scampi* are also doubtless twentieth-century introductions into English—most of them probably by way of America, where Italian cooking is more popular than in England.

German Loanwords

LOANWORDS FROM LOW GERMAN

Dutch and other forms of Low German have contributed a number of words to English, to a large extent via the commercial relationships existing between the English and the Dutch and Flemish-speaking peoples from the Middle Ages on. It is often difficult to be sure which of the Low German languages was the source of an early loanword because they are quite similar to one another.

It is not surprising in view of their eminence in seafaring activities that the Dutch should have contributed a number of nautical terms: *boom* 'spar,' *bowline*, *bowsprit*, *buoy*, *commodore*, *cruise*, *deck* (Dutch *dec* 'roof,' then in English 'roof of a ship,' a meaning that later got into Dutch), *dock*, *freight*, *iceberg*, *keel*, *lighter* 'flat-bottomed boat,' *marline* (the name of the fish *marlin* is short for *marlinespike*), *rover* 'pirate,' *scow*, *skipper* (*schipper* 'shipper,' that is, 'master of a ship'), *sloop*, *smuggle*, *split* (in early use, 'break a ship on a rock'), *taffrail*, *yacht*, and *yawl*.

The Dutch and the Flemish were also famed for their cloth making. Terms like *cambric*, *duck* (a kind of cloth), *duffel* (from the name of a place), *nap*, *pea jacket*, and *spool* suggest the cloth-making trade, which merchants carried to England, along with such commercial terms as *dollar*, *groat*, *guilder*, and *mart*. England was also involved militarily with Holland, a connection reflected in a number of loanwords: *beleaguer*, *forlorn hope* (a remodeling by folk etymology from *verloren hoop* 'lost troop,' Dutch *hoop* being cognate with English *heap*, as of men), *furlough*, *kit* (originally a vessel for carrying a soldier's equipment), *knapsack*, *onslaught*, and *tattoo* 'drum signal, military entertainment.'

---

[23] Its doublet *macaroon*, though designating quite a different food, entered English by way of French in the seventeenth century. *Maccaroni* was the plural of *maccarone*; the singular form was taken into French and adapted as *macaron*, whence the English form *macaroon*.

The reputation of the Dutch for eating and especially drinking well is attested by *booze, brandy(wine), gherkin, gin* (short for *genever*—borrowed by the Dutch from Old French, ultimately Latin *juniperus* 'juniper,' confused in English with the name of the city *Geneva*), *hop* (a plant whose cones are used as a flavoring in malt liquors), *log(g)y*, and *pickle*. Perhaps as a result of indulgence in such Dutch pleasures, we have *frolic* (*vrolijk* 'joyful,' cognate with German *fröhlich*) and *rant* (earlier 'be boisterously merry'). Dutch painting was also valued in England, and consequently we have as loanwords *easel, etch, landscape* (the last element of which has given rise to a large number of derivatives, including recently *moonscape* and *earthscape* as space travel has allowed us to take a larger view of our surroundings), *maulstick*, and *sketch*.

Miscellaneous loans from Low German include *boor* (*boer*), *brake, gimp, hanker, isinglass* (a folk-etymologized form of *huysenblas*), *luck, skate* (Dutch *schaats*, with the final -*s* mistaken for a plural ending), *snap, wagon* (the related OE *wægn* gives modern *wain*), and *wiseacre* (Middle Dutch *wijsseggher* 'soothsayer'). From South African Dutch (Afrikaans) have come *apartheid, commandeer, commando, kraal* (borrowed by Dutch from Portuguese and related to the Spanish loanword *corral*), *outspan, spoor, trek,* and *veld*.

A number of loanwords have entered English through the contact of Americans with Dutch settlers, especially in the New York area. There are Dutch-American food terms like *coleslaw* (*koolsla* 'cabbage salad'), *cookie, cranberry, cruller, pit* 'fruit stone,' and *waffle*. The diversity of other loanwords reflects the variety of cultural contacts English and Dutch speakers had in the New World: *boodle, boss, bowery, caboose, dope, Santa Claus* (*Sante Klaas* 'Saint Nicholas'), *sleigh, snoop, spook,* and *stoop* 'small porch.'

LOANWORDS FROM HIGH GERMAN

High German has had comparatively little impact on English. Much of the vernacular of geology and mineralogy is of German origin—for instance, *cobalt, feldspar* (a half-translation of *Feldspath*), *gneiss, kleinite* (from Karl Klein, mineralogist), *lawine* 'avalanche,' *loess, meerschaum, nickel* (originally *Kupfernickel*, perhaps 'copper demon,' partially translated as *kopparnickel* by the Swedish mineralogist Von Cronstedt, from whose writings the abbreviated form entered English in 1755), *quartz, seltzer* (ultimately a derivative of Selters, near Wiesbaden), and *zinc*. *Carouse* occurs in English as early as the sixteenth century, from the German *gar aus* 'all out,' meaning the same as *bottoms up*. Originally adverbial, it almost immediately came to be used as a verb, and shortly afterward as a noun.

Other words taken from German include such culinary terms as *braunschweiger, delicatessen, noodle* (*Nudel*), *pretzel, pumpernickel, sauerkraut* (occurring first in British English, but the English never cared particularly for the dish, and the word may to all intents and purposes be considered an

Americanism, independently reborrowed), *schnitzel, wienerwurst,* and *zwie-back. Knackwurst, liederkranz,* and *sauerbraten* are fairly well known but can hardly be considered completely naturalized. *Liverwurst* is a half-translation of *Leberwurst. Hamburger, frankfurter,* and *wiener* are doubtless the most popular of all German loans. The vernacular of drinking includes *bock* (from *Eimbocker Bier* 'beer of Eimbock,' shortened in German to *Bockbier*), *katzenjammer* 'hangover' (though more widely known from *The Katzenjammer Kids*), *kirsch(wasser), lager,* and *schnapps. Cold Duck,* a kind of mixed wine, is a loan translation of *Kalte Ente,* which is (according to *The Barnhart Dictionary of New English*) a remodeling of *kalte Ende* "cold ends, a phrase used to describe leftover wines mixed and served at the close of a party."

Other words from German include *drill* 'fabric,' *hamster, landau* (from the place of that name), *plunder* (*plündern*), *waltz,* and the dog names *dachshund, Doberman(n) pinscher, poodle* (*Pudel*), and *spitz.* We also have *edelweiss, ersatz, hinterland, leitmotiv, poltergeist, rucksack, schottische, yodel* (*jodeln*), and the not yet thoroughly naturalized *gemütlich, Gestalt, Sitzfleisch* 'perseverance,' *Weltanschauung,* and *Weltansicht. Ablaut, umlaut,* and *schwa* (ultimately Hebrew) have been used as technical terms in this book. *Blitz(krieg)* and *Luftwaffe* had an infamous success in 1940 and 1941, but they have since receded.

Seminar and *semester* are, of course, ultimately Latin, but they entered American English by way of German. American *seminar,* as Mathews (1951) says, is probably "independent of the British borrowing of about the same date," that is, the late nineteenth century, when many American and English scholars went to Germany in pursuit of their doctorates. *Semester* is known in England, but the English have little use for it save in reference to foreign universities. *Academic freedom* is a loan translation of *akademische Freiheit. Bummeln* is used by German students to mean 'to loiter, waste time,' and it may be the source of American English *to bum* and the noun in the sense 'loafer,' though this need not be an academic importation.

On a less elevated level, American English uses such expressions as *gesundheit* (when someone has sneezed) and *nix* (*nichts*), and German-Americans have doubtless been responsible for adapting the German suffix *-fest,* as in *Sängerfest,* to English uses, as in *songfest* and *gabfest. Biergarten* has undergone translation in *beer garden; kindergarten* is frequently pronounced as though the last element were English *garden.* By way of the Germans from the Palatinate who settled in southern Pennsylvania in the early part of the eighteenth century come a number of terms of German origin little known in other parts of the United States, such as *smearcase* 'cottage cheese' (*Schmierkäse*), *snits* 'fruit cut for drying,' and *sots* 'yeast.' *Kriss Kingle* or *Kriss Kringle* (*Christkindl* 'Christ child') and *to dunk* have become nationally known.

Yiddish (that is, *Jüdisch* 'Jewish') has been responsible for the introduction of a number of German words and minced forms of German words, some having special meanings in Yiddish, among them, *kibitzer, phooey, schlemiel, schmaltz, schnozzle, shmo, shnook, shtick*, and others less widely known to non-Jews. Other recent contributions of Yiddish are *chutzpah, klutz, kvetch, mavin, mensch, nebbish, nosh, schlep, schlock, schmear, yenta*, and *zoftig*—all distinctly ethnic in tone. The suffix *-nik*, ultimately of Slavic origin and popularized by the Soviet *sputnik*, has also been disseminated by Yiddish through such forms as *nudnik*; it has been widely used in forms like *beatnik, filmnik, neatnik, no-goodnik*, and *peacenik*.

Loanwords from the East

NEAR EAST

As early as Old English times, words from the East doubtless trickled into the language, then always by way of other languages. *Ealfara* 'pack horse' and *mancus* 'coin' have been cited as commercial loans from Arabic. Neither word has survived, and the second occurs only once in the Old English writings that have come down to us (Serjeantson 1935, p. 214). A number of words ultimately Arabic, most of them having to do in one way or another with science or with commerce, came in during the Middle English period, usually by way of French or Latin. These include *amber, camphor, cipher*,[24] *cotton, lute, mattress, orange, saffron, sugar, syrup*, and *zenith*.

The Arabic definite article *al* is retained in one form or another in *alchemy, alembic, algorism, alkali, almanac, azimuth* (*as* [for *al*] plus *sumūt* 'the ways'), *elixir* (*el* [for *al*] plus *iksīr* 'the philosopher's stone'), and *hazard* (*az* [for *al*] plus *zahr* 'the die'). In *admiral*, occurring first in Middle English, the Arabic article occurs in the final syllable: the word is an abbreviation of some such phrase as *amīr-ul-baḥr* 'commander (of) the sea.' Through confusion with Latin *admīrābilis* 'admirable,' the word has acquired a *d*; *d*-less forms occur, however, as late as the sixteenth century, though ultimately the blunder with *d*, which occurs in the first known recording of the word—in Layamon's *Brut*, written around the end of the twelfth century—was to prevail. *Alcohol* (*al-kuḥl* 'the kohl, that is, powder of antimony for staining the eyelids'),[25] *alcove*, and *algebra*, all beginning with the article, were introduced in early Modern times, along with a good many words without the article—for

---

[24] From Arabic *ṣifr* by way of Medieval Latin. The Italians modified the same Arabic word as *zero*, by way of **zefiro* (*OED*). This Italian form entered English in the early Modern period.

[25] The modern meaning, which occurred in the European languages borrowing the word, has come about in a rather complicated way. Its development from a specific powder to any powder to essence (or "spirit," as in obsolete *alcohol of wine*) to the spirituous element in beverages is traced in the *OED* for anyone who wishes to follow it.

instance, *assassin* (originally 'hashish eater'), *caliber, candy, carat, caraway, fakir, garble, giraffe, harem, hashish, henna, jinn* (plural of *jinnī*), *lemon, magazine* (ultimately an Arabic plural form meaning 'storehouses'), *minaret, mohair, sherbet,* and *tariff.* Some of these were transmitted through Italian, others through French; some were taken directly from Arabic. *Coffee,* ultimately Arabic, was taken into English by way of Turkish.

Other Semitic languages have contributed little directly, though a number of words ultimately Hebrew have come to us by way of French. Regardless of the method of their transmission, most of us must be aware of the ultimate or immediate Hebrew origin of *amen, behemoth, cabbala, cherub, hallelujah, jubilee, rabbi, Sabbath, seraph, shekel,* and *shibboleth.* Both *Jehovah* (*Yahweh*) and *Satan* are Hebrew. Yiddish uses a very large number of Hebrew words and seems to have been the medium of transmission for *goy, kosher, matzo* (plural *matzoth*), *mazuma,* and *tokus* 'backside.'

IRAN AND INDIA

Persian and Sanskrit are not exotic in the same sense as Arabic, for both are Indo-European; yet the regions in which they were spoken were far removed from England, and they were to all intents and purposes highly exotic. Consequently, such words as Persian *bazaar* and *caravan* (in the nineteenth century clipped to *van*) must have seemed as exotic to the English in the sixteenth century, when they first became current, as Chinese *wok* and Japanese *sukiyaki* seem to most people past middle age today. *Azure, musk, paradise, satrap, scarlet, taffeta,* and *tiger* occur, among others, in the Middle English period. None of these are direct loans, coming rather through Latin or Old French; later, from the same two immediate sources, come *naphtha, tiara,* and a few Persian words borrowed through Turkish, such as *giaour.*

In addition, some Persian words were borrowed in India. *Cummerbund* 'loin-band' first appears (as *combarband*) in the early seventeenth century and reappears within the last 60 years or so as a name for an article of men's semiformal evening dress frequently replacing the low-cut waistcoat. *Seersucker* is an Indian modification of Persian *shīr o shakkar* 'milk and sugar,' the name of a fabric that came into vogue in America about half a century ago. *Khaki* 'dusty, cloth of that color,' recorded in English first in 1857 but not widely known in America until much later, was at first pronounced [káki], though [kǽki] prevails nowadays.

Direct from Persian, in addition to *caravan* and *bazaar,* come *baksheesh, dervish, mogul, shah,* and *shawl. Chess* comes directly from Old French; it is an aphetic form of *esches,* but the word is ultimately Persian, as is *check* (in all its senses), from the variant Old French form *eschecs.* The words go back to Persian *shāh* 'king,' which was taken into Arabic in the specific sense 'the king in the game of chess,' whence *shāh māt* 'the king is dead,' the source of *checkmate.* The derivative *exchequer* (OF *eschequier* 'chess board') came about through the fact that accounts used to be reckoned on a table marked with squares like a chess (or *checker*) board. *Rook* 'chess piece' is also ultimately derived from Persian *rukhkh* 'castle.'

From Sanskrit come, along with a few others, *avatar, karma, mahatma, swastika*, and *yoga* ('union,' akin to English *yoke*). *Swastika* denotes in English a symbol of the Nazi party in Germany but is actually little known in that country, where the name of the figure is usually *Hakenkreuz* 'hook-cross'; *swastika* occurs in English first in the latter half of the nineteenth century. Sanskrit *dvandva, sandhi*, and *svarabhakti* are pretty much confined to the vernacular of linguistics; nonlinguists get along without them very well.

Ginger, which occurs in Old English (*gingifere*), is ultimately Prakrit. From Hindustani come *bandanna, bangle, bungalow, chintz, cot, dinghy, dungaree, gunny* 'sacking,' *juggernaut, jungle, loot, maharaja* (and *maharani*), *nabob, pajamas, pundit, sahib, sari, shampoo*, and *thug*, along with a number of other words that are much better known in England than in America (for instance, *babu, durbar*, and *pukka*). *Pal* is from Romany, or Gypsy, which is an Indic dialect. A good many Indic words have achieved general currency in English because of their use by literary men, especially Kipling, though he had distinguished predecessors, including Scott, Byron, and Thackeray.

The non-Indo-European languages, called Dravidian, spoken in southern India have contributed such fairly well-known words as *copra, curry, mango, pariah*, and *teak*. Of these, *curry* and *pariah*, from Tamil, are direct loans; the others have come to us by way of Portuguese, *mango* from Portuguese by way of Malay.

FAR EAST AND AUSTRALASIA

Other English words from languages spoken in the Orient are comparatively few in number, but some are quite well known. *Silk* may be ultimately from Chinese, although there is no known etymon in that language; as *seoloc* or *sioloc* the word came into English in Old English times from Baltic or Slavic. Serjeantson (1935, p. 237) cites *catchup* (*ketchup*), *japan* 'varnish' (from the Chinese name of the country, called *Nippon* by the Japanese), and *tea*, along with the names of some varieties of tea (*bohea, oolong, pekoe*, and *souchong*). *Ginseng, kowtow, litchi*, and *pongee* have come direct from Chinese, along with the Americanisms of Chinese origin *chop suey, chow, chow mein*, and *tong* 'secret society.' From Japanese have come *banzai, geisha, hara-kiri, (jin)ricksha, kimono, sake* 'liquor,' *samurai*, and *soy(a)*, along with the ultimately Chinese *judo, ju-jitsu*, and *tycoon*. *Kamikaze* had a certain vogue during World War II. The word, designating so-called suicide pilots, literally means 'divine wind.'

From the languages spoken in the islands of the Pacific come *bamboo*, *gingham, launch,* and *mangrove,* and others mostly adopted before the beginning of the nineteenth century by way of French, Portuguese, Spanish, or Dutch. *Rattan,* direct from Malay, appears first in Pepys's *Diary* (as *rattoon*), where it designates, not the wood, but a cane made of it: "Mr. Hawley did give me a little black rattoon, painted and gilt" (13 September 1660). Polynesian *taboo* and *tattoo*[26] 'decorative permanent skin marking,' along with a few other words from the same source, appear in English around the time of Captain James Cook's voyages (1768–79); they occur first in his journals. *Ukulele* is Polynesian, entering American English by way of Hawaii around 1900; *luau,* also Polynesian, came in fairly recently. Captain Cook also first recorded Australian *kangaroo. Boomerang* (as *wo-mur-rāng*), another Australian word, occurs first somewhat later. *Budgerigar,* also Australian and designating a kind of parrot, is well known in England, where it is frequently clipped to *budgie* by those who fancy the birds, usually known as *parakeets* in America.

Other Sources

LOANWORDS FROM AFRICAN LANGUAGES

A few words from languages spoken by blacks on the west coast of Africa have entered English by way of Portuguese and Spanish, notably *banana* and *yam,* both appearing toward the end of the sixteenth century. It is likely, as Mathews (1948, pp. 111–12) points out, that *yam* entered the vocabulary of American English independently. In the South, where it is used more frequently than elsewhere, it designates not just any kind of sweet potato, as in other parts, but a red sweet potato, which is precisely the meaning it has in the Gullah form *yambi.* Hence Mathews thinks, very plausibly, that this word was introduced into Southern American English direct from Africa, even though there is no question of its Portuguese transmission in earlier English: "Our word came to us directly from headquarters, that is from Africa," he declares, pointing out that "we had in our midst the very people who gave the word to the Portuguese."

Voodoo, with its variant *hoodoo,* is likewise of African origin and was introduced by way of American English. *Gorilla* is apparently African: it first occurs in English in the *Boston Journal of Natural History* in 1847, according to Mathews's *Dictionary of Americanisms* (1951), though a plural form *gorillae* occurs in 1799 in British English. *Juke* (more correctly *jook*) and *jazz* are Americanisms of African origin. Both were more or less disreputable when first introduced but have in the course of time lost most of their earlier sexual connotations. Other African words transmitted into

---

[26] Not the same as *tattoo* 'drum or bugle signal, (later) military entertainment,' which is from Dutch *tap toe* 'the tap (is) to,' that is, 'the taproom is closed.'

American English are *banjo, buckra, cooter* 'turtle,' the synonymous *goober* and *pinder* 'peanut,' *gumbo, jigger* 'sand flea,' recorded in the dictionaries as *chigoe,* and *zombi. Samba* and *rumba* are ultimately African, coming to English by way of Brazilian Portuguese and Cuban Spanish, respectively. There can no longer be much doubt that *tote* is of African origin; the evidence presented by Lorenzo Dow Turner (1949, p. 203) seems fairly conclusive.

SLAVIC, HUNGARIAN, TURKISH, AND AMERICAN INDIAN

Very minor sources of the English vocabulary are Slavic, Hungarian, Turkish, and American Indian, with few words from these sources used in English contexts without reference to the countries from which they have been borrowed. Most have been borrowed during the Modern period, since 1500, and practically all by way of other languages.

Slavic *sable* comes to us in Middle English times not directly but by way of French. From Czech we later acquired, also indirectly, *polka. Mazurka* is from a Polish term for a dance characteristic of the Mazur community. We have borrowed the word *horde* indirectly from the Poles, who themselves acquired it from the Turks. *Astrakhan* and *mammoth* are directly from Russian. Other Russian words that are known but hardly thoroughly naturalized are *bolshevik, borzoi, czar* (ultimately Lat. *Caesar*), *intelligentsia* (ultimately Latin), *kopeck, muzhik, pogrom, ruble, samovar, soviet, sputnik, steppe, tovarisch, troika, tundra, ukase,* and *vodka.*

Goulash, hussar, and *paprika* have been taken directly from Hungarian. *Coach* comes to us directly from French *coche* but goes back ultimately to Hungarian *kocsi. Vampire* is of Hungarian or Slavic origin (the close linguistic contact among East Europeans making it often difficult to be sure of exact sources), but the shortening to *vamp* is a purely native English phenomenon.

Jackal, ultimately Persian, comes to English by way of Turkish; *khan* occurs as a direct loan quite early. Other Turkish words used in English include *fez* and the fairly recent *shish kebab. Tulip* is from *tulipa(nt),* a variant of *tülbend* (taken by Turkish from Persian *dulband*); a doublet of the Turkish word comes into English in modified form as *turban(d).* The flower was so called because it was thought to look like the Turkish headgear. *Coffee,* as has been pointed out, is ultimately Arabic, but comes to us directly from Turkish; the same is true of *kismet.*

American Indian words do not loom large, even in American English, though many have occurred in American English writings. Most of the 132 words borrowed from Algonquian dialects compiled by Alexander F. Chamberlain in 1902 (Mencken 1945, pp. 169–71) have now gone out of use or are but dimly known—for instance, *peag, sagamore,* and *squantum.* Those that have survived are, thanks to the European vogue of James Fenimore Cooper, about as well known transatlantically as in America: they include *moccasin, papoose, squaw, toboggan,* and *tomahawk.* Others with perhaps fewer literary associations are *moose, opossum, pecan, skunk, terrapin*, and *woodchuck*. Muskhogean words are more or less confined to the southern American states—for instance, *bayou, catalpa*, and a good many proper names like *Tallahassee, Tombigbee*, and *Tuscaloosa*. Many place names are, of course, taken from Indian languages. Loans from Nahuatl, almost invariably of Spanish transmission, have been mentioned already (see p. 306).

The Sources of Recent Loanwords

English speakers continue to borrow words from almost every language spoken upon the earth. A study of the loanwords recorded in two new-word dictionaries, *6,000 Words* and *The Barnhart Dictionary of New English* (Cannon and Egle 1979), reports that, during the 15-year period 1961–76, 473 loanwords entered the language. French has maintained its position as the major contributor of new foreign words to English by supplying 30 percent of those loans. It is followed by Latin as a distant second (8 percent); the Latin contributions are primarily terms from the international scientific vocabulary that would have been quite unrecognizable to the ancient Romans. Japanese and Italian both have supplied 7 percent of the new loanwords, the former having greatly increased its importance as a source language for English in recent years. Other contributors (with the percentage of their contributions in parentheses) are Spanish (6 percent); German and Greek (5 percent each); African languages, Russian, and Yiddish (4 percent each); Arabic, Chinese, Hindi, and Sanskrit (2 percent each); and Afrikaans, Hebrew, Indonesian, Norwegian, Portuguese, Swedish, and Vietnamese (1 percent each). Collectively accounting for 5 percent of the recent loans, although less than 1 percent each, are American Indian languages, Annamese, Bengali, Czech, Danish, Eskimo, Hungarian, Irish, Korean, Mongolian, Nahuatl, Persian, Pilipino (the national language of the Philippines), Provençal, Samoan, Serbo-Croatian, Tahitian, Tongan, Urdu, Welsh, and West Indian languages.

English Remains English

Enough has been written to indicate the cosmopolitanism of the present English vocabulary. Yet English remains English in every essential respect: the words that all of us use over and over again, the grammatical structures in which we couch our observations upon practically everything under the sun remain as distinctively English as they were in the days of Alfred the Great. What has been acquired from other languages has not always been particularly worth gaining: no one could prove by any set of objective standards that *army* is a "better" word than *dright* or *here*, which it displaced, or that *advice* is any better than the similarly displaced *rede*, or that *to contend* is any better than *to flite*. Those who think that *manual* is a better, or more beautiful, or more intellectual word than English *handbook* are, of course, entitled to their opinion. But such esthetic preferences are purely matters of style and have nothing to do with the subtle patternings that make one language different from another. For, as has been demonstrated time and again in this book, language is nothing so simple as words. The words we choose are nonetheless of tremendous interest in themselves, and they throw a good deal of light upon our cultural history.

But with all its manifold new words from other tongues, English could never have become anything but English. And as such it has sent out to the world, among many other things, some of the best books the world has ever known. It is not unlikely, in the light of writings by Englishmen in earlier times, that this would have been so even if we had never taken any words from outside the word hoard that has come down to us from those times. It is true that what we have borrowed has brought greater wealth to our word stock, but the true Englishness of our mother tongue has in no way been lessened by such loans, as those who speak and write it lovingly will always keep in mind.

It is highly unlikely that many readers will have noted that the preceding paragraph contains not a single word of foreign origin. It was perhaps not worth the slight effort involved to write it so; it does show, however, that English would not be quite so impoverished as some commentators suppose it would be without its many accretions from other languages.

For Further Reading

Barnhart, Steinmetz, and Barnhart, *The Barnhart Dictionary of New English since 1963*, 1973.

Barnhart, Steinmetz, and Barnhart, *The Second Barnhart Dictionary of New English*, 1980.

Benjamin and Schneidemesser, "German Loanwords in American English, A Bibliography of Studies, 1872–1978," *American Speech*, 1979.

Cannon and Egle, "New Borrowings in English," *American Speech*, 1979.

Rao, *Indian Words in English: A Study in Indo-British Cultural and Linguistic Relations*, 1954.

Serjeantson, *A History of Foreign Words in English*, 1935.

6,000 Words: A Supplement to Webster's Third New International Dictionary, 1976.

Turner, *Africanisms in the Gullah Dialect*, 1949.

Selected Bibliography

Works cited in the text are listed here, along with some additional books and periodicals that should prove useful in one way or another to the student of linguistics. This bibliography is necessarily limited; it includes works ranging from the semipopular to the scholarly abstruse, although only a few specialized studies of technical problems have been included. A few items deal with general linguistic theory.

Abbott, E. A. *A Shakespearian Grammar*. 2nd ed. London: Macmillan, 1870.

Adams, Ramon F. *Western Words: A Dictionary of the Range, Cow Camp, and Trail*. Rev. ed. Norman: Univ. of Oklahoma Press, 1968.

Adams, Valerie. *An Introduction to Modern English Word-Formation*. London: Longman, 1973.

Akmajian, Adrian; Demers, Richard A.; and Harnish, Robert A. *Linguistics: An Introduction to Language and Communication*. Cambridge, Mass.: MIT Press, 1979.

————; and Heny, Frank W. *An Introduction to the Principles of Transformational Syntax*. Cambridge, Mass.: MIT Press, 1980.

Alexander, Henry. *The Story of Our Language*. Rev. ed. New York: Doubleday, 1962.

Algeo, John. "The Acronym and Its Congeners." In *The First Lacus Forum 1974*, ed. Adam Makkai and Valerie Becker Makkai, pp. 217–34. Columbia, S.C.: Hornbeam, 1975.

————. "Grammatical Usage: Modern Shibboleths." In *James B. McMillan: Essays in Linguistics by His Friends and Colleagues*, ed. James C. Raymond and I. Willis Russell, pp. 53–71. University: Univ. of Alabama Press, 1977.

————. *Problems in the Origins and Development of the English Language*. 3rd ed. New York: Harcourt Brace Jovanovich, 1982.

————. "The Taxonomy of Word Making." *Word* 29 (1978): 122–31.

————. "The Voguish Uses of *Non.*" *American Speech* 46 (1971): 87–105.

————. "Where Do All the New Words Come From?" *American Speech* 55 (1980): 264–77.

Allen, Harold B. *The Linguistic Atlas of the Upper Midwest.* 3 vols. Minneapolis: Univ. of Minnesota Press, 1973–76.

————. *Linguistics and English Linguistics.* 2nd ed. Goldentree Bibliographies. Arlington Heights, Ill.: AHM Pub., 1977.

————, ed. *Readings in Applied English Linguistics.* 2nd ed. New York: Appleton-Century-Crofts (Englewood Cliffs, N.J.: Prentice-Hall), 1964.

————. "Regional Dialects, 1945–1974." *American Speech* 52 (1977): 163–261.

————; and Underwood, Gary, eds. *Readings in American Dialectology.* New York: Appleton-Century-Crofts (Englewood Cliffs, N.J.: Prentice-Hall), 1971.

Alston, R. C. *An Introduction to Old English.* New York: Harper & Row, 1961.

The American Heritage Dictionary of the English Language, ed. William Morris. Boston: Houghton Mifflin, 1976.

American Speech: A Quarterly of Linguistic Usage. Journal of the American Dialect Society. 1925–date.

Amon, Aline. *Reading, Writing, Chattering Chimps.* New York: Atheneum, 1975.

Anderson, James Maxwell. *Structural Aspects of Language Change.* London: Longman, 1973.

Anderson, John M.; and Jones, Charles, eds. *Historical Linguistics: Proceedings of the First International Conference on Historical Linguistics, Edinburgh, 2nd–7th September 1973.* New York: American Elsevier, 1974.

Andrew, S. O. *Syntax and Style in Old English.* 1940. Reprint. New York: Russell and Russell, 1966.

Anglo-Saxon England, ed. Peter Clemoes. Cambridge: University Press, 1972–date.

Anttila, Raimo. *An Introduction to Historical and Comparative Linguistics.* New York: Macmillan, 1972.

Arlotto, Anthony. *Introduction to Historical Linguistics.* Boston: Houghton Mifflin, 1972.

Armstrong, Lilias E.; and Ward, Ida C. *A Handbook of English Intonation.* 2nd ed. 1931. Reprint. London: Heffer, 1963.

Atwood, E. Bagby. *The Regional Vocabulary of Texas.* Austin: Univ. of Texas Press, 1962.

————. *A Survey of Verb Forms in the Eastern United States.* Ann Arbor: Univ. of Michigan Press, 1953.

Avis, Walter S., ed. *A Dictionary of Canadianisms on Historical Principles.* Toronto: Gage, 1967.

Avis, Walter S.; and Kinloch, A. M. *Writings on Canadian English 1792–1975.* Toronto: Fitzhenry and Whiteside, 1978.

Babcock, C. Merton. *The Ordeal of American English.* Boston: Houghton Mifflin, 1961.

Bähr, Dieter. *A Bibliography of Writings on the English Language in Canada from 1857 to 1976.* Heidelberg: Winter, 1977.

Bailey, Charles-James N.; and Shuy, Roger W., eds. *New Ways of Analyzing Variation in English.* Washington, D.C.: Georgetown Univ. Press, 1973.

Bailey, Richard W.; and Burton, Dolores M. *English Stylistics: A Bibliography.* Cambridge, Mass.: MIT Press, 1968.

320 ————; and Robinson, Jay L., eds. *Varieties of Present-Day English*. New York: Macmillan, 1973.

Barber, Charles. *Early Modern English*. London: Deutsch, 1976.

————. *Linguistic Change in Present-Day English*. Edinburgh: Oliver and Boyd, 1964.

Barney, Stephen A. *Word-Hoard: An Introduction to Old English Vocabulary*. New Haven: Yale Univ. Press, 1977.

Barnhart, Clarence L. "American Lexicography, 1945–1973." *American Speech* 53 (1978): 83–141.

————; Steinmetz, Sol; and Barnhart, Robert K. *The Barnhart Dictionary of New English since 1963*. Bronxville, N.Y.: Barnhart; New York: Harper & Row, 1973.

————; Steinmetz, Sol; and Barnhart, Robert K. *The Second Barnhart Dictionary of New English*. Bronxville, N.Y.: Barnhart, 1980.

Barnhart, David K. "*Gate* Stays Open." *American Speech* 55 (1980): 77–78.

Baron, Dennis E. "The Epicene Pronoun: The Word That Failed." *American Speech* 56 (1981): 83–97.

Baugh, Albert C.; and Cable, Thomas. *A History of the English Language*. 3rd ed. Englewood Cliffs, N.J.: Prentice-Hall, 1978.

Bender, Harold H. *The Home of the Indo-Europeans*. Princeton: University Press, 1922.

Benjamin, Steven M.; and Schneidemesser, Luanne von. "German Loanwords in American English, A Bibliography of Studies, 1872–1978." *American Speech* 54 (1979): 210–15.

Bennett, William H. *An Introduction to the Gothic Language*. Introductions to the Older Languages of Europe, ed. W. P. Lehmann, no. 2. New York: Modern Language Association of America, 1980.

Benveniste, Emile. *Indo-European Language and Society*, trans. Elizabeth Palmer. Coral Gables, Fla.: Univ. of Miami Press, 1973.

Berndt, Rolf. "The Linguistic Situation in England from the Norman Conquest to the Loss of Normandy (1066–1204)." *Philologica Pragensia* 8 (1965): 145–63.

Berrey, Lester V.; and Van den Bark, Melvin. *The American Thesaurus of Slang*. 2nd ed. New York: Crowell, 1953.

Birnbaum, Henrik; and Puhvel, Jaan, eds. *Ancient Indo-European Dialects*. Berkeley: Univ. of California Press, 1966.

Björkman, Erik. *Scandinavian Loan-Words in Middle English*. 2 vols. in 1. Halle: Niemeyer, 1900–1902.

Blair, Peter Hunter. *An Introduction to Anglo-Saxon England*. 2nd ed. Cambridge: University Press, 1977.

Bloomfield, Leonard. *Language*. New York: Holt, Rinehart and Winston, 1933.

————. "Secondary and Tertiary Responses to Language." *Language* 20 (1944): 45–55.

Bloomfield, Morton W.; and Newmark, Leonard. *A Linguistic Introduction to the History of English*. New York: Knopf, 1963.

Bolinger, Dwight. *Aspects of Language*. 2nd ed. New York: Harcourt Brace Jovanovich, 1975.

————. *Language—The Loaded Weapon: The Use and Abuse of Language Today*. New York: Longman, 1980.

————. *Meaning and Form*. New York: Longman, 1977.

————. *The Phrasal Verb in English.* Cambridge, Mass.: Harvard Univ. Press, 1971. 321

Bolton, Whitney F., ed. *The English Language: Essays by English and American Men of Letters, 1490–1839.* Cambridge: University Press, 1966.

————; and Crystal, David, eds. *The English Language, Vol. 2: Essays by Linguists and Men of Letters, 1858–1964.* Cambridge: University Press, 1969.

Boone, Lalia Phipps. *The Petroleum Dictionary.* Norman: Univ. of Oklahoma Press, 1952.

Bradley, Henry. *The Making of English.* 1904. Reprint, with additional material by Bergen Evans and Simeon Potter. New York: Walker, 1967.

Brasch, Ila Wales; and Brasch, Walter Milton. *A Comprehensive Annotated Bibliography of American Black English.* Baton Rouge: Louisiana State Univ. Press, 1974.

Bréal, Michel. *Semantics: Studies in the Science of Meaning,* trans. Mrs. Henry Cust. 1900. Reprint. New York: Dover, 1964.

Brend, Ruth M., ed. *Advances in Tagmemics.* Amsterdam: North-Holland, 1974.

Bright, Elizabeth S. *A Word Geography of California and Nevada.* Berkeley: Univ. of California Press, 1971.

Bright, William, ed. *Sociolinguistics.* The Hague: Mouton, 1966.

Bronstein, Arthur. *The Pronunciation of American English.* Englewood Cliffs, N.J.: Prentice-Hall, 1960.

Brook, George Leslie. *English Dialects.* London: Deutsch, 1965.

————. *A History of the English Language.* Fair Lawn, N. J.: Essential Books, 1958.

————. *An Introduction to Old English.* 2nd ed. Manchester, Eng.: University Press, 1962.

————. *Varieties of English.* New York: St. Martin's, 1973.

Bruce-Mitford, Rupert. *Aspects of Anglo-Saxon Archaeology: Sutton Hoo and Other Discoveries.* New York: Harper's Magazine Press, 1974.

Brunner, Karl. *An Outline of Middle English Grammar,* trans. Grahame Johnston. Cambridge, Mass.: Harvard Univ. Press, 1963.

Bryant, Margaret. *Current American Usage.* New York: Funk & Wagnalls, 1962.

————. *Modern English and Its Heritage.* 2nd ed. New York: Macmillan, 1962.

Buck, Carl Darling. *A Dictionary of Selected Synonyms in the Principal Indo-European Languages: A Contribution to the History of Ideas.* Chicago: Univ. of Chicago Press, 1949.

Bullock-Davies, Constance, ed. *English Pronunciation from the Fifteenth to the Eighteenth Century.* 1934. Reprint. Westport, Conn.: Greenwood, 1970.

Burling, Robbins. *English in Black and White.* New York: Holt, Rinehart and Winston, 1973.

Bynon, Theodora. *Historical Linguistics.* Cambridge: University Press, 1977.

Campbell, Alistair. *Old English Grammar.* Oxford: Clarendon, 1959.

The Canadian Journal of Linguistics. Journal of the Canadian Linguistic Association. 1954–date.

Cannon, Garland. *A History of the English Language.* New York: Harcourt Brace Jovanovich, 1972.

————. "Statistical Etymologies of New Words in American English." *Journal of English Linguistics* 12 (1978): 12–18.

————; and Egle, Beatrice Mendez. "New Borrowings in English." *American Speech* 54 (1979): 23–37.

322   Cardona, George; Hoenigswald, Henry M.; and Senn, Alfred, eds. *Indo-European and Indo-Europeans*. Philadelphia: Univ. of Pennsylvania Press, 1970.

Carr, Elizabeth Ball. *Da Kine Talk: From Pidgin to Standard English in Hawaii*. Honolulu: Univ. of Hawaii Press, 1972.

Caso, Arthur Lewis. "The Production of New Scientific Terms." *American Speech* 55 (1980): 101–11.

Cassidy, Frederic G. *Dictionary of American Regional English*. In progress.

————. *Jamaica Talk: Three Hundred Years of the English Language in Jamaica*. New York: St. Martin's, 1961.

————. "*OK*—Is It African?" *American Speech* 56 (1981): 269–73.

————; and Le Page, Robert B. *Dictionary of Jamaican English*. Cambridge: University Press, 1967.

————; and Ringler, Richard N., eds. *Bright's Old English Grammar and Reader*. 3rd ed. New York: Holt, Rinehart and Winston, 1971.

Chambers, J. K. *Canadian English: Origins and Structures*. Toronto: Methuen, 1975.

————; and Trudgill, Peter. *Dialectology*. Cambridge: University Press, 1980.

Chambers, Raymond W. *On the Continuity of English Prose from Alfred to More and His School*. London: Oxford Univ. Press, 1957.

————; and Daunt, Marjorie, eds. *A Book of London English, 1384–1425*. Oxford: Clarendon, 1931.

Chomsky, Carol. *The Acquisition of Syntax in Children from 5 to 10*. Cambridge, Mass.: MIT Press, 1969.

Chomsky, Noam. *Aspects of the Theory of Syntax*. Cambridge, Mass.: MIT Press, 1965.

————. *Language and Mind*. Enlarged ed. New York: Harcourt Brace Jovanovich, 1972.

————. *Reflections on Language* New York: Pantheon, 1976.

————. Review of *Verbal Behavior*, by B. F. Skinner. *Language* 35 (1959): 26–58.

————. *Syntactic Structures*. The Hague: Mouton, 1957.

————; and Halle, Morris. *The Sound Pattern of English*. New York: Harper & Row, 1968.

Clark, John Williams. *Early English: A Study of Old and Middle English*. Rev. ed. London: Deutsch, 1967.

Clark, Virginia P.; Escholz, Paul A.; and Rosa, Alfred P. *Language: Introductory Readings*. New York: St. Martin's, 1972.

Coetsem, Frans van; and Kufner, Herbert L., eds. *Toward a Grammar of Proto-Germanic*. Tübingen: Niemeyer, 1972.

Copperud, Roy H. *American Usage: The Consensus*. New York: Van Nostrand, 1970.

Cottle, Basil. *The Plight of English: Ambiguities, Cacophonies and Other Violations of Our Language*. New Rochelle, N.Y.: Arlington House, 1975.

Craigie, William A. *English Spelling: Its Rules and Reasons*. New York: Crofts (Englewood Cliffs, N.J.: Prentice-Hall), 1927.

————; and Hulbert, James Root, eds. *A Dictionary of American English on Historical Principles*. 4 vols. Chicago: Univ. of Chicago Press, 1938–44.

Creswell, Thomas J. *Usage in Dictionaries and Dictionaries of Usage*. Publication of the American Dialect Society, nos. 63–64. University: Univ. of Alabama Press. 1975.

Crystal, David. *Prosodic Systems and Intonation in English*. Cambridge: University Press, 1969.

————; and Davy, Derek. *Investigating English Style*. London: Longman, 1969.

Curme, George O. *A Grammar of the English Language*. 2 vols. Boston: Heath, 1931, 1935.

Danielsson, Bror, ed. *Works on English Orthography and Pronunciation, 1551, 1569, 1570* [by John Hart]. 2 vols. Stockholm: Almqvist and Wiksell, 1955–63.

————; and Gabrielson, Arvid, eds. *Logonomia Anglica (1619)* [by Alexander Gill]. 2 vols. Stockholm: Almqvist and Wiksell, 1972.

Davis, Alva L.; McDavid, Raven I., Jr.; and McDavid, Virginia G., eds. *A Compilation of the Work Sheets of the Linguistic Atlas of the United States and Canada and Associated Projects*. 2nd ed. Chicago: Univ. of Chicago Press, 1969.

Davis, Lawrence M., ed. *Studies in Linguistics in Honor of Raven I. McDavid, Jr.* University: Univ. of Alabama Press, 1972.

DeCamp, David. "The Genesis of the Old English Dialects: A New Hypothesis." *Language* 34 (1958): 232–44.

Dewey, Godfrey. *English Spelling: Roadblock to Reading*. New York: Teachers College Press, 1971.

Dialect Notes. Publication of the American Dialect Society, vols. 1–6. 1890–1939.

Dillard, Joey L. *All-American English*. New York: Random House, 1975.

————. *American Talk*. New York: Random House, 1976.

————. *Black English: Its History and Usage in the United States*. New York: Random House, 1972.

————. *The Lexicon of Black English*. New York: Seabury, 1977.

————, ed. *Perspectives on Black English*. The Hague: Mouton, 1975.

Diringer, David. *The Alphabet: A Key to the History of Mankind*. 3rd ed. 2 vols. New York: Funk & Wagnalls, 1968.

————. *The Story of the Aleph Beth*. New York: Yoseloff, 1960.

————. *Writing*. New York: Praeger, 1962.

Dobson, Eric John. *English Pronunciation, 1500–1700*. 2nd ed. 2 vols. Oxford: Clarendon, 1968.

Dohan, Mary Helen. *Our Own Words*. New York: Knopf, 1974.

Dumas, Bethany K.; and Lighter, Jonathan. "Is *Slang* a Word for Linguists?" *American Speech* 53 (1978): 5–17.

Dunn, Charles W.; and Byrnes, Edward T., eds. *Middle English Literature*. New York: Harcourt Brace Jovanovich, 1973.

Dykema, Karl W. "How Fast Is Standard English Changing?" *American Speech* 31 (1956): 89–95.

Ehrlich, Eugene; Flexner, Stuart Berg; Carruth, Gorton; and Hawkins, Joyce M., eds. *Oxford American Dictionary*. New York: Oxford Univ. Press, 1980.

Ekwall, Eilert. *American and British Pronunciation*. Upsala: Lundequistska Bokhandeln, 1946.

————. *The Concise Oxford Dictionary of English Place-Names*. 4th ed. Oxford: Clarendon, 1960.

————. *A History of Modern English Sounds and Morphology*, trans. and ed. Alan Ward. Oxford: Blackwell, 1975.

Elgin, Suzette Haden. *Pouring Down Words*. Englewood Cliffs, N.J.: Prentice-Hall, 1975.

324 Emerson, Oliver Farrar. *The History of the English Language*. New York: Macmillan, 1894.

Emery, Donald W. *Variant Spellings in Modern American Dictionaries*. Rev. ed. Urbana, Ill.: National Council of Teachers of English, 1973.

Escholtz, Paul; Rosa, Alfred F.; and Clark, Virginia. *Language Awareness*. New York: St. Martin's, 1974.

ETC.: A Review of General Semantics. Journal of the International Society for General Semantics. 1943–date.

Evans, Bergen; and Evans, Cornelia. *A Dictionary of Contemporary American Usage*. New York: Random House, 1957.

Evans, William. "The Dramatic Use of the Second Person Singular Pronoun in *Sir Gawain and the Green Knight*." *Studia Neophilologica* 39 (1967): 38–45.

———. "The Survival of the Second-Person Singular in the Southern Counties of England." *South Central Bulletin* 30 (1970): 182–86.

———. "'You' and 'Thou' in Northern England." *South Atlantic Bulletin*, November 1969, pp. 17–21.

Farmer, John S.; and Henley, William Ernest. *Dictionary of Slang and Its Analogues*. 7 vols. 1890–1904. Reprint in 1 vol. New York: Dutton, 1970.

Fasold, Ralph W. "The Relation between Black and White Speech in the South." *American Speech* 56 (1981): 163–89.

Feinsilver, Lillian Mermin. *The Taste of Yiddish*. New York: Barnes, 1980.

Ferguson, Charles A.; and Heath, Shirley Brice, eds. *Language in the USA*. Cambridge: University Press, 1981.

Fillmore, Charles J.; and Langendoen, D. Terrence. *Studies in Linguistic Semantics*. New York: Holt, Rinehart and Winston, 1971.

Finberg, H. P. R. *The Formation of England, 550–1042*. London: Hart-Davis, MacGibbon, 1974.

Finnie, W. Bruce. *The Stages of English: Texts, Transcriptions, Exercises*. Boston: Houghton Mifflin, 1972.

Firth, J. R. *Papers in Linguistics, 1934–1951*. London: Oxford Univ. Press, 1957.

———. *The Tongues of Men and Speech*. London: Oxford Univ. Press, 1964.

Fisher, Douglas J. V. *The Anglo-Saxon Age, c. 400–1042*. London: Longman, 1973.

Fisher, John H. "Chancery and the Emergence of Standard Written English in the Fifteenth Century." *Speculum* 52 (1977): 870–99.

———. "Chancery Standard and Modern Written English." *Journal of the Society of Archivists* 6 (1979): 136–44.

———; and Bornstein, Diane. *In Forme of Speche Is Chaunge: Readings in the History of the English Language*. Englewood Cliffs, N.J.: Prentice-Hall, 1974.

Fisiak, Jacek. *Morphemic Structure of Chaucer's English*. University: Univ. of Alabama Press, 1965.

———. *A Short Grammar of Middle English; Part One: Graphemics, Phonemics and Morphemics*. Warsaw: Państwowe Wydawnictwo Naukowe, 1970.

Flexner, Stuart Berg. *I Hear America Talking*. New York: Van Nostrand Reinhold, 1976.

Forgue, Guy Jean. *Les Mots Américains*. Paris: Presses Universitaires de France, 1976.

———; and McDavid, Raven I., Jr. *La Langue des Américains*. Paris: Aubier Montaigne, 1972.

Forshall, Josiah; and Madden, Frederic, eds. *The New Testament in English, According to the Version by John Wycliffe*. Oxford: Clarendon, 1879.

Foster, Brian. *The Changing English Language*. New York: St. Martin's, 1968.

———. "Recent American Influence on Standard English." *Anglia* 73 (1956): 328–60.

Fowler, Henry W. *A Dictionary of Modern English Usage*. 1st ed., 1926. 2nd ed. Rev. Ernest Gowers. New York: Oxford Univ. Press, 1965.

———; and Fowler, F. G. *The King's English*. 3rd ed. Oxford: Clarendon, 1931.

Francis, W. Nelson. *The Structure of American English*. New York: Ronald, 1958.

Franklyn, Julian. *A Dictionary of Rhyming Slang*. London: Routledge & Kegan Paul, 1960.

Franz, Wilhelm. *Shakespeare-Grammatik*. 3rd ed. Heidelberg: Winter, 1924.

Freeman, Edward Augustus. *The History of the Norman Conquest of England*, ed. J. W. Burrow. Chicago: Univ. of Chicago Press, 1974.

Friedrich, Paul. *Proto-Indo-European Trees: The Arboreal System of a Prehistoric People*. Chicago: Univ. of Chicago Press, 1970.

Friend, Joseph Harold. *The Development of American Lexicography, 1798–1864*. The Hague: Mouton, 1967.

Fries, Charles Carpenter. *American English Grammar*. New York: Appleton-Century-Crofts (Englewood Cliffs, N.J.: Prentice-Hall), 1940.

———. *The Structure of English*. New York: Harcourt Brace Jovanovich, 1952.

Funk and Wagnalls Standard College Dictionary. New York: Funk & Wagnalls, 1963.

Furnivall, Frederick J., ed. *A Parallel-Text Edition of Chaucer's Minor Poems*. Part 2. London. Chaucer Society, 1878.

———. *A Six-Text Print of Chaucer's Canterbury Tales*. London: Chaucer Society, 1868.

Galinsky, Hans. *Die Sprache des Amerikaners*. 2 vols. Heidelberg: Kerle, 1951, 1952.

Gardner, Faith F. *An Analysis of Syntactic Patterns of Old English*. The Hague: Mouton, 1971.

Gelb, Ignace J. *A Study of Writing: The Foundations of Grammatology*. 2nd ed. Chicago: Univ. of Chicago Press, 1963.

General Linguistics. 1955–date.

Gimbutas, Marija. "The Beginning of the Bronze Age in Europe and the Indo-Europeans: 3500–2500 B.C." *Journal of Indo-European Studies* 1 (1973): 163–214.

———. "Proto-Indo-European Culture: The Kurgan Culture during the Fifth, Fourth, and Third Millennia B.C." In *Indo-European and Indo-Europeans*, ed. G. Cardona, H. M. Hoenigswald, and A. Senn, pp. 155–97. Philadelphia: Univ. of Pennsylvania Press, 1970.

Gimson, A. C. *An Introduction to the Pronunciation of English*. 2nd ed. London: Arnold, 1970.

Gleason, H. A., Jr. *An Introduction to Descriptive Linguistics*. Rev. ed. New York: Holt, Rinehart and Winston, 1961.

———. *Linguistics and English Grammar*. New York: Holt, Rinehart and Winston, 1965.

Goldin, Hyman; O'Leary, Frank; and Lipsius, Morris. *Dictionary of American Underworld Lingo*. New York: Twayne, 1950.

326   Gordon, James D. *The English Language: An Historical Introduction.* New York: Crowell, 1972.

Gowers, Ernest. *Plain Words: Their ABC.* New York: Knopf, 1954.

Greenbaum, Sidney. *Studies in English Adverbial Usage.* Coral Gables, Fla.: Univ. of Miami Press, 1969.

Greenberg, Joseph H. *Language Universals, with Special Reference to Feature Hierarchies.* The Hague: Mouton, 1966.

———. "A Quantitative Approach to the Morphological Typology of Language." *International Journal of American Linguistics* 26 (1960): 178–94.

———. "Some Universals of Grammar with Particular Reference to the Order of Meaningful Elements." In *Universals of Language,* ed. J. H. Greenberg, pp. 73–113. Cambridge, Mass.: MIT Press, 1962.

Greenough, James Bradstreet; and Kittredge, George Lyman. *Words and Their Ways in English Speech.* 1901. Reprint. New York: Macmillan, 1961.

Griffin, Donald R. *The Question of Animal Awareness: Evolutionary Continuity of Mental Experience.* Rev. ed. New York: Rockefeller Univ. Press, 1981.

Haas, William. *Phono-Graphic Translation.* Manchester, Eng.: Manchester Univ. Press, 1970.

Hall, John R. Clark. *See* Meritt, Herbert.

Hall, Robert A., Jr. *Hands Off Pidgin English!* Sydney: Pacific Pubs., 1955.

———. *Linguistics and Your Language.* New York: Doubleday, 1960.

———. *Pidgin and Creole Languages.* Ithaca, N.Y.: Cornell Univ. Press, 1966.

———. *Sound and Spelling in English.* Philadelphia: Chilton, 1961.

Halle, Morris; and Keyser, Samuel J. *English Stress: Its Form, Its Growth, and Its Role in Verse.* New York: Harper & Row, 1971.

Halliday, M. A. K. *Explorations in the Functions of Language.* New York: American Elsevier, 1977.

———; McIntosh, Angus; and Strevens, P. D. *The Linguistic Sciences and Language Teaching.* Bloomington: Indiana Univ. Press, 1964.

Hanna, Paul, R.; Hanna, Jean S.; Hodges, Richard E.; and Rudorf, Edwin, H., Jr. *Phoneme-Grapheme Correspondences as Cues to Spelling Improvement.* Washington, D.C.: U.S. Department of Health, Education, and Welfare; Office of Education, 1966.

Harder, Kelsie B., ed. *Illustrated Dictionary of Place Names: United States and Canada.* New York: Van Nostrand, 1976.

Hayakawa, S. I. *Language in Thought and Action.* 4th ed. New York: Harcourt Brace Jovanovich, 1978.

Hill, Archibald A. *Introduction to Linguistic Structures: From Sound to Sentence in English.* New York: Harcourt Brace Jovanovich, 1958.

———, ed. *Linguistics Today.* New York: Basic Books, 1969.

Hockett, Charles F. *A Course in Modern Linguistics.* New York: Macmillan, 1958.

———. "In Search of Jove's Brow." *American Speech* 53 (1978): 243–313.

———. *Man's Place in Nature.* New York: McGraw-Hill, 1973.

———. *The View From Language: Selected Essays, 1948–1974.* Athens: Univ. of Georgia Press, 1977.

Hodgkin, R. H. *A History of the Anglo-Saxons.* 3rd ed. 2 vols. London: Oxford Univ. Press, 1952.

Hoenigswald, Henry M. *Language Change and Linguistic Reconstruction*. Chicago: Univ. of Chicago Press, 1960.

Hoffman, Richard L., ed. *History of the English Language: Selected Texts and Exercises*. Boston: Little, Brown, 1968.

Hook, J. N. *History of the English Language*. New York: Ronald, 1975.

Hooper, Joan B. *An Introduction to Natural Generative Phonology*. New York: Academic, 1976.

Hopper, Paul J. *The Syntax of the Simple Sentence in Proto-Germanic*. The Hague: Mouton, 1975.

Horn, Wilhelm. *Laut und Leben. Englische Lautgeschichte der neuren Zeit (1400–1950)*, rev. and ed. Martin Lehnert. 2 vols. Berlin: Deutscher Verlag der Wissenschaften, 1954.

Horwill, H. W. *A Dictionary of Modern American Usage*. 2nd ed. Oxford: Clarendon, 1944.

Hughes, Arthur; and Trudgill, Peter. *English Accents and Dialects: An Introduction to Social and Regional Varieties of British English*. Baltimore: Univ. Park Press, 1979.

Humble, Richard. *The Fall of Saxon England*. New York: St. Martin's, 1975.

Hungerford, Harold; Robinson, Jay; and Sledd, James. *English Linguistics: An Introductory Reader*. Glenview, Ill.: Scott, Foresman, 1970.

Hussey, Maurice. *Chaucer's World: A Pictorial Companion*. Cambridge: University Press, 1967.

International Journal of American Linguistics. 1935–date.

Ives, Sumner. *The Phonology of the Uncle Remus Stories*. Publication of the American Dialect Society, no. 22 (1954).

———. "A Theory of Literary Dialect." *Tulane Studies in English* 2 (1950): 137–42.

Jakobson, Roman. *Six Lectures on Sound and Meaning*. Cambridge, Mass.: MIT Press, 1978.

———; and Halle, Morris. *Fundamentals of Language*. 2nd ed. The Hague: Mouton, 1971.

———; and Waugh, Linda. *The Sound Shape of Language*. Bloomington: Indiana Univ. Press, 1979.

Jankowsky, Kurt R. *The Neogrammarians: A Re-Evaluation of Their Place in the Development of Linguistic Science*. The Hague: Mouton, 1972.

Jeffers, Robert J.; and Lehiste, Ilse. *Principles and Methods for Historical Linguistics*. Cambridge, Mass.: MIT Press, 1979.

Jespersen, Otto. *Analytic Syntax*. 1937. Reprint. New York: Holt, Rinehart and Winston, 1969.

———. *Essentials of English Grammar*. New York: Holt, Rinehart and Winston, 1933.

———. *Growth and Structure of the English Language*. 9th ed. Oxford: Blackwell, 1954.

———. *John Hart's Pronunciation of English (1569–1570)*. 1907. Reprint. Amsterdam: Swets and Zeitlinger, 1973.

———. *Language: Its Nature, Development, and Origin*. 1922. Reprint. New York: Norton, 1964.

———. *A Modern English Grammar on Historical Principles*. 7 vols. 1909–49. Reprint. London: Allen and Unwin, 1954.

328 ———. *Progress in Language, with Special Reference to English*. 2nd ed. New York: Macmillan, 1909.

———. *Selected Writings*. London: Allen and Unwin, 1962.

Jones, Charles. *An Introduction to Middle English*. New York: Holt, Rinehart and Winston, 1972.

Jones, Daniel. *An Outline of English Phonetics*. 9th ed. 1960. Reprint. Cambridge: Heffer, 1972.

———. *The Pronunciation of English*. 4th ed. Cambridge: University Press, 1967.

———; and Gimson, A. C. *Everyman's English Pronouncing Dictionary*. 14th ed. London: Dent, 1977.

Joos, Martin. *The English Verb: Form and Meaning*. 2nd ed. Madison: Univ. of Wisconsin Press, 1968.

———. *The Five Clocks*. New York: Harcourt Brace Jovaⱼ ich, 1967.

Jordan, Richard. *Handbook of Middle English Grammar: Phonology*, trans. and rev. Eugene Joseph Crook. The Hague: Mouton, 1974.

Journal of English and Germanic Philology. 1902–date.

Journal of English Linguistics. 1967–date.

Journal of Indo-European Studies. 1973–date.

Katz, Jerrold J. *Semantic Theory*. New York: Harper & Row, 1972.

Keiler, Allan R. *A Reader in Historical and Comparative Linguistics*. New York: Holt, Rinehart and Winston, 1972.

Kennedy, Arthur G. *A Bibliography of Writings on the English Language, from the Beginning of Printing to the End of 1922*. 1927. Reprint. New York: Hafner, 1961.

———. *Current English*. Boston: Ginn, 1935.

———. *English Usage: A Study in Policy and Procedure*. New York: Appleton-Century-Crofts (Englewood Cliffs, N.J.: Prentice-Hall), 1942.

Kenyon, John S. *American Pronunciation*. 10th ed. Ann Arbor, Mich.: Wahr, 1950.

———; and Knott, Thomas Albert. *A Pronouncing Dictionary of American English*. Springfield, Mass.: Merriam, 1953.

Kerr, Elizabeth; and Aderman, Ralph M. *Aspects of American English*. 2nd ed. New York: Harcourt Brace Jovanovich, 1971.

Key, Mary Ritchie. *Nonverbal Communication: A Research Guide and Bibliography*. Metuchen, N.J.: Scarecrow, 1977.

———. *Paralanguage and Kinesics (Nonverbal Communication)*. Metuchen, N.J.: Scarecrow, 1975.

King, Robert D. *Historical Linguistics and Generative Grammar*. Englewood Cliffs, N.J.: Prentice-Hall, 1969.

Kingdon, Roger. *The Groundwork of English Intonation*. London: Longman, 1958.

———. *The Groundwork of English Stress*. London: Longman, 1958.

Kispert, Robert J. *Old English: An Introduction*. New York: Holt, Rinehart and Winston, 1971.

Kluge, Friedrich. *Etymologisches Wörterbuch der deutschen Sprache*. 19th ed. Berlin: de Gruyter, 1963.

Kochman, Thomas, ed. *Rappin' and Stylin' Out: Communication in Urban Black America*. Urbana: Univ. of Illinois Press, 1972.

Kökeritz, Helge. *A Guide to Chaucer's Pronunciation*. New York: Holt, Rinehart and Winston, 1962.

————. "John Hart and Early Standard English." In *Philologica: The Malone Anniversary Studies*, ed. Thomas A. Kirby and Henry Bosley Woolf, pp. 239–48. Baltimore: Johns Hopkins Press, 1949.

————. *Shakespeare's Pronunciation*. New Haven, Conn.: Yale Univ. Press, 1953.

Kolin, Philip C. "The Pseudo-Suffix *-oholic*." *American Speech* 54 (1979): 74–76.

Krapp, George Philip. *The English Language in America*. 2 vols. 1925. Reprint. New York: Ungar, 1960.

————. *Modern English: Its Growth and Present Use*, rev. Albert H. Marckwardt. New York: Ungar, 1966.

————. *The Pronunciation of Standard English in America*. New York: Oxford Univ. Press, 1919.

Kreidler, Charles W. "Creating New Words by Shortening." *Journal of English Linguistics* 13 (1979): 24–36.

Kristensson, Gillis. *A Survey of Middle English Dialects, 1290–1350: The Six Northern Counties and Lincolnshire*. Lund: Gleerup, 1967.

Kruisinga, Etsko. *A Handbook of Present-Day English*. 4 vols. Pt. 1, 4th ed. Utrecht: Kemink en Zoon, 1925. Pt. 2, 5th ed. Groningen: Noordhoff, 1931, 1932.

————. *An Introduction to the Study of English Sounds*. 12th ed. Rev. C. Hedeman and J. J. Westerbeek. Groningen: Noordhoff, 1960.

Kučera, Henry; and Francis, W. Nelson. *Computational Analysis of Present-Day American English*. Providence, R.I.: Brown Univ. Press, 1966.

Kurath, Hans. *Handbook of the Linguistic Geography of New England*. 2nd ed., with a new introduction, word-index and inventory of LANE maps and commentary by Audrey R. Duckert, and a reverse index of LANE maps to worksheets by Raven I. McDavid, Jr. New York: AMS, 1973.

————. *Linguistic Atlas of New England*. 3 vols. 1939–43. Reprint. New York: AMS, 1972.

————. "The Loss of Long Consonants and the Rise of Voiced Fricatives in Middle English." *Language* 32 (1956): 435–45.

————. *A Phonology and Prosody of Modern English*. Ann Arbor: Univ. of Michigan Press, 1964.

————. *Studies in Area Linguistics*. Bloomington: Indiana Univ. Press, 1972.

————. *A Word Geography of the Eastern United States*. Ann Arbor: Univ. of Michigan Press, 1949.

————; and Kuhn, Sherman M., eds. *Middle English Dictionary*. Ann Arbor: Univ. of Michigan Press, 1954–.

————; and McDavid, Raven I., Jr. *The Pronunciation of English in the Atlantic States*. Ann Arbor: Univ. of Michigan Press, 1961.

Labov, William. *Language in the Inner City: Studies in the Black English Vernacular*. Philadelphia: Univ. of Pennsylvania Press, 1972.

————. *The Social Stratification of English in New York City*. Washington, D.C.: Center for Applied Linguistics, 1966.

————. *Sociolinguistic Patterns*. Philadelphia: Univ. of Pennsylvania Press, 1972.

LACUS Forum. Publication of the Linguistic Association of Canada and the United States. 1974–date.

Ladefoged, Peter. *A Course in Phonetics*. New York: Harcourt Brace Jovanovich, 1975.

330 Laird, Charlton. *Language in America*. Englewood Cliffs, N.J.: Prentice-Hall, 1971.

Lakoff, Robin. *Language and Woman's Place*. New York: Harper & Row, 1975.

Lamb, Sidney. *An Outline of Stratificational Grammar*. Washington, D.C.: Georgetown Univ. Press, 1966.

Lamberts, J. J. *A Short Introduction to English Usage*. New York: McGraw-Hill, 1972.

Landau, Sidney I. "Popular Meanings of Scientific and Technical Terms." *American Speech* 55 (1980): 204–09.

Langendoen, D. Terence. *The Study of Syntax: The Generative-Transformational Approach to the Structure of American English*. New York: Holt, Rinehart and Winston, 1969.

Language: Journal of the Linguistic Society of America. 1925–date.

Lass, Roger, ed. *Approaches to English Historical Linguistics*. New York: Holt, Rinehart and Winston, 1969.

———. *English Phonology and Phonological Theory: Synchronic and Diachronic Studies*. New York: Cambridge Univ. Press, 1976.

———; and Anderson, John M. *Old English Phonology*. New York: Cambridge Univ. Press, 1975.

Leech, Geoffrey. *Semantics*. Harmondsworth, Eng.: Penguin, 1974.

———; and Svartvik, Jan. *A Communicative Grammar of English*. London: Longman, 1975.

Lees, Robert B. *The Grammar of English Nominalizations*. Bloomington: Indiana Univ. Press, 1963.

Lehmann, Winfred P. "Contemporary Linguistics and Indo-European Studies." *PMLA* 87 (1972): 976–93.

———. *Descriptive Linguistics, An Introduction*. 2nd ed. New York: Random House, 1976.

———. *Historical Linguistics: An Introduction*. 2nd ed. New York: Holt, Rinehart and Winston, 1973.

———. "Proto-Germanic Syntax." In *Toward a Grammar of Proto-Germanic*, ed. F. van Coetsem and H. L. Kufner, pp. 239–68. Tübingen: Niemeyer, 1972.

———. *Proto-Indo-European Phonology*. Austin: Univ. of Texas Press, 1952.

———. *Proto-Indo-European Syntax*. Austin: Univ. of Texas Press, 1974.

———, ed. and trans. *A Reader in Nineteenth-Century Historical Indo-European Linguistics*. Bloomington: Indiana Univ. Press, 1967.

———. "A Structural Principle of Language and Its Implications." *Language* 49 (1973): 47–66.

———, ed. *Syntactic Typology: Studies in the Phenomenology of Language*. Austin: Univ. of Texas Press, 1978.

Leonard, Sterling A. *Current English Usage*. Chicago: National Council of Teachers of English, 1932.

———. *The Doctrine of Correctness in English Usage, 1700–1800*. University of Wisconsin Studies in Language and Literature 25. Madison: Univ. of Wisconsin, 1929.

Lewis, J. Windsor. *A Concise Pronouncing Dictionary of British and American English*. London: Oxford Univ. Press, 1972.

Lighter, Jonathan. "The Slang of the American Expeditionary Forces in Europe 1917–19: An Historical Glossary." *American Speech* 47 (1972): 5–142.

Lightfoot, David W. *Principles of Diachronic Syntax*. Cambridge: University Press, 1979.

Lindberg, Conrad, ed. *Ms. Bodley 959: Genesis-Baruch 3.20 in the Earlier Version of the Wycliffite Bible*. Stockholm Studies in English 6. Stockholm: Almqvist and Wiksell, 1959.

Linden, Eugene. *Apes, Men, and Language*. New York: Saturday Review Press, Dutton, 1974.

Linguistic Reporter. 1959–date.

Lockwood, David G. *Introduction to Stratificational Linguistics*. New York: Harcourt Brace Jovanovich, 1972.

Lockwood, W. B. *Indo-European Philology, Historical and Comparative*. London: Hutchinson, 1969.

———. *A Panorama of Indo-European Languages*. London: Hutchinson, 1972.

Loman, Bengt, ed. *Conversations in a Negro American Dialect*. Washington, D.C.: Center for Applied Linguistics, 1967.

Lounsbury, Thomas R. *English Spelling and Spelling Reform*. New York: Harper & Row, 1909.

Luick, Karl. *Historische Grammatik der englischen Sprache*. 1914–40. Reprint. Stuttgart: Tauchnitz, 1964.

Lyons, John. *Introduction to Theoretical Linguistics*. Cambridge: University Press, 1968.

———. *Language and Linguistics: An Introduction*. Cambridge: University Press, 1981.

———. *Noam Chomsky*. New York: Viking, 1970.

———. *Semantics*. 2 vols. Cambridge: University Press, 1977.

McConnell, Ruth E. *Our Own Voice: Canadian English and How It Is Studied*. Toronto: Gage, 1979.

McDavid, Raven I., Jr. "American English: A Bibliographic Essay." *American Studies International* 17, no. 2 (Winter 1979): 3–45.

———. "American English Dialects." In *The Structure of American English*, by W. Nelson Francis, pp. 480–593. New York: Ronald, 1958.

———. *Dialects in Culture*. University: Univ. of Alabama Press, 1979.

———. *Varieties of American English*, ed. Anwar S. Dil. Stanford: University Press, 1980.

——— ; and Duckert, Audrey, eds. *Lexicography in English*. Annals of the New York Academy of Sciences, vol. 211. New York: New York Academy of Sciences, 1973.

———; and Marckwardt, Albert H. *Linguistic Atlas of the North Central States*. In progress.

———; and O'Cain, Raymond K. *Linguistic Atlas of the Middle and South Atlantic States*. Chicago: Univ. of Chicago Press, 1980–.

McIntosh, Angus. *An Introduction to a Survey of Scottish Dialects*. Edinburgh: Nelson, 1952.

McKnight, George H. *English Words and Their Background*. New York: Appleton (Englewood Cliffs, N.J.: Prentice-Hall), 1923.

———. *Modern English in the Making*. New York: Appleton (Englewood Cliffs, N.J.: Prentice-Hall), 1928.

McLaughlin, John C. *Aspects of the History of English*. New York: Holt, Rinehart and Winston, 1970.

332 ——. *A Graphemic-Phonemic Study of a Middle English Manuscript*. The Hague: Mouton, 1963.

MacLeish, Andrew. *The Middle English Subject-Verb Cluster*. The Hague: Mouton, 1969.

McMillan, James B. "American Lexicology, 1956–1973." *American Speech* 53 (1978): 141–63.

——. *Annotated Bibliography of Southern American English*. Coral Gables, Fla.: Univ. of Miami Press, 1971.

Makkai, Adam. *Idiom Structure in English*. The Hague: Mouton, 1972.

Makkai, Adam; and Lockwood, David G., eds. *Readings in Stratificational Linguistics*. University: Univ. of Alabama Press, 1973.

Mallory, J. P. "A History of the Indo-European Problem." *Journal of Indo-European Studies* 1 (1973): 21–65.

Malone, Kemp. "The Old English Period (to 1100)." In *A Literary History of England*, ed. Albert C. Baugh, pp. 3–105. New York: Appleton-Century-Crofts (Englewood Cliffs, N.J.: Prentice-Hall), 1948.

——. "Oldest England." *Emory University Quarterly* 5 (1949): 129–48.

Marchand, Hans. *The Categories and Types of Present-Day English Word-Formation*. 2nd ed. Munich: Beck, 1969.

Marckwardt, Albert H. *American English*. New York: Oxford Univ. Press, 1958.

——. *Introduction to the English Language*. New York: Oxford Univ. Press, 1942.

——. *Linguistics and the Teaching of English*. Bloomington: Indiana Univ. Press, 1966.

——; and Quirk, Randolph. *A Common Language: British and American English*. London: Cox and Wyman, 1964.

——; and Rosier, James L. *Old English Language and Literature*. New York: Norton, 1972.

——; and Walcott, Fred G. *Facts About Current English Usage*. New York: Appleton-Century (Englewood Cliffs, N.J.: Prentice-Hall), 1938.

Markman, Alan M.; and Steinberg, Erwin R. *English Then and Now: Readings and Exercises*. New York: Random House, 1970.

Martin-Clarke, D. Elizabeth. *Culture in Early Anglo-Saxon England*. Baltimore: Johns Hopkins Press, 1947.

Mathews, Mitford M. *The Beginnings of American English*. Chicago: Univ. of Chicago Press, 1931.

——, ed. *A Dictionary of Americanisms on Historical Principles*. 2 vols. Chicago: Univ. of Chicago Press, 1951.

——. *Some Sources of Southernisms*. University: Univ. of Alabama Press, 1948.

Matthews, C. M. *Words, Words, Words*. New York: Scribner's, 1979.

Matthews, P. H. *Morphology: An Introduction to the Theory of Word-Structure*. Cambridge: University Press, 1974.

Maurer, David W. *The Argot of the Racetrack*. Publication of the American Dialect Society, no. 16 (1951).

——. *Whiz Mob: A Correlation of the Technical Argot of Pickpockets with Their Behavior Pattern*. Publication of the American Dialect Society, no. 24 (1955).

Mayhew, A. L.; and Skeat, Walter W. *A Concise Dictionary of Middle English from A.D. 1150 to 1580*. Oxford: Clarendon, 1888.

Meillet, Antoine. *General Characteristics of the Germanic Languages*, trans. William 333
P. Dismukes. Coral Gables, Fla.: Univ. of Miami Press, 1970.

———. *The Indo-European Dialects*, trans. Samuel N. Rosenberg. University:
Univ. of Alabama Press, 1967.

Mencken, H. L. *The American Language*. 4th ed. New York: Knopf, 1936.

———. *The American Language*, abridged and ed. Raven I. McDavid, Jr. New
York: Knopf, 1963.

———. *The American Language, Supplement I*. New York: Knopf, 1945.

———. *The American Language, Supplement II*. New York: Knopf, 1948.

Meritt, Herbert, ed. *A Concise Anglo-Saxon Dictionary*, by John R. Clark Hall.
4th ed. with a supplement. Cambridge: University Press, 1960.

Michael, Ian. *English Grammatical Categories and the Tradition to 1800*. Cambridge:
University Press, 1970.

Miller, Casey; and Swift, Kate. *The Handbook of Nonsexist Writing*. New York:
Lippincott and Crowell, 1980.

———. *Words and Women*. New York: Doubleday, 1976.

Mitchell, Bruce Colston. *A Guide to Old English*. 2nd ed. Oxford: Blackwell,
1968.

Mitchell, T. F. *Principles of Firthian Linguistics*. London: Longman, 1975.

Mitford, Nancy, ed. *Noblesse Oblige*. New York: Harper & Row, 1956.

Moody, Patricia A. "*Shall* and *Will*: The Grammatical Tradition and Dialectology."
American Speech 49 (1974): 67–78.

Moore, John L. *Tudor-Stuart Views on the Growth, Status, and Destiny of the English
Language*. 1910. Reprint. College Park, Md.: McGrath, 1970.

Moore, Samuel. *Historical Outlines of English Sounds and Inflections*, rev. Albert H.
Marckwardt. Ann Arbor, Mich.: Wahr, 1951.

———. "Loss of Final *n* in Inflectional Syllables of Middle English." *Language* 3
(1927): 232–59.

———; and Knott, Thomas Albert. *The Elements of Old English*. 10th ed. Rev.
James Root Hulbert. Ann Arbor, Mich.: Wahr, 1955.

———; Meech, Sanford Brown; and Whitehall, Harold. "Middle English Dialect
Characteristics and Dialect Boundaries: Preliminary Report of an Investigation
Based Exclusively on Localized Texts and Documents." *Univ. of Michigan
Publications in Language and Literature* 13 (1935): 1–60.

Morris, William; and Morris, Mary. *Harper Dictionary of Contemporary Usage*.
New York: Harper & Row, 1975.

Moss, Norman. *What's the Difference? A British/American Dictionary*. New York:
Harper & Row, 1973.

Mossé, Fernand. *A Handbook of Middle English*, trans. James A. Walker. Baltimore:
Johns Hopkins Press, 1952.

Moulton, William G. *A Linguistic Guide to Language Learning*. 2nd ed. New York:
Modern Language Association of America, 1970.

Mueller, Robert Kirk. *Buzzwords: A Guide to the Language of Leadership*. New
York: Van Nostrand Reinhold, 1974.

Murray, K. M. Elisabeth. *Caught in the Web of Words: James A. H. Murray and
the "Oxford English Dictionary."* New Haven: Yale Univ. Press, 1977.

Mustanoja, Tauno F. *A Middle English Syntax, Part I: Parts of Speech*. Helsinki:
Société Néophilologique, 1960.

334   Myers, Alec Reginald. *England in the Late Middle Ages.* 8th ed. New York: Penguin, 1971.

Myers, L. M.; and Hoffman, Richard L. *The Roots of Modern English.* 2nd ed. Boston: Little, Brown, 1979.

Names: Journal of the American Name Society. 1953–date.

Nevins, Allan, ed. *American Social History as Recorded by British Travellers.* New York: Holt, Rinehart and Winston, 1923.

Nicholson, Margaret. *A Dictionary of American-English Usage.* New York: Oxford Univ. Press, 1957.

Nida, Eugene A. *Exploring Semantic Structures.* Munich: Fink, 1975.

———. *Morphology: The Descriptive Analysis of Words.* 2nd ed. Ann Arbor: Univ. of Michigan Press, 1949.

———. *A Synopsis of English Syntax.* 2nd ed. The Hague: Mouton, 1966.

Nilsen, Don L. F. "The Grammar of Graffiti." *American Speech* 55 (1980): 234–39.

Nist, John A. *A Structural History of English.* New York: St. Martin's, 1966.

O'Cain, Raymond K. "Linguistic Atlas of New England." *American Speech* 54 (1979): 243–78.

Ogden, C. K.; and Richards, I. A. *The Meaning of Meaning.* 8th ed. New York: Harcourt Brace Jovanovich, 1946.

Onions, C. T. *An Advanced English Syntax.* 6th ed. New York: Humanities, 1966.

———, ed. *The Oxford Dictionary of English Etymology.* London: Oxford Univ. Press, 1966.

Orkin, Mark M. *Speaking Canadian English.* Toronto: General Publishing, 1970.

Orton, Harold, ed. *Survey of English Dialects.* Introduction, 4 vols. each in 3 parts. Leeds: Arnold, 1962–71.

———; and Wright, Nathalia. *A Word Geography of England.* London: Seminar, 1974.

The Oxford English Dictionary. 13 vols. London: Oxford Univ. Press, 1933.

The Oxford English Dictionary: A Supplement, ed. R. W. Burchfield. London: Oxford Univ. Press, 1972–.

Palmer, Frank R. *The English Verb.* 2nd ed. London: Longman, 1974.

———. *Semantics: A New Outline.* New York: Cambridge Univ. Press, 1976.

Palmer, Harold E.; and Blandford, F. G. *A Grammar of Spoken English.* 3rd ed. Rev. Roger Kingdon. Cambridge: Heffer, 1969.

Palmer, Leonard R. *Descriptive and Comparative Linguistics: A Critical Introduction.* New York: Crane, Russak, 1972.

Partridge, Eric, ed. *A Dictionary of Slang and Unconventional English.* 7th ed. New York: Macmillan, 1970.

———. *A Dictionary of the Underworld.* 2nd ed. London: Routledge & Kegan Paul, 1964.

———. *Shakespeare's Bawdy.* New York: Dutton, 1948.

———. *Slang To-day and Yesterday.* 4th ed. New York: Barnes & Noble, 1970.

———; and Clark, John W. *British and American English Since 1900.* New York: Philosophical Library, 1951.

Patterson, Francine. "Conversations with a Gorilla." *National Geographic* 154 (1978): 438–65.

Pedersen, Holger. *The Discovery of Language,* trans. John Webster Spargo. Bloomington: Indiana Univ. Press, 1962.

Pederson, Lee. *Linguistic Atlas of the Gulf States*. In progress.

——. *The Pronunciation of English in Metropolitan Chicago*. Publication of the American Dialect Society, no. 44. University: Univ. of Alabama Press, 1965.

——. "Studies of American Pronunciation since 1945." *American Speech* 52 (1977): 266–327.

——; McDavid, Raven I., Jr.; Foster, Charles W.; and Billiard, Charles E. *A Manual for Dialect Research in the Southern States*. 2nd ed. University: Univ. of Alabama Press, 1974.

Peters, Robert A. *A Linguistic History of English*. Boston: Houghton Mifflin, 1968.

Pike, Kenneth L. *The Intonation of American English*. Ann Arbor: Univ. of Michigan Press, 1945.

——. *Language in Relation to a Unified Theory of the Structure of Human Behavior*. The Hague: Mouton, 1967.

——. *Selected Writings*, ed. Ruth M. Brend. The Hague: Mouton, 1970.

Pitman, James; and St. John, John. *Alphabets and Reading: The Initial Teaching Alphabet*. New York: Pitman, 1969.

Pokorny, Julius. *Indogermanisches Etymologisches Wörterbuch*. 2 vols. Bern: Francke, 1959–69.

Pooley, Robert C. *The Teaching of English Usage*. 2nd ed. Urbana, Ill.: National Council of Teachers of English, 1974.

Pope, Maurice. *The Story of Decipherment from Egyptian Hieroglyphic to Linear B*. London: Thames and Hudson, 1975.

Potter, Simeon. *Changing English*. London: Deutsch, 1969.

Pound, Louise. "American Euphemisms for Dying, Death, and Burial." *American Speech* 11 (1936): 195–202.

Poutsma, H. *A Grammar of Late Modern English*. 4 vols. Groningen: Noordhoff, 1904–26. Pt. 1, 2nd ed., 1928–29.

Premack, Ann J. *Why Chimps Can Read*. New York: Harper & Row, 1976.

Premack, David. *Intelligence in Ape and Man*. Hillsdale, N.J.: Erlbaum, 1976.

Priebsch, Robert; and Collinson, W. E. *The German Language*. 6th ed. London: Faber and Faber, 1966.

Prokosch, Eduard A. *A Comparative Germanic Grammar*. Philadelphia: Linguistic Society of America, 1939.

Publication of the American Dialect Society. 1944–date.

Puhvel, Jaan, ed. *Myth and Law Among the Indo-Europeans*. Berkeley: Univ. of California Press, 1970.

Pyles, Thomas. "Bible Belt Onomastics; or, Some Curiosities of Anti-Pedobaptist Nomenclature." *Names* 7 (1959): 84–100.

——. "Onomastic Individualism in Oklahoma." *American Speech* 22 (1947): 257–64.

——. *Thomas Pyles: Selected Essays on English Usage*, ed. John Algeo. Gainesville: Univ. Presses of Florida, 1979.

——. *Words and Ways of American English*. New York: Random House, 1952.

——; and Algeo, John. *English: An Introduction to Language*. New York: Harcourt Brace Jovanovich, 1970.

Quirk, Randolph. *The English Language and Images of Matter*. London: Oxford Univ. Press, 1972.

————. *Essays on the English Language: Medieval and Modern.* Bloomington: Indiana Univ. Press, 1968.

————. *The Linguist and the English Language.* London: Arnold, 1974.

————. *The Uses of English.* With supplementary chapters by A. C. Gimson and Jeremy Warburg. 2nd ed. New York: St. Martin's, 1968.

————; and Greenbaum, Sidney. *A Concise Grammar of Contemporary English.* New York: Harcourt Brace Jovanovich, 1973.

————; Greenbaum, Sidney; Leech, Geoffrey; and Svartvik, Jan. *A Grammar of Contemporary English.* New York: Seminar, 1972.

————; and Svartvik, Jan. *Investigating Linguistic Acceptability.* The Hague: Mouton, 1966.

————; and Wrenn, C. L. *An Old English Grammar.* London: Methuen, 1955.

The Random House College Dictionary. Rev. ed. Ed. Jess Stein. New York: Random House, 1975.

The Random House Dictionary of the English Language, ed. Jess Stein and Laurence Urdang. New York: Random House, 1967.

Rao, G. Subba. *Indian Words in English: A Study in Indo-British Cultural and Linguistic Relations.* Oxford: Clarendon, 1954.

Read, Allen Walker. "Could Andrew Jackson Spell?" *American Speech* 38 (1963): 188–95.

————. "The First Stage in the History of 'O.K.'" *American Speech* 38 (1963): 5–27.

————. "The Folklore of 'O.K.'" *American Speech* 39 (1964): 5–25.

————. "Later Stages in the History of 'O.K.'" *American Speech* 39 (1964): 83–101.

————. "The Motivation of Lindley Murray's Grammatical Work." *Journal of English and Germanic Philology* 38 (1939): 525–39.

————. "The Second Stage in the History of 'O.K.'" *American Speech* 38 (1963): 83–102.

————. "Successive Revisions in the Explanation of 'O.K.'" *American Speech* 39 (1964): 243–67.

Reed, Carroll A. *Dialects of American English.* 2nd ed. Amherst: Univ. of Massachusetts Press, 1977.

Reed, David Wooderson. *The History of Inflectional "n" in English Verbs before 1500.* University of California Publications in English, vol. 7, no. 4. Berkeley: Univ. of California Press, 1950.

Rex, Richard. "Five Hundred Years of *Fruition.*" *American Speech* 44 (1969): 179–90.

Robertson, Stuart. *The Development of Modern English.* 2nd ed. Rev. Frederic G. Cassidy. Englewood Cliffs, N.J.: Prentice-Hall, 1954.

Robins, Robert Henry. *A Short History of Linguistics.* London: Longman, 1967.

Robinson, Ian. *The Survival of English: Essays in Criticism of Language.* Cambridge: University Press, 1973.

Ross, Alan S. C. *Etymology.* London: Deutsch, 1958.

Rumbaugh, Duane M., ed. *Language Learning by a Chimpanzee: The Lana Project.* New York: Academic, 1977.

Russell, I. Willis; and Porter, Mary Gray. "Among the New Words." *American Speech,* passim.

Safire, William. *On Language.* New York: Times Books, 1980.

————. *Safire's Political Dictionary.* New York: Random House, 1978.

Salus, Peter H., ed. *On Language: Plato to von Humboldt.* New York: Holt, Rinehart and Winston, 1969.

Sampson, Geoffrey. *Schools of Linguistics.* Stanford: University Press, 1980.

Samuels, Michael Louis. *Linguistic Evolution, with Special Reference to English.* Cambridge: University Press, 1972.

Sapir, Edward. *Culture, Language and Personality: Selected Essays,* ed. David G. Mandelbaum. Berkeley: Univ. of California Press, 1961.

———. *Language: An Introduction to the Study of Speech.* New York: Harcourt Brace Jovanovich, 1921.

Saussure, Ferdinand de. *Course in General Linguistics.* Rev. ed. Ed. Charles Bally and Albert Sechehaye in collaboration with Albert Reidlinger. Trans. Wade Baskin. London: Owen, 1974.

Scargill, M. H. *Modern Canadian English Usage: Linguistic Change and Reconstruction.* Toronto: McClelland and Stewart, 1974.

———. *A Short History of Canadian English.* Victoria, B.C.: Sono Nis, 1977.

Schmidt, Alexander. *Shakespeare-Lexicon: A Complete Dictionary of All the English Words, Phrases and Constructions in the Works of the Poet.* 2 vols. 6th ed. Rev. Gregor Sarrazin. 1902. Reprint. Berlin: de Gruyter, 1971.

Schur, Norman W. *English English.* Essex, Conn.: Verbatim, 1980.

Scott, Charles T.; and Erickson, Jon, eds. *Readings for the History of the English Language.* Boston: Allyn & Bacon, 1968.

Scragg, D. G. *A History of English Spelling.* Manchester, Eng.: University Press, 1974.

Sebeok, Thomas R., ed. *Current Trends in Linguistics, Vol. 10: Linguistics in North America.* 2 vols. The Hague: Mouton, 1973.

Serjeantson, Mary S. *A History of Foreign Words in English.* 1935. Reprint. London: Routledge & Kegan Paul, 1961.

Seymour, Richard K. *A Bibliography of Word Formation in the Germanic Languages.* Durham, N.C.: Duke Univ. Press, 1968.

Shannon, Ann. *A Descriptive Syntax of the Parker Manuscript of the Anglo-Saxon Chronicle from 734 to 891.* The Hague: Mouton, 1964.

Sheldon, Esther K. "Boswell's English in the *London Journal.*" *PMLA* 71 (1956): 1067–93.

Shores, David L., ed. *Contemporary English: Change and Variation.* Philadelphia: Lippincott, 1972.

———. *A Descriptive Syntax of the Peterborough Chronicle from 1122 to 1154.* The Hague: Mouton, 1971.

———; and Hines, Carole P., eds. *Papers in Language Variation: SAMLA-ADS Collection.* University: Univ. of Alabama Press, 1977.

Shuy, Roger W. *Discovering American Dialects.* Champaign, Ill.: National Council of Teachers of English, 1967.

———, ed. *Social Dialects and Language Learning.* Champaign, Ill.: National Council of Teachers of English, 1965.

———; Wolfram, Walter A.; and Riley, William K. *Field Techniques in an Urban Language Study.* Washington, D.C.: Center for Applied Linguistics, 1968.

6,000 Words: A Supplement to Webster's Third New International Dictionary. Springfield, Mass.: Merriam, 1976.

Skeat, Walter W. *English Dialects from the Eighth Century to the Present Day.* Cambridge: University Press, 1912.

338 ———. *An Etymological Dictionary of the English Language*. 4th ed. Oxford: Clarendon, 1910.

———, ed. *The Holy Gospels in Anglo-Saxon, Northumbrian, and Old Mercian Versions*. Cambridge: University Press, 1871–87.

Sledd, James. *A Short Introduction to English Grammar*. Chicago: Scott, Foresman, 1959.

———; and Ebbitt, Wilma R., eds. *Dictionaries and That Dictionary: A Casebook on the Aims of Lexicographers and the Targets of Reviewers*. Chicago: Scott, Foresman, 1962.

———; and Kolb, Gwin J., eds. *Dr. Johnson's Dictionary: Essays in the Biography of a Book*. Chicago: Univ. of Chicago Press, 1955.

Smith, Elsdon C. *New Dictionary of American Family Names*. New York: Harper & Row, 1972.

Smitherman, Geneva. *Talkin and Testifyin: The Language of Black America*. Boston: Houghton Mifflin, 1977.

Soudek, Lev. *Structure of Substandard Words in British and American English*. Bratislava: Slovenská Akadémia Vied, 1967.

Starnes, DeWitt T.; and Noyes, Gertrude E. *The English Dictionary from Cawdrey to Johnson, 1604–1755*. Chapel Hill: Univ. of North Carolina Press, 1946.

Stenton, Doris Mary. *English Society in the Early Middle Ages (1066–1307)*. Hammondsworth, Eng.: Penguin, 1951.

Stenton, Frank M. *Anglo-Saxon England*. 2nd ed. Oxford: Clarendon, 1947.

Stern, Gustav. *Meaning and Change of Meaning, with Special Reference to the English Language*. 1931. Reprint. Bloomington: Indiana Univ. Press, 1963.

Stevick, Robert D. *English and Its History: The Evolution of a Language*. Boston: Allyn & Bacon, 1968.

Stewart, George R. *American Place-Names: A Concise and Selected Dictionary for the Continental United States of America*. New York: Oxford Univ. Press, 1970.

———. *Names on the Land*. 2nd ed. Boston: Houghton Mifflin, 1958.

Stockwell, Robert P. *Foundations of Syntactic Theory*. Englewood Cliffs, N.J.: Prentice-Hall, 1977.

Stockwell, Robert P.; and Macaulay, Ronald K. S., eds. *Linguistic Change and Generative Theory*. Bloomington: Indiana Univ. Press, 1972.

———; Schachter, Paul; and Partee, Barbara H. *The Major Syntactic Structures of English*. New York: Holt, Rinehart and Winston, 1973.

Strang, B. M. H. *A History of English*. London: Methuen, 1970.

———. *Modern English Structure*. 2nd ed. London: Arnold, 1968.

Stratmann, Francis Henry. *A Middle-English Dictionary*, rev. Henry Bradley. Oxford: Clarendon, 1891.

Stubelius, Svante. *Balloon, Flying-Machine, Helicopter*. Gothenburg Studies in English, no. 9. Göteborg: n.p., 1958.

Sturtevant, Edgar H. *An Introduction to Linguistic Science*. New Haven: Yale Univ. Press, 1947.

The Sutton Hoo Ship-Burial. London: Trustees of the British Museum, 1947.

Sweet, Henry. *A New English Grammar, Logical and Historical*. 2 vols. Oxford: Clarendon, 1900, 1903.

Temerlin, Maurice K. *Lucy: Growing Up Human: A Chimpanzee Daughter in a Psychotherapist's Family*. Palo Alto, Calif.: Science and Behavior Books, 1975.

Ten Brink, Bernhard. *The Language and Metre of Chaucer.* 2nd ed. Rev. Friedrich
Kluge. Trans. M. Bentinck Smith. New York: Macmillan, 1901.

Thieme, Paul. *Die Heimat der indogermanischen Gemeinsprache.* Wiesbaden: Steiner, 1954.

———. "The Indo-European Language." *Scientific American,* October 1958, pp. 63–74.

Thomas, Charles Kenneth. *An Introduction to the Phonetics of American English.* 2nd ed. New York: Ronald, 1958.

Thomas, Lewis. *The Lives of a Cell: Notes of a Biology Watcher.* New York: Viking, 1974.

Toller, T. Northcote, ed. *An Anglo-Saxon Dictionary Based on the Manuscript Collections of the Late Joseph Bosworth.* Supplement with rev. and enlarged addenda by Alistair Campbell. London: Oxford Univ. Press, 1898. Supplement 1921, Addenda 1972.

Trager, George L.; and Smith, Henry Lee, Jr. *An Outline of English Structure.* Studies in Linguistics Occasional Papers, no. 3. 1951. Reprint. Washington, D.C.: American Council of Learned Societies, 1957.

Traugott, Elizabeth Closs. *A History of English Syntax: A Transformational Approach to the History of English Sentence Structure.* New York: Holt, Rinehart and Winston, 1972.

Tucker, Susie I. *English Examined: Two Centuries of Comment on the Mother-Tongue.* Hamden, Conn.: Archon, 1974.

Turner, Lorenzo Dow. *Africanisms in the Gullah Dialect.* Foreword by David DeCamp. 1949. Reprint. Ann Arbor: Univ. of Michigan Press, 1974.

Twaddell, W. Freeman. *The English Verb Auxiliaries.* 2nd ed. Providence, R.I.: Brown Univ. Press, 1968.

———. "The Inner Chronology of the Germanic Consonant Shift." *Journal of English and Germanic Philology* 38 (1939): 337–59.

Ullman, Berthold Louis. *Ancient Writing and Its Influence.* Cambridge, Mass.: MIT Press, 1969.

Ullmann, Stephen. *The Principles of Semantics.* Rev. ed. Glasgow: Jackson, 1959.

———. *Semantics: An Introduction to the Science of Meaning.* New York: Harper & Row, 1962.

Valdman, Albert, ed. *Pidgin and Creole Linguistics.* Bloomington: Indiana Univ. Press, 1977.

Vallins, G. H. *Spelling,* rev. D. G. Scragg. London: Deutsch, 1965.

Venezky, Richard L. "Notes on the History of English Spelling." *Visible Language* 10 (1976): 351 65.

———. *The Structure of English Orthography.* The Hague: Mouton, 1970.

Vigilans [pseud.]. *Chamber of Horrors.* Introduction by Eric Partridge. London: British Book Centre, 1952.

Visser, F. Th. *An Historical Syntax of the English Language.* 3 vols in 4. Leiden: Brill, 1963–73.

Vivian, John H. "Spelling an End to Orthographical Reforms: Newspaper Response to the 1906 Roosevelt Simplifications." *American Speech* 54 (1979): 163–74.

Voegelin, C. F; and Voegelin, F. M. *Classification and Index of the World's Languages.* New York: American Elsevier, 1977.

Wakelin, Martyn F. *English Dialects: An Introduction.* London: Athlone, 1972.

340   Waldron, R. A. *Sense and Sense Development.* New York: Oxford Univ. Press, 1967.

Wardale, Edith E. *An Introduction to Middle English.* 1937. Reprint. London: Routledge & Kegan Paul, 1962.

————. *An Old English Grammar.* London: Methuen, 1964.

Waterman, John T. *Perspectives in Linguistics.* Chicago: Univ. of Chicago Press, 1970.

Webster's New Collegiate Dictionary. 8th ed. Ed. Henry Bosley Woolf. Springfield, Mass.: Merriam, 1973.

Webster's New World Dictionary of the American Language. 2nd College ed. Ed. David B. Guralnik. Cleveland: Collins and World, 1974.

Webster's Third New International Dictionary. Ed. Philip Babcock Gove. Springfield, Mass.: Merriam, 1961.

Wells, Ronald A. *Dictionaries and the Authoritarian Tradition: A Study in English Usage and Lexicography.* The Hague: Mouton, 1973.

Wentworth, Harold, ed. *American Dialect Dictionary.* New York: Crowell, 1944.

Wentworth, Harold; and Flexner, Stuart Berg. *Dictionary of American Slang.* 2nd supplemented ed. New York: Crowell, 1975.

Wescott, Roger W., ed. *Language Origins.* Silver Springs, Md.: Linstok, 1974.

Whitehorn, Katharine. "What Makyth Manners?" *Spectator,* 9 March 1962, p. 317.

Whitelock, Dorothy. *The Beginnings of English Society.* Baltimore, Md.: Penguin, 1952.

Whitney, William Dwight. *Whitney on Language: Selected Writings of William Dwight Whitney,* ed. Michael Silverstein, intro. Roman Jakobson. Cambridge, Mass.: MIT Press, 1971.

Whorf, Benjamin Lee. *Language, Thought, and Reality,* ed. John B. Carroll. Cambridge, Mass.: Technology Press of MIT, 1956.

Wijk, Axel. *Rules of Pronunciation for the English Language.* London: Oxford Univ. Press, 1966.

Williams, Edna Rees. *The Conflict of Homonyms in English.* New Haven: Yale Univ. Press, 1944.

Williams, Joseph M. *Origins of the English Language: A Social and Linguistic History.* New York: Free Press, 1975.

Williamson, Juanita V.; and Burke, Virginia M., eds. *A Various Language: Perspectives on American Dialects.* New York: Holt, Rinehart and Winston, 1971.

Withycombe, E. G. *The Oxford Dictionary of English Christian Names.* 3rd ed. Oxford: Clarendon, 1977.

Wolfe, Patricia M. *Linguistic Change and the Great Vowel Shift in English.* Berkeley: Univ. of California Press, 1972.

Wolfram, Walter A. *Sociolinguistic Aspects of Assimilation: Puerto Rican English in New York City.* Arlington, Va.: Center for Applied Linguistics, 1974.

————. *A Sociolinguistic Description of Detroit Negro Speech.* Washington, D.C.: Center for Applied Linguistics, 1969.

————; and Christian, Donna. *Appalachian Speech.* Arlington, Va.: Center for Applied Linguistics, 1976.

————; and Clarke, Nona H., eds. *Black-White Speech Relationships.* Washington, D.C.: Center for Applied Linguistics, 1971.

————; and Fasold, Ralph W. *The Study of Social Dialects in American English.* Englewood Cliffs, N.J.: Prentice-Hall, 1974.

Wood, Gordon R. *Vocabulary Change: A Study of Variation in Regional Words in Eight of the Southern States.* Carbondale: Southern Illinois Univ. Press, 1971.

Word: Journal of the International Linguistic Association. 1945–date.

"Words and Meanings, New." In *Britannica Book of the Year.* Chicago: Encyclopaedia Britannica, annual.

The World Book Dictionary. 2 vols. Ed. Clarence L. Barnhart and Robert K. Barnhart. Chicago: World Book–Childcraft, 1980.

Wrenn, C. L. *The English Language.* London: Methuen, 1952.

———. *Word and Symbol: Studies in English Language.* London: Longman, 1967.

Wright, Joseph, ed. *The English Dialect Dictionary.* 6 vols. 1898–1905. Reprint. New York: Hacker Art Books, 1963.

———. *The English Dialect Grammar.* Oxford: Frowde, 1905.

———; and Wright, Elizabeth Mary. *An Elementary Middle English Grammar.* 2nd ed. London: Oxford Univ. Press, 1928.

———; and Wright, Elizabeth Mary. *Old English Grammar.* 3rd ed. London: Oxford Univ. Press, 1925.

Wyld, Henry Cecil. *A History of Modern Colloquial English.* 3rd ed. Oxford: Blackwell, 1936.

———. *A Short History of English.* 3rd ed. London: Murray, 1927.

———, ed. *The Universal Dictionary of the English Language.* London: Routledge & Kegan Paul, 1932.

Zachrisson, Robert Eugen. *The English Pronunciation at Shakespeare's Time as Taught by William Bullokar.* 1927. Reprint. New York: AMS, 1970.

———. *Pronunciation of English Vowels, 1400–1700.* 1913. Reprint. New York: AMS, 1971.

Zandvoort, R. W. *A Handbook of English Grammar.* 5th ed. Englewood Cliffs, N.J.: Prentice-Hall, 1966.

Zettler, Howard G., ed. *-Ologies & -Isms: A Thematic Dictionary.* Detroit: Gale, 1978.

Zviadadze, Givi. *A Dictionary of Modern American and British English on a Contrastive Basis.* Tbilisi, U.S.S.R.: Tbilisi State Univ., 1973.

Indexes

Index of
Modern English Words,
Affixes, and Phrases

Index of Modern English Words, Affixes, and Phrases

Index of Modern English Words, Affixes, and Phrases

Index of Modern English Words, Affixes, and Phrases

Index of Modern English Words, Affixes, and Phrases

354

hussar, 315
hussy, 273
hype, 275

I, 157, 194
-(i)an, 266
-(i)ana, 266
iceberg, 308
icebox, 271
ice cream, 271
Iceland, 272
iceman, 272
-ician, 267
idiosyncrasy, 297
-ie, 265
ill, 217
image, 255
imaginary, 296
imitate, 296
immensely, 253
impartial, 241
impasse, 305
impassive, 288
in, 285
incense, 10
incognito, 307
index, 296
indict, 172
inferiority complex, 254
inferno, 307
inflection, 230
influenza, 307
Info-gate, 281
-ing, 6, 265
in good point, 305
inpatient, 285
input, 256
ins, 285
insane, 217
insanity, 255
instant, 296
intelligentsia, 315
interest, 296
interface, 256
intermission, 217
interval, 217
in the chips, 288
into, 271

invalid, 305
Irangate, 281
irresponsible, 288
is, 12, 38
-ish, 265
isinglass, 309
-ism, 268
isms, 268
-ist, 5
it, its, 22, 121, 156, 189, 192
italic, 287
it's, 205
it's me, 225
-ize, 267, 268

jackal, 315
jackass, 287
jack-in-the-box, 287
jack-of-all-trades, 287
jacks, 287
jail, 229
jakes, 287
jamboree, 279
janitor, 251, 296
japan, v., 313
jaunty, 304
java, 287
jazz, 234, 314
jeans, 287
Jehovah, 312
jeremiad, 286
Jerusalem artichoke, 283
jester, 179
jigger, 315
jinn, 312
jinricksha, 313
JOBS, 276
jocose, 296
john, 287
johnnycake, 287
Johnny-jump-up, 215
johnny-on-the-spot, 287
jovial, 287
jubilee, 312
judge, 301
judo, 313
juggernaut, 313

juggler, 301
ju-jitsu, 313
juke, 314
jungle, 313
junta, 306
jury, 301

kaiser, 286
kamikaze, 313
kangeroo, 314
karma, 72, 313
Kate, 171
Katy, 273
katzenjammer, 310
keel, 308
kempt, 3
Kenzie, 139
kerb, 229
Keswick, 272
kettle, 293
key, 306
khaki, 312
khan, 315
kibitzer, 311
kick, 300
kidvid, 275
kilt, 300
kimono, 313
kind, 185
kindergarten, 310
kindle, 300
kine, 115, 185
king, 301
kirsch(wasser), 310
kismet, 315
kit, 308
Kit, 171
kitchen, 293
Kleenex, 261
kleinite, 309
klutz, 311
knack, 179
knackwurst, 310
knapsack, 308
knave, 179, 247
knead, 179, 201
knee, 179
knickers, 216

Index of Modern English Words, Affixes, and Phrases

Index of Modern English Words, Affixes, and Phrases

Index of Modern English Words, Affixes, and Phrases

-th, 265
than, 168, 194
that, 6, 117, 156, 158, 188, 193, 253
the, 117, 158, 168, 169, 177
theater, 171, 229
theatre, 229
thee, 168, 169, 191
their, theirs, 121, 145, 157, 158, 186, 189, 223, 258
them, 121, 145, 157, 168, 223, 258, 300
Theobald, 62
theory, 297
these, 117, 159, 188
thesis, 171
they, 121, 145, 157, 223, 258
thine, 189
thing, 246
think, 196
this, 6, 117, 156, 159, 188
-thon, 280
thorough, 231
those, 117, 158, 188
thou, 190
thought, 172
thrall, 300
three, 80
thrice, 119
thrive, 197
throne, 171, 178
throughout, 271
throw, 202
thug, 313
thumb, 284
Thurston, 273
thy, 189
tiara, 312
ticket, 277
tide, 110
tiger, 312
tile, 295
tilt at, 288
tinkle, 261
tiptoe, 284
tire, 229

titmouse, 283
toboggan, 315
toby, 287
toe, 284
toilet, 250
tokus, 312
tomahawk, 315
tomato, 226, 306
tomb, 4
tomboy, 287
tomcat, 287
tomfool, 287
tommyrot, 287
tomtit, 287
tong, 313
tongue, 142
tonic, 240
Tony, 171
too, 253
took, 173
tornado, 306
torso, 307
tortilla, 306
tory, 298
tote, 315
tovarisch, 315
towards, 119
tractorcade, 280
traffic, 230
trait, 225
transient, 296
treacle, 217
tread, 200
trek, 309
tremble, 4
trial balloon, 305
trillion, 217
trio, 307
troika, 315
trombone, 307
truck, 217
tryst, 225
tsk-tsk, 263
tuberose, 283
tulip, 315
tummy, 250
tundra, 315
turban(d), 315

turkey, 246, 287
turn, 284
tush, 262
tut(-tut), 263
tuxedo, 287
TV, 219, 275
twice, 119
twirl, 279
two, 80, 146, 147
two weeks, 219
tycoon, 313
-type, 267
typewrite, 278
tyrant, 297
tyre, 229

ugh, 263
uh-huh, 263
ukase, 315
ukulele, 314
ultimate, 296
umbrella, 307
umlaut, 310
umpire, 147
un-, 264
uncanny, 288
under-, 264
under, 109
underbred, 271
underbrush, 215
underprivileged, 251
understand, 201, 245
undertaker, 249
unkempt, 3
up-, 265
upon, 271
upscale, 270
upset, 285
urban, 296
urge, 296
urinalysis, 279
ush, 277
utopia, 287

valentine, 286
valet, 225
valour, 304
vamoose, 306

Subject Index

F
G 8
H 9
I 0
J 1